Satanic Mills To Galilee

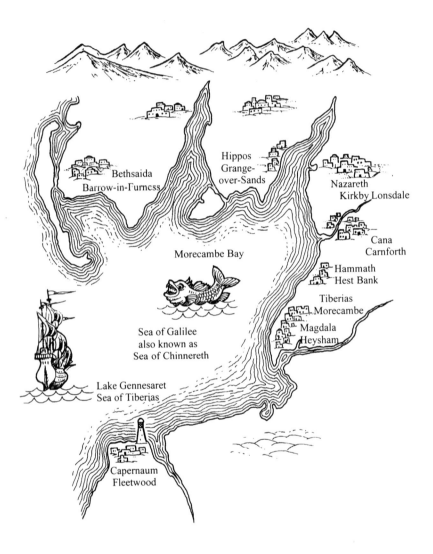

But if we Desire Him,
He is close at hand;
For our native country
Is our Holy Land

Satanic Mills To Galilee

John Knape

The Pentland Press Limited
Edinburgh • Cambridge • Durham • USA

© John Knape 1998

First published in 1998 by
The Pentland Press Ltd.
1 Hutton Close
South Church
Bishop Auckland
Durham

British Library Cataloguing in Publication Data.
A Catalogue record for this book is available
from the British Library.

ISBN 1 85821 581 1

Typeset by CBS, Felixstowe, Suffolk
Printed and bound by Antony Rowe Ltd., Chippenham

This book is dedicated to
DAD
who always made everyone feel better

Believe not those who say
The upward path is smooth, . . .

. . . It is the only road
Unto the realms of joy;

Anne Brontë (1820–1849)

CONTENTS

ILLUSTRATIONS

FOREWORD

I have known John Knape for over thirty years in the capacities of lawyer, Methodist lay preacher, and friend.

When I started my own accountancy practice in Morecambe, in 1964, John's father, Senior Partner in the firm of solicitors Jobling & Knape, took me under his wing and greatly helped in the ultimate success of the practice. I have a shrewd suspicion that young John may well have been behind his father's 'adoption' of me!

My abiding memory of John, from those days, relates to a particular Sunday evening. I had only just started my practice and I wasn't making the progress I had hoped. I went to my local church that evening more out of habit than expectation. John was in the pulpit and I came away from that service knowing that all would be well. His sermon, based on verse three of Psalm 56, lifted me and gave me a new sense of confidence for the future. John was well known as one of the better preachers in our Methodist circuit, including the ministerial staff! He conducted services with a deep sense of worship and what he had to say was based on wide reading, thoughtful interpretation, and an awareness of the needs of his hearers.

John has had more than his fair share of crises to deal with. It must have come hard to him to have had to face up to personal problems when for so much of his life he had been advising others on how to deal with their problems. However, he has come through and is the stronger for it. He also now has his own experiences to pass on to others who find themselves in similar situations. May John have the strength to do just that and may others have the sense to listen, to understand and to respond.

John had, understandably, a strong affection and respect for his father. As had many of us. I wonder, though, whether that respect turned into a sense of worship which could only be demonstrated in trying to emulate him. It may well be that if John could have come to terms with his feelings for his father he could have more easily accepted himself for what he undoubtedly is, a warm, sensitive, highly aware person with so much to offer, irrespective of any abilities of his father which he could not hope to match.

I commend John's book to anyone (which perhaps includes us all) who is trying to solve that great question of life . . . 'what's it all about?' Here is the story of the life of a man who is (still?) coming to terms with life but who wishes to share the lessons he has learnt with others that they may be more able to confront and overcome the hazards and problems which life inevitably brings.

Eric D. Armitage OBE, FCA
1998

Mr Eric D. Armitage opened an accountancy practice in Morecambe in 1964.

He answered a call from the Methodist Missionary Society to go to the Caribbean and take control of difficult administration and finance problems at the Methodist Queen's College, Bahamas, a task he completed with distinction over a period of three years. He was also able to train a Bahamian to succeed him before his return.

Awarded the OBE (for services to Housing) in 1991, he recently retired as Chief Executive of the North British Housing Association, the largest Housing Association in the country, handling millions of pounds of government money.

He is a former Chairman of the National Federation of Housing Associations, and was recently elected to the Board of the National Housing Corporation.

Eric is a Methodist local preacher and Sunday School teacher.

PREFACE

The aim of the book is to answer the simple question so many ask – 'What's it all about?' – based on my pilgrim way through the events and experiences of a varied life.

The thread which I seek to weave through life's rich tapestry is spun from a spiritual experience in childhood, through the joys, trials and tribulations of everyday events, to the certainty of a faith now being lived out on the gentler slopes of later years.

The title illustrates the aim. Born in one of the 'satanic' mill towns of Lancashire, I have lived for most of my life overlooking a lovely bay with a background of Lakeland hills where Wordsworth felt the power of an unseen and eternal presence. The bay in many ways reflects the geography and other features of the Sea of Galilee.

My late father's favourite hymn begins with the line 'Yes, God is good'. I seek to show by personal testimony, assent to the truth of those words.

My personal faith is also reflected in the words of St Paul in his letter to the Church at Rome: 'All things work together for good to those who love God.' There have been moments in my life when my faith has been severely tested, but I hope my story will be a source of hope and encouragement to those passing through similar times, and of identification for those who, like me, have 'won through', not because of any merit of their own, but by the free unmerited Grace of God. It is important to remember that we must press on in our pilgrim way to the very end.

AUTHOR'S NOTE

The original manuscript for my autobiography was delivered to the Publishers in the Spring of 1995. For reasons which will become apparent to the reader, it has only now become possible to publish.

Obviously a great deal can happen in three years, and my life has been no exception. It includes a divorce, the tragic death of my younger brother, an Easter pilrimage to the Holy Land, and the recurrence for a time of my incurable illness.

It has been necessary, as the reader will readily appreciate to re-read and update my life story with that in mind. I felt it would be helpful to mention these circumstances at the outset.

ACKNOWLEDGEMENTS

I owe a debt of gratitude to many for practical help and encouragement, and without which my story would not have been published.

Firstly to Hilary Marfleet, and Sarah Mainwaring with her assistant Elton. Hilary and Sarah gave me efficient, kindly and helpful assistance in typing the manuscript and putting up with my longhand. I could not have wished for more help in this important area. Sarah was quite outstanding in the help she gave me immediately prior to receipt of the proofs and in the general finishing and updating of the manuscript. I was extremely fortunate to be able to enlist her help again, after the enforced delay in my being able to publish.

My friend Bob (Group Captain R.G. Nuttall OBE RAF (Retd)) was a source of support throughout and in particular spent many hours photocopying my handwritten pages in the early days.

My cousin Bobby (Air Vice-Marshal R.M. Robson OBE RAF (Retd)) and his wife Brenda gave me valuable help and generous hospitality when researching the family ancestry.

Dr W. Graham Orr MB BS MRCGP showed skill and patient understanding over many years. I am deeply indebted to him.

Mr R. Bell of Wisbech and Fenland Museum gave expert and friendly advice and service at short notice when researching the family ancestry.

Miss M.B. Jobling MBE DL LLB (Lond) assisted me with background information about the family legal practice.

Miss M. Humble MA and Mr E.D. Armitage OBE FCA of Torrisholme Methodist Church, Morecambe supplied helpful information.

Mr Michael L. Charlesworth MA (Oxon) was helpful on several occasions with information about Shrewsbury School. He wrote promptly and helpfully, not only on specific points, but with general encouragement and interest. He also helped me with several other aspects in regard to illustrations. His helpful and ready replies to correspondence were much appreciated.

His Honour Sir (Ernest) Sanderson Temple MBE MA QC, Circuit Judge 1977-91, Honorary Recorder of Liverpool, Kendal and Lancaster gave me permission to publish information. His help was particularly appreciated coming at the time of the death of his wife Lady June.

The Rt Hon Sir Christopher D.R. Rose PC LLB BCL (Oxon) QC, a Lord Justice of Appeal, gave me permission to publish personal details and wrote words of encouragement.

I am similarly indebted to Sir Richard H. Tucker MA QC, a Judge of the High Court with whom I shared house and form at Shrewsbury School.

Mr Eddie Shapland FCIB DMS MIMGT, Director and Chief Executive of Marsden Building Society, gave help in connection with building society matters. He was a source of great encouragement, kept constantly in touch and maintained a close friendship formed over the years. His tragic death at the time of going to press was a great blow, but I am glad to have had the opportunity of thanking him for all his support in many ways, and of paying tribute to his life.

Ayrshire Cattle Society of Great Britain and Ireland gave permission to use extracts from 'The Ayrshire Cow' leaflet.

Farmers' Weekly gave permission to use the leaflet 'Hard Lines' originally published in 1964.

James A. Dickson (Books) of Christian Bookshop Edinburgh gave permission to reprint *The Incomparable Christ.*

Methodist Recorder gave permission to quote freely from their weekly publication and assisted me in several ways.

The *Financial Times* gave permission to reproduce the article 'Peeled in the pink with pride' first published by them on 25 & 26 April 1992. Mr Bob Baxter gave valuable assistance.

The sisters of the Monastery of Our Lady of Hyning gave me help throughout my writing as over the past ten years. I found much of my strength to write in the chapel and their company.

Epworth Press and particularly their former Editorial Secretary Dr C. S. Rodd were of great help.

Oxford University Press of Walton St, Oxford gave permission to print an extract from *A Diary of Private Prayer* by Dr John Baillie DD DLitt STD. The book is still in print.

Alcoholics Anonymous World Services Inc. gave me permission to print the Twelve Steps (acknowledged on the appropriate page) and also excerpts from pages 31, 43, 58, 76, 291 and 292 of *Alcoholics Anonymous.*

Extracts from 'Hymns and Psalms' and the Covenant Service in the Methodist Service book reproduced by kind permission of the Methodist Publishing House © Trustees for Methodist Service Book.

Victoria Edlington of the *Burnley Press* was most helpful and particularly in connection with the local historian Mr John Monk to whom I have expressed my thanks.

I also thank the *Burnley Express* newspaper for permission to use photographs and various extracts.

The *Lancaster Guardian* and the *Morecambe Guardian* for permission to use extracts; and generous help. Mr Craig Jackson was of particular help.

The *Lancashire Evening Post* gave permission to use extracts, and general help.

Westmorland Gazette gave permission to use a photograph taken at Westmorland County Show 1965. Mr Will Mapplebeck wrote a generous and helpful article.

The sisters of the Monastery of Our Lady of Hyning and Visual Image Production of Morecambe gave permission for the photograph of Hyning.

Rev. B.J.W. Cave MA, Anglican Chaplain of the University of Lancaster, was a great help with general advice when I first started to write.

Mr Alan D. Tennant of Bolton-le-Sands, nr. Lancaster prepared the original sketch of Morecambe Bay seen as the Sea of Galilee and brought to fruition an idea of many years.

Professor Philip Leather gave permission to include an extract from a paper prepared by the National Housing Forum which featured Marsden Building Society.

Rev. Graham A. Vickers, the Minister of my church at Bare, has given me encouragement and permission to reproduce his Minister's Letter from our Church magazine 'The Messenger' in connection with a visit to Handel's *Messiah* at Huddersfield.

Rev. G. Roy Chapman of Christ Church URC, Broadway, Morecambe gave me sound advice from his publishing experience.

Rev. Ken Clapham of St Cuthbert's Over Kellett, nr. Carnforth gave me helpful information.

Rev. David Pike MA BD, as through the years, has been a constant source of strength and wise counsel.

Rev. H. Foster and Mr J.W. Pratt in connection with their respective addresses at Vera's funeral.

Dr A. Brown-Lawson BD MLITT was of great help with general advice about publication and comments on the Reader's Report.

Mr Roger Knape of Luton was a great inspiration in the early days of writing. He first wrote to me in 1985 when investigating the history of the 'Knape' family and encouraged me along with my cousin (Air Vice-Marshal R. M. Robson OBE RAF (Retd)) to continue and complete the family genealogy.

Mr Eric D. Armitage OBE FCA for kindly agreeing to write the Foreword and for all his support.

Sister Dolores of Verlag Evangelische Marienschwester Schaft for permission to use extracts from The Holy Places Today by M. Basilea Schlink.

I thank Mr Mike Whalley, Editor of my local newspaper, Morecambe's *The Visitor*, has been a source of inspiration and encouragement throughout. He was the first to share the report from the Publishers and the Reader's Report on my return from the Holy Land in 1995. Always available, he is a fine example of a 'hands-on' Editor.

To everyone who has assisted in any way I extend my grateful thanks. If I have omitted anyone it has been through inadvertence and I apologize for any shortcomings.

It would be remiss of me if I failed to express my deep gratitude to all my friends at The Pentland Press Ltd. I feel to have become part of the 'family'. Without their help, I could have found the task other than the delight it has been. My special thanks to:

Mrs Jill R. Cole (former Executive Editor) who showed such patience and skill and 'bore the heat and burden of the early days' without complaint.

Mrs Mary Denton (Publishing Manager) for her professional skill and friendliness, and readiness with advice whenever asked.

Mr Anthony Phillips (Editorial Director) for 'settings things up'.

Mrs Rachel Gowling (Promotion Manager) for her enthusiasm and advice.

Chapter I

A REASON FOR WRITING

Fear and anxiety have plagued me nearly all my life. When I was eight years old I was asleep one evening in my own little bedroom, next to my mother and father's room. It was probably about 11 p.m., when I was awakened by the hysterical voice of my mother running along the corridor and shouting repeatedly, 'Your daddy is going to leave us all, your daddy is going to leave us all.'

Some people talk of butterflies in the tummy, others of a knotted stomach, or use some other phrase which describes a vague fear of life in general, and nothing specific. There is an endless list of specific fears, but perhaps worst of all is the shapeless, nameless dread which seems to have no definite source or cause, on which we cannot put our finger, but which saps our energy and vitality. Kneeling up on my bed, I placed my hands together, closed my eyes, and said, 'Please God, don't let Daddy leave us.' Mother was sitting on one of the beds in the adjoining bedroom where three of my sisters had been sleeping. She was sobbing.

I got out of bed, walked along the corridor, and into the bedroom where Father, dressed only in his shirt, was pulling on his pyjama trousers. Flinging my arms round his waist I pleaded, 'Daddy, please don't leave us.' The words of reply were indescribably comforting. 'It's alright John. I'm not going to leave you.' And he didn't. And through all the trials and tribulations of life, I believe God has never done so.

I do not live now with anxiety and fear, and can testify to a life lived with an almost constant quiet peace and joy. It has taken a lifetime to find, but I believe that to have been God's plan for me.

The 'sanctification of the secular' is not a phrase likely to draw enthusiastic crowds. When expressed as in Brother Lawrence's experience, it is quite different. He said that he felt as close to God when washing the dirty dishes in the refectory, as when kneeling for the elements at the communion rail. Consciousness of God in every waking moment is the secret.

> So shall no part of day or night
> From sacredness be free;

1

> But all my life, in every step,
> Be fellowship with Thee.

Whenever I find myself 'out of sorts', pondering a problem which is not yielding a solution, having a bad day or time, experiencing a general feeling that I am not enjoying life as I would have expected, I often look at a small piece of wood in my study, or if elsewhere, think about it in my imagination. It would not bring much at a car boot sale. It was given to me by two dear friends with whom I had been discussing the importance of the words for my life:

> God is.

As soon as I draw Him into the situation or allow Him to enter, as soon as I invite Him into whatever may be concerning me, I see a change in the situation, there are new angles, and a transformed attitude. More often than not, there falls on me a measure of peace, with myself, my fellow man, and with God. And that leads me on to Christ. I believe He is a gift. In the words of a great man, the essence of the matter is the simple acceptance of the gift of the friendship of Christ. All we have to do is to hold out our hands and take it.

The late Dr Leslie D. Weatherhead writes in his book *The Transforming Friendship*, about a new beginning with a penitent who wishes to be done with the past. Knowledge of his circumstances, praying and reading the Bible, belief in salvation by Jesus Christ, imitating Christ, a matter of the will, the straightening out of intellectual difficulties, were all given to him as the way forward. They were partially true. But it was when he turned to an old man he had previously thought narrow-minded, that he was given the answer. The new life was a gift from God. 'You simply had to kneel down and ask for it, go out and live as if you had received it, only to find that it was yours indeed.'

I also believe the gift to be the solution to most of the problems of the world, and my hope is that this simple fact and belief will permeate all the words I write about the joys and sorrows, the successes and failures, the pain and suffering, hopes and disappointments, and unfulfilled aspirations, of an ordinary but varied life. I apologize to anyone who finds my language emotive, when I say that I feel I have tried and been led to affirm the eternal truths, and testify to them in my own experience. There have been moments when I was transported in time, oblivious of it, and of place and reality, and when tears flowed freely in sadness and remembrance, but primarily in joy.

When I first made a decision that I could no longer postpone the writing of my life story, I considered several possibilities so far as the actual work was concerned. These were reduced to renting a Lakeland cottage for three months, or taking a cottage at Hyning Hall, a nearby monastery of which I shall write further.

In the event I wrote three pages at the weekend of the 14/15 October 1994. This was to enable me to say I had started. After a busy but enjoyable week involving many activities, I returned from golf on 21 October and put pen to paper. I can only say that I seemed to have been taken over in the following days. I could not put my pen down and wrote not only during the day but in spells of several hours, through broken nights, for twenty-three days. I was intent on just producing page after page of mixed content, as the spirit moved me, leaving grammar and punctuation, order and style, editing and deletions, additions and alterations, until later. Occasionally I would wonder for a moment if I would have sufficient material, but in the event the fear was unfounded. Towards the end there was a pause, when I felt certain items were not being addressed in a proper manner, and I suspect when I was very tired, that the ending and balance of the book would fail me. The next day, after an hour of quiet reflection and meditation, the pen began to flow again, uninterrupted to the end of my manuscript.

I shared with a friend my amazement that a work which I had anticipated taking several months of disciplined work should be completed in twenty-three days. He is a man of music and reminded me that Handel wrote *Messiah* in twenty-four days. A sense of proportion was restored.

My hope and prayer is that the reader may find a little of the strength, the joy, the hope, and above all the love, which is in my present daily experience.

Chapter II

THE FAMILY NAME AND BACKGROUND

I was born on 10 January 1930 in Burnley. The town will not be found on the English Tourist Board's routes, nor in holiday brochures, but it has a character of its own, with direct, friendly Lancashire folk, and many memories for me. My grandparents are buried there and the family's roots go back a long way.

Situated between Rossendale and Pendle, it was second only to Blackburn in the weaving towns of south Lancashire. Wool and cotton weaving were the basic industries, and there were coal pits on the outskirts. In 1952, 49 per cent of the adult insured females were employed in cotton. The population was about 80,000. Mother's family were farmers and butchers, and my grandfather on my father's side, was engaged in the motor car business.

I have a photograph from the *Burnley Express* showing a bus built in 1906. The photograph bears the words 'Burnley Motor Pleasure Co. Ltd. June 1st 1906' and the copy underneath reads:

C.W. 182 – built by John Knape, of Bank Top Garage and Motor Works, the 'Habergham' bus had motors by Critchley and Norris of Bamber Bridge, and was fitted with a Crossley engine. It was registered in June, 1906 in the name of F. Groome, motor engineers, of Whalley, who presumably supplied it to the Burnley Motor Pleasure Company. A second vehicle was registered a few days later – C.W. 190. The 'Habergham' could carry 40 passengers, had 4 cylinders and a 40 h.p. motor. It was capable of 15 m.p.h. and fitted with garden seats inside and out. Mr W.E. Cooke was manager of the Company.

Another showing the vehicle parked outside York Minster, reads:

Probably the most famous of the early motor buses in the Burnley areas, the Habergham, was operated by the Burnley Motor Pleasure Co. Ltd with Mr W.E. Cooke as manager – his family has had a long connection with local motor transport. The vehicle C.W. 182, was registered in June, 1906, built by F. Groome, motor engineers of Whalley, and John Knape, of Bank Top Carriage and Motor Works. It had a top speed of 15 m.p.h. – fast compared with the horse-drawn wagonettes which it replaced. Powered by a 40 horse power Crossley engine, made by Critchley-Norris, of Bamber Bridge, it carried 40 passengers on slatted seats, and ran on solid tyres. It must have been an adventure to ride to York Minster, where this photograph was taken in front of the south door.

My surname is something of a mystery and appears to be of Dutch or German origin. Many years ago I read in the press of a lady Olympic high diving board Gold Medal winner, who shared the name. So far as I know it is limited in Great Britain to my relatives, and a branch of the family in the King's Lynn area of Norfolk. My cousin Bobby and I are at present intending to explore in the Wisbech area of Cambridge which he has already researched.

The following is a copy of a letter I received in March 1985:

Dear Mr(s) or Ms Knape,
    You may be interested to receive a letter from a fellow Knape of whose existence you were previously unaware.
    Having reached the age of 65 (but not yet retired) I have set myself the task, purely for my own interest, of getting in touch with all the Knapes in the United Kingdom (there are only 27 entries recorded in telephone directories, partly to see if there is any common family origin traceable).
    My own interest was stimulated many years ago by a great uncle, John Knape, who was the Accountant to the old Great Eastern Railways. When this line was merged with others in 1922, he spent his time partly delving into Knapish origins. He certainly proved to his own satisfaction that there was an influx of Knapes into the country during the 16th century from Holland, who came to assist the draining of the Fens in East Anglia. Subsequently the trail goes a little dim, enlivened chiefly by deportations for sheep stealing and the like.
    My grandfather was a stone mason in Cambridge and my father an office manager in Epping. I had a brother, Alan, who was killed during the war serving in the RAF. I have two daughters and one son, Richard and ten grandchildren of whom only Alan the last and recently born is a male Knape, thereby – I hope, saving this line of Knapes from extinction.
    It would be of great interest if you could drop me a line indicating the extent of your own family and where it has been for the last three generations.

If any interesting information arises from answers to this letter (and 26 similar) I will embody the findings in a further letter and circulate it.

Yours sincerely,

Roger W. Knape

Unfortunately, I did not receive and was not able to elicit, any further information.

My German master at Shrewsbury School called me 'Canarber' (the German for boy is knabe) and it has been used in jest over the years, rhyming as it does with many other words! Certainly the family legal practice name of Jobling & Knape was distinctive, and also has given rise to a few smiles and corruptions down the years, from friend and foe alike.

I wrote the first part of this Chapter in late October 1994, soon after I first started to write. It has not been altered in spite of a quite remarkable turn of events which has been typical of so many since I first began to tell my life story. I cannot help but feel an overriding purpose and plan for the completion of my work. The happenings have been too frequent and substantial to be explained away as good fortune, chance or coincidence. None illustrate my conviction more than investigation into the family background.

As I was meditating before Christmas on the paucity of information about my ancestors and immediate predecessors, and feeling a little disappointed about my inability to acquire and give more detail, the telephone rang. A voice said 'Is that you, John?' I did not recognize the caller and said so. 'It's Roger from Luton' came the reply. I had only heard from him in the one fulsome letter I have mentioned, in 1985. There had been no reply to my letter of reply or to an enquiry which I sent at a later date. My assumption was that Roger had died or had abandoned his project.

Our conversation revealed that advancing years and ill-health had prevented him completing the task on which he had embarked, and he was asking me if I would assume his mantle and complete the task I readily agreed, and asked him about the progress he had made and the point he had reached. Roger said he had got as far as Walsoken in Norfolk. He suggested a visit there to the church would reveal numbers of gravestones of 'Knapes' and in conjunction with a search of the church records would enable us to complete a successful investigation.

My cousin Bobby (a retired Air Vice-Marshal) who lived in Lincolnshire, had contacted me on hearing about my book, to say that he had been researching the family tree and had traced it as far as Wisbech in Cambridgeshire. When we consulted the map we concluded that Walsoken and Wisbech were only a few miles apart. Bobby investigated further and found the distance was even shorter. He invited me to visit him and his wife Brenda early in the New Year, and suggested we motor down to Wisbech which was only forty miles or so from his home. We both became excited at the prospect of the visit and what it might reveal. I had a picture in my mind of knocking on doors, inspecting telephone directories and all manner of things, in addition to the suggested visit to the church.

On 2 January 1995 I travelled by train across country to Bobby and Brenda's home. I had not been there previously, and indeed had not seen them for many years. The following day was cold but sunny and bright, ideal for our plans, and we entered Wisbech by road, quickly finding the church. We established that although Walsoken was in Norfolk and Wisbech in Cambridgeshire, they were in effect one and the same place, with the county boundary running through the middle. Walsoken and Wisbech had grown together over the years and were rather like Bare and Morecambe where I live. Bare is a part of the town, but originally separate from it.

The building was surrounded by very old graves, and although we separated for search purposes, it soon became clear that it was going to

Four Generations: Grandmother, Author with son John, and father John on Christening day (1962).

7

be extremely difficult, if not impossible, to decipher the words on the headstones of a very old burial ground. I spotted three men working over the wall in a new burial area, and they directed me to the modern Rectory building a few yards away. The Rector was at home and proved most helpful, but pointed out that the graveyard had been closed since the beginning of the century and the best course of action he could suggest was a visit to the local authority offices in Wisbech, where the records were kept.

As it was the first day after the bank holiday the offices were busy but whilst waiting, my cousin engaged in conversation with a young man who had become aware of the purpose of our visit. He informed Bobby that as a member of a YTS scheme he had been involved in placing on microfilm the Parish records of births, marriages, deaths and baptisms of the surrounding large area, and with the help of the receptionist we were directed across the square outside to the Wisbech and Fenland Museum. A wonderful surprise awaited us.

The Steward, a Mr Robert Bell was both interested and helpful to us in our quest and within a minute or two had produced some index cards. One of them showed the birth of a 'Knape' in 1561. I later received the following from Mr Bell:

Wisbech St Peter's Baptisms – KNAPE.
[St Peter's was the Church we had visited]
26.5.1561	Robert son of John
15.9.1566	John son of Robert
8.10.1810	William Jarry son of Elizabeth
21.12.1825	Charles son of Edward & Susannah
4.2.1837	William son of William & Sarah
1.10.1837	Sarah Ann daughter of Henry & Frances
31.1.1838	Sarah daughter of William & Sarah
3.11.1839	Sarah daughter of William & Sarah
3.11.1839	Hannah daughter of Henry & Frances
27.11.1839	Susan daughter of Edward & Mary

It was pointed out to us discreetly that the absence of a father's name in the one instance denoted the child was 'base born'. Rather polite, I thought, and wondered how many other families had similar skeletons in their cupboards. In later years Aunt Ruth, my father's eldest sister, who took a great interest in the family history, was wont to remark (*sotto voce*) that a member of the family (she did not specify further detail) had been found on a doorstep. There were thirty-two Parishes listed in all. Only Wisbech St Mary with a General Register of 1557-1813 had an earlier date than that of Wisbech St Peter, from 1558-1812.

I paid a small amount for copies of hand-written documents of title and a letter dated 17 January 1995 from the Museum reads:

Dear Mr Knape
  You will find enclosed the photocopies which you ordered during your recent visit.
  As you left your change from the shop I took the liberty of copying the other Manor entries from the court books of West Walton Colerane, as well as entries from West Walton cum Membris and used the change to pay for the other copies – I hope this was OK?
  With regard to the index cards, as these were in pencil (and as such would not photocopy well) I have transcribed them for you.
  Yours sincerely
  R Bell

  Robert Bell
  Steward

Even forgetting my change had produced good fortune!
  An entry for Walsoken dated 23 December 1801 reads:

23 Dec 1801
They also Present that Edward Knape a Copyhold Tenant of the said manor is by reason of his Tenure according to the custom thereof chargeable with the office of collecting the Quit rents due to the said manor on the part of Walsoken at Saint Michael Old Stile in the last year. And he is thereupon elected to the said Office.

I was sure that searches in the other Registers would produce many more 'Knapes' but we had achieved our main purpose, because in some old cuttings from the *Burnley Express* newspaper, which I only discovered by chance a few days before our visit to Wisbech, there was a reference to the death of Mrs Isabella Knape in 1934, which linked Wisbech to my family roots in Burnley. It read:

DEATH OF MRS KNAPE

Loss To Bethel Primitive
Methodist Chapel

We regret to announce the death, which took place on Tuesday at 66, St Matthew Street, the residence of her daughter and son-in-

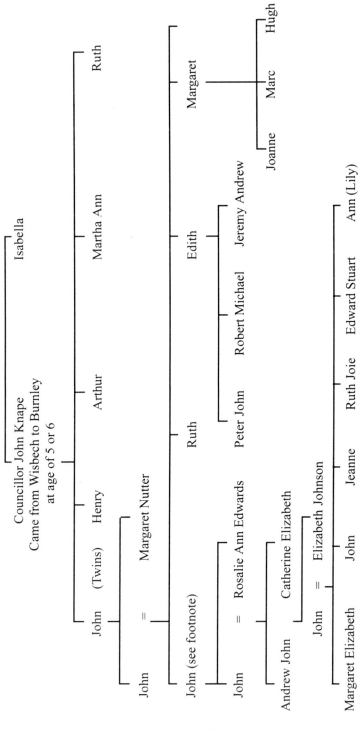

Councillor John Knape
Came from Wisbech to Burnley
at age of 5 or 6

Isabella

John (Twins) Henry Arthur Martha Ann Ruth

= Margaret Nutter

John

John (see footnote) Ruth Edith Margaret

= Rosalie Ann Edwards Peter John Robert Michael Jeremy Andrew Joanne Marc Hugh

John Catherine Elizabeth

Andrew John

= Elizabeth Johnson

John

Margaret Elizabeth John Jeanne Ruth Joie Edward Stuart Ann (Lily)

The distaff side is shown in the lower half for interest

law (Mr and Mrs H. Mitchell), of Mrs Isabella Knape, the widow of the late Councillor John Knape, who as a Liberal was the representative of Stoneyholme Ward for some years. Mrs Knape who was in her 79th year, leaves three sons and two daughters to mourn their loss. She was a native of Burnley, and was the oldest member of Bethel Primitive Methodist Chapel, Hammerton street. From childhood she had been one of the most regular members of the congregation at the various services, and was, in addition, while not an active participant, speaking generally, in the manifold activities of the church, a generous patron and supporter of any undertakings, such as bazaars and sales of work, which were organised for the benefit of the church.

Her connection with the chapel commenced 72 years ago, and was only terminated when her health began to fail recently. Her husband the late Mr John Knape, although not a native of Burnley – he came from Wisbech in Lincolnshire*, when a child of five or six years old – could claim an almost equally long term of service with the same church and Sunday school, as during his lifetime he was Sunday school treasurer, a circuit steward, and a president of the Burnley and District Sunday School Union. In May, 1911, he had completed a term of 50 years as Sunday school superintendent, and carried on afterwards until he sustained a breakdown in health. The late Mr Knape pre-deceased his wife eight years ago. He died in 1923, and a circumstance which is not without an element of pathos, in connection with the passing of Mr and Mrs Knape – both more devoted to their home and church than to any outside interest – is that Mrs Knape passed away on the anniversary of her late husband's interment eight years previously.

And so we were able to unearth over 430 years of family history in an hour or two. I thought of many who spent a lifetime tracing their roots. Our family had come from Holland, worked on the draining and farming of the Fens, and thence I would guess moved in part to the cotton town of east Lancashire, where there would be work.

I sent copies of the relevant documents to Roger and the following is an extract from his reply of 26 January 1995:

Dear John,
    Many thanks for the sheaf of paper received earlier during the week which has proved to be very interesting. The somewhat abstruse legal language of the court records will mean more to you

---

I assume this was before boundary alterations.

than to me but at least they enabled me to fill in some gaps and to make some assumptions.

I enclose a copy of a record dated 1933 which gives a rough plan of the family from 1803 onwards. This to the best of my knowledge was completed by Cllr. John Knape of King's Lynn who would be the one shown as being born in 1874 and who died, I believe, in the 1950s. I have brought this up to date as far as my own family is concerned.

Reverting to the court records. The Edward referred to on transcripts 247/8 and whose death is mentioned on page 270 is obviously our common ancestor but I cannot place Edward his son on the tree. The William who died in 1823 (transcripts 389 & 75) is obviously the above mentioned Edward's son, his wife was Mary and his son Edward (page 258) who seems to have died in 1875. Your great grandfather would seem to be the John referred to as John (Burnley) born 1851.

[This John Knape is my great grandfather. Obviously he did not come on his own from Wisbech at such a tender age, and I intend to follow up this lead in the records at Burnley, and which in view of the local authority connection, should not prove difficult.]

Your baptismal record from Wisbech St Peters is very interesting but it would appear that for 250 years most activity must have been in the neighbouring parishes and no doubt we can collectively do some research to enlarge the picture, particularly on the distaff side.

The death in the 1950s to which he refers was in fact that of my grandfather and not great-grandfather.

Bobby, Brenda and I felt well pleased with our morning's work in Wisbech and had a splendid lunch there before returning home.

I had an idyllic two days at North Rauceby sharing so much with Bobby and Brenda, enhanced by an overnight stay by Simon, the youngest son of Bobby's eldest brother, Peter John, of whom I write later.

Those press reports from the *Burnley Express* which appeared miraculously in my filing cabinet a few days before my visit, and which must have fallen out of an old file of my father's which I had not previously examined, referred to a Councillor John Knape who had arrived in Burnley from Wisbech as a boy of five or six years of age.

The chain was complete.

There are still many details to collect, but we now have a family history of over 430 years and undoubtedly showing a continuous line of the name of John Knape which I and my son bear today.

I telephoned Roger immediately on my return, and there is no need to emphasize our family delight.

In December 1997 a report was published in the Burnley Express about my forthcoming Autobiography. Shortly afterwards the following letter was published from Mr John Monk:

On the Trail of Well Known Coachbuilder

I was interested to read the article in the *Burnley Express*, December 12th, about John Knape, a solicitor whose family had had a coach building firm in Burnley earlier this century.

The name Knape first appears in a local directory in 1868, found under Marshall & Knape, coach builders.

The men involved were Richard Marshall and John Knape, who both lived in Cuerden Street. By 1872, John Knape was in business on his own at 1 Railway Street, though he still lived in Cuerden Street.

On further investigation I found the name John Knape in the 1881 census. This John Knape was a 64-year-old coach builder and livery stable proprietor employing 17 men and living at 11 Cuerden Street.

His place of birth was given as Wisbech, Cambridgeshire. He was married to Sarah, a 57-year-old native of Accrington. There was also an 18-year-old daughter Susanna, living with them.

Nearby at 4 Blenheim Street was living John Knape, the son of John Knape. He was also a coach builder, aged 29 years. He was married to Ruth, a Burnley woman of the same age whose occupation was given as a dressmaker. They had three daughters aged between two and six years.

The elder John Knape died in March 1890. There was a very brief obituary in the local newspaper saying that for many years he had carried on an exclusive carriage repository near Bank Top.

The younger John Knape appears again in the 1891 census. He is now living at 11 Cuerden Street. Sarah the wife of the original John Knape, is now living at 65 Rectory Road. The name of John's wife is now given as Isabella, and the number of children has grown to seven, three sons and a daughter having been added to the family.

The two eldest boys, John and Henry, seem to have been twins, as the age of both of them is given as nine. The other son was five-year-old Arthur. The four daughters were 16-year-old Susanna, Martha Ann (14), Florence (12) and Ruth (3). The oldest girls were cotton weavers and the third daughter and the three sons were scholars.

John Knape continued to run the business started by his father until he died in April, 1923. His obituary notice gives much information.

He was said to have been born at Wisbech and came to Burnley as a baby. He attended Bethel Primitive Methodist Chapel in Hammerton Street.

With the advent of the motor vehicle, there was a fall in the demand for the horse-drawn coach. John Knape was one of the first to convert the business to making motor bodies, for both vans and cars.

He built up one of the largest firms of its type in the area. His son, John, was the representative of the company. He was well known at Olympia and other trade shows in the U.K.

John Knape was connected with Bethel Chapel as a teacher and superintendent for over 50 years. He was a staunch Liberal and in 1913 he was elected councillor for Stoneyholme ward.

About 1920, he went to live at St Annes for a while but he later returned to Burnley and his home was at 'Studleigh', Watt Street, where he died aged 71. He left a widow and seven children.

After his father's death, the third John Knape was now in charge of the firm. The firm was now described as John Knape and Son Ltd., coach and motor engineers, Bank Top and Canning Street Works. John was now living at 53 Scott Park Road. By 1927, as well as the works, they had a showroom in St James's Street.

The 1930s were difficult times and the name of the firm does not appear in the directories of the time.

In 1937, John Knape was living at 55 Glen View Road and he was described as a motor salesman. By 1941 a new firm has been formed. John Knape was still living at 55 Glen View Road but he was now the managing director of Jubilee Garages (1940) Ltd, Trafalgar Street.

After the war, the firm is described as commercial vehicle specialist, Trafalgar Street and Station Garage, Padiham Road. The managing director was now F. H. Last.

John Monk
Hollingreave Road, Burnley

I am most grateful to him for the trouble he has taken in adding so much interesting further detail, and which also confirms my own research into the family history in Burnley. A matter of some relief to me.

International research records that the name is probably occupational in origin, the German meaning 'One who was a young servant'. There are 778 Knape families, which makes us quite an exclusive bunch!

The number of Countries, States, Territories or Provinces where households reside i.e. 778 shows 272 (estimate) in the USA, 48 in Australia, 493 in Germany, 152 in Netherlands and 90 in Great Britain. The majority in Great Britain are to be found in the North-West (largely Lancashire and Cheshire) and Scotland. I look forward with great anticipation to making contact, now the record has been completed.

It is yet another story which I find it impossible to describe as a coincidence.

Chapter III

MOTHER AND FATHER

It would be impossible for me to write about my life without stating from the outset that the two most important influences were my mother and father. I do not find it easy to write.

Mother was little more than a domestic slave in our earliest years. With two daughters and a son born within three years and two months, another daughter after an interval of 2½ years, and another son and daughter in a year less one day of each other, her life was not easy. She was six years older than my father and he was only twenty-one when they married. Both lived in Burnley, attended the same church, and were largely brought together through the influence of my father's eldest sister, Aunt Ruth. I was given to understand that Mother suffered much under a cruel stepfather.

As they left the church, Father dressed in formal wear, with spats and a wing collar (known colloquially as a 'come to Jesus' collar), feeling happy and rather pleased with himself, heard one of the ladies in the gathered spectators say, 'Ee look, he's nobbut a lad.'

Mother worked night and day in her domestic duties. She loved to rise at 5 a.m. or earlier and work until late evening, washing, scrubbing, cleaning, baking, sewing, polishing, knitting and darning. But in all our years of childhood not one of us sat on her knee, had a cuddle, except as a babe in arms, or a bedtime story. She had favourites. My eldest sister Peggy (Margaret Elizabeth), I, as the elder son, sister Joie (Ruth Joie) and brother Stuart (Edward Stuart) were the apple of her eye. Sister Jeanne was often ill-treated and contracted a nervous complaint. Youngest sister Ann was the most unfortunate of all. She has recently retired after a lifetime of teaching including latterly a period as a dedicated headmistress. Her qualifications and interests are in Infant Teaching. When she was born, my mother nearly died.

Special prayer meetings were held at our church for Mother in what were regarded as her final hours, but she survived, and stayed in the private nursing home where my sister was born, for six months. Not until after the death of both my parents did Peggy reveal to me that Ann's treatment became such that she was to be adopted by Aunt Ruth and Uncle Andrew, who had married late in life and were childless.

They were my godparents. Jeanne qualified as a nurse and midwife and took the early opportunity of an exchange visit to the USA, apparently for twelve months. She never returned except for normal short visits and is happily married to an American doctor of Brazilian birth, whom she met in hospital while nursing. Theirs was, and is, an ideal marriage. I miss her greatly and a visit is something I have much in mind. On the occasion of her marriage and at other times I was naturally expected to look after the family legal practice, and so enable Father to go.

My sister Ann was baptized Lily because of the fact that my mother, of that name, was not expected to live. Mother's name was Elizabeth but she was always called Lily.

Everyone married early, except the elder son, and father told me in later years that he felt entitled to keep one of us at home in return for his having stayed with my mother for our sakes. I was thirty-one when first married, which was late in those days.

While Mother was in the nursing home, we were very fortunate to be looked after by her then unmarried sister, Auntie Hattie. Auntie applied herself unceasingly to our care and showed us great affection. It would be difficult to pay too great a tribute for all she did. She later married a widower who became our Uncle Fred, one of the most charming and unassuming of men. His daughter Marjorie has been close to us over the years, and I am now in regular contact with her.

The following is a report of Auntie's death in a local newspaper:

A former Chairman of the old Spenborough Urban Council and a prominent figure in the business and public life of the district, Mr F.A. Brown, has been bereaved by the death of his wife, Mrs Harriet (Hattie) Brown, of 120, Westfield Lane, Wyke.

Mrs Brown, who died on Sunday in the Duke of York Home, Bradford, was an enthusiastic supporter of her husband in his interests in public affairs and in her younger days was a talented musician and accomplished concert pianist. She was a member of a musical family originating from the Burnley district of Lancashire, and her cousin, Mr Lawrence Turner, was a former leader of the Halle Orchestra.

She leaves a widower.

A service at Whitechapel Church on Wednesday preceded internment at Cleckheaton New Cemetery.

The story of my life would not be complete nor would it be honest without commenting on the difficult relationship which existed throughout between my mother and father. In the early years I loved my mother and the opening words of my story reflect the natural attraction to the one who performs the daily domestic chores, tasks and duties, for a young child. Mother always seemed to be there and my early affection was for her.

There is no doubt at all in my mind that Father stayed with Mother for the sake of their children, and that he sacrificed so much in the way of happiness, friendship, leisure and achievement because of his love for us. He had pet names for some of us. Peggy, my eldest sister (christened Margaret Elizabeth) he called 'Peter'. I heard him explain more than once that it was a reference to Peter the Apostle and the words of Jesus at Caesarea Philippi after Peter's bold statement 'Thou art the Christ, the Son of the living God.' There followed the words of Jesus that 'upon this rock I will build my Church'. Father was referring to his dynasty!

These words of Jesus, of course, have become controversial and a matter of unending debate among scholar and Church member alike. The Roman Catholic Church refers to it as justification and reason for its primacy, whereas others refer to the 'rock' as meaning Peter's affirmation of his belief in Jesus being the Messiah.

Jeanne was often referred to as Monte Bré, a hill near Luzano which Father, Peggy, Jeanne and I had climbed on our visit to Switzerland in 1946, and which was intended to refer to her ample schoolgirl figure.

Sunny Jim was often my name, and Joie was 'Off at Boggart' which may sound offensive to strangers. It was simply a Lancashire phrase Father once used to describe her action of walking quickly ahead of the rest of us, when on holiday abroad in the South of France.

Stuart had to suffer 'Neddy' or (from his brothers and sisters) 'Num num' which was his way of referring to a sweet, for which he regularly asked from his pram.

Ann unfortunately became 'Loopy' but it was used good-naturedly and she was far from being backward, as her subsequent career proved. I cannot remember its origin.

It was not possible to discuss anything with Mother. On one occasion I said something was black and she insisted it was white. Eventually, in frustration, I brought the article to her. Her reply 'I still say its white' was typical of so much about her. We so much wanted to love her but her continual and constant criticism of all and everything made it very difficult. She had few good words for anyone and was very conscious of being slightly better than most other people because of my father's occupation and our material possessions.

I remember asking on one occasion why we didn't shop at the local Co-op where many of my friends and their mums went. I knew about the 'divi' they paid. 'We don't shop at places like that,' was her reply.

But there were happy times, and above all we had great fun among ourselves as children. We never were short of home-made entertainment. Cricket, football, cards, houses, hospitals, skating, skipping, snakes and ladders, chess, draughts, Monopoly, conkers, tree-climbing, camping, and a hundred other enjoyable games and pastimes ensured a balanced upbringing. Our numbers alone cancelled out any possibility of selfishness.

Our holidays in childhood consisted almost entirely of two weeks in Abersoch in north Wales. We went in the late spring and it was entirely a beach holiday. Lovely golden sands with a large beach hut rented for £1-1-0d per week, a canoe hired for 7/6d per week, a football, cricket bat, ball and wickets, buckets and spades and deckchairs were all we needed for a wonderful time. There must have been wet days because I remember going to the cinema in Pwellheli, seven miles away, on a few occasions. Many identify with me when I seem to recall endless hours of sunshine not only then but in all summer holidays from school. There are memories of Mother gently applying lotion to sunburnt backs and arms.

We stayed with Mrs Wheeler in her small guest house and when I walked out of the front door in the morning, a clap of the hands, and dozens of rabbits ran hither and thither in the field across the lane. I understand it is no longer a sleepy village with largely unmade roads, but have not visited since those days.

Dad seemed to spend most of the morning on the telephone to the office. I am sure he had every letter read to him and directed operations in the practice almost as if he were there.

One year he bought a trailer for our enormous pile of luggage and we called it 'Jumbo'. On our first trip with Jumbo hitched to the car we were stopped by police. I think it was a matter of the trailer not bearing the car's registration number. It was very hot, the sun-roof was drawn back, Dad was in trousers and shirt only, and he was accompanied by mother and six children. The officer took one look at him, assimilated the position instantly and waved him on with a brief word to have it seen to on return from holiday, and accompanied by a sympathetic look.

Mother had a lovely soprano voice and used it to good effect in choirs and as a soloist over the years. Father fell in love with her as she sang 'Oh for the wings of a dove' in the choir at Bethel Primitive Methodist Church in Burnley where so much of the life of their families was spent. She was the only one with musical talent in the family. Father bought a baby grand piano in later years. Some of us could play a little but it was much underused. It has been a source of great pleasure to me that on Mother's death we decided to make a gift of it to the Church, and it has had a place of honour in the children's corner of Bare Methodist Church since 1979. The pianists tell me it is a lovely instrument, and above all it is used regularly in worship and at other services. A minister of our Church, the Rev. John Harris BA, who recently retired, played it a great deal and told me he found much pleasure in doing so.

As I have said, it is not easy to write about Mother. I, above all of us, have the most regrets. I lost my temper repeatedly when Mother's words and actions seemed uncalled for, but I think I upset myself more than her. Certainly my sisters and brothers showed greater tolerance, although in extenuation perhaps I should add that I was at home for many more years than any of them.

I have asked for divine forgiveness for many unkind words, and particularly after my father's death when Mother became a virtual recluse for eight years. Few people visited her, she lived a strange and unnatural life within the four walls of Clevelands on which I do not propose to elaborate, except to express my gratitude to my sister Peggy who lived nearby and attended to her needs and foibles unceasingly during these years, when she herself was leading a busy life.

I look back on my relationship with Mother, as with so many other things, with a great measure of sadness and regret but also as part of God's plan for my life, and without which I would not have found the path I tread, and the joy I experience in these later years of life.

Father and I were more like inseparable brothers, than father and son. We shared the same professional life as solicitors in the practice he founded, farmed in the Lake District together for twenty-five years until his death, played golf, spent much of our leisure time together as keen supporters and season ticket holders of Burnley and Preston North End football clubs, and generally enjoyed each other's company. I came as close to worshipping him as is possible. He was a Churchillian figure to me and all with whom he came into contact, full of common sense, having a deep care and compassion for all, generous and full of a driving life spirit.

My dedication of this book, which was easily settled, reflects the feelings of countless men and women who have reason to give thanks for his life, selfless service and love.

In spite of thinking otherwise, during my first forty-one years, I never had a real problem in life. And then he died on 24 April 1971 aged sixty-four. Our farm manager's wife, in whose arms he died, said 'Mr John,' (for so I was called), 'my mother is in her eighties, little more than a cabbage, visited regularly in hospital but unable to communicate, and has been like this for years. Why should she still live on and a man like your father, with all he had to offer, pass away?'

I was to be asked a similar question on the death of my wife Vera at thirty-seven, from cancer.

Why does God do this? Why does God do that? Why does God allow

20

this to happen? Why does He allow that to happen? Always the question is an open one. I believe if we knew with absolute certainty that God exists, that right will ultimately triumph over wrong, that there is a new and better life for each of us hereafter, then there would be no room for a free-loving response to the love of God. We would be little more than puppets. Life without faith would be 'a tale told by an idiot, full of sound and fury, signifying nothing'. The mind revolts at the idea.

To give up, to give in, is to make the final surrender. My mind and everything in me rebels against the idea that there is no meaning or sense, or purpose in life or history; that 'when you're dead you're done'. Always there is mystery, and the faith that bets your life on there being a God.

Many years ago I read in the *Westmorland Gazette*, a letter to the editor complaining about the state of the road from Kendal to Bowness, a narrow, winding, country road with hedgerows encroaching on the drivers who passed that way. Why did the Council not get their act together and clear the offending growth? The following week came a reply from a country lover pointing out the wealth of beauty and interest in the hedgerows. Blackthorn and hawthorn, and many other treasures of nature were there to be seen, by those who knew and loved their nature. And so it is with those who know God. Jesus said 'Blessed are the pure in heart: for they shall see God.'

Paul wrote to the Corinthians in the great hymn of love: 'For now we see through a glass darkly, but then face to face.'

When we attain unto a measure of the fullness of the stature of Christ, 'His servants shall serve Him: and they shall see His face.'

> But what to those who find? Ah! this
> Nor tongue nor pen can show:
> The love of Jesus, what it is
> None but His loved ones know

> (Bernard of Clairvaux 1091-1153;
> Tr. by Edward Caswall 1814-78)

21

Chapter IV

SATANIC MILLS TO GALILEE

In lighter moments, I have wondered if the reason my family left Burnley when I was four years old, was because of my eldest sister's pink knickers. Father augmented his income for mother and four young children by keeping poultry. The thought of a solicitor, for such he was, having to do this in my time, or even today, seems far from reality.

My mother and father told me in later years that it was my practice from time to time to slip through the wooden palings surrounding the hut and land close to our home, where he kept the hens and cockerel, remove the eggs and throw them to the ground. I then substituted 'pot' or porcelain eggs which Father kept, and which were a well-known method of encouraging backward hens to start production. I plead neither innocent nor guilty, because I cannot remember.

The shame fell upon me one day when I fell into a water-filled hole in the ground, on returning from the hut to the road on one such mischievous expedition. Memories are vivid of standing up to my waist in cold water, with three or four laughing mums, staring at me from a distance of a few yards. They were too ample of girth to climb through the gap in the fence which I had used. Somehow rescue came.

Mother made it clear that the only available article of clothing for the lower half of my body was my eldest sister's pink knickers. My friends were playing cricket outside our home, using one of the gate pillars as wickets, and although embarrassed and the object of ridicule when I emerged, not even self-conscious confusion kept me from joining in the game.

In later years I would speak of my unwillingness to leave the town of my birth at the tender age of four years, by relating the events of the day we left. Father had gone ahead to Morecambe. Mother and four children, who then formed the family, left later in the day, in a large car, with many of our belongings. I remember seeing clearly, as I sat in the back, that the rear offside door was not fully closed. Chamber pots were stacked close to it and as I moved restlessly to and fro, I leaned against the door. We were turning the long bend outside Lowerhouse Cricket Club on the outskirts of Burnley, when I fell out. I can recall the experience of rolling over and over down the road which joined the one on which we were travelling, and seeing in the distance the approach of another car. The next thing I remember is of being nursed comfortingly in the arms of a kind lady from one of the adjoining houses, who had obviously come to our rescue. I suffered nothing more serious than cuts, bruises and bumps which were bathed and dressed. A pair of velvet green leggings I was wearing probably saved me from serious injury and for the active sporting life I was to lead. There were large holes in the knee areas and my own knees today bear the considerable scars of the incident.

In later years when I saw the film of John Wesley's life, when he was plucked from the fire at Epworth as a babe, I was reminded of events in all our lives which, though at the time apparently meaningless, and often unfortunate and tragic, nevertheless are later seen as having a purpose and meaning in the vast eternal plan.

My grandfather was determined that my father would not enter the cotton trade, as would have been expected of many boys educated at Burnley Grammar School. The booms and recessions of the industry were notorious and family folklore tells of fortunes made and lost.

John Knape was the name given to the eldest son for as far back as can be remembered, as I have already mentioned, and my own son bears the name of Andrew John. Grandfather was an identical twin, and many are the stories of girlfriends shared and other escapades.

And so Father was articled to Mr George W. Jobling, a solicitor of good repute in the town, who practised with his brother, Mr Tom Jobling, under the firm name of Jobling and Jobling in Hargreaves Street in former bank premises. Mr Tom was employed in the Blackpool office of the partnership. Living was not easy as the keeping of poultry indicates. Father told me of writing to the local paper, asking if they could offer him weekend employment as a football reporter. The editor replied, enquiring from my father about the possibilities of employment in the law firm!

Taken into limited partnership, Father soon opened a branch office in Morecambe which he attended on one day a week. Business prospered in a rapidly developing town to such an extent that he had to decide either to close or to move. He chose the latter course, a brave decision in uncertain times, with a wife and four young children, but thereby demonstrated his belief in his own ability. It was to prove a wise choice.

The following is an extract from a booklet entitled *Southern, Jobling & Ashworth Solicitors 1792-1991* which I recently received from Miss Muriel Jobling, the daughter of Mr George and an outstanding solicitor in her own right:

This firm of Jobling Jobling & Knape (Joblings) was founded in Burnley in about 1889 by Smith Lawson soon after he had completed his Articles of Clerkship with, of all firms, Artindale & Artindale! Apart from his legal ability, he was a talented musician being Organist at Worsthorne Parish Church and then at St Pauls in Burnley. Quite apart from all this, he was one of the first three residents at Burnley to own a motor car. Lawyers to the fore!

When he died at Easter, 1919 in his fifty-fifth year Mr Lawson had established in his practice 'An extensive connection, chiefly in conveyancing and County Court work', to quote his obituary in the local paper. In particular, he was solicitor to the Burnley Grocers' Association and this link remained until the late 1960s leading to the amalgamated firm of Southern, Jobling & Ashworth acting for Burnley Wholesale Grocers Limited which seemed to rise phoenix-like from the ashes of the Grocers' Association.

Mr Lawson was clearly a man of ability and force to establish Joblings in the town and expand it to the stage where he was able to take into partnership in about 1917, Thomas Ernest Jobling, who had been articled to him and to whom he was related by marriage. Tom Jobling (as he was usually known) built vigorously on this foundation and when his brother George was admitted as a Solicitor in 1922 after service in the Great War, they went into partnership together under the style of Jobling & Jobling. They were an effective partnership, because George was the lawyer and the workhorse in the firm, while Tom was the business and organizing partner.

Whilst Joblings prospered locally, they also developed a talent in the 1920s for expansion into different parts of the county. Because his wife was advised by her doctor that her health required such a move, Tom moved to and opened an office in Blackpool in 1924 which became another thriving practice. He still continued to travel to the Burnley office each Monday to oversee the work of that office which was really being done by George.

In the early 1930s John Knape, who had served his articles with the firm, persuaded the brothers to open an office in Morecambe where there were builder clients, and soon after that an office in Barrow-in-Furness followed. The office in Morecambe was to grow into one of the larger firms of solicitors in north Lancashire, bearing the name of Jobling, Jobling & Knape, as John Knape had emulated the business capacity of Tom, by becoming a director of a number of companies including Loxhams Garages, the West End Pier and also the Marsden Building Society.

Throughout this time, George continued to work in the Burnley office but also lent his conveyancing expertise to all offices and was accustomed to going to the Morecambe office one day each week until the Second

World War. The outbreak of this war caused great upheavals. John Knape was called up to serve as an officer with the Royal Air Force and George lost his articled clerk and all other male members of staff within a matter of weeks. Coincidentally, George's daughter Muriel had entered the practice as an articled clerk on 3 September 1939 and she recalls spending her first week in travelling to the Blackpool and Morecambe offices to bring clients' title deeds into the strongroom at Burnley in the bank premises which they occupied. The purpose of this was to safeguard the deeds from 'imminent enemy action'.

On the death of Tom Jobling in 1954, John Knape and his sons and other partners took over the Morecambe and Barrow practices entirely, and George and Muriel were left with both Burnley and Blackpool practices to run. This they did successfully until 1958 when there was an opportunity for an articled clerk from the Blackpool office who had then qualified to take over that practice. At the same time Muriel was approached by Guy Southern, John Southern and William Ashworth (Partners in Southern, Ritchie & Ashworth) to consider a merger with their firm and this took place on 1 April 1958. George retired then as a Partner and happily settled into his natural role as an invaluable backroom conveyancer where he continued with the newly merged firm for many years.

Muriel Jobling

Apart from her work in the Practice, which was principally in the field of family and matrimonial law and conveyancing, Muriel also achieved local, regional and national recognition in several fields. The Girl Guide movement was her first and perhaps most abiding love and Muriel became an International Trainer and Commonwealth Headquarters Guide Adviser.

Her involvement with the Health Service went back to her membership of the Burnley Executive Council which was concerned with the doctors, dentists, chemists and opticians in the Health Service. She was also a member and indeed chairman of other Health Service committees over many years and it is interesting to reflect that one of Muriel's first jobs as an articled clerk had been to collect debts for a General Practitioner from patients who struggled to pay his fees of 6d per week!

For much of her practising life, Muriel had been the only female solicitor in the town but this had never daunted her. Muriel was the first woman to propose the toast to the Bench and Bar at a dinner of the Burnley & District Law Debating Society in 1954 and Neville Laski QC, who was then Recorder of Burnley, said her speech should be reprinted and circulated. Muriel then became the first woman President of the Burnley & District Law Society and the first woman in the country to achieve such distinction. Her role as a 'statutory woman' (to use her own words) have also led to her serving as a General Commissioner of Income Tax for Burnley and District and as a lay member for the Parole Board for England and Wales upon which she served for four and half years. She has also worked in a judicial capacity as an Adjudicator for Immigration Appeals and continues to sit as a Society Security Appeal Chairman at the present day.

Muriel served for four years as Chairman of the Burnley Pendle & Rossendale Health Authority in the 1980s and since then she has helped to found and remains Chairman of the very successful Burnley & Pendle Hospice movement. Her appointment as Deputy Lieutenant for the County of Lancaster epitomizes her many other local activities and indeed she is one of only two Women Deputy Lieutenants in the County – out of a total of more than fifty. This reflects her standing in the community at large and her devotion to the people of this district who always came first with Muriel.

Muriel was awarded the MBE in 1994 in recognition of her services to the community in Burnley.

And so we moved to Morecambe.

Chapter V

EARLY SCHOOLDAYS

I shall always remember Miss Wilson and her father for giving me a solid grounding in the 3 R's. They lived in a detached bungalow round the corner from my home and had about a dozen boys and girls from the immediate area under their care. On the first morning, at the age of five, I arrived with Father at the front door. I can remember the tension as I stood there, and Miss Wilson opened the door. After a pregnant pause, I lashed out with my legs and arms, kicking the door, struggling and crying with fear. Thus I began my education.

Life thereafter was a pleasure and I looked forward to each day with anticipation. Mr Wilson marked my sums with a short stub of a pencil, we read a great deal, and wrote sentences and short essays. Games on the lawn at the rear enabled me to show and develop my running and ball skills. When I left at seven, Father told me that Mr Wilson informed him I would have no difficulty in getting to Oxford. It remained my ambition which turned to regret when, in later years, Father would not allow me to enter. Everyone is a Cambridge or Oxford supporter in the Boat Race, and perhaps my support for Oxford stemmed from this, but at the time it seemed to me to be nothing more than a preference for the sound of the name. I was to see the fulfilment of my dream in my daughter.

In 1937 I entered Euston Road Primary School in Morecambe at the age of seven, and soon became aware of the benefits flowing from a good grounding in the 3 R's. Taken into the first class in the school on arrival, I was asked to do a little sight-reading. After two or three sentences I was taken to the second form room for a repeat performance, and finally settled in the third form.

I had an excellent teacher when I was in the class preceding the 11-plus year, or scholarship class as it was then known. Miss Harrison was everyone's idea of a model teacher. Always smartly dressed in twin set and pearls, she spoke clearly and calmly and was able to keep order without asserting her authority. She educed a desire for learning in me and involved us all in her work.

My concerns were twofold. I was quite useless at Art, taken by the Headmaster, and was moved down for that subject to 2b, from 3a. This was ignominy of the worst order, but alleviated by Miss Annie Laity, the teacher who took me under her wing, recognizing my embarrassment. She was later to be the Sunday School Superintendent at the church I have attended all my life. She started her own Independent School in the town and devoted her life to children. I remember her saying on retirement, as Superintendent, that the one thing above all others she had tried to instil was a sense of worship. Miss Laity had the faith and presence for that laudable aim. The other problem was the teacher of the 11-plus class. 'Lofty' Holdsworth was a terror in the classroom. We formed the view that he caned several boys each day as a matter of principle. The thought of spending a year in his class terrified me. My eldest sister Peggy did so, but she was of a much calmer temperament. In addition, his temper seemed to be concentrated on the boys.

I won a national handwriting competition whilst there. We sat in class and the girl next to me nudged my arm from time to time. I had thought her far better than me and my ink had bits in it. Thin upstroke and thick downstroke was the order of the day. When Mr Drummond, the Headmaster, said in assembly that the winner, when announced, should walk up the middle aisle to receive his or her prize, I was only half listening, and hardly heard my name. Others pushed me forward and several tried to trip me up on the way to receive my book. Father disposed of the book, with others, when clearing out in later years and never knew the loss I felt. It was a valued possession.

I passed the scholarship examination to the Grammar School, but Peggy failed.

We had three papers – Arithmetic, English and Problems. I cannot remember there being any pressure on me, as is the case today. This may have been because I was in the preparation class and not expected to pass until the following year. The dress rehearsal turned out to be the real thing. Peggy was a good all-rounder and proved it in later life. There was apparently a system for fee-payers to obtain places for their children who had failed the examination, and Peggy obtained entry in this way. I was told to be nice to her and I remember the tears.

I have never been able to understand the reason for the abolition of Grammar Schools, orchestrated by Shirley Williams, and Anthony Crosland later, for two reasons. The first is that every child, regardless of status or wealth, had the opportunity of a route through such schools to University. The other is more fundamental to our social fabric. Children in secondary modern schools were regarded as failures. I had such friends and invariably they had practical skills I never enjoyed. One of them made a car when in his early teens. Another would take a wireless set to bits and put it together. Others were outstanding with woodwork and working with other materials. I envied them. It seemed then and now that such a person is of at least equal status, and particularly in a manufacturing economy which has now been so largely destroyed. I was a 'pen-pusher' with so-called academic ability. In Communist Russia the engineer enjoyed superior status to that of the doctor. At least they had one thing in balance.

When my children came to take their 11-plus examination in later years, I was confident they would pass. I felt embarrassed at parents' evenings, spending as little time as possible with each teacher. Perhaps I was fortunate, but the life and death manner with which some parents captured each teacher's attention for an inordinate length of time, appalled me. I am sure it did harm to the children who could not fail to feel the vibes. Many of my children's contemporaries were offered bribes by ambitious parents and a few were threatened with the results of failure.

To return to my exam. I was average in Arithmetic (hopeless later when it came to Algebra, Geometry and Logarithms), slightly below average in Problems, but well above average in English. I am sure this was reflected in my papers and increased my inability to understand my sister's failure. She was a good steady all-rounder.

A few weeks before I had been reading about clouds, and had assimilated a great deal of information about, and was familiar with, the names of Cirrus, Cirrostratus, Cirrocumulus, Altostratus, Altocumulus, Stratocumulus, Stratus, Nimbostratus, Cumulus and Cumulonimbus. The exam paper offered three options for the essay and one was – yes – 'Clouds'! The examiner must have thought I was a genius. I sometimes wonder if that, and that alone, got me through, and shivered at the prospect of what would have happened if I had gone into Lofty Holdsworth's class.

I am certain Mother and Father did not expect me to pass. On returning home with the papers, he questioned Peggy, my best friend Ernest and myself about the papers and our answers. I remember we had to give the meaning of several words in the English paper. One was 'impenetrable' and I cannot remember the answers of the others. He turned to me and I said, 'Cannot be got through'. I think I noticed a flicker of hope on his face about my prospects, as he said, 'Excellent, that's it.'

When I first was shown round Morecambe Grammar School along with my parents, it filled me with a feeling I find difficult to describe. Euston Road was an old building erected in Victorian times. There was a hard-surfaced playground and we had to walk a mile to our football pitch. The Grammar School had only been erected some ten years previously. Its red brick exterior, with gymnasium, science laboratories, spacious classrooms, a dining room, and other facilities, the like of which I had never imagined, were even surpassed by the library. I cannot remember a room which appealed to me more on first acquaintance. The whole was surrounded by magnificent level playing fields, providing football, cricket and hockey pitches, and tennis courts for the girls.

My best friend, Ernest, and I were to reach a high standard of play on those courts, by playing on Saturday mornings when nobody was about. Ernest lived opposite the school. It was a very good school under Mr H.H. Palmer JP, a strict disciplinarian, but held in great respect in the town.

On one occasion we were visited by Harry Healess, who had captained Blackburn Rovers in the FA Cup Final of 1928. A Lancashire CC Education employee, he came to coach us for the day. He taught me the way to take corners and noted my name. Dick Taylor, known affectionately as 'Toffee Taylor', a well-known local figure and keen supporter of football, watched one of our games, and presented a few sticks of his renowned Morecambe rock to me as his choice as outstanding player. 'Uncle' Dick was standing outside the dressing room in 1952 to shake my hand as I ran out for my home debut, playing for my home team of Morecambe, in the Lancashire Combination at Christie Park. It is now the GM Vauxhall Conference.

Peter Gambrill comes to mind. He was a boy of my age with a lovely soprano voice, and the Headmaster often included him in morning assembly to sing the third verse of the hymn 'Praise, my soul, the King of Heaven.' In those days I did not appreciate the purpose of the first comma, and often thought it was strange to ask God to praise my soul.

The third verse reads:

> Father-like he tends and spares us
> Well our feeble frame He knows
> In His hands He gently bears us
> Rescues us from all our foes
> Praise Him! Praise Him!
> Widely as His mercy flows

Unfortunately when his voice broke, the quality was not the same and tragically he died, not many years later.

My class when I left were, on average, thirteen years of age, and the boys and girls were beginning to organize dances. It was a small disappointment to leave. The Headmaster was kind enough to come to the classroom to wish me farewell in front of my friends. I had no really deep feelings and accepted my parents' plans for me. Probably the thought that I was going to a soccer school buoyed me up.

Chapter VI

SHREWSBURY SCHOOL

Father and I travelled by train to Shrewsbury from Lancaster. I was not frightened or depressed, and felt that there was a reasonable equanimity in me for the first part of the journey. I say part of the journey because the position changed when we joined the Shrewsbury train at Crewe.

In our carriage were two mothers and their sons, also travelling to the same school for their first term. Mother to mother, son to son, they never ceased to talk all the way, excitedly, interestingly, with a *joie de vivre* and maturity which simply overwhelmed me. Prepatory school had done its job. They knew where they were going. Their manner was confident, but above all their accents were so upper class that I felt completely out of my depth and remained silent all the way. Father, a sociable, outgoing, relaxed person must have sensed it was the time for him to do the same.

Things have changed enormously since 1943 as in so many areas of life. I can testify to some of them through my brother, who went in 1952, and my nephew in 1967.

When I look through the Shrewsbury School Register of the 183 boys who were new that term, I see an orthopaedic registrar MA MB BChir FRCS; an MA Univ of London (RAF Chinese Language Course); two with MA MB BChir DCH DObst RCOG; one with MA MBChir MRCS LRCP MD (Maryland); a Chief Accountant to BSA Guns Ltd; nine Cambridge MAs and two BAs; three Oxford MAs and one BA; one other MA; a Captain RN of HM Submarines *Artemis* and *Andrew* (a nuclear submarine specialist); four solicitors; one barrister; two Oxford blues; a well-known TV actor (now deceased); and several Sandhurst graduates. Many others were clearly in successful occupations. In all, a typical example of the school.

On arrival at the school we were greeted by my Housemaster, Major A.E. Taylor TD MA of Queen's College, Cambridge, who served the school from 1928 to his death in 1952, and was a Housemaster from 1943. This was his first term as such. I came to love and respect him. He was efficient, hard-working, a little aloof, but above all for me, had played outside right for the English amateur soccer side. He played for the amateur Corinthian Casuals, as well as Cambridge. At the time the former

31

were as formidable as the professionals. I remember being told he played in a side which held Newcastle United to a 2-1 scoreline when the Magpies were at the top of the First Division. He was in charge of school soccer.

The school motto is '*Intus si recte, ne labora*', and no one seemed to know its meaning. I think it denotes that inner strength is sufficient for life, but we each had our own views. One school of thought said it translated as 'If you are alright inside, there is no need to work'. Another more engaging translation was dedicated to the virtues of Andrews Liver Salts. Incidentally my father always had a glass of the product in the bathroom every day I lived at home, and I suspect, thereafter – constipation and inner cleanliness were never a problem for him. But it was a strange motto for a school with a great classical tradition.

It was wartime and this was almost certainly the reason for my easy entry. The custom was for a father to put down his son's name at birth and entry had been, and came again to be, very competitive. Entry to a public school was a standard Common Entrance Exam for which all the other boys had been trained during years at prep school. Most of them started their education at the age of seven, or even younger. I had not received any special coaching and was not aware of the importance of the exam. One day, the Headmaster's secretary extracted me from my form room, sat me at a desk in a room next to her office, and, in effect, told me to get on with it. I cannot remember the content of the papers, or feelings about my performance. One handicap certainly was that at prep school, Latin was taught from the beginning. I had only begun in my second year at the Grammar School, when aged eleven. Shrewsbury had a reputation for being one of the very best in the country for the Classics. The house complement was not full and Major Taylor had been eager for me to enter his house, largely I suspect because Father had earlier briefed him on my soccer skills.

Father had looked at several outstanding public schools before choosing Shrewsbury and the balance which swayed him was the soccer reputation. He knew of my almost fanatical love of the game, and that a rugby-playing school would have severely handicapped my happiness and scholastic progress. How right he was. Shrewsbury had not then lost a school match for nine years, and were unbeaten at home for fourteen years.

My house was Churchill's (the name of a previous Housemaster and unconnected with the great statesman) and I joined two older boys in my study. I was fortunate they accepted me for what I was, a new boy who had never been to a prep school, completely ignorant of their way of life and, worst of all, with a Lancashire accent. Such were called Oiks, and I was known as one for a long time.

It was Major Taylor's custom to invite three or four boys to Sunday breakfast, with his wife and children (if at home) being present. The invitation was extended to me on the Saturday evening, during his round of the dormitories, and of course was obligatory. He invited me on my first Sunday as a very new boy. I remember standing on my bed, paying particular attention to my dress, and using Brylcream for my hair. As I turned from the mirror the other boys were standing and staring, with grimaces. This really was an Oik. One did not use hair cream. At breakfast the conversation was stilted, and I disgraced myself by severing the black, hard crust of my sausages, and sending pieces flying all over the long table. There was a long silence with not a word to ease the traumatic moment. I wished myself afar.

By the end of term I had acquired their accent, and when my erstwhile friends from Morecambe Grammar School came to my home to greet me at the end of term they stayed but a few minutes, noting I had become a 'posh snob' and wanted nothing more to do with me. I could not win.

On the first day I was standing with a group of other new boys in the corridor and proffered a sweet to each. The Head of House came out of the monitors' study, and sneered, 'After today, scum will not eat out of their studies.' New boys were known as scum. Some weeks afterwards, during a meal in hall, he barked my surname in front of fifty boys and summoned me to his table. A noisy room subsided into complete silence. After a pause he said, 'Knape, I am told you are an Oik. Cut me a slice of bread.' Shades of Tom Brown's schooldays. I will leave it there. I came to hate the Head of House and Praepostor (School Prefect) with a burning ferocity, and his departure at the end of that academic year was both a great relief and marked the end of the old regime, or nearly so.

The surviving relic was the school bully who was in my house. One of his dormitory pleasures was to swing me round in circles by the feet, for long spells, with my head missing the iron bedsteads by the narrowest of margins. But do not let all this detract from my happiness there. My sporting ability was a sound foundation in my life. If it had not been for Jonathan Clegg, I would have been the 1st XI outside right, in spite of my tiny stature and slight frame.

I met Jonathan at a friend's wedding in later years and he greeted me by my soccer name of 'Twinkle Toes'. Jonathan became a Praepostor, played cricket, soccer, fives and athletics for the school, was an Oxford Soccer blue in 1950, 1951 and 1952 (when the match against Cambridge was played at Wembley), gained an MA there, and subsequently became Headmaster of Holmwood Prep School in Formby, Lancs from where he sent many boys to Shrewsbury via the entrance exam. A great all-rounder and a winsome personality.

A formidable rival indeed, but he would be the first to admit I kept him on his toes and I knew that Major Taylor was on occasion tempted to play me. On one occasion he told me that he would like me to play at Charterhouse, a ground known for its dry condition, which he felt would suit my physique and style of play. I was a regular in the second XI.

There was a special sporting experience for me when Tommy Lawton, my boyhood football hero, came to the school at the invitation of my Housemaster, Major Taylor, to coach the 1st XI. My sense of a special relationship, compared with the other boys in the dining hall of our house, stemmed from him being a Burnley player at the start of his career before moving to Everton, then Chelsea, and finally becoming the first of a new breed – player-manager of Notts County. I saw him score a hat-trick at Turf Moor for Burnley when he was seventeen. The players of the 1st XI were exceedingly impressed.

I played cricket and Eton fives to a good level, and took part in cross-country runs for which the school was well-known. The annual Tucks involved the whole school and many of the masters. Major Taylor did not approve of these runs for his soccer players, being of the view that they required long strides, anathema to a mán who knew the importance of the short, sharp sprint in soccer.

Although the choice was between rowing and cricket, I was occasionally pressed into service as a cox on the River Severn, because of my diminutive stature. One day, when coxing an eight, we sprang a leak. Our coach, on his bicycle and shouting instructions through his megaphone, ignored my pleas.

'We're sinking, sir.'

'Yes, but stroke, get your hands forward.'

I took my life in my hands, ignored his shouts and returned to the boathouse in the nick of time. The coach was Rev. J.O. Whitfield MA former housemaster of my house and my form master. He was very deaf!

Starting in the third form, the bottom class for duffers, and those not yet properly assessed, I made steady progress, streaming on to the Classical side at an early stage, and producing in my School Certificate a pass in Maths, credits in French, German, Roman History, History, Greek and English language, and distinctions in English Literature and Divinity (RE or RI as we know them today).

Father would not let me stay beyond a fourth year which was a source of great disappointment. It meant I could not take my Higher School Certificate (A levels) and seek to enter Oxford, which remained a burning ambition, or, and at the time this seemed more important, give me the opportunity of making the 1st XI soccer side. It has remained a source of diminishing regret all my life, but Father thought it wise for me to start my five-year articles, in his solicitors' practice, commencing as an office boy and work my way up. I saw my Oxford ambition fulfilled in my daughter Catherine, who attained an Honours degree in Chinese (Mandarin) at Wadham College, Oxford.

Life at Shrewsbury was disciplined but always enjoyable. We had compulsory cold baths in the morning, entailing leaping into a full bath of icy water, pausing for a few seconds, and then leaping out for a brisk towelling. The warm glow which followed made it almost worthwhile, even in the depths of winter. First lesson followed, which meant a forty-minute teaching session in the school buildings before breakfast. Chapel was compulsory after breakfast and the making of beds. Also compulsory were Matins and Evensong on Sundays. Morning Chapel lasted some twenty minutes, and I owe a great debt of gratitude to the Anglican Church for teaching me the Collects and Creeds, the beauty and dignity of worship, not always found in Methodism, and for a daily reminder of things eternal.

Chapel was followed by morning lessons until midday, with a break (and for some a mad rush to the school tuck shop). In the winter, games followed lunch and lessons continued in the late afternoon. In summer the order was reversed. After the evening meal the younger boys did their prep in the dining room, under supervision of a House Monitor. At 'lights out' the Housemaster would visit each bedroom and have a few words with us.

When I reflected in later years, it was clear that I spent much more time at sport, and less in class, than at Morecambe Grammar School. There, in a co-ed school, I was below the average age and working with the top stream of the year. I was below halfway in the order of merit and it may well have been that standing on my own two feet, in a public school, helped to raise my self-esteem and encouraged me to work harder. The Headmaster of the Grammar School, an outstanding man and friend of my father, had wished me well before I left, but said he regretted my father's decision and indicated I would achieve just as much with him. I doubt it and have no regrets at all for this widening of my horizons and experience of life, but Oxford still hurts a little!

The school was founded by Edward VI in 1552. In the late seventeenth and eighteenth centuries it had its ups and downs, partly because of loyalty to the Stuart cause. At the end of the eighteenth century three great headmasters, Butler, Kennedy and Moss, made great improvements in its academic standing and started a remarkable run of university successes, which made it famous as a centre of classical teaching. They covered the whole of the eighteenth century and during this period the school was without rival in classical successes at Oxford and Cambridge.

Situated, since 1882, on a superb site overlooking the Severn and the town, it always had a fine reputation for rowing as well as Association Football.

We had many ordained Anglican clergymen on the staff, but the one I remember with the greatest affection was the School Chaplain, Rev. C.G. Furnivall MA, formerly scholar of Trinity College, Cambridge, who was my form master for some time. As an impressionable boy I not only recognized his classical scholarship, but his sporting prowess. He had won three university blues and to me was all a man should be. He retired in later years to Crete.

Major H.H. Hardy CBE MA was Headmaster from 1932-44, but in my second year was succeeded by J.F. Wolfenden CBE MA, who at thirty-eight years of age had previously been appointed the youngest Headmaster of the Headmasters' Conference Schools, at Uppingham. He was later to be knighted and become the Chairman of the Wolfenden Report, Vice-Chancellor of Reading University and Director of the British Museum.

On Speech Day in 1944, Major Hardy's last as Headmaster, the guest of honour was Archbishop William Temple, one of the greatest of the Archbishops of Canterbury. As a young first-year boy I sat on the platform only half a dozen strides from the great man. Even at that age, his spirituality and wisdom were plain for all to see and hear and feel. He had been a contemporary of Major Hardy at Rugby and had promised to come before the end of his headmastership – a close-run thing. There was lively banter as Major Hardy disclosed that the Archbishop had assisted him with his religious studies, and the Archbishop retaliated that it was in return for help with his prep (homework) in the Classics.

The most famous old boy is generally regarded as Sir Philip Sidney, and I passed his statue as I went to and fro from my house situated only a few yards away, near the main school gates. An embodiment of chivalric virtue and the nobility of his bearing set the nation's seal on his reputation. Mortally wounded at the Battle of Zutphen in 1556, he is said to have handed a cup of cold water to a dying soldier with the words 'Your need is greater than mine.'

The perceived wisdom of my contemporaries ranked the school as fifth after Eton, Harrow, Winchester and Rugby. I feel that there was little to choose when compared with such schools as Repton, Malvern, Charterhouse, Millfield, Sherborne and several others. Certainly brothers of Salopians were at some or all of these during my time, separated by parents who felt this an advantage.

Many boys had no idea of how the other half lived. Some saw their parents infrequently, especially when the latter lived and worked abroad. This had been their position since going to prep school at six or seven years of age. The stiff upper lip is now seen as a handicap or suppressing healthy emotions and the cause of problems in later life, but it was plain to see in my time at Shrewsbury. A telephone call from the parents of

36

one of my closest friends, inviting me in the school holidays to their substantial country estate, was politely turned down by my parents because of our modest home, albeit a modern, detached house.

One of my closest friends was Richard Tucker. We were in the same house and form. Richard arrived at Shrewsbury a year later than me. He was the only boy in Churchill's in our class, and where our education was very much involved with the Classics with which the school was associated. It was clear that he had a good mind. In addition I found him always equable, friendly and given to a more retiring than forward disposition.

He was fond of rowing. Our interest in the legal profession was mutual as Richard's father was a County Court Judge. In later years I consulted him professionally on my matrimonial affairs and met him in Stoke-on-Trent after he had spent a busy day in court. He was then a Queen's Counsel. His entry in *Who's Who* is as follows:

TUCKER, Hon. Sir Richard (Howard), Kt 1985; Hon. Mr Justice Tucker; a Judge of the High Court of Justice, Queen's Bench Division, since 1985; b. 9 July 1930; s of Howard Archibald Tucker, later His Honour Judge Tucker, and Margaret Minton Tucker; m 1st, 1958 Paula Mary Bennett Frost (Marr. diss. 1974); one s two d; 2nd, 1975. Wendy Kate Standbook (d 1988); 3rd 1989, Jacqueline Suzanne Rossvell Thomson, widow of William Thomson, artist. Educ: Shrewsbury Sch: The Queen's Coll., Oxford (MA; Hon. fellow, 1992). Called to Bar, Lincoln's Inn 1954; Bencher, 1979, QC 1972: a Recorder, 1972-1985; Mem. Senate, Inns of Court and the Bar, 1984-86; Dep. Leader, 1984-85, and Presiding Judge, 1989-90. Midland and Oxford Circuit Mem., Employment Appeal Tribunal, 1986-. Recreations: sailing, shooting, gardening. Address: Royal Courts of Justice, Strand, WC2A 2LL. Clubs: Garrick: Leander (Henley-on-Thames)

Another close friend, Tony Pack, lived in nearby Church Stretton. I cycled there with him on many occasions on Sundays. He was adopted by a village doctor and his wife, with others of varying ages including a young lady, commissioned in the ATS. We played tennis and enjoyed delicious high teas, and a warm family atmosphere. After leaving school I read in the national press of the award to him of the MC for rescuing a soldier under fire in Korea as an officer of the King's Shropshire Light Infantry. A few days later I read in the same paper of his death, shot in the head by a sniper.

Wartime presented staffing problems and many masters were brought out of retirement, but still presented a formidable array of teaching and other talent.

Because of the Severn and rowing, passing the school swimming test was obligatory. Often with little heating and sometimes with ice on the surface, I had to go to the school baths twice a week until I learned to swim (the one sport I disliked) and complete the regulation five lengths in shorts, shirt, stockings and gym shoes. The air bubble in the shirt provided buoyancy for about three lengths and then was a considerable impediment. I walked the last few yards at the shallow end with relief.

One of my contemporaries was Michael Heseltine. The much publicized photograph in the national press at the time of the Westland helicopter problem, when he walked out of Cabinet, showing him from the rear, walking along Downing Street with golden mane and papers under his arm, was exactly as I remember him walking across the site at Shrewsbury. Old boys will remember him as follows:

LENT TERM, 1947
Heseltine, Michael Ray Dibdin (M) 1 1951. Pembroke Coll:
Oxf. BA. Dir: of publishing and property cos.

He seemed, and this was confirmed to me in later years by a ministerial colleague, a very private person. I never saw him with other boys nor do I remember him on the sporting field.

Ruth Ellis was the last woman to be hanged in the country. The mass press publicity narrated a sorry tale of this poor woman, from a different social class, and her volatile relationship with the Mayfair playboy, David M.B. Blakely. He was her victim. We were in the same house and shared a dormitory for several terms. I remember him as having little enthusiasm for, or interest in, school life, intellectually below average in achievement, interested in rowing and an excellent gymnast. He talked a good deal of the circles in which he moved, which was clearly the high society of London life. Interested in car racing, he later achieved some success in this field. He was also, unfortunately, involved in the darker side of life at a boys' public school.

J.F. Wolfenden (later Lord Wolfenden) was a formidable Headmaster during my last three years. These three incidents in particular portray something of the man.

As a Methodist, I was excluded from the confirmation class on arrival. I attended Holy Communion before Sunday breakfast for many weeks before my Divinity tutor, Rev. J.O. Whitfield MA, spotted me and told me I should not be there. He had asked me to leave the first preparation class for Communion which I attended and which had revealed me as a Methodist. I felt to be an inferior creature in his eyes.

After a few weeks' absence, the school Chaplain, Rev. C.G. Furnivall

MA, who was my form master at the time, commented about my absence, and I explained. Within a short time J.F.W. sent for me, was aware of the position, said I had a choice and could attend if I wished. I solved the sensitive problem by absenting myself when J.O.W. was officiating: ecumenicity had not then arrived.

J.F.W. interviewed all leavers and interested himself in their futures. My proposed entry to the family legal practice evoked little comment, but he was not impressed when I said my chief form of sporting activity would he golf. He knew of my soccer talent and particularly as a member of the school XI which played a formidable combined Manchester Grammar Schools XI, home and away. A civil reception at the Town Hall in the away game was disappointed by the absence through illness of Ellen Wilkinson, the Labour Minister of Education. 'Golf isn't a sport' was his disdainful reply and he exhorted me to join a leading amateur soccer team of ex-public schoolboys, based in Manchester.

The most revealing experience of the man occurred when I was completing my National Service in the RAF in London. On my way to a dental appointment at the RAF surgery in Harley Street, I spotted his familiar figure some one hundred yards away. I had not seen him since I left school in 1947 and this was 1953. I was in uniform. He had no particular reason to remember me. 'Good morning, Knape,' he said as I was passing him. He was reputed to know the name of every boy in the school at any time, but I found this later experience quite amazing.

Bumpers at Shrewsbury School
(Painting by John Alford)

39

The playing fields of Shrewsbury were extolled by the late Sir Neville Cardus, music and cricket correspondent of the *Manchester Guardian* who was cricket coach from 1912-16 and Secretary to the Headmaster, the Rev. Dr C.A. Alington (later Bishop of Durham). He wrote with affection of his time there. These fields played a large part in my life. Soccer and cricket were my staple diet. I sat on a glorious summer's day watching the 1st XI, seated in a deckchair beside the Headmaster and General Sir Miles Dempsey, an OB and at the time Deputy to Viscount Montgomery. The war in Europe was in its final stages and he had come for a brief break from his onerous duties. I confess to eavesdropping on their conversation and sometimes wonder whether the situation was covered by the Official Secrets Act.

An annual event was Bumpers, a rowing event similar to those at Oxford and Cambridge, where a line of eights try to touch the boat in front. The event lasted for several days. I was asked to sell the occasional school magazine *The Wollopian* which was a satirical riposte to *The Salopian*, the authorized school magazine, and published at irregular intervals. Wearing a bill-board, and standing on the Kingsland toll suspension bridge which led from the school site to the town, I was approached for a copy by a retiring gentleman.

He said he was the father of Richard Hillary. Hillary was a famous battle of Britain fighter pilot, involved in countless plastic surgery operations at the hands of the pioneering surgeon, Sir Archibald McIndoe. School folklore had it that he had flown his Spitfire under Kingsland bridge which would have been consistent with the daredevil exploits of the pilots of this heroic band of men. He had been in my school house and we found a 'grave' in my study one term. These were pieces of wood carved from the furniture where names were written on pieces of paper and concealed. Richard Hillary's name was on one of the pieces. The following details are in school records:

Hillary, Richard Hope (JOW) 1 1937. Trinity Coll: Oxf. HOR Crew. Trials. Ft/Lt: RAF. Wounded, Battle of Britain 1940, Staff Coll: RAF, 1942. k on active service 1943. Publication – *The Last Enemy.*

Many interesting personalities visited the School during my time. Lady Mountbatten took the salute at a parade of the St John Ambulance Brigade. In my first year we had lectures in the School's Alington Hall in successive weeks by Anthony Wedgwood Benn on 'The Case for Socialism' and by Viscount Hailsham on 'The Case for Conservatism'. It seems strange that the former, a Socialist, was then Viscount Stansgate, and the latter, a Conservative, was then Quintin Hogg. The former, of course, renounced his peerage. I remember a slide lecture on ornithology by Eric Hoskins which showed (*inter alia*) an owl, pictured by Hoskins at night and showing a claw. It was the claw which blinded him in one eye.

Old boys included, in addition to Sir Philip Sidney, soldier and poet, Fulke Greville, his friend and biographer, George Savile ('The Trimmer'), Charles Darwin, Walsham How, Francis Paget, Stanley Weyman; and in a later generation, General Sir Bernard Paget, General Sir Miles Dempsey and P.G. Wodehouse. Other famous old boys included the feared Judge Jeffreys, who became Common Serjeant of the City of London in 1671. In every state trial he proved himself a tool of the Crown. Titus Oates and Richard Baxter were tried before him, and those involved in Monmouth's rising. During the 'bloody assize' in Dorset and Somerset, 320 were hanged, 841 transported, and still more imprisoned and mercilessly whipped. The only good thing said in his favour is that he was honest enough not to turn Catholic to please his master, James II. After the latter's flight, he tried to escape, but was caught in disguise, and sent to the Tower to save him from the mob.

The author P.G. Wodehouse was not often spoken about as there were rumours of Nazi sympathies during my wartime years at the School.

Salopian nomenclature was distinctive. Evening prep was called Top Schools, the Captain of Cross-Country running 'The Huntsman', and the next senior colours, the senior and junior whips, all in the traditional form of a hunt. The winner is said 'to kill', and the runners were counted in couples. Fags were douls (from the Greek for slave). All sorts of privileges existed for Praepostors (School Prefects), House Monitors, holders of school sporting colours, and others. After the first year pupils could walk with one hand in their pockets. The pupils lived in separate buildings on the site and daily routine was supervised in large part by the Monitors. There was a janitor, matron and domestic staff. A housemaster's wife, invariably in my experience, played a major supporting role.

I left at the end of the Summer Term in 1947.

It would be remiss of me not to pay tribute to Major Taylor's wife, Mary. Major Taylor tragically collapsed and died of a heart attack while playing fives. My brother Stuart was a boarder at the time. Major and Mrs Taylor were moved from my house, Churchill's, in 1948 to School House, twice the size of the other houses. It was a tribute to her gifts of management that she was asked to live on in School House. Mrs Taylor made a tremendous contribution to the School over many years.

She died on 4 October 1990 at the age of eighty-two. The tribute at her funeral ended with these words:

We are gathered here to remember, to mourn and to give thanks.

Jane, Mark and Marianne have suffered a deep and sudden shock; so has the family; so have we all. We feel an aching emptiness and loss. But through the years we have surely also greatly gained. Let us pray for the soul of Mary Taylor and give thanks for her example. 'And behold, the half was not told me'. But her full story is known to Him who is the root and the offspring of David, and the bright and morning star, the High Steward of Eternity; and I dare to hope that in His book of accounts is inscribed against Mary Eleanor Bradshaw Taylor: she used well her talents and returned them with no small interest. I pray it be so written. Amen.

Chapter VII

THE SECOND WORLD WAR

On 3 September 1939, I heard Neville Chamberlain's broadcast on the radio when he announced the outbreak of the Second World War. A Sunday morning, and we must have stayed away from church for the momentous occasion. Mr Simpson of gentle manner and permanent smile was laying carpet in the lounge, kneeling and tapping in the tacks, continually muttering, as was his practice, 'Hum Ha, Hum Ha'.

He paused as the words came informing us that a state of war already existed between this country and Germany. A final ultimatum had not drawn any response. I imagined hordes of bombers appearing overhead within minutes. There was no great fear but apprehension and a childish ignorance of what was really involved in war.

We saw little action. German bombers were heard returning from bombing raids on the docks at Barrow-in-Furness, a few incendiary bombs were dropped on Heysham, and I was driven through a devastated city centre in Manchester.

Shrewsbury School, for the years of my stay, was a quiet backwater.

I did not have a 'good' war, but a quiet one. In direct contrast to Dad, who as recorded in Chapter XXVIII, had a very 'busy' war.

Dad had built a house in 1938 and had the foresight and premonition to build an air-raid shelter under the garage floor. I still have a vivid memory of Mother waking me about 3 a.m. shortly afterwards, saying quietly that the air-raid siren had sounded, to put on my dressing gown and slippers and go to the shelter with the aid of my torch.

Gas masks were always carried. I used to be frightened when Father would leave the shelter and go out into the street. With the benefit of hindsight it was probably as much to smoke a cigarette as to see if there was anything in the night sky. I can still smell the musty atmosphere and feel the slight trepidation as we sat for varying periods, often shivering. But we were some of the fortunate people.

Chapter VIII

FIRST FOREIGN HOLIDAY

In 1946, Father planned a holiday for Peggy, Jeanne (my next youngest sister) and myself, with him, in Switzerland. Mother stayed at home with the younger children.

The first year after the War, and our first time abroad, there was a great thrill and excitement about the journey. Passports, Dover to Calais by ferry, a train from there to Paris for an overnight stay and a show, followed by breakfast with white rolls on the station platform at Basle, and seeing a hand-cart outside the station. It was loaded with pineapples, bananas, coconuts and other fruits and edibles, the like of which we had not seen since before the War. It all added up to a memorable time.

A lighter moment was enjoyed as we passed through Lyons. An elderly couple were in the corridor of the train. As we hurtled through the station, the lady asked the husband to identify the place. Peering through the window, he joyfully exclaimed 'Hommes, dear.'

We stayed at the Weisses-Kreusses Hotel, overlooking Lake Lugano. We found the hotel porter could speak fluently in seven different languages. Outstanding memories were of sailing across the lake, boarding a mountain train and looking from the summit of Mt Genoroso to the long line of the Alps including the Jungfrau.

We had a day trip to Milan and viewed Leonardo da Vinci's *Last Supper* on the wall of the church where it was being restored. We wandered round the square where black marketeers sold silken goods. We saw the spot where Benito Mussolini was hanged by the crowd and viewed the splendour of the cathedral. We read much of Italian corruption. Father took his travellers cheques to the bank and was advised to change them for lira in the street where the rate of exchange was much better!

Leonardo da Vinci's *The Last Supper* was far bigger than I had expected and I stood gazing at it with some awe, as expert artists were engaged on retouching it.

Father did not like the smell of garlic and his return journey was spoilt by the presence in the carriage of four plump, black ladies, enthusiastically chewing generous quantities of the bulbs.

Chapter IX

MY DAD – A GREAT MAN

I would like to try and summarize my thoughts and feelings about Father for my own benefit, for those who knew him well or more distantly and for the reader to whom I am trying to convey the story of a remarkable man.

One evening as I came home from the office about 10 p.m. after yet another three-hour spell of work at my desk, I turned off the seafront into Broadway where I lived. As I turned the corner I could see the 'portholes', the round windows in the lounge wall of my parents' house, just fifty yards away. The light was shining brightly from each. I knew this denoted Father was sitting in his armchair at home and all was well. All *was* always well when he was there. It was like saying 'God's in His heaven – all's right with the world.'

Dad, so will he always be to me, was the finest man I ever met.

A few months ago there was a distressing time in a church near Reston, only twenty miles or so, from Morecambe. An Anglican clergyman had exercised his right to refuse permission for a family to include a term of endearment on a headstone in the church burial ground. To me my father will always be Dad, and 'Father' seems remote, impersonal, and far from displaying the man I, my four sisters and my brother Stuart, came near to worshipping.

As small children we would argue in our nursery over the question of who was his favourite. We all claimed the title but there was never much conviction about the argument because even at that tender age we knew, different as we all were in temperament, ability, looks and so much else, that he loved us all equally.

In my writing about preaching I refer to an occasion when a young Chartered Accountant was to open his practice in Morecambe the day after I conducted worship at his church and when he found strength and comfort in the words of my text: 'What time I am afraid, I will trust in the Lord'. That man is Eric Armitage. He kindly wrote the Foreword and I also refer to him elsewhere.

Eric will tell you that the most important thing in his life is his Lord and Saviour Jesus Christ, and it shows in all he does, modestly, lovingly, with great care and efficiency, and to the benefit of all who come into contact with him. He would deny this, but then he would, wouldn't he?

Eric once said to me that when he came out of my father's office, he felt ten feet tall. That was the sort of effect my father had on people. If the office girl was 'out of sorts', he knew, would sit her down, would be able to gain her confidence to tell of her problem and would offer wise help and advice. Only a few weeks ago I was chatting to a lady in a car park near to the offices we shared for so many years. She said that I did not know her but would know her daughter who worked for us many years ago. I remembered the person concerned as soon as her name was mentioned. The lady said she had been very troubled years before about her daughter's expressed wish to go abroad to the other side of the world. There was no one with whom she could share the problem, when my father contacted her and showed he too had been aware of the situation and was also concerned. It had been such a relief to her that she could share the anxiety. This was typical of my father and of his individual caring and concern. The problem resolved itself.

Many, many elderly widows have told me over a lifetime that they would never have 'managed' without his help, guidance and advice. I wonder often how he managed to do all he accomplished. The staff 'worshipped' him. The farm workers he employed would have done anything for him. But there was not the slightest trace of arrogance, cleverness or superiority in him. He was always himself, and while with the office girl or some of the great captains of industry with whom he mingled in business, he never altered.

Dad would say, when I asked him, that his secret in business was common sense. But it was a quality I never saw so strongly in any other man I have ever met. Dad was not an intellectual. He did not have a degree, was not the sort to be found delving deeply into legal textbooks, but he always found the answers to business problems by cutting through the peripheral and unimportant, and looking at the heart of the matter.

I have in front of me, as I write, the following letter dated 30 July 1971, written by Eric to me and to Colin, my colleague who succeeded me as Senior Partner. The letter was written before Eric's departure for the West Indies:

Dear John and Colin,

On this my last day at the office, I feel it only right and proper that I should send a few lines to you, with whom I have been so close in my professional life.

In the early days, the connection with Jobling & Knape, and particularly the late Mr Knape, was a great source of help to me and in many ways, was the springboard for the success of the practice.

My Father

More importantly, of course, I have come to know you both in a personal capacity and trust that distance and time will in no way affect our friendships.

I would, therefore, wish your two goodselves, your families and all your staff the very best in both health and happiness.

My kindest regards.

Yours sincerely,

Eric

Another client once presented him with a briefcase with the letters L.L. inscribed on the exterior. He was puzzled for a long time, until the client explained that it recorded the many occasions when he came into my father's office like a lion, and went out like a lamb.

It was not for nothing I dedicated this book to him, with the words: 'To Dad who always made everyone feel better.'

He had a great sense of humour and a buoyancy which never flagged, and made those near him feel that everything would be alright. Except for one great flaw. If Burnley (or 'the Clarets' as he preferred to call them) were winning 1-0 in a football match with ten minutes to go before the final whistle, and the ball came anywhere near the Burnley penalty area, his hands began to tremble, he drew more heavily on his cigarette, and in loud and panicky voice he would dispense the deep wisdom and advice of soccer supporters down the years: 'Get rid of the thing.'

I found a postcard with the following printed on it, among his personal file on his desk, after his death:

A lady in search of a quiet resting place rents a cottage in Switzerland, but just after signing the agreement she remembers that she has forgotten to enquire whether the house contains a comfortable W.C., so she writes to that effect.

W.C., thought the owner on receiving her letter. I wonder what those initials stand for, as he makes enquiries amongst his neighbours, and finally in desperation goes to the old Curé of the Village, who after careful consideration, declares that W.C. must stand for Wold Cappelle, which means 'Chapel in the Forest'. So the owner, well satisfied, writes as follows to the Lady:

I must regret the delay in replying to your letter, I am pleased to be able to tell you that you will not have to be without a W.C.

This building is situated five miles from the house and right in the middle of the Forest. It can hold 250 people, and because of its picturesque surroundings people come from far away to it. It is open on Fridays and Sundays. This is very regrettable if you are accustomed to going regularly. You will be comfortable there, as there are sixty reserved seats and also standing accommodation near the entrance, so there is enough room for the whole village. You will be pleased to learn that quite a number of people bring their meals and spend most of the day there, and others not wanting to lose any time arrive hurriedly in their cars, just in time as they cannot wait. It is now over six years since my wife and I went there and it was then so full we had to stand the whole time. You can, if you wish, go to the men's side or stay in the Ladies. If I may give you advice, I suggest you go there on Sundays because then you would be accompanied by the Organ.

Mergers, takeovers and public flotations were bread and butter to him, and his advice was widely sought. On one occasion one of the North's leading businessmen had clinched a major commercial deal in the City. When asked for the name of the solicitor who would be acting for him, the man replied, 'My usual solicitor, John Knape of Morecambe.'

'Morecambe?' replied the City flyer. 'You can't have anyone of the calibre for this job in Morecambe.'

To which the man replied, 'If John Knape doesn't act for me, the deal's off.'

He had a great sense of justice and fair play. Father was a Methodist local preacher for many years and played an influential part in many ways. Through him, a well-meaning but occasionally impulsive minister of our Church was saved from having to leave, which would have been a grave injustice, because my father was the only one prepared to stand up to the person causing the trouble and carried the day.

I found the following children's address in his file which speak a great deal to me of his nature and kindness to all:

In a wonderful old book there is a story of three young princes, who lived in a splendid palace with the Sultan, their father. There also lived in the palace a young princess, their cousin. She was, of course, very beautiful, and all the princes loved her. But as they could not all marry her, the shrewd old Sultan proposed a plan for deciding in a peaceful way, which of them should. He said, 'You know that I am very fond of rare and precious things. Now you must all go from here and travel and explore in different directions for a year and a day and the one who brings me back at the end of that time the most wonderful and valuable present shall have the princess for his bride.'

The young princes immediately consented and started off the next morning. They rode together for one day and then parted, after agreeing to meet at the same spot a year later. Each had many adventures and when they met again each informed the others that he had certainly got the best present and would win the hand of the princess.

The first had bought a magic carpet: you had only to sit on it and wish yourself at any place – and you were there immediately.

The second had found a curious tube, like a telescope, but more remarkable, because if you just looked through it and wished to see any sight, at once it was visible to you.

The third had procured a very singular apple, which had the power to cure all diseases; whatever you suffered from you had but to sniff this apple – and you were perfectly well.

As they compared their marvellous finds, their thoughts turned naturally to the princess, for whose sake they had gone exploring. 'Why,' said the second, 'how foolish I am. If I like I can see her.' He lifted his tube to his eye, and at once his face became pale. 'She is ill,' he cried. The others looked in turn and saw that the princess was indeed at the point of death, lying in her room, and surrounded by her maidens.

'Oh, if only I were there,' said the youngest prince, 'my apple would cure her, but we shall not arrive in time.'

'Yes,' said the eldest, 'we will go on my carpet.'

So they all sat down on the magic carpet and wished themselves in the princess's room, with the result that they were immediately there. It was then only the work of a moment to hold the apple before the dying princess's face. At once she revived, the colour rushed back to her cheeks, her eyes opened, and she smiled on her cousins, and began to ask them about their adventures. She was, in fact, perfectly well.

The next morning the young princes anxiously awaited the decision of their father. The old Sultan was much pleased with their gifts and promised that the carpet, the tube, and the apple should have honoured places in his museum. He acknowledged that their worth had been practically proven by the restoration of the princess.

But which was the best gift? Which did he value most? Which prince had won his cousin's hand? 'Ah,' he said, shaking his wise old head, 'not one of you has done better than the other. Indeed, not one of you would have been of the slightest use to your cousin apart from the others. Do you say your apple restored her? Yes, but you could not have applied the remedy in time had not your brother brought you on his carpet. Was your carpet then the cause of the cure? No, for but for what your brother saw through his tube you

50

would not have known the need for coming so hastily. The truth is you have worked together and helped one another, and your cousin's recovery is due to your united presents, and your united wisdom and kindness is using them.'

So the troublesome question as to whose bride the princess should be remained undecided and was left to be settled in some other way.

But the three young princes had not wasted their year and a day, for they had learned a great lesson – that 'none of us liveth to himself', that we are of very little use alone, that we all depend upon other people, and that we ought to be willing to help one another because we are helped so much ourselves.

Now there is a rather big word which describes all that, a word which I want you to try to remember, because you will meet it later on; it is co-operation. And that is a very fine lesson for all young folks to learn, whether they are princes and princesses, or ordinary boys and girls.

So let us carve deeply on our minds our two texts. First, 'None of us liveth to himself.' That means, don't be conceited. Nobody can live alone. We all depend upon other people. Second. 'Bear ye only another's burdens.' That means, always be ready to lend a helping hand. You are helped by a multitude of hands yourself. Lend a hand in return whenever you can. And these two texts together spell – co-operation.

In 1945 he was offered the opportunity by a local businessman, Mr James Wilson, to join him in a builders' merchant business in Morecambe by the name of Dent & Wilson Ltd. It is a measure of his ability that, although breaking the rules of the Royal Air Force, he was able to run that business (Mr Wilson playing very much a subsidiary role), the legal practice of Jobling & Knape, his own job as Senior Admin Officer in the RAF stationed at Morecambe, where he also did much of his Commanding Officer's work as well, together with welfare work.

When I speak of breaking the rules of the Royal Air Force, I mean that he was not supposed to have any other employment. There was no suggestion of him working during RAF hours in other areas.

He did this by being at Dent and Wilson Ltd from 7 a.m. to 8 a.m., at the office at Jobling and Knape from 8 a.m. to 9 a.m., when he reported at the nearby RAF Headquarters. Evening work also included a great deal of welfare work for the RAF and many people have told me down the years of his help in solving legal and personal problems. But I do not think his action would have commended itself to the authorities.

He was also in charge of sport for some time. With so many men in the town, the team resembled a First Division side, and when playing Blackpool RAF, who could choose from an even larger number, it was like watching a full international.

I remember seeing Stanley Mortensen as a youngster. He went on to score a hat-trick in the legendary Matthews Final at Wembley in 1953.

I also remember my father at the Morecambe ground, Christie Park, shaking hands with a very tall Scottish soldier wearing a kilt. He was then a Lieutenant, and went on to become a Brigadier and Churchill's special envoy to Marshal Tito. It was Sir Fitzroy-MacLean, later to become our MP.

The builders' merchant business flourished and on its sale a few years later, he made a substantial capital profit for the first time in his life. But to do so he had to borrow first. He told me, with deep emotion in his voice, of travelling to Burnley to see his father, explaining the opportunity, and that he would need his father's help in the form of a deposit of my grandfather's securities with a bank. Without hesitation, my grandfather put on his coat and they went together in the snow on a bitterly cold winter's day to my grandfather's safe at his office in the town, where he handed the papers without hesitation to my father.

The promissory note he signed is in front of me and reads:

27th January 1945.
Six months after demand I promise to pay to John Knape (senior) of 55 Glen View Road Burnley, and Margaret Knape his wife the sum of three thousand pounds value received and until payment to pay interest thereon in the meantime at the rate or five pounds per centum per annum to be payable by equal half yearly instalments on the thirtieth day of June and the thirty first day of December in every year and to be calculated from the first day of January instant. This note embodies and includes all moneys owing by me to the Lender down to the date hereof.

Father could never speak of this event without tears in his eyes.

It was a similar position with the West End Pier at Morecambe, subsequently purchased by my brother after Father's death, and which was destroyed in the great storm of 1977.

Here are the words of the document he asked my grandfather and grandmother to sign:

To:- Barclays Bank Limited.
WE, the undersigned, JOHN KNAPE of 55 Glen View Road Burnley in the County of Lancaster and MARGARET KNAPE, his wife HEREBY CONFIRM that of the shares in West End Pier

(Morecambe & Heysham) Limited totalling 6125 Ordinary Shares of One pound each held by our son John Knape, We are interested therein to the extent of One thousand nine hundred and seventy five thereof. It is with our knowledge and consent that our son the said John Knape is depositing the whole of the Share Certificates with your Bank to be secured against accommodation being granted to him and Mr Harry Wood on a joint account in a sum of Ten thousand pounds.

Date this 20th day of January 1945.

Father died on 24 April 1971 at his farm bungalow Greenhills, Crook. He had attended an important business meeting on the previous day and our farm manager Ted spoke of his unusual reluctance to leave in the morning, standing in the barn where the orphaned lambs were kept and fed.

On the 24th, a Saturday, I was working in the office when Ted's wife Edith phoned about 10 a.m. She had been trying frantically to contact one of the family and broke the news of my father's death.

I went to the farm immediately with Rosalie and did what was necessary. He had suffered from angina and we found an empty bottle of his little white pills. Who knows?

Late that evening I returned home in the state you would expect. Before retiring I switched on the television. The sound came before the picture and the first words were: 'And so Burnley are relegated from the First Division for the first time since the War.' It seemed to fit in with the great blow earlier in the day.

I shall not see his like again.

It has been a matter of the most profound satisfaction, however, that so far as his professional business acumen and commercial expertise are concerned, I have been able to write Chapter XIII of my life story.

Thanks Dad, for everything.

Chapter X

A SOLICITOR OF THE SUPREME COURT

There was never any doubt about my job in life. I was to be a solicitor, in my father's provincial family practice, with the main office in Morecambe, and a branch office in Barrow-in-Furness. From my earliest years I knew this was to be my work. Whether Father gently brainwashed me or not (and I suspect he did), and although I did not really understand the nature of the work, there was an early feeling that it was connected with books, and writing, and papers. These I loved.

As a young boy I travelled with him on many occasions to our Barrow office, some fifty miles from Morecambe. We lunched on the way and I understand I sat patiently for hours at these and other times, sitting in the front passenger seat with my hands folded in the glove compartment. On the way home, nearing Levens in the dark, and on a stretch of the road where subsidence warnings were displayed, Father would suddenly switch on his headlights, press his horn and we would enjoy the sight of dozens of rabbits, darting to and fro in the blinding light.

The office seemed rather cold and impersonal, furnished in a rather spartan way with linoleum on the floor. I remember press-copy letters and long, rather boring conversations which must have been on current office business. Activity seemed desultory and there was little to impress or attract me.

Even when at Shrewsbury my father pressed forward with his plans. My disappointment on realizing there would be no Oxford, and no degree, was mollified to some extent by the knowledge that I was to take a Bachelor of Laws degree. Although I did not realize it, Father had in mind a London University external degree, which would be attained by study at home, a correspondence course, be sandwiched between the Law Society exams, and enable me to work full time in the office. It was not, for me, a proper degree, and would not offer university life and soccer.

Five years of articles of clerkship could have been replaced by an Oxford degree in law, with all which the life there could provide, and three years reduced articles. I have never been able to accept my father's reasoning in wanting me to qualify in the shortest possible time, and I was to be proved right for two reasons. Perhaps he thought Oxford might change my attitude to law. Firstly, I know Oxford would have given me a broadened mind and greater self-confidence. More importantly I came in to the office as a very young man of seventeen and a half. The practice was small and some of the senior members instantly saw me as a threat. They felt it would be a case of working themselves out of a job, by training the boss's son. Many solicitors I knew later ensured that their sons were properly trained elsewhere, and joined them in the family practice as mature men and as qualified solicitors.

Father decided I should be called Mr John by everyone. This would have been perfectly in order after a few years, but sounded rather pompous for someone of 5' 2½" in stature, just over 6½ stones in weight and looking more like a young choirboy, than a partner in embryo. Father determined that I should learn every facet of the job (never allow yourself to be in a position where you are in someone else's hands, was his philosophy), and so I began by clearing out the cellar, wearing old clothes. Sea water had come through the floor over the years, soaked the lower racks of stored papers and resulted in a multi-coloured mess, which I shovelled into sacks and took to the Corporation destructor, where I had personally to supervise their departure in the furnace on the grounds of confidentiality. The work lasted two weeks.

His error was heavily compounded by sending to me, in my last term in Shrewsbury, a book of Roman Law in Latin, with a translation. When his accompanying letter revealed that mastery of the book would enable me to pass only one subject of the inter-LLB examination, my stomach churned. He was being advised by his cousin, John Knape Holmes, MB ChB LLB. Cousin John had been a medical doctor until fifty years of age, had been compelled to retire from practice because of ill-health, and was taken into the office by my father, where he proceeded to obtain his London University external degree and pass his Solicitors' Finals, all in five years. What he could do at that age, I could surely do, starting at seventeen and a half, and straight from school.

Cousin John looked like 'Sherlock', his fictional namesake. Aquiline features covered a sharp and incisive brain which excelled in many fields. He knew virtually every postage stamp ever printed, *Bradshaw's Rail Guide* almost by heart and as much about politics and history as any Member of Parliament. He also suffered from asthma, smoked incessantly, talked constantly and occupied the office room adjoining mine.

His idea of fun was to take home the massive legal work called *Snell's Equity*, of several hundred pages, and read it over the weekend. And yet, practically, he was lost when an old lady came in and wanted to make a simple will, or a man asked for his help in buying a house. They were bewildered by lengthy expositions of the law. As a back-room boy (much needed and valued, I stress) he was unsurpassed. And he had a heart of gold.

I signed my articles on 12 August 1947. Before I left Shrewsbury in July 1947, I visited the office of solicitors in Shrewsbury to be sworn to a statutory declaration about my articles, by a Commissioner for Oaths. I began to feel the excitement of knowing I would shortly begin training for a lifetime in law.

A partially compiled testimonial was also forwarded to me by Father for completion by Major Taylor. The documents, when completed, were in the following form:

To The Secretary,
Law Society's Hall,
Chancery Lane,
London. W.C.

I, JOHN KNAPE, Junior of 'Clevelands' 38 Stuart Avenue Bare Morecambe and Heysham in the County of Lancaster hereby apply to the Registrar of Solicitors under Section 29 of the Solicitors' Act 1932 as amended by section 26 of the Solicitors' Act, 1941 for exemption from the Preliminary Examination.

I make this application in the following circumstances:

1. I was born on the Tenth day of January 1930.
2. I was educated at The Schools, Shrewsbury.
3. In 1946 I obtained the Oxford and Cambridge Schools Examination Board School Certificate gaining 'Very Good' in Scripture Knowledge and English Literature, 'Credit' in English Language, History, Latin, Greek, French (written and Oral) and 'Pass' in Elementary Mathematics.
4. I send herewith in support of this application (a) a letter from John Knape of 19 Northumberland Street Morecambe and Heysham Solicitor expressing his willingness to take me as his Articled Clerk and (b) testimonials as to my standard of general education from at least two persons to whom I am well known, who are able to speak thereto.

I solemnly and sincerely declare that the facts set out herein are true.

And I make this solemn declaration conscientiously believing the same to be true and by virtue of the Statutory Declarations Act 1835.

Declared by the above
named John Knape Junior
at Shrewsbury in the   John Knape Junior

County of Shropshire
this 23rd day of June 1947.
Before me.
S.E. Corser
A Commissioner for Oaths

Testimonial in support of application for Exemption from the
Preliminary Examination
The Solicitors' Act 1932 Section 29
as amended by
The Solicitors' Act 1941 Section 26

I, A.E. TAYLOR of Churchill's Hall The Schools Shrewsbury in
the County of Shropshire T.D., M.A., Queen's College Cambridge,
Housemaster certify that John Knape Junior has been personally
known to me for upwards of four years past.
From my personal knowledge of the applicant I am able to give the
following particulars for the information of the Council as to his
standard of general education, namely:
J. Knape passed the Oxford and Cambridge School Certificate in
July 1946 with a pass in Mathematics, Credits in English language,
History, Greek, Latin, French and Very Goods in English Literature
and Divinity. He therefore matriculated.
He has studied here for the past year with marked progress.
My personal knowledge of the applicant is based on acquaintance
extending over four years.
DATED this 23rd day of June 1947.
A.E. Taylor, M.A. Cantab
Housemaster, Shrewsbury School
To: The Secretary,
Law Society's Hall,
Chancery Lane,
London. W.C.2.

After the clearing-out of the cellars, I turned to tea-making, answering
the telephone, delivering local letters by hand, and acting as general
dogsbody. I did not mind, but it was yet another instance in my young
thoughts of the way life never allowed me to go quite to the summit.

Removed from the Grammar School before I was old enough to play
soccer for the school, removed from Shrewsbury without the normal
fifth year (which my father later allowed my brother to take on my
recommendation, and which was wasted) when I could have become a

House Monitor, take my Higher School Certificate ('A' levels) and endeavoured to make the soccer first XI, not allowed to go to Oxford, and then be asked to clean cellars and make tea, did not seem the fairest of all worlds.

I tried hard, so hard, to please the shorthand typists and others with my tea, by giving them in turn the cream from the top of the milk bottle. The mixture was yellow and only in later times did I recollect their grimaces (silent, because I was Mr John). I was also frightened of the telephone which seemed a technological monster. We had open fires and press-copy letters.

On my first day at the office I was given the job of indexing the press-copy letters, which were kept on a daily basis in a folder. The office girl had numbered her last entry as 63, and so I followed with 64. Her entry should have been 53, and so all my work was wrong. Father whisked me away for the day on some business trip, and when we returned home in the early evening, sister Peggy, who was assistant cashier, rushed out to the front door to greet me with a gloating cry of 'You got the letter book wrong.' Not an auspicious start.

Worse was to follow. After a few days in the general office, Father decided I should sit at a desk in his room, and presumably assimilate a vast amount of knowledge. He handed me a set of title deeds of a house, a printed contract form and asked me to draft the document. I did not know a set of title deeds from a pink elephant, much less how to draw up a contract. As a result I was on my feet incessantly asking for advice. With his telephone ringing constantly and clients coming in almost all the time, he decided enough was enough, and I returned with much relief to the general office.

Gradually I began to see through the mists of conveyancing, County Court debt work, probate, wills, company formations, writs, and the general giving of advice, over a wide range of legal and non-legal problems. No one ever came to a solicitor without a problem, I declared, and Father assenting, said it was our task to take it from them, so that they went away feeling it had been left on our desk.

My first hurdle was the Intermediate Examination, normally taken after twelve to eighteen months, and then the Final at the end of the five years of Articles of Clerkship. As in all professions, great changes have been made since then. The Intermediate consisted of papers on several legal subjects including Contract, Torts, Constitutional Law, Land Law, Criminal Law, and a separate examination on Trust Accounts and Book-keeping. They could be taken separately, but Father pushed me in at the deep end after twelve months, when I sat both, comfortably passing the first, but failing the other. This was a subject unlike any at school, but Father had been taught book-keeping at Elmfield College, the Methodist

School near York, which he attended after Burnley Grammar School. I had to resit a few months later and was sent on a refresher course for three weeks before the exam, which I passed.

The following year I sat and passed the London University Inter-LLB exam. It was clear to me that I could not possibly attempt the LLB final course without seriously jeopardizing my Solicitors' Final Examination, and this was agreed.

Father was in a worse state than I, when awaiting the results of the Final, which would mean, if I passed, the end of my Articles and qualification as a Solicitor of the Supreme Court (what a grand title!).

Unbeknown to me, Father had told a member of the Law Society Council, with whom he was in contact regularly on substantial professional matters, of my sitting the examination, along with Charles Altham, our Managing Clerk. Charles was one of the large number of legal clerks of those days who were the backbone of the profession. They had been unable to pay the fees which were asked by the principal for Articles, or to study, because of age, or domestic or other reasons. Our practice never charged anyone a premium for articles but we were an exception.

When my father started his practice in Morecambe, the largest firm was Bannister, Bates & Son who practised in the same street. Shortly after his arrival, my father was summoned to the presence of the Senior Partner, Mr Alfred Bates and asked why he had commenced practice in the town without first calling on him. I remember saying to my father when he first told me, 'Why didn't you tell him to go and jump in the nearby sea?' or words to that effect. But as usual Dad was correct. 'That's alright,' he said, 'but he could have made life impossible for me if he had combined with his colleagues to obstruct my work and made me look incompetent and slow.' So my father had swallowed hard and apologized.

Later Mr Bates became Sir Alfred Bates DL, Chairman of Lancashire County Council, and received His Majesty King George VI and Queen Elizabeth at Lancaster station shortly before the King's death. He was a leading figure in the public life of the county for many years. He was also Chairman of the Governors of Royal Lancaster Grammar School, of rich tradition and achievement, which produced Lord Cecil Parkinson and many other leading figures in public life.

His son Michael also followed his father as Senior Partner and on my father's death wrote to me as follows:

Dear John

I was shocked to hear of your father's sudden death this morning, because he seemed so fit and well when I saw him last a few weeks ago.

59

Although I know our two fathers had their differences over the years this did not involve me and particularly over the past four years I felt that your father and I had grown closer and he was on many occasions extremely kind to me.

I am therefore very sincere when I say how very sorry indeed I am that his life has been cut so short and I hope you and your family will accept my deepest sympathy.

If there is anything I can do to help you at the present time please don't hesitate to ask.

I am afraid I have never really known your mother but I hope you will also extend my sympathy to her and I know she will gain strength from her family, to support her at this difficult time.

Yours aye
Michael

Michael was a good and close friend of Father and myself. He, too, dedicated himself to the work of the Lancashire County Council, and although never Chairman, chaired several important committees and held various offices.

The firm was run on a day-to-day basis by those 'treasures' of the legal profession, the unqualified clerks. Mr J.W. (Johnny) Bell was the doyen and was at one time, before my father's day, perhaps the most influential legal figure in the town. He was noted for appearing in the wills he made, for modest legacies. His spectacles were held together on one side by plaster. He was always kind to me, but so were Alec Harper, Ted Slater (who later crossed the road to rival Ratcliffe & Bibby), Mr Bartlam, Mr Harker and others.

These men were never able to afford the fee to take Articles of Clerkship. The normal charge was about £300. Although as I have said, my father never charged for Articles, in fairness he did not pay much of a wage before the articled clerk had qualified.

Before the Finals, Charles and I had spent four and a half months in London and Guildford respectively, on a course organized by Law tutors, Gibson and Weldon (later The College of Law). Father thought it better we should be apart. The course was taken by virtually all entrants for the Final. There was a six months' course, but Father thought we could manage with the shorter one, and he wanted us both back in the office.

The stay in the lovely town of Guildford was a happy one. The goal of the Final examination was in sight and we studied hard. Afternoon lectures were largely a case of scribbling down the lecturer's notes furiously, committing them almost to memory later in the evening, and then reading a chunk of a textbook in preparation for the next day's lecture. Frequent exams were held, with an order of merit published for each. Some time was spent on drawing attention to possible questions in the real examinations, and concentrating on those questions which had not appeared for some time.

At the end of the course, a final list was pinned up, expressing the confidence of the experienced lecturers, by bracketing the 'will pass', followed by the 'should pass', and followed by the borderline cases. My name was bracketed at the bottom of the first group and the beginning of the second, and so I was included in both. Well pleased, I noted all those above me were graduates.

A few days before the results were due, Father spoke to me, said that the Law Society's Council member had been able to access the examiners' findings during his normal duties, and that Charles and I had comfortably passed. He then went round to Charles's home to impart the good news to him and his wife, Claire. The overwhelming joy had to be hidden by us both, and the procedure followed in our office for all examination results, strictly followed. Our London agents sent someone along to the Law Society's Hall in Chancery Lane, inspected the displayed notice of results, and telephoned to my father as Senior Partner. I could hear the call being put through, as my office was next to the switchboard. I heard his door open, then the crossing of the general office, the opening of my door, and the extension of his hand in congratulation, before repeating the exercise with Charles. Incidentally I found out later that Charles and I were not the only people to receive their result before the official date.

Cakes for everybody was always the order of the day. I felt well pleased later, on hearing that the percentage failure rate was about 58 per cent, then the highest in the history of the exam. When it is considered that those who sat had been studying law for at least five years, the high standard then prevailing is clear.

I have my Final Examination papers in front of me as I write. I consider that in many ways my task was much more difficult than later, when there was an easier way to sit the papers. I had six papers of twelve questions each, and *all* had to be answered. The time for each paper was 10 a.m. to 1 p.m. and 2.30 p.m. to 5.30 p.m. on Monday, Tuesday, and Wednesday. It was a physical and mental test. One of my friends was unable to sit the last paper because his hand had ceased to function in the writing process. I had heard of this possibility several times, and when I began my last paper I was terrified for a few seconds as my fingers seemed to stiffen and I feared I would not be able to write.

Another very testing requirement was that we had to obtain a minimum on each paper, and a minimum aggregate. I can say with confidence that anyone who passed the Final Examination in my day was fit to practise as a solicitor.

Here are the heading and questions for the papers:

61

1. The Law of real and personal property, with special reference to the principles and practice of conveyancing, and the principles and rules of equity.
2. (a) The Law relating to negligence and nuisance: including liability for dangerous property and dangerous things. (b) The law relating to defamation. (c) The law of evidence. (d) Criminal Law. (e) Proceedings in criminal cases before magistrates other than magistrates sitting at quarter sessions.
3. (a) The law of wills and of intestate succession and of the administration of assets: including the procedure and practice of the probate court in non-contentious matters. (b) The law relating to death duties. (c) The law relating to income tax.
4. (a) The law relating to contracts generally; and (b) the law relating to (a) sale of goods; (b) negotiable instruments; (c) master and servant, including the law relating to industrial injuries; (d) hire purchase; (e) insurance (other than marine insurance).
5. The law relating to (a) companies; (b) agency and partnership; (c) bankruptcy; (d) arbitration.
6. (a) Conflict of Laws; and (b) the law and procedure in matrimonial causes usually determined or administered in the Probate, Divorce and Admiralty division of the High Court of Justice, and before magistrates.

I attended court quite regularly. I loved this aspect of legal work, but it was a time-waster. A solicitor could sit in court all day, awaiting his case being called, while work was piling up at the office. I wanted to be a good advocate as part of my aim to know every part of a family solicitor's work, which was possible at that time, until increasing specialization changed the system. Unfortunately our partner who specialized in advocacy, and was accepted by local practitioners as the local expert, saw me at times in the role I have described earlier, as a threat.

One day he was on annual holiday when a young policeman called at the office. He had been charged with stealing a purse, containing three or four shillings. Such a serious matter of a 'bent copper' attracted wide attention. He asked me to represent him. It was a case of pleading guilty and offering a plea in mitigation. I knew an emotional appeal containing such phrases as 'broken on the wheel on life' would bear no fruit and I said so in my opening remarks, thus making the point.

My tactics were dictated by the presence on the bench of a chairman who was more impressed by cold facts, and not attempts to pull at the heartstrings. An appeal to the emotions would have been a waste of time. The Editor-Proprietor of our local newspaper (*The Visitor*) for many years, and a formidable figure in the town, James Caunt JP, was the son of its founder. The newspaper at the time bore, below the title at the head of the front page, the following words:

Founded in 1873 when Income Tax was 2p in the £.

Mr Caunt was involved in a famous seditious libel case, a rare type of prosecution, following an editorial which was alleged to be anti-Semitic. He was acquitted and displayed in his office the framed cheque for the fees of the leading barrister he employed. I think the figure was £900.

With the young man seated a few feet away in the dock, and weeping, I did my best to present a balanced plea for a ruined career. The Chairman returned with his fellow magistrates to announce a fine of £20 and added, 'If it had not been for the words of your solicitor, the punishment would have been greater.'

I confess to feeling on 'a high'. The court room was crammed with police officers of every rank, and the Press. I had briefly to ask the Detective Chief Superintendent of Lancashire about loss of pension rights, and after the hearing, he came to shake hands with me.

'I have heard Marshal Hall, Norman Birkett, and all the great barristers of the day, but never a better plea than that,' he said.

I walked on air for several weeks. I remember a letter, couched in generous terms, which greatly moved and pleased my father from Richard ('Dick') Quick, a legendary journalist in my part of the world, which he wrote as a reporter in court.

I had no leaning or special aptitude towards Father's special field and was content to carry the mantle of office administration and a vast amount of routine work. A measure of the workaholic in me is that I had in hand at one time, 300 conveyancing matters and a host of miscellaneous matters in addition to the office administration. I also read every letter which came in and went out. A normal workload for a competent legal executive would be about sixty conveyancing matters.

At holiday times every executive prepared a 'list of matters' giving a brief résumé of the individual's current files, to assist the person dealing with them in his absence. I remember telling Father, before an annual holiday, of the 300 cases and he refused to believe me, until I produced my list and counted them in front of him. Nine shorthand and other typists (two part-time) were fully employed in dealing with the endless tapes and dictation I produced. It was foolish, but although I was a worrier, I revelled in it, and the weight of matters never affected my efficiency and care. It was a golden rule, more observed today in the breach rather than the observance, to reply to all letters by return of post, by acknowledgement or in detail. Telephone calls were returned at once, if received when engaged. If a professional colleague from another firm telephoned, it was normal etiquette to take the call, explain that you were presently engaged and that you would return the call as soon as free.

I do not think today's practitioners will find it easy to believe and I have a certain regret at today's situation, so far as I observe it. Times have changed dramatically. The old family solicitor who knew his clients intimately, and their family affairs, has disappeared along with the family doctor, who often called at homes, and never seemed to be rushed. I see today pressure, impersonal attitudes, the constant concern with cash flow, expenditure as a result of rising overheads, competition and more of a view of the work as a necessary means of making a living, rather than a way of life, with personal contacts to be savoured, and cultivated.

Conveyancing, with scale charges, of course, enabled solicitors in those times to earn their bread and butter, without difficulty. Other work, such as probate, was the icing on the cake. My own practice carried out a great deal of work without charges. The making of a will was free, although of course the solicitor saw the document as goodwill, a future source of work, with hundreds placed with the client's title deeds in his strongroom for safe custody and without storage charge. Solicitors were expected to repay their privileged life by such service, both in the office, and in the life of the community.

Generally we were an object of affection and reassurance. I now see the solicitor in private practice regarded primarily as an expensive luxury, to be avoided at all costs. We were the last bastion of freedom against authority, bureaucracy and the establishment, a defender of individual freedom, which upheld the Rule of Law. I return to the subject of the profession.

Some people took a short cut by purchasing a will form (in early days for 6d in old currency) at their stationers, and following the written instructions printed on the reverse side. In every case where I was involved, this foolish, although understandable practice, resulted in an expensive application to the Court to determine the will's true meaning. As an example, I remember a man who had left 'all my cash' to a beneficiary, which he thought would ensure virtually all his assets passing to that person. In fact 'cash' in legal understanding and interpretation meant 'cash' in the pocket or wallet and current account at the bank.

Today charities and many other bodies produce literature on, and emphasize the importance of, making a will. Charges are now made and may appear high, but the peace of mind from knowing that all your wishes on death will be carried out, and those you love properly safeguarded, is cheap at the sort of price I see of £30/40 for a straightforward case. Every word of a will is important and needs to be carefully drafted. Intestacy (the absence of a will) can be disastrous in effectively carrying out the individual's wishes, and the common view about the notion 'I don't need to make a will because I haven't got any (or much) money' is a foolish one. It is a surprise to many people to see the total, when their assets are set down in an orderly fashion. The couple, husband and wife for example, who had bought their house and paid off the mortgage, through a life of hard work, and built up a small nest egg in a building society, shares or material possessions, can find that Inheritance Tax, and other matters, can impinge upon their particular situation.

It is also true that little changes people more than a will, when death occurs.

A favourite episode in the *Steptoe and Son* series showed Harold and his father furtively leaving the wake and heading for the deceased's residence. The astonished faces on seeing a home stripped of every single item by people more astute than themselves reflected a situation I have seen on countless occasions. Lifelong friendships broken, litigation benefiting only the lawyers, years of silences, and severance of contacts, and much more, can be the result of failure to make a will. Many people, and particularly ladies, have shed tears at my desk when signing their wills, believing in some way it denotes an early demise. I could often leave them happy by simply saying, 'You're good for another fifty years now,' and 'It's when wills are not made that the problems usually arise.'

There is humour in court. In my early days a local farmer appeared before the magistrates on a charge of allowing four horses to stray on a major local highway. He strenuously denied his guilt and finally, in exasperation, the Chairman said, 'Well, if you deny the evidence, what *did* you have with you?'

Came the reply, 'Three horses and a mare, Your Worship!'

I suppose I must tell a story against my profession. The bishop, the actress and the solicitor drew lots as they floated on their raft, close to the desert island. The purpose was to establish who should swim ashore with the rope, through shark-infested waters, and pull the raft in to safety. The solicitor drew the short straw and began to swim. As the sharks drew back and allowed him through the actress shrieked, 'A miracle, a miracle!'

The bishop dryly observed, 'Professional etiquette, my girl.'

A friend compares my kind to a rhinoceros – thick-skinned and always ready to charge.

My first appearance in the County Court was rather like a scene from the film *Brothers-in-Law*, a story of practice at the Bar. Arriving early, I put on my collar and tabs, followed by the obligatory black gown, and felt very important as I looked in the mirror. Both my father and our expert partner advocate had advised me to wear an old collar and tabs so that His Honour would not see me as a new boy. A debt procedure, called a judgement summons, was in force at that time. Some dozen of my experienced brethren sat with me. I was first on my feet. His Honour paused, peered at me over his glasses, and said. 'I will not have advocates in my Court improperly dressed.' A lesson in humility. Bill Oglethorpe, a clever lawyer sitting beside me, muttered, 'Ask him for a 138.' No such number in procedure existed and it took me all my time to avoid bursting out laughing, with all my colleagues stifling giggles at the remark.

It would be remiss of me if I omitted to mention the quality and loyalty of the staff of the practice, down the years. We grew rapidly and became one of the largest provincial practices in the area, handling matters of a very varied nature, and with specialists in all but the most specialist subjects.

It would be invidious to mention the length of individual periods of service, but I must mention Miss Dorothy Davies, who was a faithful, efficient and loyal member of the firm for over forty years. She spent a period at the practice in Barrow-in-Furness, but her main contribution was as my father's secretary, and our cashier. The latter involved great responsibility in regard not only to the sums handled, but the pressure of work in a rapidly expanding practice. I cannot speak too highly of her dedicated service.

I think too of Elizabeth (née Redmond), assistant to Miss Davies as cashier for many years; of 'Joe' Unsworth, a conveyancing man; of 'Vi' Hartley (secretary to our late partner Mr Frank (Mac) McHugh – litigation expert and advocate); Joyce Biggs, a fine shorthand/typist who assisted me for many years, and overcame a serious illness; Irene Roberts and 'Jo' Anderton, assistants to partners and able to carry out executive or secretarial functions – most valuable assets of the practice. ('Jo' also was a secretary and general assistant to my late brother Stuart in his separate practice); Jean Cornford, shortly to retire after many years outstanding service as our cashier, insurance expert, and a worthy successor to Miss Davies; Stanley Taylor, a diligent and hard-working conveyancer with great personal qualities, and Robin Baines, our Legal Executive who has served faithfully now for very many years. Winnie Shenton served my father faithfully for many years as a shorthand typist and now lives near me in retirement.

It would be remiss of me not to mention Ronnie Hampson, who ran our Barrow-in-Furness office for many years. It was a happy day when he came to join the Morecambe practice where he still does valuable work and defies his years. I could write a separate book on a long and happy relationship and thank him for all his support to my father and myself.

Michael 'John' Easthope and Michael Woods were outstanding partners, and sadly suffered untimely deaths.

The pressures were great and constant and I record thanks and deep appreciation for every remembrance of them.

Chapter XI

NATIONAL SERVICE

I can perhaps best illustrate the continuing, but lessening, influence of the old school tie, by speaking about my National Service.

After qualifying as a solicitor in 1952, I wrote and asked for immediate call-up, seeing no purpose in delaying the two-year period of service, from which I had received deferment, until completion of my articles of clerkship. This was a common practice and I was persuaded by the realization that I could the more easily assimilate the required knowledge of the law by continuing to study after leaving school, than by the hiatus of a two-year stint in the RAF.

I reported to RAF Padgate, near Warrington. We stayed only a few days for kitting out, before leaving for RAF Hednesford in the Staffordshire hills, for the prescribed twelve weeks of initial training or 'square bashing'. It presented no fears for me after schooldays. One young man at Padgate listened to the sergeant in the canteen address given to us at our first meal, reassuring us of his fatherly regard, and asking us to let him know at once if there was anything bothering us. The young man was aged eighteen and had never previously been separated from his mother's apron strings. He approached the NCO and pointed out the caterpillar in his lettuce. Whispering quietly in his ear, the sergeant advised him not to make the matter public, 'or everyone else will want one'.

Homesickness was fairly common and reminded me of my own at Shrewsbury.

I was physically fit and still enjoying the feeling of being a qualified solicitor after five years of hard study. I took in my stride the disciplined regime of rising at 6 a.m., washing and shaving in cold water, with no plugs in the basins, in uncovered Nissen huts, in the depths of winter. The drill movements came with ease to one who practised them with his friends at home in the early years of the War. I had also been in the Junior Training Corps throughout my time at Shrewsbury School. I could take a Bren gun to bits, put it together and fire, shoot well with a .38 revolver, and had ridden in tracked vehicles on manoeuvres, in addition to the usual drill and use of a .303 Lee Enfield rifle. The 'bull', shine and polish, painting white everything which did not move, the shouting and bawling, the sometimes pointless orders, merely toughened me further and increased my appetite. I was made leader of my hut and felt thoroughly at home with men from all walks of life.

Whilst at Hednesford I heard from the Careers Officer of the existence of the Directorate of Legal Services, sited in Northumberland Avenue, London. I applied for interview and during a six-week stay at RAF Ruislip, following completion of initial training, I was summoned for an interview with Air Commodore J.B. Walmsley CBE DFC QC. His details were: 'RMC Sandhurst, First War RFC and RAF, 1924 Barrister (Gray's Inn), 1933 RAF Legal Branch, 1936-40 Deputy Judge Advocate General of Army and RAF in Middle East, 1948-57 Director or Legal Services, Air Ministry ret. 1957 Holder of Greek MC.'

His PA, Squadron Leader Gilchrist marched me into the room. I saluted smartly and was asked to sit. The great man was in civvies. His first question was to ask me which school I had attended.

'Shrewsbury?' he said, with a note of surprise. 'Which house were you in?'

'Churchill's, sir.'

'Churchill's?' he said. 'So was I.'

The rest of the interview was a series of questions to update him on developments since his days. He had fought as a pilot in the First World War, was a guest in Westminster Abbey at the imminent Coronation, and although I did not see much of him, I was occasionally ordered to take what I assume were confidential papers to his home in Oxted. The Air Commodore said I could either be usefully employed for eighteen months, or probably 'twiddle my thumbs' as a Pilot Officer dealing with admin at some remote station. The Squadron Leader was not amused to be told that the only vacancy which existed was mine. His ornate language when we left the room left me in no doubt that I was not to think it would be a holiday. At the end of my two years he shook my hand, laughingly referred to his earlier feelings, and told me that I had done 'a damn good job'.

Miss Janet McKay, my Commanding Officer, was an unusual person. In a major feature article about her, in the *Daily Express* of 18 February 1958, Squadron Officer McKay was described as a woman solicitor in the Royal Air Force – not (as the article pointed out) as you may imagine, in the Women's Royal Air Force. In referring to sexual discrimination, the writer revealed that Miss McKay received £183 a year less than her male colleagues of equal age and seniority, and then continued:

Women just do not want to be equal to men. They do not want to be treated like men. These days, they even hate being told they are career women.

National Service at Hednesford – square-bashing. Author is next (right) to drill Sergeant (or Corporal in this case) – front centre.

Not, I think, the message of today.

An able and demanding CO, qualified in Canada as a barrister and solicitor, as well as her English qualification, Squadron Officer McKay taught me much. She responded generously to effort and right attitude and had a very real command of her job.

After a short time as assistant to her PA, I spent the remainder of my National Service as her PA, apart from a short period at the end when I was placed in charge of my colleagues dealing with the general administration of the department. The establishment was non-commissioned and I was promoted to Flight Sergeant, with three stripes and a crown. My guess is that I may have been unique in this, perhaps the only National Service Flight Sergeant in the RAF, a rank usually held by long-serving regulars. The Squadron Officer and I were certainly unusual species.

We were a small group of some fifteen newly qualified English and Scottish solicitors. After years of study, we had our National Service to complete in London. We worked in civvies and I had a room in Kensington. It was a wonderful opportunity to acquire legal experience as well as allowing us to see and enjoy London. We made the most of it. Theatres, famous landmarks and all the attractions of the capital came as a real contrast to years of study. But we worked hard as well. I handled, with my CO, hundreds of divorces, preparing them for legal aid, and then handing the papers for the actual Court proceedings to many London firms.

We handled every type of legal problem for serving men and women and travelled round the country to RAF stations. The Station CO and other officers to whom we had to report often asked for ad hoc advice on a multitude of matters. The Air Commodore's remark at my interview that I would be far better off at the Directorate as an NCO (it was, as I have said, a non-commissioned establishment) than as a Pilot Officer twiddling my thumbs at some remote station proved absolutely correct. I gave evidence in many cases at the Royal Courts of Justice in the Strand, in the days when divorce was serious and detailed, and cases were heard by a High Court Judge.

Arthur Askey and Thora Hird in *The Love Match*, Brian Rix in *Reluctant Heroes* at the Whitehall Theatre, Richard Burton and Claire Bloom in *Hamlet* with Michael Hordern at the Old Vic, Norman Wisdom at the Palladium, and Al Read in his own show in the Strand were but some of the entertainment I enjoyed.

Several of these shows I attended with my cousin Ann along with days at weekends at the home of her parents in Esher. Cousin Tom was a college lecturer who had gained good degrees at a lesser-known university, and gained them again at a better-known establishment to enhance his career prospects. On Ann's twenty-first birthday I was invited with one of my sisters to join the family at the Café de Paris. The glittering assembly sang 'Happy Birthday' as the cake was delivered to our table and I was invited to accompany Ann to a private meeting with the cabaret star – no less than Marlene Deitrich. She gave me a signed photograph.

I was spellbound by the sheer magnetism of her personality. When she descended the stairs for her appearance, every eye seemed to be riveted on her, dressed in shimmering lace dress and white fox furs. There seemed to be no great voice, but for entertainment value she was the tops. Each evening she was introduced by a different star and when we were there, it was John McCallum, the film star, accompanied by his wife, Googie Withers.

I sailed down the Thames to Kew, sauntered around Windsor Castle, visited magnificent Knowle in Kent, spent hours in Foyles Bookshop, among its three million volumes, and where I left much of my hard-earned money, visited nearly every London football ground including Highbury (Arsenal), White Hart Lane (Tottenham Hotspur), The Valley (Charlton Athletic), Stamford Bridge (Chelsea) and Craven Cottage (Fulham). There was cricket at Lord's and the Oval.

On the occasion of the annual RAF v Royal Navy cricket match at Lord's, we were given the day off to support our team. There was a young fast bowler completing his National Service in the RAF side who was said to be a promising prospect for the future. He played for Yorkshire and his name was Fred Trueman.

Many weekends I went home on the Heysham boat train from Euston, enjoying a relaxing dinner. This involved catching the 9.37 p.m. train from Lancaster on Sunday evening for the return journey, and arriving at a dark and deserted Euston at 3.30 a.m. before getting a train to my digs and arriving for work at 9 a.m. Not for me today! During our lunch hour we usually walked through Horse Guards Parade and through St James's Park.

A great experience was to attend morning worship at Kingsway Hall led by Donald (now Lord) Soper. For Methodism, the service was 'High Church' and the liturgy, dress and ceremonial were more than I had experienced at home. In the afternoon, what a contrast! On his soap box in Hyde Park, where he still appears in his nineties, he was a source of wonderful entertainment and instruction. The humour was rib-shaking and as he often said, although he did not know all the answers, he had heard most of the questions.

On one occasion a heckler shouted, 'We've had Christianity for two thousand years and look at the state of the world,' to which the reply came, 'Yes, and we've had water for two million years and look at the state of your neck.' He never put down his questioners but rather made them face their questions. His faith and joy shone through every moment. As a prominent figure, he was a target for the media. In reply to a questioner who asked for his opinion about the Royal Family, he spoke warmly about them, but said he wished the Duke of Edinburgh didn't play so much polo on Sundays. A national newspaper the following day had the blazing headline 'Methodist leader makes violent attack on Royal Family'.

Other gems I remember reading about were when the heckler enquired about the Biblical authority against drink. As quick as a flash Donald Soper said, 'Proverbs Twenty-Three, verses Thirty-One and Thirty-Two – "Look not upon the wine when it is red, . . . for at the last it biteth like an adder, and stingeth like a serpent".'

A wag called out, 'Blimey Guv, he's been looking for that stuff for twenty years.'

Again, someone asked him to explain when discussing the evils of gambling, where it differed from life insurance. 'Have you ever known anyone who wanted to win?' he enquired.

In 1960 I attended the Methodist Conference at Stoke-on-Trent, as a representative of the North Lancashire District. There I saw and heard the great men and women of the day in Methodism. Dr Marjorie Lonsdale MA BD, who was headmistress of the Methodist Trinity School for Girls in Southport, and Vice-President of the Conference in 1961, was expressing her concern one evening to a group of us about Lord Soper's health. She was clear that he did not look after himself as he should, neglecting meals and working long hours. He always attached great importance to the National Children's Home and Orphanage (NCHO) rally at Conference, (now the NCH) and a leading national charity. He described it as probably the best work which Methodism did and he usually added greatly to the Conference NCHO rally by playing his tin whistle. That evening he was leaving the Conference, addressing a meeting on the way to London and would be at his desk at the Kingsway Hall at the usual time the following morning. As Superintendent of the West London Mission his responsibilities included Hungerford Hostel where about 100 people he described as the poor relations of the 'down-and-outs' were cared for. 'Delinquent girls' were also cared for in the Katherine Price Hughes Hostel.

In 1938 at the Bradford Conference, it is said that the then President of the Conference begged someone to 'get hold of that young man and warn him to slow down or otherwise he will wear himself out before he is forty.' He is now in his nineties. One of my all-time pin-up boys.

It was a wonderful period of my life and one of which I feel I made the maximum use. Qualified for my profession, five years of hard study completed, twenty-two years of age and the freedom of London, it was not the place I had disliked when I visited the capital briefly for examinations on previous occasions. Indeed I did not want to return to what seemed the quiet backwater of my home town, Morecambe, and to my father's legal practice.

My stationing in London covered the whole of the eventful year of 1953 – the Stanley Matthews Cup Final, Gordon Richards at last winning the Derby on Pinza, the conquering of Everest by Hillary and Tensing, and above all, the Coronation of our Queen. We were offered window seats on the route in Northumberland Avenue where we worked, but I chose to go to Esher and join cousin Ann and other local residents at a neighbour's house where there was TV and the opportunity to watch the moving and magnificent Abbey service.

I particularly remember the offering to her of a Bible with the words:

Take this book, the finest gift this world affords. Here is wisdom, this is the Royal Law, these are the lively (living) oracles of God.

Chapter XII

PRESIDENT OF THE (LOCAL) LAW SOCIETY

One of the more pleasant honours accorded a solicitor in my geographical area of the profession is the appointment for a year as the President of the Morecambe, Lancaster and District Law Society.

In 1969 I entered my Presidential year in unusual circumstances, as the youngest member ever to hold the office. Taken in order of entry to the Law Society's Roll of Solicitors of the Supreme Court, the appointment was made at the Society's AGM annually in February. The year was preceded by one as Vice-President, which enabled a member to learn the ropes. Unfortunately my predecessor as Vice-President died during his year of office. My resultant catapulting straight into the Presidency was a little nerve-racking.

My deceased Vice-President colleague was Francis Gerald Dromgoole who was not a Bachelor, but a Master of Laws. He had served on the British party of lawyers at the Nuremberg trial of Nazi war criminals, charged with crimes against humanity. Goering, Goebbels and Hess were but a few of the Nazi leaders arraigned before the tribunal in the greatest indictment in the history of mankind. Himmler, the dreaded Gestapo leader, had committed suicide with a capsule of cyanide. Hitler himself had died in his Berlin bunker.

Francis Gerald Dromgoole had one of the most mellifluous voices in my experience. With an artificial leg, he walked with some difficulty. An indication of his intellectual brilliance can be gauged by the knowledge that the thesis for his Master's degree was on the transitional provisions of the Law of Property Act 1925. In 1925 the introduction of a vast range of legislation, included the Law of Property Act 1925, the Trustee Act 1925, and others.

It is a measure of resilience of practitioners like my father, who was admitted to the Roll of Solicitors of the Supreme Court in 1929, that they had to cope with the old and new legislation in their Final examination. The day-to-day conveyancing dealt with by the profession involved great adaptation and change, and the smooth transition from old to new was a credit to its quality and skills. My father had to sit his Intermediate Examination on the old law, and the Final on the new.

Francis was a sole practitioner in Lancaster. At one Annual Dinner when the distinguished guest of honour and speaker was the Deputy and later Secretary of the Law Society, he whispered to me in a voice that could be heard across the room that he was finding the speech a bore. Seated next to him, he asked me, 'Do you find him a bore, John?' After a few minutes of further delivery by the speaker, Francis rose, rather unsteadily, to his feet. Fortified by the juice of the grape and having arrived by taxi already replenished, he turned towards the top table and called out, 'Sir, you are a bore. You are moreover a Socialist.' I had already been regaled in emotional terms with the wonderful qualities of the Holy Father and a visit to the square in the Vatican for a Papal address, his willingness to admit the merit of other denominations including my Methodism, and solutions to other problems which afflicted the world. The speaker handled the situation with a calm ease, indicative of great experience of post-prandial jollity, and Francis resumed his seat. His mutterings continued.

The other guest of honour was Sir Harold Parkinson KBE who, as he said, had only to venture across the road from his nearby Hornby Castle home in carpet slippers. Sir Harold had played a great part in the wartime National Savings movement and was a good friend of the Marsden Building Society which honoured him in 1964 with an invitation to open their new head office in Nelson. My father was then a director of and solicitor to the Society, of which I was to become a non-executive director on his death, and later non-executive and (for a time) Executive Chairman.

At the same AGM as my appointment as President, George C. Howson was appointed Hon. Secretary. George, an able and highly respected solicitor, remained a good friend over the years and to this day. He is currently HM Coroner for north Lancashire, an office held within his practice for 140 years and with great distinction. George himself was appointed full Coroner in 1979.

It was the beginning of an anxious period for the legal profession, when legislative proposals attempted to simplify the conveyancing system, the bread and butter of the profession, by differing methods. In my own year George and I made several trips to meetings in London of Presidents and Secretaries of local Law Societies throughout the country, to discuss proposals and convey the individual views of each Society. I remember one of the platform figures was Sir David Napley, later President of the Law Society, accepted as the outstanding solicitor advocate of his day, apart possibly from Lord Goodman, and who later defended Jeremy Thorpe, as well as the man who attacked the Princess Royal in the Mall. A brilliant advocate, he wrote a book on the subject, accepted as a standard work of the time within the profession. He represented for me all that was best in the profession and the Law Society was well served by his prodigious talent and skill. He was guest of honour in later years at our annual dinner when my good friend, Jim Wilson, was President.

The main proposal during my year, to be followed by many others, was a sort of logbook which would have been administered at local authority level. There were those outside the profession who saw the well-argued point that you could not deal with a house, with rights of way, easements, restrictive covenants and many other complex matters like the sale of a car. The proposals frightened and threatened the future of the profession which was seen as protecting its vested interests. One of the eventual results was a modified system of separate registered conveyancers. Austin Mitchell, MP for Grimsby, was the most ardent proponent of reform and often referred to his love of the friendly building society, against the much less-loved legal profession.

At the annual dinner of my local Society, the President spoke, along with his own selected guest of honour. My choice, who graciously and readily accepted the invitation, was E.S. Temple MBE MA QC of the Northern Circuit of the Bar. He has recently retired as Judge Sir Ernest Sanderson Temple, former Recorder of Liverpool, a much loved and respected figure. The following are details from *Who's Who:*

TEMPLE, His Honour Sir (Ernest) Sanderson, Kt 1988: MBE: MA; QC 1969; a Circuit Judge 1977-91; Honorary Recorder of Kendal, since 1972, of Liverpool 1978-91; s of Ernest Temple, Oxenholme House, Kendal; m 1946 June Debonnaire d of W.M. Saunders JP, Wennington Hall, Lancaster; one s two d Educ: Kendal School; Queen's Coll., Oxford. Served in Border Regt in India and Burma, attaining temp, rank of Lt-Col (despatches 1945), Barrister-at-Law 1943. Joined Northern Circuit 1946: Dept Recorder of Salford, 1962065; Dept Chm., Agricultural Land Tribunal (Northern), 1966-69, Chm. Westmorland QS. 1969-71 (Dep. Chm 1967); a Recorder of the Crown Court, 1972-77; Mem., Bar Council, 1965 Chairman: Arnside/Silverdale Landscape Trust 1987-; NW Area Point-to-Point Assoc. 1987-; Pres. British Harness Racing Club, 1991- Jt Master, Vale of Lune Hunt 1963-85. Hon FICW Hon. Citizen of Kendal 1992. Recreations; farming and horses. Address: Yealand Hall, Yealand Redmayne near Carnforth Lancs. LA5 9TD. T: Burton (Cumbria) (0524) 781200.

'Sandy', as he was known to his friends, was, as I described him in my speech, 'one of us', i.e. of particular closeness to the solicitors practising in the Society's area and a personal friend of many. He held us spellbound and helpless with laughter, as in so many of his brilliant after-dinner speeches of those years, repeating almost verbatim a recent exchange in a Court where he had been appearing, between the Judge and a Counsel who had arrived late at Court, after an arduous journey in extreme weather conditions.

At the 105th Anniversary of the Lancaster, Morecambe and District Law Society, Lord Justice Rose or Mr Justice Rose, as he then was, described 'Sandy' Temple as (in his opinion) the outstanding criminal defence counsel in the country.

It is worth recording that the President usually selected a venue close to his own residence. And so it was with me. It was the second dinner at The Elms on the first of such occasions immediately after the War. On the former occasion the number of courses which could be eaten was restricted by a continuation of wartime regulations. With the end of the War and the return of many members from the Armed Forces, it was a time of great celebration. The restriction on courses was broken and for a time the spectre of all the members of the local legal profession being arraigned before the local magistrates was a real possibility.

At the time it was the custom for the youngest member of the Society to propose a toast to the guests. This was a real ordeal for a newly qualified solicitor to speak to his elders. I made reference to this earlier occasion in my speech. The gentleman concerned had returned home on foot to his nearby home. There were two parallel roads near his home. The first was a cul-de-sac, but he failed to negotiate his way past the entrance in order to gain entrance to the next road which led to his home. Proceeding down the cul-de-sac, he turned right, or tried to do so, only to find, as I observed in my speech, that an enterprising local builder had erected, during his time at the dinner, a pair of freehold semi-detached dwelling houses, so blocking his way. This necessitated him negotiating rose bushes, a brick wall and other obstacles which he surmounted with extreme difficulty, before regaining his proper route and staggering home to his spouse. As I finished my account, the member concerned rose to his feet with the words 'You rotter, you ******* know it was me, John.' As I dropped my father at home after the dinner, he expressed his pride at my performance and I enjoyed a moment of quiet gratitude to him and life in general.

Sandy Temple and father enjoyed a common view that their farming activities, though differing in nature, kept them sane for the arduous calls of the law on their time and skills.

The following appeared in the *Lancashire Evening Post* of 17 November 1994 under the headline 'M'Lud's zonked out!! "Experiment" is no Ass!' and accompanied by appropriate photographs:

A retired judge is proving that the law is not an ass . . . it's a Zonkey!

The new arrival at Sir Sanderson Temple's country home in Yealand

Redmayne, near Carnforth, is a hybrid between a donkey and zebra.

And he and his wife believe it could be the first of its kind in Britain.

But much of the animal's background remains a mystery, although the couple believe the four-year old animal may have started life as an experiment at a research centre near Newmarket.

One thing is certain – the new cross is smarter than the normal mule, although he does share some traits.

Lady June Temple said today: 'He's really got brains. Mules can be a bit slow taking things on, but he's a lot quicker. He's got a beautiful character.'

The couple spotted a newspaper advert and travelled down to Weymouth for their first glimpse of the beast and were taken by its character.

The hybrid bears its father's darker zebra stripes on its legs but is believed to have inherited its mother's colouring.

Judge Temple – the former Recorder of Liverpool – drives his four-year-old Zonkey between the shafts of a trap.

He said:

> 'I bought him because of his unique character. He is probably the only animal of his kind in Britain.

> 'He is a mule because he is hybrid. A zebra is an ass not an equine.

> 'He came to us unbroken but I have broken him to harness and we drive him around the country lanes. He is a grand little thing.

> 'The only thing the new arrival at Yealand Hall lacks at the moment is a name.'

A lovely man who belies on his farm his brilliant legal career. It was with great sadness I heard from him a few days ago of the death of his wife.

When I was a young Articled Clerk I attended the office of his father in Kendal. Sandy's father was a solicitor of the old school and was wearing jodhpurs and boots at his office desk. I was dressed in black jacket and pinstriped trousers as a rather over-proud, newly-articled teenager. Mr Temple was polite and helpful to me. This was my first 'completion', the occasion when a solicitor acting for a buyer attends the office of a solicitor acting for the seller, examines the title deeds to the property, hands over the money, collects the keys and deals with several other important details of the transaction. A day and experience to remember.

It was a happy year and gave my father a lot of pleasure.

I am reminded of another solicitor who in that year gave the legal profession of the district great amusement. Harry Gorton spent the mornings in his downstairs office attending to conveyancing matters, with an hour's coffee break out of the office. In the afternoons, he ascended to an upper room, donned a blue velvet jacket and attended to probate matters, wills and the administration of the estates of deceased clients. Harry Gorton did not smile, but the day came when he did. A report in the local newspaper described a road traffic offence when he had proceeded through the traffic lights on the A6 at Carnforth when the lights were red. A fine of £5 was imposed but the quiet smile of satisfaction on Harry Gorton's face for several weeks afterwards arose from the fact that his age was described as fifty-six years. He was in fact a splendid sixty-five years old.

Chapter XIII

A SINGULAR MAN

Continuation of a Life's Work

David Harrison is a singular man and my story would be far from complete without him. We first met in April 1969 when Jobling and Knape had advertised for an articled clerk and I was interviewing. He was one of many applicants and came (without much in the way of real expectations and enthusiasm he later told me) on a Saturday from his home in Preston, which found me working at the office as usual. He became a partner in January 1972.

The first impression was of a reserved and rather shy young man, which belied his CV, indicating a first-class honours degree in Law from Liverpool University and a glowing testimonial from the Dean of the Faculty. His was the only first of his year. He combined that rare combination of the intellectual and the practical common-sense approach to matters. My father always claimed the latter as the more important requirement for life, and the source of his business acumen and skills, but David enjoyed both qualities. He was divided between the attractions of a cloistered academic life and that of a professional life, with all its variety of opportunities, both of expertise and financial advancement, offered by private practice, dealing with every facet of legal affairs. He chose the latter, but there were times in later years when I suspect he was drawn to the other way of life.

I had always thought that on Father's dreaded death the firm would revert to being an average conveyancing and probate practice, with some litigation and miscellaneous matters. There were several examples in the vicinity, all perfectly respectable firms of integrity, and all earning a comfortable livelihood.

Father's domain was an empire. He had the ability to convey to his ever-increasing number of clients the impression that he was dealing with their affairs personally. It was not a deceitful practice because his excellent memory enabled him to retain a vast amount of detail and keep his 'hands on the wheel', popping in for a few words with clients when they were being dealt with by other partners and staff, and always with that common touch which made them feel special. His practice and manner sprang from a genuine care and concern for everyone and endeared him to a multitude of people from all walks of life.

There was, however, the matter of his extensive commercial interests. Increasingly involved in takeovers, mergers, company affairs, dealing with captains of industry, and always available for the ever-increasing demand for his services in this specialized field, which he enjoyed enormously and which were very rewarding financially, he needed assistance, and David arrived to become his right-hand man. 'Cometh the hour, cometh the man' is a splendid and accurate description of the situation.

The commercial work demanded much travelling and could not be executed satisfactorily at the same time as the requirements and demands of a normal family practice.

He spent three years in the 'heat and burden' of my father's work. His travelling companion and PA, David carried the bags, drove the car and generally attended to the practical matters. But more importantly he absorbed what he saw and heard, and ensured his own aptitude for the work was developed by everything in which he was involved from all those with whom he came into contact, and not just his principal. It was a great partnership. I know how much help and assistance he gave to Father, and I know the esteem in which David held his mentor.

I am sure David could write a book of memoirs, of their travels and activities. Many were the times when, returning by car after a hard day's work on substantial matters, Father would say, 'It's too early to be late, David, and too late to be early' in justifying a leisurely dinner. Father could enjoy a drink with his meal, knowing that his 'chauffeur' was going to drive. When the wine waiter turned to David for his order the reply was always the same and swift: 'He's driving. Thank you.' David retained the connections when my father died and I suspect in some cases against his own expectations. He had been with his teacher long enough, not only to be known to our clients for his own ability, but for his detailed knowledge of their affairs. The continuity was a source of great happiness and satisfaction to all the partners, not primarily for the retained business, but the further extension of the work to which both had contributed so much.

I speak elsewhere of the other valued connection which I was able to retain with the Building Society.

It is a strange happening – I will not call it a coincidence – that on 24 April 1971, the day my father died, David had an appointment at Liverpool University with the Dean of the Faculty, in connection with that academic life which I have mentioned.

David today is a competent and able Senior Partner in a practice which continues to expand and has branch offices. The problems and stresses, the difficulties and strain of running such a practice today, I confidently assert, are far beyond those of my day. It is an added bonus that he seeks to maintain in the practice those principles of integrity, personal attention and caring so dear to my father.

I am grateful to David for so much, and not least his personal friendship and understanding for me at all times. I know that in great measure, but not entirely it has been in memory and appreciation of one we both loved so dearly. Thank you David.

I write these lines on 5 November, Guy Fawkes Day and my father's birthday. As I visit his grave later today, I shall remember David with so many other people who have played such an important part in my life.

Chapter XIV

GIFTS AND TALENTS

A surprising number of men and women do not always show their talents and gifts in early life. I have referred to David Harrison in Chapter XIII. David told me that in his first two years at university he was an average student and only in his final year did he recognize his ability which enabled him to attain the only first-class honours degree of his year. Another similar and more extreme case is that of Lord Justice Rose.

Christopher Rose was a bright, intelligent boy, educated at Repton. He was articled to my firm for three years before deciding he wanted to be a barrister and studied for the Bar.

There was every indication when he came to the office that he would be an able young solicitor, passing his exams without difficulty. There was no indication of this, from *Who's Who* 1994:

ROSE, Rt Hon. Sir Christopher (Dudley Roger) Kt 1985; PC 1992: Rt Hon. Lord Justice Rose; a Lord Justice of Appeal, since 1992; b. 10 Feb 1937; s. of late Roger and Hilda Rose, Morecambe; m. 1964 Judith d. of late George and Charlotte Brand, Didsbury; one s and one d. Educ. Morecambe Grammar Sch.: Repton; Leeds Univ.; Wadham Coll., Oxford (Hon Fellow 1993), LLB and Hughes Prize, Leeds 1957; 1st cl. hons BCL 1959, Eldon Scholar 1959. Oxon. Lectr in Law, Wadham Coll., Oxford 1959-60: called to Bar, Middle Temple, 1960 (Bencher 1983); Bigelow Teaching Fellow, Law Sc., Univ. of Chicago, 1960-61; Harmsworth Scholar 1961; joined Northern Circuit 1961; QC 1974: a Recorder, 1978-85; a Judge of the High Court, 1987-90. Mem., Senate of Inns of Court and Bar. 1983-85. Recreations: playing the piano, listening to music, golf, travel. Address: Royal Courts of Justice, Strand, WC2A 2LL. Club: Garrick.

Lord Justice Rose has never forgotten his roots. I have many happy memories of childhood spent with him and his sister Annette. For many years I lived in St Christopher's Way in Morecambe, named after him and where he spent much of his childhood with his parents in a detached house close to where I later lived.

He was a very happy, sociable articled clerk to whom people readily responded. I remember his outstanding ability as a pianist and of him playing duets with his sister in our local musical festival.

In later years he invited several members of the local legal profession to meet him together in his rooms when sitting as a Judge of the High Court at Lancaster Assizes. He also attended the 150th Anniversary Dinner of the Lancaster, Morecambe and District Law Society where he made, as usual, an eloquent, witty and fascinating speech.

Lord Rose's father was Mr Roger Rose, Town Clerk of the old Borough of Morecambe and Heysham from 1937 to 1961. The local newspaper *Morecambe Guardian* reported on 10 June 1960:

Town Clerk of Morecambe since 1937 Mr Roger Rose, told Morecambe Finance Committee at its meeting yesterday that he intended to retire by next February.

Mr Rose was appointed Town Clerk of Morecambe from a short list of six in May 1937. He was then 40 years of age and had at the time 25 years experience of local government work. Born at Burton-on-Trent he began his municipal career in the Town Clerk's office in that town in 1911. On the outbreak of the first world war he joined the Infantry and saw service with the Royal Engineers.

For two years he was in the thick fighting on the Western Front and was mentioned in despatches at the first battle of Cambrai.

On demobilisation in 1919 he returned to work at Burton-on-Trent and was there until 1926 when he was appointed Chief Assistant to the Town Clerk of Chesterfield, Major Parker Morris, who was later knighted and became Town Clerk of the City of Westminster.

In 1929 he qualified as a solicitor of the Supreme Court and two months before being admitted in March 1930, he became Deputy Town Clerk and Deputy Clerk of the Peace of Dudley. His stay there was very brief for in November of the same year he became Town Clerk and secretary of Education to the Borough of Glossop, where he remained until January 1935 when he was appointed Town Clerk of Hyde. Two years later he came to Morecambe.

During the last war he was Civil Defence Controller, Food Executive Officer and National Registration Officer for the town. He has worked strenuously for Morecambe and through his efforts as a representative in the Association of Health and Pleasure Resorts, the name of Morecambe has often been to the fore.

In 1948 he became vice-chairman of the Association, has been assistant secretary and only a few months ago became the

Association's honorary secretary, a position which will afford him ample opportunity for furthering the interests of the town of his adoption. He is a past president of the Lancaster and Morecambe Law Society.

Nowadays his chief recreation is gardening but in his younger days he was a keen Rugby player and an oarsman. He played Rugby with Burton R.F.C. and with the North Midlands County and he was vice-captain of the Burton Club when they were finalists in the Midlands Counties Cup. As an oarsman he competed at most of the provincial amateur regattas with the Burton Leander Rowing Club.

In 1957-58 his wife, Mrs Hilda Rose was Mayoress. There are two children, Mrs Annette McIntyre, of Bare Lane, Morecambe, and Mr Christopher Rose, who is a lecturer in law at Wadham College, Oxford.

The Town Clerk and my father were close friends and in fact Mr Rose joined our firm for a short time following his retirement. He and my father were largely responsible for effectively carrying through the very considerable work involved in requisitioning hundreds of hotels and boarding houses in the town during the Second World War, for use by the Royal Air Force.

It is a matter of considerable satisfaction and some pride that so many of us can look on the career and achievements of Lord Justice Rose. On a personal note, he wrote me a gracious letter in consenting to my use of his entry in *Who's Who* for inclusion in my writing and I thank him.

I have met many people who have discovered latent talent in early or later life. A boy from a secondary modern school in Lancashire obtained a first-class honours degree at Oxbridge. The most usual case is the discovery by older friends and acquaintances of the ability to paint, sometimes as septuagenarians. A friend discovered after retirement that he had a natural talent for DIY around the house and beyond which has given him great pleasure and satisfaction.

Many, of course, are unable because of work and other matters to cultivate and use known talents until retirement. Although many people, including myself, feel as we say, 'they have a book in them', they do not convert the feeling into action until later years.

I think we should take great pleasure in seeing the large number of people who, in the autumn of their lives, are finding fulfilment, happiness and joy in doing things requiring skills, and which they have either discovered or developed in themselves.

It would be wrong to leave this subject without referring to the Open University and all the courses of further education which are available today. I have nothing but respect for a man or woman, perhaps deprived through no fault of their own of a good education in childhood, studying, often with other demanding duties, and certainly in many cases working unsociable hours, to the end of acquiring a degree, other qualifications or the sheer fulfilment of completing a course of study.

As we live longer, so I believe there will be an ever-increasing demand for education, hobbies and pastimes in every area of life.

Chapter XV

YOUR LOCAL FRIENDLY BUILDING SOCIETY

I had a long association with the Marsden Building Society. Founded in 1860 it remains to this day one of the few Societies which has remained in its original form, without merger or takeover. The Chief Office is in Nelson. Father was invited to join the Board in 1946, as a non-executive director and later appointed Solicitor to the Society. He was one of several men responsible for steady growth. He was Solicitor to the Society until his death in 1971. My family practice of Jobling and Knape were the Society's official solicitors for many years and a strong working bond and relationship was established.

After my father's death I was unexpectedly invited to join the Board, as a non-executive director. I had always understood from Father that the connection would close on his death, and so I felt overjoyed and honoured. The assets were £17 million in 1971 and when I left the Society in 1990 they had risen to nearly £200 million. The number of societies has reduced dramatically over recent years. The Society is the largest of only two which exist in Lancashire. Its policy has always been based on the friendly, personal approach, a position taken until recent times at least by most Societies.

In 1973, I was appointed Vice-Chairman and in 1984 invited to the Chair, again in a non-executive capacity.

On my appointment to the Board, my mind went back to the visit of a former Chairman, Mr J.W. Haythornwaite JP, the proprietor of the famous Victory V lozenge factory in Nelson, to my father for a social evening when he was holidaying with his wife in Morecambe. Requested to accompany them back to their hotel, we walked along the promenade together and Mr Haythornwaite intimated that he would like me to follow my father one day. A young, inexperienced solicitor, I felt honoured but rather apprehensive. In reality the prospect was remote and not in Mr Haythornwaite's disposition.

The work of a Society is interesting and rewarding, and in my time a welcome contrast with and departure from the more abrasive atmosphere of a private legal practice.

The earliest Building Societies were often simply clubs formed mainly by workers employed in factory, mills and workshops, to provide housing.

They often met in the local inn. Regular subscriptions were paid and funds were accumulated to provide each member in turn with a house. A ballot was taken before each house was started. Rules were drawn up.

Probably the first Society was at Longridge, nr. Preston, some twenty miles from my home. There were about twenty members including farmers, stonemasons, weavers, spinners and a shopkeeper. Most of the early Societies were terminating Societies, i.e. they ceased to exist once their object of providing a home for each member was accomplished.

Gradually Societies ceased to build houses themselves and simply advanced the money to a member to build or buy. Eventually permanent Societies were established. They were open-ended, allowing new savers at any time and making advances to borrowers subject to funds being available. Often differing arrangements were made with each borrower as to the terms and repayments.

And so a share in a Building Society is essentially different from a share in a joint stock company or a limited company. Building Societies have proved themselves very popular since inception, providing as they do a safe haven for savings with a reasonable return on their capital, and a popular place for loans required by borrowers purchasing a home, with reasonable rates of interest and other assistance. 'Your local friendly Building Society' is an apt term.

Reduced to its very basics, it involved in my time borrowing money from investors, lending it to borrowers for house purchase at a slightly higher rate than paid to the investors and leaving a comfortable surplus (it was not called a profit for reasons I explain later), after deducting tax and management expenses. Today the picture is much more complex and competitive and I have expressed my views of the legal profession and the building society today in Chapter XVI.

During my period of office as Chairman of the Society, The Building Societies Act 1986 was enacted which marked very significant changes for all Societies. It entailed a great deal of work for everyone. We held a meeting at Chief Office when the Bill was introduced into the House of Commons, which was attended by Mr John Lee, MP for Pendle, who is a Chartered Accountant and had served as a Building Society Director. The members of the Board, senior management, branch managers and others were able to listen and offer opinions as well as asking questions.

The basic object of the Act was to enable Societies to compete with banks and other financial institutions for both savings and mortgage business. Competitors had been able to offer wider services.

The main features of the legal framework under which Societies were allowed to operate under the 1986 Act are:

a) The supervisory body is the Building Societies Commission, with the Registry of Friendly Societies retaining certain functions with respect to registration of documents.

b) Societies are mutual institutions owned by investing and borrowing members.

c) Societies are able to do only those things laid down in the Act and subsequent statutory instruments.

d) Societies are required to raise at least 60 per cent of their funds from retail sources.

e) Societies' assets must be predominantly in first mortgage loans to owner-occupiers of residential property, although they are allowed a limited proportion of their assets in unsecured loans, residential land and certain other assets.

f) Societies are empowered to offer a range of house-buying and financial services.

g) Societies must meet capital adequacy requirements as set out in the relevant Prudential Note.

The services which a Building Society were empowered to provide either itself or through a subsidiary included:

a. Banking Services
b. Investment Services
c. Insurance Services
d. Trusteeship
e. Executorship
f. Land Services

The Annual Conference, with distinguished speakers, was always a time for social intercourse and getting the 'feel' of current changes and exchanging views. I list William Waldegrave MP, Peter Lilley MP, Sir Gordon Borrie then Director of the Office of Fair Trading, the last Governor of the Bank of England, Sir David Frost (as after-dinner speaker) and Lord Whitelaw as a few of the distinguished speakers over the years. The usual delightful places for the annual Building Society Conference included Bournemouth, Torquay, Guernsey and Brighton. The structure of the Association has now been affected by the creation of the Council of Mortgage Lenders.

As with many commercial businesses today, the Society was involved in sponsorship. One particularly pleasant occasion was in May 1984 when Marjorie, as the wife of the Chairman, renamed a boat at Blackpool and Fleetwood Yacht Club. It was owned by yachtsman, Mr Frank Wood, a member of the Club, who was preparing to sail it in that year's *Observer* single-handed race from Plymouth to Newport, Rhode Island. The 45-

foot trimaran's new name was naturally Marsden.

We sponsored other events at Fleetwood in connection with the annual Tall Ships race and held receptions and evenings on the SS *Winston Churchill* and SS *Malcolm Miller*. A senior member of staff, Dennis Capstick, was a former Merchant Navy officer with considerable navigational skills, and was involved in the races. The Marsden Building Society is based in the North-West and has some fifteen branches.

My address at the first Annual General Meeting of the Society as Chairman in 1984 was reported in a local newspaper *The Nelson Leader* as follows:

YEAR OF CHANGES, SAYS CHAIRMAN

It would be difficult to think of a year which had seen more in the way of change and difficulty for building societies than 1983, said chairman Mr J. Knape presenting his report at the 123rd annual meeting of the Marsden Building Society.

There had been a substantial increase in business activity, technology had developed, the Marsden was studying the implications of joining a proposed cash-dispenser network, the Mortgage Interest Relief at Source scheme (MIRAS) had been introduced, and there had been other heavy pressures on resources and time.

All this, combined with growth in competition, and replacement of the recommended interest rate system by a system of advised interest rates, meant that a far greater burden of decision-making had been placed on the boards of building societies. Far more attention had to be paid to the financial strength of a society than its rate growth. Reserve strength, from now on, would be a prime objective of a building society.

He was happy to draw attention to the strong reserves of the Marsden which at the year end were 4.96% of total assets, with a high liquidity representing 25.04% of total assets.

Throughout a difficult time, the Marsden, because of its strong position, had been able to continue to pay extra interest on personal paid up share accounts, and to offer investors a most attractive range of investments for varying periods. Assets had increased from £74m. to over £83½m. and the society increased its lending by more than 52% over 1982 to a record level of over £17m.

Mr Knape mentioned the opening of the Barrowford branch last year, and the forthcoming opening of a new branch in Colne. The society, he said, was well placed to take advantage of the increased demand for mortgages expected during the coming months.

He paid tribute to the work of the late Mr T.A. Baker, former general manager and director, who over 35 years saw the Marsden grow from a small and comparatively unknown position with just a head office in Russell Street, Nelson to its current position as the largest building society based in Lancashire, with branches throughout the North West.

'It is a difficult and demanding era, but I cannot emphasize too strongly that the continuing policy of the Marsden is to remain independent as a strong regional society with the emphasis on providing a friendly, efficient and personal service to all its members. We are confident that this policy will be successful as long as we are not subject to intense outside interference and pressures over which we have no control. Size is not everything.

'We consider that we can give a better service in our own region to our members and borrowers, than many of the national societies. We know the area and are aware of the types of homes and problems in the North West. These factors are, I suggest, becoming more important and present increasing problems to the large conglomerates,' said Mr Knape.

The approaching 1986 Act was clearly in my mind at the time.

I was Chairman, as I have said, at the introduction of the Building Societies Act 1986, which wrought many changes and greatly increased the powers of the Society and its competitive edge. I saw a good deal of Mr John Lee, the MP for Pendle and Minister for Tourism in the Thatcher Government, who rendered great assistance to us in connection with the Act and other matters. He will be remembered by many for his resignation on the Poll Tax affair where he took a brave stand.

One of the highlights of my time as Chairman was the opening of a new computer centre in Nelson, but away from the Chief Office site. Mr John Lee MP was to open the building at the official ceremony, attended by a large number of invited guests, but because of voting commitments in the House of Commons that day, he was unable to attend. It was a happy decision to invite three YTS trainees to carry out the formal cutting of the ribbon.

I made it my task to visit the branches regularly and I like to think my own particular contribution was the raising of staff morale over a period of time. Management problems resulted in my being invited to act as Executive Chairman for a spell, during which time the Board and Senior Management carried out a great deal of reorganisation and forward planning.

A charge of nepotism and closed-shop attitudes has been levelled at Boards of Building Societies and competition for places on the Board has increased to an intensely fought nature. I feel, however, that a group of local professional and businessmen, who know each other and the areas where they operate, is a valuable asset. There has been an increasing tendency to appoint senior management to the Board.

I set out in another chapter my short views on Building Societies today and on the legal profession where I spent virtually all my professional life – from the vantage point of age and experience.

Mergers and takeovers began to take place on an ever-increasing scale as competition, technology and other factors began to take effect. One of my great feelings of satisfaction in building society life was that I know I played a prominent part, and at times a decisive one, in preserving the independence of the Marsden Building Society.

There are three instances in particular which I will mention as typical of the situation. The MP for Pendle wrote to my predecessor as Chairman in 1982 when I was Vice-Chairman in an effort to bring together three local societies. For reasons of which he was unaware and although he was plainly trying to act in everyone's best interests, such a merger would, in my view, have been disastrous. Another occasion saw me deliberately absenting myself from a meeting when I knew my support would be essential for a proposed takeover from which I personally would have benefited, but which I felt was not in the best interests of the Society. The third illustration was when I attended what was virtually a final meeting to agree a merger with another Society of about our own size. Again I would have benefited in status and financial terms but I felt it was being looked upon as a takeover by the other Society. Subsequent events in this last case proved me right. There were many other cases.

I have a treasured note from a branch manager at the time who, when writing to me on a routine matter, added as a postscript, 'Thank you for saving the Society.' I didn't do so on my own, but I think I helped.

I look back with pleasure on many happy memories and friendships.

Only two weeks before I put my manuscript 'to bed', I have learned of the tragic death of Eddie Shapland, the Society's Chief Executive, and a Director. He is referred to in the Acknowledgements and gave me the benefit of his experience and views about the future of the Building Society as an institution as he saw it.

He quickly made his mark in the Society and his death is a great loss. Burnley born and bred, Eddie joined the highly respected Burnley Building Society which eventually merged with the National and Provincial in one of the largest and most controversial of the early takeovers and mergers in the movement. I ask my reader to turn to Chapter XL where I have written about him at some length.

He was a Building Society man through and through, appointed as Assistant General Manager in 1980 (I was a member of the three-strong

Marsden Building Society Board of Directors and Senior Management 1984
Back row (l to r) J Atkinson ACIS ACBSIU MBIM, Assistant Secretary (Later Secretary), R G Glover AIDPM, Assistant General Manager (Later Deputy General Manager and Group Secretary), K Nutter, Mortgage Manager (Later Assistant General Manager (Mortgages)), R M Parkinson BSc FRICS, Director (Later Vice-Chairman), R L Cornes FCA, Director (Later Chairman), B W Haigh ACIS FCBSI, General Manager & Secretary, E Shapland ACBSI DMS MBIM, Deputy General Manager (Later General Manager, Chief Executive and Director)
Front row (l to r) M Wiltshaw PhC, Director; L P Smith MA (Cantab), Vice-Chairman (Later Chairman), J Knape, Chairman, R H Reed OBE, Director (Later Vice-Chairman), Dr L B Ashworth JP MBBS LRCP MRCS, Director

sub-committee which interviewed the applicants and recommended his appointment to the Board), Deputy General Manager in 1984, General Manager in 1986 and Chief Executive in 1988. He made rapid progress.

During the period I acted as Executive Chairman he was a tower of strength. Friendly, open, Eddie was a leader of original thought, who nevertheless commanded the respect and affection of all the Society's staff. Everyone has been stunned by his tragic death.

The policies and schemes he espoused may be summarized as follows and be implemented by other Societies who have not already done so:

Housing renewal and renovation with a subsidiary, a Home Improvement Agency which received an annual grant from the Department of the Environment and local authority.

Purchase by the Society of a property needing renovation, returned to owner occupation and giving confidence to adjoining owners to spend money on renovations.

Equity release – enabling the elderly to 'unlock' the value of their property on a year-by-year basis, and often without any payment until death, or a very small interest only payment spread over many years. Many a widow scraping by on her pension, with no dependants, has found a wonderful release from financial worries by this method.

Allowing young couples about to be married to choose a run-down property, the Society then buying and renovating, and allowing the couple to choose the final fittings e.g. bathroom suite and kitchen furnishings. The property is then sold to the couple.

A private sector landlord with a difference. I refer my reader also to Chapter XVI.

I have in front of me as I write some papers about non-urgent matters which I had intended to discuss with him in the near future. One was a personal matter asking for the recommendation of a valuer in connection with a property formerly owned by my late father; another concerning the content of my writing in this my autobiography about the Building Societies Movement, and to refresh myself again in up-to-date views of the future; and confirmation that the mutual nature of Building Society, the strength of their reserves, their ability to deal with a variety of specialist housing matters, and particularly in local areas by local, smaller Societies, would ensure their future survival and importance.

In a news-sheet published by the Marsden Building Society shortly before I left, Eddie wrote:

The Marsden in the 90s: A personal view.
by Eddie Shapland, Chief Executive

During the 1990s, Marsden Building Society will continue its traditional role of supplying housing and investment services for the benefit of its members.

It will continue as a mutual institution based in Lancashire, having a strong affinity with this area of the country.

Although the Society will continue on traditional lines it will not be slow to innovate, but will only offer new services and products which will not endanger members' funds.

During the 1990s I see the Society becoming more directly involved in housing projects, both new building and home renovation schemes. It will be one of the Society's major aims to help improve the housing stock of the area in which it operates, particularly around our Lancashire base.

The Society will continue as a completely independent organisation owned by its members and will seek to expand by natural growth offering a secure future to its current and future staff. As the services offered expand, high quality job opportunities will be provided for people within our home area.

The Society being based in the area provides business opportunities for many local companies and the Society will continue to spend money locally which in turn will improve the economy of the area.

Many people will be aware of the strong commitment the Society has had over many years to sponsoring local charities and worthwhile causes, and this policy will continue, thus assisting the community generally.

I mentioned that the Society is owned by its members and I would urge the people of this area to support 'their' Society during the 1990s so that we can continue to offer mutual support to the community.

Eddie never forgot his friends, and he wrote to me on 14 December 1994 and again on 31 March 1995 when I was writing my story.

31st March 1995
Dear John
Many thanks for letting me have a copy of the letter from The Pentland Press Limited, together with the other enclosures, via Morecambe Office.

Simply for the sake of accuracy, I am returning a photocopy of the acknowledgement sheet with my name on as there have been a number of changes over the last few years. The Chartered Building Societies Institute has now amalgamated with The Chartered Bankers Institute. The British Institute of Management has become the Institute of Management and therefore, my designatory letters have changed. I was, of course, never Eddie 'S' Shapland, but I presume the 'S' may stand for Stanley, after Matthews!

I understand that you are going on holiday to the Holy Land at the end of next week and at the same time Janet and I will be in Malta. (Perhaps Janet and I are following in the footsteps of St Paul!)

I hope you have an enjoyable holiday.
Kind regards
Eddie
E Shapland
Chief Executive

He wrote to me yet again:

9th December 1997
Dear John
Many thanks for your letter of 25th November, together with other correspondence. I have, over the last couple of weeks, tried to ring you on a considerable number of occasions, but unfortunately there has been no answer. Perhaps when convenient you would like to ring me either at the office or on my home number, which is . . .

I am sure we can find plenty of things to talk about!
Kind regards.
Yours sincerely
Eddie
E Shapland
Chief Executive

There are two matters, one from the business world, and the other from my own experience on a personal note, which I would like to pass on to the reader.

The 'Gospel according to Eddie' was excellently summed up in a report from a forum he attended. It reads:

Serving the local community: what a building society can do

One of the few building societies to have retained interest in housing renewal projects is the Marsden, based in Nelson, Lancashire. The

Marsden is a regionally based society, operating in north and east Lancashire and Cumbria, with 15 branches. The society does not aim to compete with the larger national societies in providing financial and banking services, but instead sees itself as playing a full role in meeting housing needs in the local communities which it serves. In addition to the normal range of savings and lending services, the Marsden operates directly through its subsidiary Marsden Home Renovations to purchase and improve vacant properties for sale or rent.

Marsden Home Renovations also acts as a home improvement agency in the Nelson area. In addition, the society provides development and mortgage finance for housing associations to undertake renewal or redevelopment projects, and works closely with the local authorities in the areas it serves to support their housing renewal strategies. The Marsden's close links with the local community also enable it to tailor financial products to the needs of individuals. Amongst other measures the society has developed equity release mechanisms which enable older people in the area to get small lump sum payments when they are needed.

The Marsden aims to develop a role in the local community which distinguishes it from the larger national societies. Its close knowledge of the local housing market enables the society to invest in projects which financial institutions lacking this community base would consider too time-consuming. Restrictions on the extent to which the society can lend for projects of this kind make it difficult to expand this role to meet the potential demand, but the society has succeeded in selling some loans on to other lenders after their profitability has been demonstrated, enabling it to recycle resources for housing renewal.

The other matter is quite different. There was a very large congregation indeed at Eddie's funeral. People who had not met for years and many business associates, staff and others were there to support Janet, Mark, Kay, Eddie's mother and the rest of the family. Everyone still appeared stunned and unable to take in the events of the previous few days.

I gave thanks for my faith. I drew back from thinking how I might have felt if I had thought that this was the end.

Why does God do this, why does God do that? Why does He allow this to happen or that? Why do the good seem to suffer when others appear to prosper? These questions must have been troubling many of that large congregation. It was written on their faces. Many of them, I am sure, hid feelings of anger towards God, an uncaring Providence, or whoever or whatever was responsible.

I reminded myself that it was all right to be angry with God, that He understood our tantrums, that there will always in this life be an air of mystery about many things. I also remembered that if we knew all the answers *we* would be God. God has given us the precious gift of free will, or we would be puppets on a string. I refer my reader to the contents of Chapters XXXV and XXXVI.

The address at the funeral service was delivered by the Rev. Geoffrey F. Nadin, Superintendent Minister of the Morecambe & Heysham Methodist circuit. The Rev. Nadin spent eleven years as a Minister in Burnley until his transfer in September 1977. He knew Eddie and the family well.

I was able to spend some time with him on the evening before the funeral and was greatly comforted to learn that he intended to speak about 'Eddie, the man'.

EDDIE SHAPLAND
1947–1998

I ask my reader to turn to Chapter XL where I have written about him at some length.

Eddie Shapland 1947-1998

Chapter XVI

THE CHANGING FACE OF WORK

Having reached retirement age, I cannot write the story of my life without looking back on the far-reaching and fundamental changes which have occurred in the workplace. My experience has naturally been largely in the legal and building society fields where I have spent nearly fifty and twenty years respectively. On these I will concentrate. I have already written a little in relation to my chosen profession.

In the case of a family legal firm there has, as elsewhere, been a complete transformation since the day I joined as a young articled clerk aged seventeen. Without doubt my main impression is of the changes in the relationship between solicitor and client.

One of my favourite TV programmes over the years was *Dr Finlay's Casebook* which has recently been revived. At the time of writing I confess I have not watched the new series, largely from fear, as has happened in other cases, of spoiling my memories. Dr Cameron was my idea of the perfect family doctor and I knew many solicitors in my early days who seemed to display similar qualities. They were predominantly men with a sound knowledge of their chosen subject, an interest in their patients and clients which extended to knowing their families, their interests, their particular circumstances, interest in the growing family, and above all the time to sit in surgery, office or home, in spite of whatever pressures may have been present, and make those with whom they were concerned feel they were the practitioner's main concern.

I hope I shall not be accused of prejudice and ignorance of the need for change. I seek only to portray the situation as it existed yesterday, and exists today, and to make a few helpful suggestions.

In my earlier days the solicitor was treated with considerable deference and respect by clients. A visit to his office demanded the making of an appointment well in advance, best clothes, prompt arrival and waiting on the proffered advice in a manner which was not far distant from showing awe and unqualified acceptance. It was possible for me as a newly-qualified solicitor in 1952 to have a general knowledge of virtually all but the most abstruse subject which a client brought before me. The term 'General Practitioner', used in the medical profession today, was applicable to the lawyer of the time, in the sense that he was competent to deal with the larger part of problems extant in a client's daily experience.

Today, almost without exception, the solicitor must specialize. The vast increase in legislation, the complexity of the law and daily life, and the need to keep up with constant changes in every field make it impossible for the general practitioner of old to survive today. And I feel too that unless he is prepared to limit himself to one particular area, e.g. conveyancing and probate or litigation, the single practitioner will find it increasingly difficult to survive.

It is always helpful to share a difficult point or case in discussion with a colleague and in many cases 'two heads are better than one'. In addition, and regrettably, the standards of honesty and integrity in the profession, as elsewhere, are in my estimation much lower than forty or fifty years ago and are continuing to decline. Solicitors have always prided themselves on the fact that nobody has ever lost financially because of the dishonesty of any member of their profession. Many Building Societies today will not send a cheque for a mortgage advance to a single practitioner. It would be easy in these days of swift travel and modern technology for a fraudulent lawyer to amass a large sum of clients' money and be in a distant part of the world in a matter of hours. And this has happened all too often in recent times.

In my view the pendulum has swung too far. Much legal knowledge and practice was dressed up in 'red tape', when a simple explanation would have left the client much happier. Today the average citizen is much more knowledgeable and will rightly demand explanations previously accepted without demur.

The matter of dress is not without interest. As I came to the end of my busiest practising years it was not uncommon to see a solicitor in polo-neck sweater and/or jeans. I do think the public in general expect a certain standard of their professional advisers. It was a treat for the men in my younger days to be allowed the luxury of a sports jacket and trousers on a Saturday morning. Most offices of lawyers are of course now closed on such occasions, but then it was often impossible for the working man to have time off during the week, and as a result the morning was almost entirely devoted to interviews from 9 a.m. until 12.30 p.m. or later. Often were the times when it was a rush to get home, have a quick meal, and travel to a soccer match at Preston or Burnley for a 3 p.m. kick-off.

A skeleton staff of typists sufficed on a Saturday because of the time devoted to interviewing. Today many firms advertise clinics when advice is offered (often with a free preliminary interview) in the evening on certain days of the week, and at other unconventional times. These are to be commended. This brings my mind to the important matter of Legal Aid. I do not propose to comment on specific matters as the whole subject is presently in the public arena and is giving rise to considerable concern. Vast sums appear to have been paid to applicants of substantial means, there has undoubtedly been a content of fraudulent claims and abuse of the system and some areas of need are outside the scheme. I consider it a matter of great importance that there should be a good Legal Aid scheme available to those who could not otherwise have recourse to law.

I feel that some of my colleagues in their and other professions are unaware of the fear and trepidation with which the ordinary citizen views professional charges in the law, medicine, dentistry, accountancy, surveying and many other fields. It is not an easy matter to resolve. During most of my professional life Conveyancing and Probate were our bread and butter and gave any reasonably hard-working solicitor a good living. Because of this, two important matters resulted.

The first was that we were able to carry out a large amount of legal and what I would term quasi-social work, without any charge at all. I do not think I ever charged for the preparation and execution of a will, and if I did it would be for a minimal sum and at the insistence of the client. We were not benevolent institutions. In due course the will would become a probate matter where good remuneration could be earned. Very often wills were dealt with when clients bought and sold their homes. 'We might as well make our wills whilst here,' was a common remark. Title deeds of the home were left in our strongroom for safe custody where there was no mortgage involved, and often placed there at the client's request after it was discharged. It was a particular pleasure to see clients who had paid off their mortgage, often in middle or later life, after many years of hard work. There was a real sense of achievement.

It was my custom in the case of deeds and wills to write to a client and confirm that the documents had been placed in our strongroom for safe custody, that they were available at any time (or copies) and that there was no charge for the facility. This, to me, was intangible goodwill and took a long-term view of the practice. I can speak of one colleague in particular in my family firm who has weathered the recession better than most because of a long-term fund of goodwill built up over a lifetime of dedicated service.

Overheads, cash flow, technology and other matters present problems today which did not exist throughout most of my professional life. I was staggered when I heard recently of the premiums which are paid (they are obligatory and not optional) by solicitors in insuring against professional negligence. We are going the way of the USA where vast sums are recovered by claimants in this area. No professional man could sleep soundly in his bed without the cover and these premiums with the usual staff salaries and wages, the cost of ever-increasing technology and usual overheads mean that a solicitor today must charge for every minute of his time. It is often forgotten by the public that time and skill are the only things a professional man possesses for sale.

It is not unreasonable, I feel, in appropriate cases to ask for a modest payment 'up-front' and certainly in the case of disbursements, i.e. such matters as stamp duty, search fees, survey and valuation fees for mortgages, court fees and many other expenses. A solicitor cannot, as in my earlier days, be expected to pay them out of his own pocket and add them to the bill at the end of what could be a lengthy transaction, in some cases lasting for months or even years.

I feel there is still much satisfaction to be enjoyed from working as a family solicitor and the downside is largely the same as in every other area of life today – too great a concern with money and materialism, too much rush and hurry, too little concern in realizing the supreme value of every individual, too much regard for the easy and fast buck, and a general dissatisfaction with life. I will receive little support when I refer to the lack of a real aim and purpose in life.

Without the God of my understanding, my Christian faith, I feel I too would be like so many of my colleagues I see today, burdened and lacking in peace and contentment, and a feeling of fulfilment.

And so to what for me was the gentler area of the Building Society. I have said in my words about building society life that there was a friendliness about it which was not seen in my own profession. I believe this was in large part due to the little understood conception in those days of the mutuality of Building Societies. The word does not convey its real meaning which is simply that the Society belongs both to the investor and borrower.

Reduced to its simplest basic format, as I have said, the investor received a good rate of interest on his money which was lent to the borrower who paid a rate which was large enough to enable the Society to pay the investor, its tax liabilities and management expenses, and leave a reasonable surplus which served to strengthen the financial position of the Society for everyone's benefit. Investor and borrower were equals. Today the word 'surplus' is scarcely heard, and a young man in financial circles might look rather strangely at anyone who used the word. The ruling word today is 'profit'. A simple definition of a Building Society but which seems increasingly out of place today, is a club for pooling funds to build houses.

The first really important legislation was the Building Societies Act 1874 which enabled permanent societies to be registered and incorporated. In 1890 there were nearly 3,000 Building Societies in Great Britain. Today the number is about eighty to ninety. In 1986 a further Building Societies Act brought about great changes, to which I referred previously.

It is in my view a pity that Building Societies in general have lost sight of their original aim. Their loss however could well be the gain of other societies. I have received a great deal of pleasure and satisfaction in observing the progress of the Society with which my father and I were so closely connected for nearly fifty years.

It is ranked about fortieth at the time of writing in the league of size of assets, but I believe some of its pioneering projects being developed and carried through today are more in keeping with the original aims of the Building Society, meet local needs in a way which could never be done by the larger Societies or other financial institutions, and in so doing retain and strengthen that personal factor and relationship which in my view is of the essence in life.

There is insufficient space for me to write at length on this 'pet theme' of mine but there are two which were begun during my term as Chairman of the Society which illustrate my case.

The first is often called the 'equity release' scheme. An elderly couple, widow or widower are owner/occupiers of a house. The mortgage was paid off at retirement or before. The property is in need of repairs and the owner has just sufficient income to live reasonably well. The children have grown up and have left home.

The Society arranges a loan which fulfils several purposes:

1. The house is put in good order, pleasing occupier and family.
2. The owner can draw an agreed sum each year which can be used as income or for any other purpose.
3. There are no repayments. The loan is repaid on sale or death.

The children are often brought into the situation and are pleased to see that an asset which they will inherit one day is keeping its value and condition, and that parent or parents do not have any income problems. There are other similar schemes in operation but all need to be carefully scrutinized. Some in the past have been found wanting. Naturally the scheme is one for later life and not normally completed unless the owner is aged over seventy. I have completed several such loans with great satisfaction for all clients.

At the other end of the scale we have a young couple who have just got engaged and are to marry in twelve months. They are thinking of buying a house and 'doing it up' before the wedding. The Society can do this for them, carrying out the work to an agreed plan and standing the cost. The property is then sold to the couple who are granted a mortgage by the Society. The overwhelming benefit is in the young couple being relieved of all the worry and anxiety of supervising or carrying out the work at a very busy time for them, and most importantly, allowing them to obtain tax relief on the whole of the mortgage. If they bought the property in its original condition and carried out the work themselves, they would not obtain tax relief on the expenditure.

It is of crucial importance that the Society is a local one, knows the area, is aware of the fundamentally good structure of the property which has fallen into disrepair, and is generally on the spot to deal with all the matters, big and small, which may arise and are to be trusted to act fairly, reasonably and without trying to make an unjustified profit. These are matters where the original concept of a Building Society is seen at its best.

There are other schemes and a good Society will create more and more good and flexible schemes to meet local demand. There is a place for the large financial institution. There is also, I believe, a very real place for the smaller local Society which finds its niche. In spite of heavy and strong competition the Marsden Building Society has increased its surplus again during 1997 and I am proud to have been associated with it. May it long continue to prosper and remain independent.

It is ranked about fortieth at the time of writing in the league of size of assets, but I believe some of its pioneering projects being developed and carried through today are more in keeping with the original aims of the Building Society, meet local needs in a way which could never be done by the larger Societies or other financial institutions, and in so doing retain and strengthen that personal factor and relationship which in my view is of the essence in life.

I would like to end with an extract from a paper prepared by the National Housing Forum entitled 'Papering over the cracks' which was compiled with the assistance of the Society.

Involvement of lending institutions.

During the early 1980's, the government made attempts to involve the private sector in housing policy. One major initiative was the development of housing renewal initiatives by lending institutions such as building societies. These included home improvement agencies such as Care & Repair, financial advice services and mortgages in local authority housing renewal areas, and subsidiary companies to undertake or organise redevelopment projects. But the advent of financial deregulation in the mid-1980's increased competition in the savings and mortgage lending markets, leading most institutions to focus their efforts on potentially more profitable areas such as the provision of banking services. The boom in the property market in the late 1980's also led to an emphasis on estate agency and the sale of endowment insurance products linked to mortgages. Most of the societies involved in housing renewal activities wound down their efforts in this field, and few now show any interest in returning.

Initiatives such as those being developed by the Marsden Building Society (see case study opposite) are vital to supplement the resources available to local authorities and housing associations. Other small regional societies have already shown an interest in developing this role, but it is also important that the larger national societies should again begin to play a significant part in housing renewal by developing initiatives of this kind. In the long term, it is in the interest of all lenders that property values and security are maintained by the encouragement of repair, improvement and maintenance investment. In addition to direct financial involvement like that of the Marsden Building Society, there are also promotional and educational roles which financial institutions could perform, as set out on page 96, *serving the local community: what a building society can do.*

Chapter XVII

DOWN ON THE FARM

Farming played a prominent part in my life from 1947 until my father's death in 1971. As a young boy he had spent a good portion of his summer holidays on the farm of Uncle Parker and Auntie Janie, near Skipton. Auntie was my paternal grandmother's sister.

He acquired a love of the farming life which remained with him until 1946 when he purchased Middle Fairbank Farm, Ings, between Kendal and Windermere. It consisted of 134 acres and was one of a number forming part of a large estate which was broken up in 1946. The farm was actually bought by one of Father's best friends, who quickly lost interest and resold to my father for the princely sum of £2,600.

The farm was tenanted at the time and I remember John Gleaves having a terrible time during the winter of 1946/47, which was one of the worst in memory. The farm was cut off from the main road for six weeks by deep snow and the tenant lost cattle from starvation. The livestock was quite insufficient, properly to stock the farm, and the tenant had no financial resources to do so. He left after the winter and my father bought such cattle and implements as remained.

The centre of our interest was a dairy herd, and the Shorthorn breed was by far the most predominant in Westmorland. The reasoning was that the Shorthorn cow produced a reasonable quantity of milk, and after its useful life, a carcass of value remained for disposal. It was a fallacy.

A manager, George Brumwell, was appointed from many applicants. He was given authority to buy cows at Kendal Auction Mart and quickly acquired sixteen newly-calved cows which filled a modern shippon. The milk churns were deposited with others, early in the morning, at the milk stand in Ings, which was a meeting place for the local farmers and where I always felt many of the world's problems were settled.

A Ferguson tractor was purchased. Costing £325 it became the workhorse (largely replacing the horse itself) of the tractor world. Smaller and less expensive than others such as the David Brown, it was an all-purpose vehicle which was seen on almost every farm for years to come. They are still to be seen.

Grass is the crop which grows best in Cumbria (formerly Westmorland and Cumberland) and dairy herds predominated. We grew a quantity of oats which were planted in the first year of a three-year rotation, followed in the second year by a 'green' crop usually of turnips, cabbages or kale for feeding to the livestock. This crop was called a 'cleaning crop' because it reduces the level of weeds. In the third year the field was put back to grass with a cover crop of oats.

Conditions were spartan and primitive. Access at first was through another farm from the main road and involved some three-quarters of a mile of rough track, and three gates to open and close. There was no mains electricity, and power was supplied by a generator after a short period. At first, however, storm lanterns were used. I knew what it was, in short spells, to rise at 5 a.m. in the winter, have a cup of tea, trim the lamps and milk the dairy herd by hand, before rushing the milk by tractor to the stand, and returning for breakfast.

In the first year we carried out the hay-making entirely by hand, apart from the cutting of the grass, which was done by mowing machine attached to the tractor. Turning and shaking out, forking the hay onto carts, forking off in the barns and stacking were all carried out manually. One year we made ninety acres of hay in a glorious spell of weather in June lasting about ten days. It was exhausting but reassuring to know the winter supply of hay for the cattle had been secured.

June hay was said to be worth twice the feed value of July hay because it was cut before the seed head was formed fully, and so more of the nutrition was retained in the grass as a whole.

After two or three years we decided to establish a pedigree Ayrshire herd. Ironically when I had visited my great-uncle's farm at Horton-in-Craven as a small boy, I was attracted to the British Friesian breed because I liked the black and white colour. They were the bitter rival of the Ayrshire among dairy farmers. The Friesian was a larger animal and it was said by the Ayrshire supporter that you could keep three Ayrshires for two Friesians. However, it was gradually and grudgingly conceded that the Friesian produced more milk than the Ayrshire. The former, in a good lactation, would produce something like 1,300 gallons, but the Ayrshire about 1,000 gallons. But again the Ayrshire produced better quality milk, with average butter-fat of about 3.8 per cent against the Friesian 3.5 per cent. This was before the days of skimmed and 'healthy' milk, and cholesterol, and there was a bonus payment for the higher quality. It explained why some farmers cleverly kept a few Jersey cows with the Friesians, producing an even richer milk. Again, the Ayrshire farmer claimed that his breed was a more thrifty animal, foraging and flourishing on less favourable and rocky pastures, whereas the Friesian required lusher pastures. The Jersey and Guernsey are noted for their exceptionally high butter-fat milk. The Friesian was called a 'black and white' and, as I have indicated, they were our sworn enemy in the shippon

THE GREENHILLS HERD OF PEDIGREED ATTESTED AYRSHIRES

NAME __GREENHILL CELIA__ H.B. No. __P13544__ Ear Mark __662856-622C3__

Sex __F__ Born __23.11.62__ Bred by __J. KNAPE__

PEDIGREE

Crown Thor 146176	Bargower Bow Tie (Ann) 96633 12 daughters average 7944 lbs actual 9995 lbs M.E. @ 4.08% in 305 days.	Bargower Cup Tie 38770	Bargower Rothesay Bay 55682
			Bargower Silver Bell 10th 13647
		Bargower Miss Donald 56th 88718	Bargower Reunion 41901
			Bargower Miss Donald 13th 79266
	Kingfield Tiara 3rd. 115479 (App) 100,000 lbs Club.	Bargower Eage Boy 64529	Bargower Legacy (App) 47939
			Bargower Cherry 39th 45497
		Kingfield Tiara 26761	Gregory Victor 53994
			Relief Tiara 5th 27457
Gowan Sophie 2nd 663256	Crown Hallmark 140635	Bargower Dollar Crown (App) 128083	Bargower Crowning Glory 81878
			Bargower Dollar Princess 4th 272413
		Crown Noreen 129274 100,000 lbs.Club.	Bargower Field Marshal 60058
			Park Norina 73115
	Gowan Celia 363755	Monktonhill Magnet 93249	Bargower Silver Ace 54771
			Monktonhill Princess 57851
		Auchencloigh Minnie 42558	Ardroscadale Winston 52850
			Auchencloigh Moss By 4th 47014

MILK RECORD

Calving Date	No. of lbs.	% B.F.	lbs. B.F.	Days in Milk	REMARKS
9.10.65	10264½	3.94		323	Heifer lactation.
15.10.66	9681	3.86		288	
14.10.67					

Ref. : RD 259

MILK RECORDS of DAM, G. DAM AND SIRE'S DAM

DAM					G. DAM					SIRE'S DAM				
Calving Date	lbs. Milk	B.F. %	B.F. lbs.	Days in Milk	Calving Date	lbs. Milk	B.F. %	B.F. lbs.	Days in Milk	Calving Date	lbs. Milk	B.F. %	B.F. lbs.	Days in Milk
23.11.62	11761	3.61	10	308	8.2.56	10874½	3.77	8	315(E)	3.10.51	9413	3.99		350
25.11.63	9190	3.46	10	307	16.4.57	8944½	3.22	6	288	20.12.52	10673	3.36		305
1.12.64	12751	3.51	10	309	13.5.58	6778½	3.40	4	190	15.1.54	16128	3.69		285
17.12.65	10822	3.41	10	315	14.6.59	10626	3.31	7	332	25.1.55	15654	3.84		295
4.1.67	13342	3.57	10	289	6.11.60	10257½	3.61	7	304	31.1.56	15103	3.64		337
13.1.68					15.11.61	9191	3.46		279	6.2.57	14115	3.70		308
										8.2.58	13489	3.89		333
										22.2.59	12615	3.23		304
										5.1.61	13857	3.57		305
										22.2.60	14738	4.03		366

BREEDING RECORD

Sex	Born	Tattoo Mark	NAME OF CALF	Herd Book No.	SIRE'S NAME
F	9.10.65	813544-622CK	Greenhills Countess	906383	Greenhills Talisman
M	15.10.66	-	-	-	Ewart Hunter
M	14.10.67	-	-	-	Overtoun Victory Day

REMARKS

To Whom Sold _____ Delivered _____

Date_____ Signature_____

and on the show field.

I still have a pamphlet called 'The Ayrshire Cow' written by James Howie OBE of Muirside, Dumfries. The North-Western Counties Ayrshire Breeders Club, of which we were members, visited his famous herd on many occasions. He had several sons with outstanding Ayrshire herds. In later years his herd contracted foot-and-mouth disease in a widespread outbreak and, as was the rule, had to be slaughtered. Full compensation was paid by the Ministry of Agriculture, Fisheries and Food.

Mr Howie writes of the outstanding characteristics of the good Ayrshire cow, with a broad, wide muzzle, a sweet, open, clear eye and showing a mild temperament. It also displayed a flat crown, moderately sized horn and smart, well-carried ears. Tight, neat feet should support straight hind legs to stand the strain of the milking gear. Above the feet the bone should be moderately sized and very good in quality. And so on, with reference to the front shoulder, spring and depth of rib and at the 'business end', a nice length and development of quarter thigh, and a large, well-developed and well-balanced udder. The teats should really be about 2½ inches long and there should be strong milk wells, twisting from far forward on the belly, to the udder. Mellow, loose skin with a soft, moosy coat and a good balance, completed a good, decent-paying animal. And that's about all!

I have stressed the intensity of purpose of the dairy farmer of my time with a pedigree herd. Bloodlines were studied, milk records kept and processed. In the case of pedigree Ayrshires, the Ayrshire Society required ear-tattooing for identification purposes, the completion of a detailed form and issue of a certificate showing what was virtually a family tree of the animal. I have still in my possession the register of our herd immediately prior to its disposal, neatly typed and with up-to-date breeding, lactation records and other details. A typical front and back page are shown.

The outstanding Ayrshire herd belonged to Bertie Drummond of Bargower, Hurlford in Ayrshire. All Ayrshire breeders made an annual November pilgrimage to his bull sale. Only twelve months old in most cases, they were studied, taken apart and discussed endlessly in the shippons or byres until late into the night. The catalogues were compulsory reading and a document to keep and refer to often in the years to come. Bertie had two brothers who jointly shared the sale. James's herd prefix was Overtoun and John's was Burnnockstone. It was Bertie who always made the highest figures. I remember Bargower Crown Diamond, a young bull I did not rate as highly as others, selling for 9,000 guineas. We purchased an Overtoun bull and had several cows in our herd from time to time with Bargower and Overtoun prefix. Father loved to wave his catalogue at the sale, partly out of fun, and partly to test the nerves of those of us who were with him. The sale was in a huge barn and we sat on the stacked bales of hay.

On one occasion we had, as usual, stayed late, looking at the bulls for sale on the following day. Aunt Ruth would have our dinner ready promptly at 7 p.m. including Father's favourite lemon meringue pie. At 9 p.m. we arrived in a guilty state. 'Throw your hat in the door' was the order to our farm manager, David Scott. The hat was thrown out almost before it had touched the ground.

We were fortunate in having a good farming friend in Willie Bone of Auchencloigh, near Galston, in the heart of Ayrshire country. My Uncle Andrew, who was a woollen manufacturer in Kilmarnock, was responsible for the introduction. Willie had a fine pedigree Ayrshire herd and we bought many cows and heifers from him over the years. A canny, quiet Scot, he was generous and helpful in all our dealings and passed on a great deal of sound advice and help. Willie and his wife May always offered us generous hospitality. May died some years ago.

I was proud of our Gowan herd of pedigree attested TT Ayrshires. The name was taken from the river which ran through the farm.

Vast sums of money changed hands in those days, and the Scottish farms must have enjoyed nothing less than a financial bonanza, even though I have yet to hear any farmer admit to anything other than a bad year. It is accepted that he does not, in general, enjoy a great return on his capital, but after the War the price of land and cattle rose dramatically, and when farming was at its peak many owners and tenants were wealthy men. Many inexperienced men and women from England, who had bought farms, spent small fortunes in areas such as the one where my father and I concentrated – the pedigree Ayrshire dairy cow. It was a good thing for British agriculture, but two salient points need to be mentioned.

Many were 'fireside' farmers with little or no experience and I know several who burnt their fingers. My father used to say that there was no easier way to lose money than in farming, without thorough knowledge and experience. He benefited from his boyhood days but he had very much a 'hands-on' approach. Every evening he spoke on the telephone to the manager, planning the work, checking on progress, increasing his knowledge by reading a wide range of books and the usual weekly publications like *The Stockbreeder* and *Farmers' Weekly*. I participated to a lesser degree, although I claimed a much deeper knowledge of bloodlines, milk records and individual performances of our milking herd. Father was more practical. He spent virtually every weekend on the farm and in later years lived in a new bungalow which he built after fighting the planning authorities. They clearly thought he was a hobby farmer, picking a choice spot looking down the Lyth Valley for luxury and comfort. He had to build nearer the farm buildings than he would have wished, but proved beyond argument that he was building to enable him properly to supervise the running of the farm.

Father purchased Greenhills and the adjoining Tarn Close farms in 1950. In total with Middle Fairbank we had some 350-400 acres. Middle Fairbank became Gowan Bank. It was a hard farm, north facing, with endless stone walls to repair and more than its fair share of ditches and hedges requiring constant attention. The north-facing aspect made it a 'cold' farm, where the growth was not as great as the more sheltered farms across the valley.

A very important event for us was when we acquired possession of three fields alongside the main Kendal to Windermere road. Until then we had to travel a long way through another farm, opening several gates, before reaching our farmhouse and buildings. The previous owner had shrewdly retained the tenancy of the three valuable fields which were excellent land. There was a very contentious action when Father sought possession.

The case was heard before an Agricultural Land Tribunal following service of a notice to quit, and Father was put under severe questioning at the hearing in an effort to show he did not have the necessary real knowledge of farming or interest in it. Father conducted the hearing himself and was, as always, equal to the occasion.

We were able to construct a road straight through from our own road to the main highway, which added very substantially to ease of working the whole, and to its value. Later Father acquired the adjoining High Fairbank Farm and when we sold to John Redmayne after Father's death in 1971 the total area was about 212 acres. This was in addition to Greenhills and Tarn Close. Father had decided to cut down his farming commitments and had let Gowan Bank to John Redmayne some years earlier which necessitated building the bungalow at Greenhills, as I have mentioned.

Greenhills and Tarn Close were sold at public auction in 1971 after Father's death. I was too upset to attend the farm sale of stock and machines, but I knew that with all the responsibilities which fell on my shoulders when he died, it was foolish to keep the farms even though we had in Ted Mitchinson, a loyal and able manager, and in his wife Edith, a caring and dedicated wife to Ted and friend to my parents. One of the saddest days of my life was when Edith, frantically trying to trace one of the family, tracked me down fortuitously at my office, on the telephone, to say Father had died in her arms. The date was 24 April 1971.

Shortly after the farm sale, I attended the sale of the farms and bungalows by public auction at Kendal Town Hall in a legal and personal capacity. It had become the pattern to divide land into parcels and thereby encourage adjoining farmers to buy and so enhancing the total sale value. Everything sold well, apart from the bungalow, which I allowed to go slightly below the reserve price, simply because everything else had gone. Sadly it remained empty for many years, for reasons unknown, and its condition deteriorated.

We were not to know, however, that this was the beginning of the inflationary spell which was to run and run. If I had sold in the following year, the prices would have doubled. And they continued to rise.

When I look at the problems of farming today, where a holding of less than 500 acres is probably not profitable, and with all the problems of the Common Market quotas and other controls, I am glad I am not farming. Together, although Father was much more involved than me, we were not just 'fireside' farmers, and knew the ins and outs and practical daily work of the farm. The identity of the cows for instance, even at a great distance in a field, became as familiar as family.

When we first farmed Middle Fairbank, we tried most forms of livestock, including turkeys (then difficult to rear), pigs, poultry, ducks and from beginning to end, the 'golden hoof' as sheep were called. This valuable animal could often produce twins for rearing and sale, provide further income from its annual shearing and clear the clumps of grass during the winter, which enabled freer growth to take place in the spring.

The other salient point to remember about farming in this generally prosperous era was that for some years a loss from one business could be set off against a profit from another. Thus while we were becoming established, losses from the farm could be offset against the healthy profits from the legal practice and this again resulted in substantial investment throughout the country. Profit was never our primary motive. Father loved his farming as I did, but capital appreciation was always an attractive and on-going feature. As long as the business 'washed its face', Father was content.

We virtually rebuilt the old buildings at Gowan Bank and carried out extensive drainage and other vital work. Again much of this was subsidized in the early days by the Government. We were the second people in the district to make silage. The neighbouring farming community who were set in their ways said it 'rotted the cows inside'. Nowadays, silage is the rule, rather than the option, and enables two crops of grass a year to be harvested, and without the need for the good weather which hay demands.

The Shorthorn cow fallacy was gradually exposed. The extra milk produced by the Ayrshire and Friesian more than compensated for the lack of carcass on disposal. The 'black and white' became the accepted cow in ours and many other areas. The 'pedigree business' gradually

Bargower Queenie 118th Supreme Champion Westmorland County Show 1965
'Ted' Mitchinson – Farm Manager.

Author with Malcolm Gorst (Marie's son) and 'Bob' Stables (Farm Manager) with
Show Contenders.

disappeared for economic reasons and it was a sad day when we sold our herd in total to a Cheshire farmer and purchased 'black and whites'. The sale was fortuitous. Cheshire had suffered badly from an outbreak of foot and mouth disease, just when we were contemplating the change. The purchaser of our dairy herd had lost his entire dairy herd of Ayrshires in the mandatory slaughter and was able to replace it with the government-paid compensation. He bought the whole herd.

Visits to the auction; the burden of stone-picking (in which father was often able to inveigle my sisters); trips to Scotland, the heart of the Ayrshire breed; hay-time and harvest; damson-picking and sheep-shearing; and all manner of country work and pastimes added up to a happy and often idyllic life on the edge of Lakeland in the Lake District National Park.

Humour and anecdotes are not hard to come by in farming.

I would like to share with the reader, the contents of a leaflet 'Hymns Trenchant and Modern' which I have kept for some thirty years. It is reprinted by kind permission of the *Farmers' Weekly*, which I have already mentioned, and was read by Father and myself throughout our farming days.

Hard Lines

Sir, Perhaps these verses based on 'We plough the fields and scatter
. . .' would now be appropriate for harvest festivals:

> We spray the fields and scatter
> The poison on the ground
> So that no wicked wild flowers
> Upon our farms are found.
> We like whatever helps us
> To line our purse with pence;
> The twenty-four hour broiler house
> And sweet electric fence.
>
> All concrete yards around us
> And Jaguars in the yard
> The tele lounge and deep-freeze
> Are ours from working hard.
>
> We fire the fields for harvest
> The hedges swell the flame,

The oak trees and the cottages
From which our fathers came,
We give no compensation,
The earth is ours today,
And if we lost on arable,
Then bungalows will pay.

All concrete yards . . . etc.

John Betjeman
Cloth Fair,
London EC1

'The poison on the ground' Betjeman out-rhymed.

John Betjeman's parody of the harvest hymn 'We plough the fields
. . .' in last week's FARMERS WEEKLY led a large number of
readers to answer him in kind – in protest, and in verse. We print
just a few of the counter-parodies which Betjeman's skit evoked,
and express our apologies to those farmers whose voices cannot be
contained in this issue but who are clearly in the great tradition of
farmer-poets – Editor.

Merry friends

Sir –
When TV poets, round and bland.
Pontificate about the land,
We farmers, not being men of letters,
Must harken and respect our betters

Let yokels wade through scenic mud,
Concrete for farms is much too good,
Let's wear our smocks in pony cart
And touch our caps to men of arts.

Do you ask of Tootes, Rinso or Wills
To make their goods in rustic mills?
In firms which pay your dividends
Are men and master merry friends?

Nostalgia for antique tables
Or imitation Flemish gables

That's your trade – we wish you luck
But think we'll borrow your next book.

A.M. Wood
Melton, High Wood
Barnetby, Lincs.

We plod the fields . . .

Sir – Mr Betjeman is right. I will heed his advice and mend my ways. Perhaps the following lines will be appropriate for my 1965 harvest festival.

> We plod the fields, our tractor
> Stands hated in the yard,
> Symbol of the decadence
> Detested by the bard
> Grimy shirt and threadbare cap
> Urge Dobbin to his best
> We picturesquely play our part
> Despising ease and rest
>
> All weeds and mud around us
> Make yeoman's paradise
> So thank the bard, O thank the bard
> For he is wise.
>
> Who wants a modern motor
> A telephone or fridge?
> Hens are free, the bacon's salt,
> The privy's by the hedge,
> Our rustic joys are simple:
> Our pleasures cannot cloy
> We keep the townsfolk happy
> Delighting in our joy.
>
> All weeds, etc.

Peter Adorian
Gibbons Mill Farm
Billinghurst, Sussex

All bugs and beetles

Sir – I feel John Betjeman's little parody calls for some reply:

> Let insects all run rampant
> Let weeds grow in the earth
> But where lies our salvation
> In the ensuing dearth?
>
> The taxpayers with their millions
> In subsidies and grants?
> The Min. of Ag. and Fisheries
> And all its Sainted Aunts?
>
> All bugs and beetles gather
> Give thanks with heart and voice:
> The farm's gone back to nature
> John Betjeman's had his choice.

P.R. Stevens
St. Margarets Farm
Whitfield, Dover

Castle critic

Sir –

> Betjeman in his castle
> The farmer at his gate
> John made us, high or lowly,
> And ordered our estate.

T.H.O. Stanley
Rectory Farm
Stanton St. John
Oxford

Humble hymn

Sir – Mr Betjeman has unfortunately omitted the final verse of his new Harvest Festival hymn which, I fancy, goes something like this:

> So make us farmers humble,
> Take all our perks away
> Convert the rippling cornfield
> And sweet green clover ley
> To wilderness or ragwort,
> Of couch and scrub and gorse.
> God, make the rabbits flourish,
> Turn tractor into horse.
>
> Make concrete yards to crumble,
> Give Jags to those who seek
> To live life as it should be:
> The townsman's four-day week.

C.J. Jessel
South Hill Farm
Hastingleigh
Nr Ashford, Kent

Lend him a hoe

Sir, Parody, like sarcasm, being the lowest form of wit, and Mr John Betjeman having need to make use of them both. I am driven down to his level to answer him:

> We plough the fields, no matter
> If we don't get a crop
> For man shan't live by daily bread
> But glib poetic rot.
> We only want to flatter
> The dim aesthetic eye
> And ears are deaf to pleading
> When hungry bellies cry.
>
> All good gifts around us
> The weeds and thistles grow
> O say a prayer, put up this prayer
> Lend Betjeman an hoe.

Let Betjeman design then
The chicken house and byres
with cornucopian cornices
And lofty dreaming spires
Let buttercups and daisies
abound the fertile earth
While beauty's eye beholds them
Our children curse the dearth

All good gifts around us, etc., etc.
Lend Betjeman a hoe!

P.J. Vine
Talbot Village Farm
Wallisdown Road
Parkstone, Dorset

Bread and scrape

Sir, –

Come fill the church with thistles,
Put docks all up the aisle,
Bring sheaves of stinging nettles,
Bring cleavers by the mile;
Away with bounteous corn crops,
For which we thanked our Lord
If Betjeman can find wild flowers
Upon his walks abroad.

Oh! back to mucky farmyards
So beautiful to see
Oh! back to 1930
And bread and scrape for tea.

J.Poi
Cotmore Farm
Chillington
Kingsbridge, S. Devon.

Ungrateful band

Sir, – A counter-doggerel for Mr Betjeman please:

We plough the fields and scatter
The good seed on the land
Despite the gibes of Betjeman
And his ungrateful band.
To try to feed the millions
Our energies are bent
And if we make a profit
We are more than content.

All critics are around us,
Their Jaguars in the yard,
The tele-lounge and deep-freeze
Are theirs for working hard.

They fire the fields for picnics,
Their rubbish swells the flame,
They take scant thought for those who toil
To feed them just the same.
They give no compensation,
The earth is theirs today
And if they should go hungry
The farmer is to blame.

All critics are, etc.

It needed saying!

T.E. Richardson
Low Farm
Harpham, Yorks

Oft in danger, oft in woe,
Out of British farms there flow,
Spite John Betjemanic grief,
Eggs and pork and barley beef.

Let not sorrow dim your eyes
When production multiplies;
Mortal men must live and eat,
Empty stomachs made replete.

Let your dropping hearts be glad,
Things are really not too bad . . .
Even with the Min. of Ag.
Not all farmers own a Jag.

Onward then in battle move,
Let us all efficient prove,
While poetic wrath abates,
Watching our conversion rates.

Pigs and poultry, beef and sheep
Never-ceasing vigil keep
On the ever-present need
For a proper balanced feed.
Hymns of glory and of praise
Sing aloud for all our days;
When there comes the final test

VITAMEALO IS THE BEST.
F.L.F.

I attended a farm sale of a neighbour. A calf was put up for bids. It was a female, twin to a male. Such an animal is sometimes infertile and the term used in my part of the world to describe the poor creature was 'freemartin'. The auctioneer was a real character, known to every farmer in the North-West of England. Sam Hodgson of Kendal Auction Mart knew his stuff as a farmer and auctioneer. Referring to the characteristic I have described he endeavoured to raise the expectation and hopes of seller and buyer alike, with the words 'I have seen 'em go both ways.'

When Middle Fairbank was being spruced up, after the takeover from the tenant, the front garden was cleared, apart from a Christmas rose bush underneath the lounge window.

'Let's have that out, George,' Father said to our manager.

He replied protestingly (he had a speech impediment), 'B-b-b-b-b-b – but Mr Knape – it'll out by Christmas' (referring to its flowering).

Father briefly observed, 'You never said a truer word, George.'

A characteristic of farm talk in Cumbria is the use of the word 'like' which could be injected into a sentence three times, with comparative ease.

We were about to leave the farm for Scotland and our manager at that time was a supreme example of the art form I have described. On an impulse, I made a bet with my father (£5, which showed my confidence) that our manager would say 100 'likes' before we reached the summit of

Shap, perhaps ten miles away. I counted *sotto voce* as we motored, our very deaf manager in the back blissfully unaware, but as the total was mounting and increasingly drawn by me to Father's attention in the front passenger seat, he had to keep himself from bursting into laughter and cover up as best he could, but with difficulty. 'Shut up,' he repeatedly hissed.

I won the bet with ease.

Although it is not a farming story, I must mention Bill Sanders. He was my father's first client in Morecambe. A builder by trade, he was in the barber's shop with another builder when my father called for his first haircut in Morecambe. Reading his newspaper, he heard one say to the other, 'I've found a solicitor who can get you your money in three to four weeks.'

'Never,' was the rejoinder.

'Yes, it's true. A young bloke who's just started up in Victoria Street. Name of Knape.' Father raised his newspaper further to ensure it covered his face.

Bill was entrusted with carrying out renovations and general rebuilding at Middle Fairbank, as it then was. Each Friday evening we called at his house, where he lived with his wife and daughter. We were always welcome and I feel Bill was rather 'chuffed' that two solicitors called every week to see him. The primary purpose was to ascertain progress during the week, but we were well fed and enjoyed the company. Bill invariably mentioned some new defect which needed to be remedied, but a regular expression which never varied was: 'Your feathers [something to do with chimneys] or your roof, or your shippon wall, or whatever, is disinterrogating.' As long as our eyes did not meet, all was well, but on one occasion we only partially succeeded and Bill's quizzical look contained a suspicion that we were 'taking the mickey'.

As I write, I realize that all three stories I have recounted are about matters of speech – perhaps a throwback to my public school days. Bill Dodd was a loveable farm labourer who never aspired to anything else. He lived in the village of Staveley, some two miles from the farm, and served us faithfully for many years. Bill was a 'chunnerer', which is one who endlessly talks and mutters to himself about things unknown. Lean and fit, with no bad habits, he took the hard physical life in his stride. He was not an intellectual. I have seen him on many winter evenings sitting by the open log fire, reading the *Telephone Directory* by way of relaxation. On more than one occasion it was upside down.

One spring day, Mother and Father were on holiday and as we had just the one car at that time I was asked to take the weekly wage packets to the farm. This entailed a long and wandering bus journey from Lancaster, through tiny villages away from the main road, with many stops. A normal 45-minute drive lengthened into two hours or more. As I walked up the unmade farm road from the main road I espied Bill. He was 'thinning' turnips. This involved crawling along a row of seedlings, protected by sacks tied round the knees, pushing most of the growth and leaving one plant to grow, at intervals of about twelve inches. Not the worst job on a farm, but also not the most interesting. I have served my time to it. As I approached, I greeted him cheerily, not appreciating that he had not heard my footsteps. I swear he left the ground on all fours as he twisted round in surprise. This evoked a fresh spell of 'chunnering' as I left him and proceeded on my way.

I had never seen a dead body until I saw Bill in his coffin. A well-lived, hard-working earthly sojourn duly ended and the farm manager, Father and I went on the obligatory visit to his cottage. His widow, a cheery, friendly lady who had spent a happy but childless life with him, invited us in. Unaware of the need to view the body, we chatted for some time. 'Well, let's go and see him,' she said. I later found it was the unchanging custom. I probably share a common experience with many people in contemplating such an occasion for the first time. I did not know how I would react. We climbed the rickety, winding stairs of the tiny dwelling to the bedroom. I shall never forget the experience, but not for the reasons I had anticipated. The overwhelming feeling was of a shell and the absence of the essential life in the body. Departed soul, life force, call it what you will, but this was not the Bill Dodd I had known, loved and respected all those years.

In later days it was easy to understand my grandmother's expressed wish not to be taken into the church which she had faithfully attended all her retirement days, and which meant everything to her. 'There's nothing there' was her comment on the situation of a body lying in a closed coffin in front of the Communion rail during a funeral service.

I do not wish to traverse the various theories about the moment of the soul's departure from the physical remains. What I do wish to say is that I realized at that moment, the body is the temple of the Holy Spirit, that we are body, mind and soul, that the physical and material things of life are transient, and that the body is but the servant of our immortal souls. The experience strengthened my faith and I knew a gentle peace and sense of the eternal in that tiny room. I shall remember Bill.

Chapter XVIII

A MATTER OF SPORT

Sport has been a joy and an essential part of my life since earliest childhood, as the reader will have already gathered.

I wrote of the 'sinister' pink knickers affair in my fourth year of life in Burnley and the game of cricket which followed. Cricket had already seized hold of my imagination and interest. I remember that Sir Donald Bradman spent hours knocking a golf ball against a house wall with a cricket wicket to give him his wonderful reflexes and eye for a ball. Anything involving a ball, drawing out natural skills, drew me close.

I am of the school which is convinced that a George Best, a John McEnroe, a Donald Bradman, a Martin Offiah, a Seve Ballesteros, a Roger Bannister and Mohammed Ali were born and not made. Training, coaching, tactics, adjustment of temperament and many other factors play a considerable part in the finished article, but the fundamental, essential, primary element of skill was there at birth. Stanley Matthews and Bobby Moore, Pele and Maradonna, Carter and Mannion, the Busby Babes and Bill Shankly developed and honed their in-born talent by kicking a tennis ball, or a tin can, in every spare moment in back streets, or on rough fields, with jackets as goalposts.

The famed 7-a-side games of Liverpool, in training, in the glory days, exemplify this conception, with the stories (some undoubtedly apocryphal) of Shankly continuing the games until his side was leading, and declaring the game to be much more serious than a matter of life and death. I was standing on a platform at London's Euston Station, waiting for my train home after another England v Scotland biennial game at Wembley, when Shankly appeared on the platform. I can only describe his presence as giving out a restless dynamism and electricity, which must have been the catalyst for all he and his merry men achieved over the glory years. Restless pacing to and fro, gesticulating and talking ceaselessly about the game, which was his lifeblood, is an unfailing memory. He lead out Preston North End before a capacity crowd at Maine Road, Manchester in an FA Cup semi-final in 1954. His clear, bubbling enthusiasm and vigour defied description and fleetingly gave the impression that he had 'flipped' with the excitement of the moment.

Of course coaching is essential. A few days ago, I was listening to the commentator on a UEFA Cup game between Aston Villa and a Yorkshire side. A brilliantly taken first-touch ball near goal was prevented from counting by the momentary hesitation of a player who should have shot with his left foot, but waited a fraction of a second to shoot with his favoured foot, with which the first touch was effected. The commentator expressed surprise that so many players at this level had a 'better foot'. I find it incredible. At my modest level I spent hour after hour on my own, with seven or eight balls, endlessly dribbling, shooting and taking corners, using my left foot almost exclusively, until it was almost as effective as my natural right foot.

Of course we all have our favourites, but for me the greatest player who ever walked onto a soccer field was 'Sir Tom', the Preston plumber, Tom Finney, a one-club player with seventy-six caps for England. Never booked by the referee, ceaselessly fouled by frustrated defenders, he never retaliated. As I write we are hearing of the imminent return of the Matthews, Finneys and Bests of yesteryear, because of changing rules and better protection from fouls. Yet in the video 'Tom Finney – the perfect player', Jimmy Hill says it has been calculated that he was fouled nearly every 4½ minutes, and this never affected his brilliance.

Sir Tom could play on either wing and in his latter days proved himself a complete centre forward. A powerful shot in either foot, good in the air, in spite of his average stature, a dribbling ability with hardly an equal, a strong tackler, a brave player always involved in the play, and a scoring record at club and national level which alone ranks him as an all-time great as a winger, make up the picture of a legend in his own time. Sir Matt Busby and Bill Shankly drool over him in their writings. I was privileged to watch him in almost every home game during his career, and was present at his emotional last game. Everyone came to see Tom, unassuming, a man who gave freely of his time after his playing days to worthy causes, including the chairmanship of the Area Health Authority, and much work for charities.

As I check the first proofs of my book, I hear of the conferring of a knighthood on one we always called 'Sir Tom' – a richly deserved honour to add to his OBE and CBE.

A few years ago I spoke in my usual animated way about him to a keen young Preston fan who was carrying out joinery work at an office in Preston. Eventually I paused for breath and said, as I ended my eulogy, 'Didn't you feel the same?' Quietly and sympathetically he said, 'You talk just like my dad. I wasn't born until after he finished.'

The worst game he ever played was in the Cup Final of 1954 against West Bromwich Albion. He has spoken of the emotional and physical tiredness which had unknowingly been overtaking him in the preceding weeks, and which he recognized only on the field of play. It was the year after the 'Matthews' final and the media were building up the inevitable comparison for weeks before. Preston lost 2-3. Tommy Docherty, when asked about him, said that when the rest of the team felt tired, they would give the ball to Tom for ten minutes. 'I just feel sorry for those who never saw him play,' he concluded. And so say I.

The old *Picture Post* contained a feature about him just after the War, showing him pushing a handcart and climbing ladders in his plumbing business, which today is a large and thriving concern with about 100 employees. 'Is this the new Matthews?' it asked, arousing my indignation that they could talk of anyone in the same breath as Stanley Matthews. My admiration for Sir Stanley remained undiminished, but 'Sir' Tom was the more complete player and always in the game. Sir Stanley demanded service, 'Sir' Tom went searching for the ball. Sir Stanley rarely headed a ball or tackled. He remained on the wing from which he seldom strayed.

I boarded a train one year at London's Euston Station after attending another England v Scotland international. There were two seats, one of which was occupied. I sat down and, looking up, saw my hero. We talked 'shop' all the way to Preston. He was so approachable, talking like any other football fan and expressing his views about every aspect of the game and players.

In the 1950s I went to the England v Scotland game at Hampden Park, Glasgow with 140,000 others and heard again the 'Hampden roar' which could 'freeze' a player. My Uncle Andrew had forgotten his ticket. Father gave him mine and purchased a cheaper ground ticket (standing room only) from a ticket tout, against his normal principles. Handing it to me he said, 'This is on condition that you promise not to speak a word during the game.' Tom played a 'blinder', made all the goals in England's 4-0 victory, and was vilified by the Scottish supporters round me, who suggested in colourful language his disembowelment and other horrors, while I, inwardly ecstatic, remained as silent as the grave.

I was foolish enough to dedicate myself entirely to studying for my chosen profession from the age of seventeen to twenty-two, and never kicked a ball until I qualified. Within weeks I was picked for my first game for my home town of Morecambe, who played in the Lancashire Combination, and were a semi-professional side. The centre forward was Harry Jackson, one of my past heroes in the Burnley side, my life-long favourite club in the town of my birth. I had replaced a popular regular in the side, and was not surprised at the greeting I received from one of the senior semi-professionals. He muttered 'How green can you get?' I was too excited to bother but I did not see as much of the ball as I should have done. The local newspaper *The Visitor* described my performance as follows:

LOCAL HOPE

In his first senior team game, local player outside right Knape showed flashes of tricky ball control that could make him a constant danger. His corners were on the mark.

I walked on air for days.

My call-up for National Service the following week ended my dreams, but I continued to think and speak of the famous trio of outside rights – Matthews, Finney and Knape! Season ticket holders at Burnley and Preston, we enjoyed those never-to-be-forgotten years of vast, well-behaved crowds, of pies and peas, and witty banter admirably portrayed by the comedian, Al Read. Bob Lord was the controversial and much-disliked Chairman for many years, but he was a great servant of the Club. The secret was largely in the scouting system in the North-East, where a scouting genius, David Blakey, picked up a constant stream of promising youngsters who were placed with a motherly landlady, made to train for a trade, and sold at the rate of one a season to balance the books. It worked until other clubs muscled in on their territory. 'Bob's' practice was, if possible, to welcome the visiting team, soundly thrash them, give them pie and peas, and send them on their way. Father was at school with 'Bob' and bore to his dying day on his legs the scars of a vicious tackle by the Chairman-to-be in the playground.

When John Bond was the controversial manager for a time, I spoke in an official capacity at a get-together after a game sponsored by Marsden Building Society of which I was then the Chairman, and presented the man-of-the-match award. I reeled off the following team and asked him if he could remember it: Strong: Woodruff; Mather; Attwell; Brown; Bray; Chew; Morris; Harrison; Potts and Kippax. 'Never heard of it,' he said. It was the Burnley Cup Final side of 1947, of which I have written elsewhere.

Father never ever got into a flap about anything in his life, except as I have said elsewhere when Burnley were winning 1-0 with ten minutes to go and the ball was near their goal. He could not bear to watch Sir Alf Ramsey, when playing for England before becoming the national team's manager, so often passing the ball in the penalty area.

My earliest memory is of being held up in the crowd at Turf Moor when Burnley played the mighty Arsenal before the War, in a cup-tie, and lost 7-1. Salt was rubbed in the wound on the way home when we purchased a paper and saw the score in the Stop Press given as 14-1!

In 1947 Burnley reached the Cup Final. After drawing with Liverpool in the semi-final, they won the replay at Maine Road, Manchester City's ground. I was at Shrewsbury and did not see the first game, but was present to see Ray Harrison, Burnley's centre forward, swivel on one leg in the closing minutes of the replay to score the only goal of the match. We travelled to Wembley by car with a close family friend, Edward Ernest Howarth, after whom my brother was given his first name. A resident of Nelson, he was Secretary of Marsden Building Society, which was to play such a big part in my life. He died, leaving a considerable estate, which must have been acquired by northern thrift – never the owner of a car, never the owner of an inside WC, the wearer of the same hat and mackintosh for countless years, a carrier of sandwiches for his lunch wherever he went, and yet a warm, friendly and charming man. We stopped at a small roadside cafe called Mary Pratt's near Watford for tea and biscuits and for which he paid 3/6d. Ernest complained about the cost all day and for years afterwards. It was always a source of laughter between Father and myself.

Perhaps it is best to draw a veil over the match. I enjoyed the pre-match build-up and seeing the VIPs, one of whom and sitting immediately in front of us was Jerry Desmond, who was then playing fall guy for Norman Wisdom. But Burnley lost 1-0 with a speculative shot from outside-left Chris Duffy, in extra time, winning the game for Charlton. I hardly spoke for days. At half-time I was later told, I consumed a bag of grapes and can of lemonade, but I cannot remember.

In the evening we attended the ice-hockey match in the stadium complex. Sitting with us at the dinner table which ran alongside the rink was Bill Kitchen, then the World Speedway Champion, who lived in Galgate near Lancaster, where he owned a garage. He was a quietly spoken, modest young man with a friendly disposition. In spite of such a treat, and being taken into the dressing room to shake hands with some of the players, I was miserable. Such is the lot of the fanatical soccer supporter.

Peter Kippax, Burnley's outside-left, was an amateur and had been a fighter pilot in the War. A local man, he was the object of hero-worship for boys of my age. As with Tom Finney in Preston's 1954 Cup Final, he had one of the few poor games I ever remember, and his relationship with the team never seemed the same afterwards. He had been selected to play for England against France for his first cap in the preceding week, but had to withdraw.

My father, like every other fan, knew where every error was currently being made. In 1970 Burnley had a poor spell and Father was convinced the answer lay in the need for a cultivated right half-back. He could restrain himself no longer and wrote to the Chairman. Bob Lord replied as follows:

Dear John,

Many thanks for your letter of the 19th ultimo, I extend my apologies very sincerely to you for not replying before now, but this Football game creates a tremendous amount of work and takes a lot of time, so therefore you will have to very kindly accept my reasons.

Regarding your meeting with a Mr Mosscrop who was the son of Mr Terry Mosscrop the ex-Burnley player was very interesting what you had to write about him, I am quite in the same mind as you and if Burnley Football Club had a man of the calibre as a Captain of the type of Tommy Boyle at the moment we should certainly not be in the position where we are today, but you find me one, we have been searching the Country for the last eighteen months for such a man and you can take it from me it is just impossible to get your hands on anything like that type of man. I am not saying there are not any but where they are you just could not buy them for all the tea in China. No we shall have to wait until we find one amongst our own staff, this we are constantly trying to do, and only this week have we appointed Martin Dobson the Captain of the team, you will I have no doubt remember that Martin broke his leg in an August practise match and he's only just come back into the side, but he is a man of calibre only a young man but never the less he is well above average both in ability on the field of play and also a man of principles and morals.

I do hope you are keeping well, and it was a pleasure to receive your letter, I take this opportunity of wishing you and yours the Compliments of the Season and perhaps, who knows, we may come across one another in the near future.

Yours very sincerely,

R.W.LORD

Father never forgave him for referring to Terry instead of Teddy Mosscrop, but I think this was a typing error, (like the others!).

A football club exercises a great influence on the pride and general morale of a town or city. Whenever Burnley or Preston North End were winners, a friend who travelled with us would invariably say, 'Production will be up in the town this week.'

In 1938 I met Sir Donald Bradman, generally acknowledged as the greatest batsman of all time. The encounter was brief, unexpected and left an indelible memory. England were playing Australia at Headingley in the series when the late Sir Len Hutton scored his then world record 364 runs in an innings at the Oval. Jim Wright was the English physio and was employed at the time in Morecambe, at the new Broadway Hotel, where an indoor swimming pool, Turkish baths and many of the features of a modern keep-fit gymnasium preceded their time. Father knew him through business and we eagerly anticipated the use of the two tickets he was given by Jim, and the invitation to look him up in the pavilion during the tea interval.

The white-coated attendant courteously took our name at the dressing-room door. A Mr Wright appeared, looking rather puzzled, and indicated that he did not know a Mr Knape. It was, in fact, Doug Wright, the Kent spin bowler. As the mix-up was being sorted out, the Australian team came through the door to take the field. I was standing against the corridor wall immediately in front of the great man and he looked down and smiled at me. I often feel that he must have been thinking that this eight year-old boy would remember the moment all his life. And he has done.

The Don scored 103 that day before being clean bowled by Bill Bowes, the Yorkshire pace bowler. He had seemed to me to be of medium pace until I saw Bradman's wickets cartwheeling all over the field.

Many who played for England that day did not survive the War. Ken Farnes, a young fast bowler who played for Sussex, was killed in 1941. His bowling was once described as 'as fast as any man ever bowled' and one can only project about his loss to the game. Hedley Verity, the Yorkshire spin bowler, died in Italy from his wounds at the age of thirty-eight as a POW and his last words were 'keep going'. Ken had a run-up which made him appear like a galloping horse, black hair streaming in the wind and with all the vigour of a sportsman in the prime of life. Jim Wright obtained autographs of the team on a neat card which my father's office boy painted round the edges. It became one of the favourites in my autograph album which sadly was lost in one of my many moves. It included Walter Hammond, the England captain, Len Hutton, Len Barnett, Norman Yardley, Bill Edrich, Dennis Compton and many other greats of the day.

I played golf in spasms, feeling I could put the game on a back-burner until middle-age. I now enjoy at least two rounds a week. As I walk up the hill on the 13th hole, in three or four strides, Morecambe Bay comes into view. When the sun is shining and a blue sky rests above a full tide, and with the Lakeland mountains as a backdrop, I say a silent word of gratitude to the Maker of it all. 'Every prospect pleases and only man is vile.'

I do not subscribe to the view that golf is a fine form of relaxation, in spite of offering a long walk and exercise, fascinating play, separation from the telephone, enjoyable friendship and good company. The non-playing reader may be puzzled.

Every golfer knows that you can play one day and feel you are Nicklaus or Palmer and have 'cracked it', only to wonder the next why you ever took up the game. A few months ago I was standing on the 15th green at Morecambe. Two players on the adjoining 14th tee were banging the ground with their clubs in exasperation with their poor drives; my partner had just used barrack-room language when missing an easy pitch to the flag from just off the green, and another member of our foursome produced equally basic expletives when missing an easy putt.

A good friend, the recently retired Superintendent Minister of the Morecambe and Heysham Circuit, Rev. Allen Fisher, is a member and excellent player. He recently appeared in the local newspaper, having done a hole-in-one on the Heysham course. Allen is the butt of many a joke which he takes in good part. A passing funeral cortège, a missed and easy putt, the inference that he has 'outside' help, have potential for harmless fun. Allen asserts that many of his best sermons are constructed on the course. His ministerial colleagues and church members do not spare him. I am sure he can handle it all. I know I could, if I did a hole-in-one, as he has done more than once.

During recent months I played eighteen holes on my own. I have found this a great help when writing. One cold but sunny Monday morning in January I left the first tee at 7.45 a.m. when there was just sufficient light. I finished in five minutes under two hours. With the course almost to myself, I was able to enjoy a wonderful sunrise and from the 6th tee look back across the lush green of the turf to the strip of bright blue sea beyond, denoting high tide. Across the bay the sun was shining on Grange-over-Sands against a background of purple but partly snow-covered Lakeland hills and mountains.

Above them the blue sky was broken by a vivid vapour trail – a photographer's dream, and my delight. For the rest of the week, play was impossible because of heavy rain. Retirement brings with it the opportunity to play when the weather permits. The weekend, mainly for working golfers, seems all too often to have the worst of it.

When in my teens, I completed a round in hurried fashion early one Saturday morning in 1½ hours. Nobody ever believed me, but completing my recent round in under two hours at the age of sixty-seven enabled me at least to prove the point to my own satisfaction.

I heartily oppose the current trend of eliminating competition in sport in schools. It is, in my view, healthy and vital. The will to win must be tempered with the acceptance of losing in a proper, if disappointed manner, but to abolish competition is to stifle proper ambition and attainment of standards, of benefit in later life.

Tennis was one of my favourite summer sports and on one occasion I shocked every member of the club by beating the outstanding player, in the men's singles final.

Keenly fought matches in a full fixture list on summer evenings,

Bare Tennis Club
Unbeaten Winners
Lancaster and District League Division II, 1959

C. Udall
D. McTaggart

H. Cochrane
A. Griffin

B. R. Worthington (Captain)
A. Brown

J. Knape
E. Walker

playing hard, sitting in deck chairs and enjoying social talk and refreshments, was a way of spending a happy three or four hours.

When I see the young people of a local school, girls and boys, jogging along the promenade, I see many obese and panting figures, with faces more suited to the torture chamber. Only a few natural loose-limbed athletes, clearly working towards the essential combination of healthy body, mind and spirit, are to be seen. This country has given so many games to the world with Association Football, Rugby, Cricket, Tennis and more. It is an essential ingredient in our national well-being and character.

Football enjoys its own brand of humour. On one occasion Father and I went to an important soccer fixture at Turf Moor. We were a little late and just before we arrived at our seats, I felt the urgent call of nature. Father waited somewhat impatiently, urging me with the words, 'Come on, John, they're on,' which meant the teams had taken the field and were carrying out shooting-in practice prior to the kick-off.

An elderly felt-capped supporter came to my rescue with the admonition, 'Leave him alone. He's 'appen one of them as 'es to look for it.'

I think God endowed us both with a small bladder. At least that is my medical theory, and many are the times of discomfort and anxiety which I have had to endure. Many years ago I conceived the brilliant idea of a 'Loo Directory' for the North-West. Convinced it would be a best seller, I began to take the thought seriously and was about to make a small beginning when I came across a book review of such a publication. It is not a laughing matter, and particularly when travelling from Blackpool Illuminations back to Morecambe, after the prolonged drive along the promenade, and unarmed with the knowledge of Great Eccleston, a small village off the main road from Bispham to the A6, where relief is at hand. When in locations such as the one I described at Burnley FC, it was often my father's practice to proclaim aloud to all and sundry, 'Well lads, it's still the cheapest luxury in life.'

The intense rivalry between Lancashire and Yorkshire is well documented and not least on the sporting field. There is a story (I suspect, apocryphal) of the Lancashire supporter attending a Roses Match at Old Trafford, becoming irritated by the Yorkshire fanatic who had conducted a running commentary throughout the day. The exasperated fan, in a reference to his rival's habit of eating his native dish before and separate from the practice of everyone else, turned and enquired, 'What's tha' know abaht it? Thee as eats thi puddin' before thi dinner.'

Chapter XIX

WHY CHRISTIANITY?

I believe the atheist and his camp followers have much to offer in evidence when they assert that religion is to blame for many of the wars and much of the suffering of the human race down the centuries. That view owes more to the sin of man than the inherent defects in the great religions of the world.

I will defend to the end the right of a man or woman to his or her own beliefs, and mine to the uniqueness and primacy of Jesus Christ. There is some merit in the view that we are all climbing the same mountain by a different route and I can find an attraction in some part of many world religions, the chief of which are Christianity, Buddhism, Hinduism, Islam and Judaism. I have read about and tried in some measure to understand their beliefs, while at the same time being 'ready to give a reason for the hope that is within me'. Not many of those with whom I come into contact in my Christian life can explain or discuss their own religion with reasonable intelligence and understanding, much less the other faiths of a multi-racial society. The Jew has much to teach the Christian about family life and the Moslem about diligent worship.

In a confused and a dangerous world, becoming ever smaller through travel, television and all manner of communication, religions have become a unifying force for newly independent countries and a stimulant to the nationalism of others. In a world which appears to many objective viewers as being in total confusion and an utter mess, traditional beliefs have in the immediate past given way to Communism, now seen to be breaking up, and by humanism which affirms the ability of man to pull himself up by his own shoestrings.

We are not short of those ready to prove that their religion can bring peace, stability and sanity to a crazy world, and those ready to believe them. It seems to me that all religions ask fundamental questions about man, the meaning and purpose of life, the need for forgiveness and the longing for immortality or a life beyond this one. I believe religions to be literally a matter of life and death, and to involve the attempt to explain the meaning and purpose of life and man's attempt to live a good or better life, which is rooted in his very being.

I believe I have found in my own searching how the Gospel of Jesus

Christ, the good news for all, which the Christian seeks to proclaim, is yet relevant to the ultimate values of a particular faith. But I hold fast to the view that in Jesus we have the supreme revelation of God. On this I take my stand in the words Martin Luther used at the Reformation: 'Here I stand. I can do no other.'

This is not always easy in a world of militant atheism where intolerance and a ruthless attempt to impose one set of beliefs all too often bring death, destruction, cruelty and which to many seems to be the very antithesis of that which they seek to establish. I see no way round the argument that you have to say one of three things about Jesus:

1. He was an impostor, fraud, cheat, and worse.
2. He was a good but misguided man.
3. He was what He claimed to be.

The reason I say so is quite simply because of the claims Jesus made. Here are some:

1. He who has seen me has seen the Father.
2. No man comes to the Father but by me.
3. All things have been delivered unto me by the Father.
4. I and the Father are one.

I believe that once a man has seen Jesus as He really is and knows Him and not just about Him, he has found the Way, the Truth, and the Life.

As the hymn says, and I have quoted elsewhere:

> But what to those who find? Ah! this
> Nor tongue nor pen can show;
> The love of Jesus, what it is
> None but His loved ones know.

> But they know

I affirm that I have found that to be true as my daily living experience in a confused and dangerous world.

Chapter XX

WHY GO TO CHURCH?

The question has been asked a thousand times, and a similar number of answers have been given. I write in Chapter XXI of the times I have walked into my own church, tired and soul-weary from the dangers of a week of modern life, and have come out restored in mind and soul.

You don't need to go to church to find God has been the cry of many down the years. What of the solitary Christian? A man who was faced with this statement and question by a friend as they sat by the fireside on a dark and stormy winter's night, thought for a moment, and then without speaking, leaned forward. He drew with his tongs from the centre of the fire a white-hot coal, placed it on the hearth, and watched it turn slowly to a glowing red, then fade into a dirty grey. The essential heat and warmth had gone. He did not speak, but his companion with the question nodded. He had his answer.

But someone says, I can find God in the countryside as I go there from the inner city into the trees and flowers and lakes, and waterfalls of a sunny English summer's day, the toil and problems of the week temporarily suspended and forgotten. But do you actually seek Him on these occasions?

Look at Mrs Jones. Never misses church on a Sunday. 'I know things about her. She's no better than me. Hypocrite if you ask me.' But there are some Mrs Jones's who know they are sinners and go to church for forgiveness, and in true penitence. Yes, there are many church members who have attended every Sunday of their lives, listened to a thousand sermons and sung more hymns, for whom worship has meant no change. Some go out of habit, because of loneliness, social custom, to be seen, because the people who go are 'nice'.

There are Mr and Mrs Brown who have always centred their whole life on church and all its coffee mornings, fellowship meetings and cosy gatherings. They treat the church like their club, a gathering of like-minded people, with friends of similar, respectable tastes. They never think about turning outwards to their local community and the needs of the world, but content themselves with the comfortable, undemanding life of their local church, oblivious of the needs of a hungry, starving, sick, bored and tired world. Respectability, without demands upon them, other than the coins they place in the collecting box, a few pence from their ample purses. They are high in numbers.

They have not experienced, in all its awesome demands, the Church which exists not for itself but for others, and which, unless it spends its spiritual and material resources for others, will wither and die. It has been well said that the Church is the only organization which exists for a purpose other than its members.

But does God need our worship? Certainty he is omnipotent, the Great Creator of all things, beyond our comprehension, His ways past finding out. Nothing can add to or take away from the truth of that statement. When she was very young, my daughter Catherine loved to pick flowers from our garden, gather them into a bunch and hand them to her mother and father. Although Rosalie and I owned the house and the garden, and all which lay within them, nevertheless Catherine's action gave us much pleasure and brought joy to our hearts because she had seen something of the wonder of the place, and wished to give something of it to us. She could be a source of embarrassment when repeating the exercise in the gardens of friends and many have been the times when this happened, but for the larger part, she warmed our hearts. So, I believe is God's heart toward us as we take ourselves apart for the noise and stress, confusion and problems of a needy world, to offer Him our worship, praise and thanksgiving.

And what else of worship? It feeds our souls. In our hymns and songs and prayers, our hearing of the Word of God and the proclamation of the Good News of the Gospel, in the uplifting music, in prayer of adoration, praise and thanksgiving, of confession, intercession and petition, we can be brought to the very gates of Heaven; to return refreshed to the place where we must go.

We love the place, O God
Wherein Thine honour dwells;
The joy of Thine abode
All earthly joy excels

As we worship we become more like the one we come to worship. Abraham Lincoln said, 'Who worships greatness passing by, himself is great.' Any happily married couple can give evidence of the truth of this fact. A good husband and a good wife become more like each other in that goodness. I have often found in my work as a solicitor further evidence of this growing together in the likeness of the handwriting of each to the other. On occasion, indeed, I have had to check that both signatures were not made by the same hand.

And again, as we worship, we regain our sense of perspective and proportion.

When Father and I were farming at Gowan Bank I often strolled up the hillside on a sunny day and lay on the ground. In peace and solitude, apart from birdsong, I gazed at the ribbon of the main road from Kendal to Windermere winding its way along the valley floor far below. In the summer and particularly at Bank Holiday and weekends, the road was jammed with cars and vans, with lorries and motorbikes, hikers and buses.

As I gazed up at the blue sky and the unhurrying clouds I regained peace and contentment, a sense of the eternal. I wanted often to shout out to those below, 'To what end? Whither goest thou?'

But above all I believe it is in worship in church that we regain our sense of perspective and proportion. I believe that it is supremely in worship that we find God.

> Let me with my heart today,
> Holy, holy, holy, singing,
> Rapt awhile from earth away,
> All my soul to Thee upspringing,
> Have a foretaste inly given
> How they worship Thee in heaven.

Chapter XXI

SPIRITUAL GROWTH AND PREACHING

I cannot make sense of life without God, His unique revelation in Jesus Christ and the life, death and Resurrection of our Lord. Strong claims, but as I look back over my sixty-eight years I believe there has been a Divine plan for me, as for everyone else, and to quote, I can

> Give a reason for the hope that is in you
> *1 Peter 3 verse 15*

My first recollection of Church is of being taken there in 1934 by my father. Bare Methodist Church (or rather the present building) was opened on 15 January in that year, the one in which we moved to Morecambe from Burnley.

During our Diamond Anniversary celebrations I wrote a short contribution to our Church Magazine *The Messenger*, under the heading 'Memories of Earlier Days' and which reads as follows:

Memories of Earlier Days

My family came to Bare in 1934, shortly after the present Church was opened. Father loved to tell the story of entering the vestibule for morning worship on our first Sunday here, with my two elder sisters and myself. The door steward welcomed him and said 'The Sunday School is in the afternoon.'

Fred Driver, John Driver and Irene Lynch need no introduction. All of them were my Sunday School teachers at various times, and Fred was also scoutmaster of the Sea Scouts when I was a member. His wife, Rene was 'Bagheera' of the Wolf Cubs from where I graduated to the Scouts. It was a great joy to say a few words in the pulpit on the recent 60th Anniversary of the Scouts in answer to questions from our minister, the Rev. Andrew Hill. I mentioned the many trips we made in the Cubs when Fred drove Rene home to Hest Bank in their 'courting' days. We were, as I said, a very real threat to a successful courtship.

Miriam Driver, now ninety-six (1998) and living in Harrogate, conducted morning worship on her return from China where she was a medical missionary and interned by the Japanese. My Uncle Bill (a doctor) and Auntie Margaret (a nurse) were also serving there in the same capacity and knew Miriam well. She brought chopsticks to sell for MMS funds. Our Sunday lunch of roast lamb, potatoes and peas on that day was a hilarious affair.

John is ninety-four this year (1998.)

Another of my Sunday School teachers whom I also remember with love and affection was Pastor Sayer. Blinded in a quarry accident in his early twenties he sat with us when teaching, with his fingers moving over his braille notes. It was always a moving experience from a man of deep spiritual insight. He preached regularly at Bare and I still remember one of his texts (from Psalm 34 v 13): 'Keep thy tongue from evil, and thy lips from speaking guile.'

It gives me much happiness to see the continuing publications of *The Messenger.* I was privileged to start the magazine in the 1950s. Most of the other Methodist Churches in the circuit (then ten in number) had them, and my main purpose was to reach the house-bound. The first issue was twenty-eight pages long! I had a copy until our last flood in Morecambe.

The sketch on the front of the church now appearing on the first page and on our church notices was drawn by the late Mr Normal Ball, Art Master at Lancaster Royal Grammar School. He lived in Burlington Grove and worked on the drawing from the forecourt of Margaret Hodgson's newspaper shop in Seaborn Road. His initials were to be found in the bottom right-hand corner, and the drawing formed the front cover of the magazine for many years. It was typed on wax sheets – no modern technology then.

I have only written a few of my memories as did Irene and John. Like them, I give thanks for so many blessings over the years. I am sure we and others could write at great length about people and events.

Perhaps I could end with a verse of a hymn with which I ended the Foreword of the Souvenir Handbook commemorating the opening of the new Sunday School on 25 April 1959:

> And as the years roll onwards,
> And strong affections twine,
> And tender memories gather
> About this sacred shrine,
> May this its chiefest honour,
> Its glory every be,
> That multitudes within it
> Have found their way to Thee.

In a souvenir handbook which I helped to compile in connection with our 60th (Jubilee) celebrations at my church I added to the above:

> I have been given permission by Bob to add another 'memory' which I know will be of interest and which I was precluded by pressure of space from including in my *Messenger* contribution. In 1941, and 11 years old, we were told in Sunday School that we were going into Church for a special event, instead of following our usual form of service. It was a marriage service. The bride looked so attractive and happy. The smiling bridegroom was on RAF week-end leave resplendent in his uniform. I can see the RAF propellers on his sleeve in my mind's eye as I write. Who were they? Steve and Mary Champley!

Steve is our caretaker with Mary and they have worked unceasingly for the Church over the years. Their son is the Rev. Andrew Champley MA, a Methodist minister who grew up in the Church and is presently serving at Richmond in Yorkshire.

I can remember the small room in the basement which was then used by the Beginners' and Primary departments of the Sunday School, and during the week by the uniformed organizations, and walking round with the other children singing 'Hear the pennies dropping, one by one' as we placed our collection into the box. This was the Beginners' Department. Soon I moved across the passage to the Primary Department. Irene Lynch, Joyce Coole, Violet Collins, Florence Myers and Iris Hodgson are a few names which readily come to mind as our teachers. We sat in circles, on small chairs, with our teacher leaning forward, with hands folded, as the story for the day was said. Simple prayers were said and children's hymns were sung.

There was a warm feeling of love and gentleness, and I believe God was beginning to work His purpose out in my life even in those first formative years.

The main body of the Sunday School met in the old wooden building, which was opened as the original church in 1907 and replaced in 1959 by the present Sunday School and church hall.

I did not know the pre-union days of the Primitive, Wesleyan and United Methodist Church. Union had come in 1932.

Sunday morning worship has remained for me the centre of my life for sixty years.

The building itself is of average size, holding about 400 people. The wood is an unusual African pine, and throughout my life there has always been a congregation at morning worship which has filled, or in recent years nearly filled, the pews. This good attendance helped to generate a

God consciousness, which produced a reverent service with hymns, prayers, offering and dedication, anthems from the Choir, Children's addresses, and above all for me, solid and sound sermons, with clear expositions of the Word of God and affirmation of the eternal truths, and with relevance to daily life. I give thanks for the countless occasions when, after a busy week, I entered spiritually hungry and out of sorts, and left at peace with myself, with my fellow man and with God. I see in my mind's eye, generation after generation of faithful, mostly older souls, eager for the Word of God, fervent in their singing, attentive to the proclamation of the Gospel and the reading of the Word.

At one service when I was seven or eight years old I sensed what I now recognize as the first stirrings of the Holy Spirit within me. I did not see any great vision, nor hear some great word, but there was no mistaking a sense of what I can now describe as the Living God, placing His hand on my life. It was not emotion, although that was present in some measure, and I believe with all my heart that the moment was not manufactured. 'The wind bloweth where it listeth, and Thou heareth the voice thereof, but knoweth not whence it cometh, and whither it goeth: so is every one that is born of the Spirit' (John 3).

The church was the centre of my life outside school. Sunday morning worship, Sunday School, Wolf Cubs, followed by the Sea Scouts, Youth Club, special anniversaries, bazaars, other fund-raising activities and sporting events, formed a sound foundation on which to build a good, loving and caring life. I hope that over the years I have increasingly come to realize, and be grateful for, the dedication of men and women who were concerned for my spiritual well-being.

Diamond Days

Twelve months of special events, services and celebrations to mark the diamond anniversary of Bare Methodist Church ended on Saturday.

It was on January 15, 1934, that the church opened in Seaborn Road and during the past year the important milestone has been marked in various ways.

On Saturday members of the church attended a thanksgiving service and enjoyed refreshments in the church hall, where there was also a fascinating exhibition of memorabilia reflecting the church's 60 year history.

From *The Visitor*

Thanksgiving Service, tea and exhibition of memorabilia. Bare Methodist Church Diamond Anniversary – 1994

From left to right (front)

Mrs E. Blease (friend of Mrs Reece); Dr M. Timpany; Mrs I. Lynch; the late Mrs K. Adshead; Mrs I. Proctor; Miss D. & Miss E. Pollard (or 'the twins' – the author does not accept responsibility for correct identification!).

From left to right (back)

Mrs K. Leece; Mr D. Youle; the author, the late Mr A. Smith; Miss M. Binning MA; Mrs E. Youle; Mrs K. Hustwick; Mrs M. Everett; Mrs C. Holt; Miss Edith Pollard (partially hidden by her 'baby' sisters); Mr N. Holt; Group Captain R. G. Nuttall OBE RAF (retd) – better know as 'Bob'; the late Rev. Eric D. Roberts; and at the back (next to the 'No Smoking' sign!) our minister Rev. G. A. Vickers.

The group includes a Circuit Steward; 3 local Preachers; Covenants and Management Secretary; Chief Executive of the Printing Department and a thousand other things; Guild, JMA Secretaries, Welcome Secretary as well as co-Editors of the Church Magazine *The Messenger*, and organisers of annual and other outings; penny bag collectors etc. (the 'twins' of course); Bible Society Secretary; Sunday School Secretary; Womens' Fellowship Secretary; Flower Secretary.

It is really invidious to select individuals because almost all the group are outstanding and devoted workers in our Church life.

The author would however feel remiss if he neglected the opportunity to mention Mrs Irene Lynch. There are several references to Irene in Chapter XXI. There can be few Sunday School teachers anywhere who have served longer. She was already a teacher sixty-four years ago when I arrived in the Beginners' Dept, at the age of four.

Irene is also (with one exception) the longest serving member of our Society at Bare. Her contribution and that of her late mother, father, sister and her children has been incalculable.

The 'twins', Doreen and Eileen Pollard have been members for forty-one years. Their contribution also has been constant and considerable in every area of Church Life. Many who are not active members have also been given great happiness and created lasting friendships as a result of the 'Happy Wanderers', coach parties organised by Doreen and Edith to many attractive places throughout the land including Eastbourne, Crieff, Torquay, Bournemouth, and many others.

'Bob' Nuttall is someone to whom the author is deeply indebted in a hundred ways, and can never repay. I knew him with his late and charming wife Lena before they came to Morecambe and Bob was still active in the RAF. The death of Lena in 1986 was a great loss to us all as well as to Bob.

In trouble and in joy he has been a constant and unwavering support. At the time of writing he has taken his first break for many years in joining his son, Hedley, in Oman. We look forward eagerly to his return. Bob's work in the Church at Bare is legendary.

The following appeared in the December 1997 issue of the Bare Methodist Church Magazine in respect of the late Rev. Eric D. Roberts:

THE REVEREND ERIC DESMOND ROBERTS (1916–1977)

Our late friend and fellow pilgrim got the send-off he wanted and planned himself down to the last detail. There were tears a-plenty at the funeral service at Bare on October 1st as the Chairman of the North Lancashire Methodist district, The Rev. G. M. Wearing, paid tribute to the man of God whose passing we mourned. Few seats were empty in the chapel which had become his spiritual home in retirement and the choir also gathered to remember their fellow chorister, now at rest after long suffering from cancer.

At Dolphinholme, in the Garstang Circuit, the place was packed for a second service, which was in part a repetition of the first, arranged specially for the benefit of the godly folk in the hills to whom he had ministered himself in former days and who to the end continued to welcome him into their homes, always with generous fare. The Rev. Allen E. Fisher drew a warm and appreciative picture of a travelling Methodist preacher, totally dedicated to his Lord.

Afterwards, in the chapel graveyard, in a brief service conducted by our Superintendent, the Rev. Geoffrey Nadin, Eric was laid to rest as the crowd sang one final favourite request by their friend, 'In the Sweet Bye and Bye'. We had a good sing!

In all of this, his widow Eileen, daughter Margaret and son David, together with the extended family, were lovingly remembered, that they might know God's comforting peace.

Eric Desmond Roberts is sadly missed in our church now. We are thankful for all that he was able to do at Bare and within the Circuit until the very end of his life. His soul rests in peace.

G.A.V.

I held (as they say) just about every office in the church including Sunday School teacher, Youth Club Leader, Secretary of the Devotional, and Musical and Social Committees of the Wesley Guild, Overseas Missions Secretary, Editor-Founder of the Church Magazine, member of the Leaders' Meeting, Trustee of the church buildings, a member of District Committees, a District representative to the Methodist Conference, and Local Preachers' Secretary.

I remember coming home after my first formal committee meeting, when I had been appointed Overseas Missions Secretary. Father, sitting in his armchair and speaking from his own experience, drew my attention, without having to ask me, to the warmth within me which the beginning of service to the Church bestowed. A small reflection of John Wesley's experience on his conversion on 24 May 1738. He records as follows: 'I think it was about five this morning that I opened my Testament on these words, "There are given unto us exceeding great and precious promises, even that ye should be partakers of the divine nature." (2 Peter, 1.4). Just as I went out I opened it again on these words, "Thou are not far from the kingdom of God." In the afternoon I was asked to go to St Paul's. The anthem was, "Out of the deep have I called unto Thee, O Lord: Lord, hear my voice." In the evening I went, very unwillingly, to a society in Aldersgate Street, where one was reading Luther's preface to the Epistle to the Romans. About a quarter before nine, while he was describing the change which God works in the heart through faith in Christ, I felt my heart strangely warmed. I felt I did trust in Christ, Christ alone, for salvation. And an assurance was given me that He had taken away my sins even mine, and saved me from the law of sin and death.'

In my later twenties there came the call to preach. Mr A.T. Humble was appropriately named. A retired schoolmaster from a village school at Yanwath, near Penrith in Cumbria, he had preached in nearly every rural Methodist church in the North of England. His daughter Miss Monica Humble MA, a member of the Torrisholme church in our Morecambe & Heysham Circuit trained as a teacher at St Hild's College, Durham and taught for two years in Chichester Girls' High School. She then offered herself to the Methodist Missionary Society for service as a teacher. She was sent to the Methodist Church, Nigeria where she taught in a girls' high school and in teacher training colleges. On her return to the UK she was appointed as Overseas Service Secretary of the Methodist Church Overseas Division. (After her parents' death, she went overseas again, this time to the Methodist Church, Sierra Leone, from where she retired in 1986).

His nature was like his name, and he loved nothing more than prompting, encouraging and even gently prodding young men he felt were ready to respond to the call to preach the Good News of the Gospel. I can remember sitting in my car, near his home, before I left him one evening when he planted the seed. There are many local preachers of my age who were led to their calling through his ministrations, and to whom we all instinctively turned for advice and wise counsel. In due course I was given a note to preach and accompanied a fully-accredited local preacher, taking ever-increasing parts in leading the worship. The Local Preachers' Meeting placed me on trial soon afterwards and I could then take appointments and lead worship on my own.

One day, before I was placed on trial, Mr Humble told me I was to preach on Local Preachers' Mutual Aid Association Sunday at Storth, a small village chapel near Arnside. I protested that I was only 'on note', and not authorized to go on my own. 'No one will know,' he said, 'and send your hymn numbers in early to the organist.'

As I stood in the pulpit on that Sunday afternoon, I little realized the importance this village would play in my life. It was a tiny, unspoilt, rural community, standing on the Sandside Estuary at the furthest reach of Morecambe Bay, looking out to the Lakeland hills and mountains and surrounded by unspoilt countryside. My first sermon. Later it was to be the place where, on retiring as Senior Partner of my legal practice, and assuming a consultancy, I built a house for my wife Rosalie, and two children, John and Catherine. Later still, after a painful divorce, I was to return to another house in the village with Vera and the three children of her first marriage, where she died of cancer in 1978, at the age of thirty-seven.

I passed my Old Testament, New Testament and Christian Doctrine written examinations with some credit, conducted a trial service in the presence of several ministers and a good congregation, and came to my oral examination at the Local Preachers' Meeting, the final step before full accreditation. My trial service was at the Torrisholme Church in the circuit. It was a great help to have the support of a good congregation, including many from my own church, and of several ministers of the circuit. It is not an easy act of worship to conduct, as any local preacher will testify, and I spent a considerable time in preparation, study and prayer.

I commenced my sermon by referring to the various ways in which God seems to hide Himself, and quoted as my text the words of the prophet Isaiah: 'Verily Thou art a God that hideth Thyself.' Wars, aggression, suffering, pain and disasters of all kinds seemed so often to hide Him from us.

I then referred to three particular ways in which God hides and reveals Himself:

1. In nature. Wordsworth felt the power of an unseen and eternal presence in the Lakeland mountains which we could see from the seafront a short distance from where I was preaching. 'The heavens declared the Glory of God' in a very special way to those of us living in that particular part of the world, but what of flood, and storm, and earthquake, and all manner of natural disasters? The laws of nature are the same for the good and the bad.

2. In history. Good does not always triumph over evil. Not all history

inspires and quickens our faith.

3. In Grace. Jesus was born to an insignificant family in an insignificant part of an insignificant country.

There has to be mystery. What sort of a God would He be if we could completely understand Him and His ways? 'Now we see through a glass darkly' as part of the price we pay for our sin.

And if we knew with absolute certainty that good will triumph over evil, that there is another and better world for us beyond this one, where would be the place of faith? Faith is to bet your life that there is a God, the refusal to give up or make the final surrender.

(I love the words used as a text which I heard in later years when we were reminded that Shadrach, Meshach and Abednego in the burning fiery furnace expressed a faith that God would deliver them. The preacher went on to stress that the next bit was the most important: 'But if not'. Even if he did not deliver them, they would still believe. That is the ultimate faith).

The challenge of the call to worship is:

Who shall ascend into the hill of the Lord? Or who shall stand in His holy place? He that hath clean hands and a pure heart . . .

Blessed are the pure in heart: for they shall see God. The supreme gift of God to man is the gift of a cleansed heart. Growth in Grace brings growth in sight.

His servants shall serve Him: and they shall see His face.

In the oral examinations the local preacher was asked to start by giving an account of his conversion, his call to preach and present Christian experience. After doing so I was 'grilled' by a circuit minister, the Rev. S.K. Chesworth, who later became Chairman of the London North-Western District, and is now living in retirement a few miles from Morecambe. The first question was to explain the difference between telepathy and prayer. The second was to describe the distinctive doctrines of Methodism. I had committed these to memory, years before, as follows:

The Methodist Church claims and cherishes its place in the Holy Catholic Church which is the Body of Christ. It rejoices in the inheritance of the Apostolic Faith and loyally accepts the fundamental principles of the historic creeds and of the Protestant Reformation. It ever remembers that in the Providence of God

Methodism was raised up to spread Scriptural Holiness through the land by the proclamation of the Evangelical Faith and declares its unfaltering resolve to be true to its Divinely appointed mission.

The Doctrines of the Evangelical Faith which Methodism has held from the beginning and still holds are based upon the Divine revelation recorded in the Holy Scriptures. The Methodist Church acknowledges this revelation as the supreme rule of faith and practice. These Evangelical Doctrines to which the Preachers of the Methodist Church both ministers and Laymen are pledged are contained in Wesley's Notes on the New Testament and the first four volumes of his sermons.

I felt better after that! The Supt. Minister was overheard afterwards, saying that he could not have recited the words. My Christian experience, strength and hope, and call to preach were stretched to the full by the examination! Although training has changed in many ways, I am sure that Methodism equips the men and women for the privilege and the responsibility of making known to others the unsearchable riches of Christ.

There were several thoughtful and kind folk who offered encouragement and went to the trouble of putting pen to paper over the years. I conducted worship at Silverdale Methodist Church in October 1959, and received a letter from William Riley, an author of some reputation and particularly loved by Methodists. He had been in the congregation and wrote as follows:

Yew Tree House
Silverdale. Nr Carnforth
Tel. 229

Oct 12th '59

Dear Mr Knape,

I was interested & impressed by your sermon this morning, & would urge you to continue to emphasise the duty & privilege of constant prayer.

I have found the value of intimacy in prayer – in the sense of oneness or power. Urge on our people this aspect of prayer – opening our hearts to a Friend who is always at our side, wherever we are & whatever we are doing, and listening for the reply.

God bless you & make you useful!

Yours cordially,

W. Riley.

PTO
PS
I have disposed of most of my books: but this I wish to retain.
There is, however, no hurry for its return.

Some would telephone and occasionally a special need was met. In 1967 I received a letter in the following terms:

Ulvik
31 Norwood Drive,
Torrisholme
Morecambe
8-11-67

Dear Sir

I write to express my appreciation of the Service at Torrisholme Methodist Church on Sunday morning.

As a retired lay preacher (Baptist) for about 50 years I was much helped and inspired.

The prayers were reverent and healing, the exposition of the Holy word wise and helpful in the worship of praise. I valued the qualities and expressions of supplication and joy.

My principal reason for writing to you is something which I hoped to express to you after the service.

During the service my memory returned to your grandfather, John Knape of Burnley. Being a motor trader I knew him very well and I remember how proudly he spoke of his son who was a solicitor in Morecambe, and of his daughter, so I just wish to tell you how gracious he always was to me and how on all occasions he showed me great kindness.

I was much moved, particularly by the last paragraph. I noted also that the name of the house (on the road where the church is built) was 'Ulvik', my favourite place in Norway! (See chapter XXVII.)

Thus does God use us, as channels of His grace.

My recognition service in my own church was conducted by my late father-in-law, Rev. J.E.P. Edwards, and the charge given, at my request, by Mr Humble.

I chose a Revised Standard Version of the Bible which has the following inscription:

151

Presented to   *November* 1961.

John Knape

on Recognition as a Fully-Accredited
Local Preacher in the Methodist Church

Maximin L Edwards
President of the Conference

Josie W. Tinsdale.
Vice-President of the Conference

David Francis
Connexional Secretary

Geo W Weathrill
Superintendent Minister.

" DO THE WORK OF AN EVANGELIST "

With young fellow local preachers, I have travelled extensively in the North-West, taking appointments in circuits, where there were difficulties in making the plan. In churches where no preacher is available, when the plan appears, the word SUPPLY is printed, denoting the responsibilities of the church itself, for the conduct of worship on that date. In rural areas, the word appears all too often, whereas throughout my life, in the Morecambe & Heysham Circuit, we have been able to call on a considerable number of local preachers and retired ministers as well as the serving ministers.

Anecdotes abound among us. At a Lancaster Chapel I was assured by the stewards before the service that when snoring was heard in the sermon, it was not my lack of ability to hold the congregation, but the weekly practice of an elderly male member. He was right on cue as I announced the text.

On another occasion I had a lesson in humility. Appointed to King's Road Church in Lytham St Anne's, I saw a huge banner outside the church bearing my name. The church was well supported and I had taken my 'best' sermon. An elderly lady in the front row coughed loudly and continuously throughout and although a steward solicitously brought her a glass of water, I am sure little was heard, and my delivery was certainly disturbed.

Mrs Clifford-Brown, with Irene Lynch, were those I held most dear at Sunday School. Mrs Brown was better known to me as Miss Gertrude Parrington, our Sunday School Superintendent for many years. She lived with her sister and father. He was a local preacher and I attended a service at Heysham Methodist Church, in my earlier years, conducted by his twin brother to commemorate the latter's 50th Anniversary as a local preacher.

I digress.

Miss Parrington, who became Mrs Clifford-Brown on marrying a retired Methodist minister, told me of a church service she attended. The preacher forcefully made his point, as his fist was brought down swiftly and noisily on the open Word of God. A man in the front row stirred and said, 'It's all right, Elizabeth, I'll be down in a second.'

Irene Lynch taught my children and is still serving, and presently taking care of Jamie, the five-year-old grandson of my former wife Marjorie. She has over sixty years of loving service to her credit. Only recently I learned from her that my arrival was similar to my first day at school. I lay on the floor, screaming and kicking, on the first Sunday, and contented myself with just crying on the second occasion.

I have always tried to be sincere in the pulpit. Preachers have their good and bad days. It is essential to remember that we go into the pulpit as sinners, and also to be aware that we are 'six feet above criticism'. I have seen in some pulpits a printed text: 'Sir, we would see Jesus'. I have sometimes found organists who are sensitive about tunes and regard this area as their domain.

Some churches have an order of service set in stone, others leave it to the preacher. A sensitive vestry before the service can affect considerably the appointed preacher. A famous preacher once descended from the pulpit to be told that he had delivered a brilliant sermon. 'I know,' he said, 'the Devil told me as I descended the steps.'

When on trial, I conducted worship at Arnside Methodist Church. On lifting my eyes, when in the pulpit, I saw seven elderly ministers with dog collars leaning on walking sticks in the front row, only a few feet away (a minor Synod!). The local preparatory school boys were there in large numbers and the church was full. The learned gentlemen gave me the impression, which I am sure was mistaken, that they were going to 'weigh up' the new generation of young local preachers. I preached on love and was told by one of them that it was an excellent service, but my sermon had 'gone on' for five minutes too long, and an earlier point would have been the time to finish. Constructive criticism is something for which I yearned, but rarely came because of the time factor at the end of the service, and the custom of most people to say a polite 'thank you' as they left. It was my custom in earlier years to leave the pulpit and go straight to the vestry after the service. It was entirely because I was thinking of myself and wanted to hold the atmosphere I hoped I had created, to myself. It was gently pointed out to me that another interpretation could be placed on my action, and ever afterwards I went to the entrance and greeted the congregation as each member left.

Sixty years at one church in the one circuit leave enough memories to fill a volume, but I will content myself with three:

We had a week's visit from the Methodist Exhibition, starting on the Sunday evening, with a torchlight procession from the West End to Green Street. John Wesley and Charles Wesley on horseback and in period costume were played by two circuit ministers, Rev. Stanley K. Chesworth and Rev. Tom R. Jenkinson. We walked along the promenade for an evening of Wesley hymns and a brief comment about each. Among the ministers, and the one I heard that evening at West End, was the late Rev. Edward Rogers MABD, a former President and Secretary of the Methodist Conference. I remember his 43-minute sermon seemed like ten, and no one wanted him to finish.

The Rev. J. Athinson, who travelled the country with the Exhibition, was a sector minister, i.e. he worked in a specialized field. He entertained us all with his eccentric ways but did a fine job. A Brains Trust with a distinguished panel, the showing of the film *John Wesley* and a host of other activities through the week accompanied a fascinating Exhibition, open throughout the day, and left a deep impression on us all. I was responsible for the publicity and during the week the Rev. Athinson asked me if I had considered offering for the full-time Ministry.

In March 1965 the Green Street and Clarence Street churches merged into Central, and retained the Green Street building. For years there had been fruitless efforts, but the Superintendent of the time, the Rev. Kenneth Mackenzie, finally brought the two societies together. I was invited to take the Chair. Two well-known Methodist ministers, the Rev. Frank Thewlis and the Rev. Reg Walker, addressed a packed church and representatives of the Connexion, together with the Chairman of the District, were present. The church had been modernised with seats downstairs similar to those in a cinema. The young minister, the Rev.

Arthur Dean, energetic and dedicated, had queues of young people on Sunday evenings for a long time afterwards.

The third occasion which comes readily to mind was the visit, when I was a young boy, to the West End Church, of a famous figure of the time, Romany, and his faithful dog Raq. Romany was a popular broadcaster in the even more popular *Children's Hour* programme, on the BBC radio programme of the time. His real name was the Rev. Bramwell Evans, an ordained Methodist Minister. In later years I read that his ashes were scattered in one of his favourite spots, open country near Kirkoswald in the Eden valley of Westmorland (as it then was), where my late father-in-law was stationed for four years.

Chapter XXII

A WEEK WHICH CHANGED MY LIFE

One of the great spiritual and religious experiences of my life was undoubtedly the second British Conference of Christian Youth, in 1956, at Bristol. We were accommodated in the University during vacation, and the Conference lasted a week.

Before this event, I knew little or nothing about other denominations, apart from the Anglicans, drawn from my experience at Shrewsbury School. This itself was not at all an entirely happy one, showing divisions even among the School's Anglican clergy about communion, as I have recorded earlier. I shall always be grateful, however, for the experience I received at Shrewsbury, of the dignity and beauty of worship, a not over-elaborate ritual, the Book of Common Prayer, Matins and Evensong, Collects and great music.

When I passed members of the Anglican Church situated some 100 yards from my own church, I would nod in a polite greeting, but without any real warmth. It was the same with the United Reformed Church. Roman Catholics were beyond the pale and if I had to give a reason, it would be a vague mass of superstition and some fear. They were not like me.

In Bristol, as a member of the North Lancashire District delegation of the Methodist Church, I mixed all week with Anglicans, Roman Catholics, Quakers, Baptists, Congregationalists (now the United Reformed Church), Salvationists and others.

We enjoyed differing forms of worship. I remember in the Great Hall the silence of Quaker worship, among the gathered assembly of some 600 young people from many countries of the world. Worshippers stood and prayed as they were moved by the Holy Spirit. There was no music.

One of my first lessons was that we could have unity without uniformity. It would not be a case of everyone singing the same hymns, saying the same prayers, and generally having a strict uniformity in all things. Every denomination had something to contribute.

Bible study, small prayer groups, addresses and discussion groups made up a varied programme which had been carefully planned.

One of the best speakers was Rev. Philip Potter, then Youth Secretary of the British Council of Churches. A West Indian, he gave a powerful address, lifting us above the insular view of the average Englishman and his memory of Empire. A vision of a World Church, lifted up and united in Christ, erased the primacy of the Union Jack in my mind.

Philip Potter worked for the Methodist Missionary Society for many years and went on to become General Secretary of the World Council of Churches in Geneva. A giant in stature, a faith and intellect to match, our lives crossed unexpectedly some years later. I was Secretary for Overseas Missions at my church, and one of my duties was to arrange a deputation for the annual OM weekend. After I married Rosalie, I sent an invitation to him which he accepted. Her father, the Rev. J.E.P. Edwards, the minister of our church, had served with him in the Caribbean.

He stayed with his wife in our home for the weekend. I remember going with him and my father-in-law to see a retired missionary who lived some fifteen miles away, and listening with great interest to their shared experiences. In particular they were unanimous that there was too much declamatory preaching today, and a need for affirmation of the central truths of the faith.

On the Sunday morning Philip Potter used our WC facilities before leaving for worship. The lock on the door was in disrepair and we did not use the key at the time. The great man turned the key but could not unlock the door. His huge frame would clearly not pass through the window if I procured a long ladder. I well remember something of the panic which laid hold of me, including a vision of hurrying to the church and advising the vestry stewards that they would have to announce the minister's unavailability. The mind boggles at the words in which the information would be conveyed to the congregation. One last desperate try and the key turned. We had a wonderful day!

Janet Lacey, who founded the Inter-Church Aid and Refugee Service, which later became Christian Aid, opened our eyes to the poverty, disease and living conditions of the Third World.

Dr Kenneth Slack was Secretary of the British Council of Churches, and in overall charge of the week. He later became Director of Christian Aid, Moderator of the Free Church Federal Council and held other high office. He conducted the Bible Study with which we commenced each day, and was based entirely on the Lord's Prayer, studied phrase by phrase.

The late Dr Leslie Newbiggin addressed us. He was perhaps the first really ecumenical clergyman I had met. He was the first bishop of the Church of South India comprising the union of several denominations, and in the 1960s led the 'missionary' studies sponsored by the World Council of Churches. He therefore had first-hand experience of denominations coming together.

Rev. Edward Patey contributed greatly to the week. He conducted the

Sunday half-hour service of hymns which was broadcast live by the BBC and which was a much-loved radio programme at that time. The Rev. Patey had been Youth Chaplain to the Bishop of Durham, Secretary of the Youth Department of the British Council of Churches, Assistant General Secretary to the British Council of Churches, Canon Residentiary of Coventry Cathedral and from 1964, Dean of Liverpool. He is the author of the immensely successful book for young people entitled *Enquire Within*, and has done a good deal of radio and television work.

We had leisure time and I went with a party to see Peter Scott's Wildfowl Trust at Slimbridge. We could see some of his original paintings through the windows of his residence. It was a most informative time and we came away thankful for the life of this son of the great Antarctic explorer.

The climax of the week was the Methodist Covenant Service at Bristol Cathedral. I know that other denominations covet this service which is used annually in each Methodist Church.

The background to the Covenant Service is as follows:

On 25 December, 1747, and on many other occasions, John Wesley strongly urged the Methodists to renew their Covenant with God. His first formal Covenant Service was held in the French Church at Spitalfields on 11 August, 1755, when he used the words of Joseph and Richard Alleine which he published in 'The Christian Library'. This service was issued separately in 1780, and was the official Wesleyan form for nearly a century. Each of the other Methodist traditions developed its own form. As a result of Methodist union, a single, thoroughly revised, form was authorised in 1936, and has now been further revised. In addition to its regular use in Methodism it has been widely used in other Christian communions.

These words from a well-known hymn which we sang in the service left a deep and lasting impression on me:

And this shall be their anthem
One Church, one Faith, one Lord.

We left Bristol to return to our own churches, buoyed up by a vision of unity 'that they all may be one, as Thou Father art in me, and I in Thee, that they also may be one in us THAT THE WORLD MAY BELIEVE' (the prayer of Jesus in John 17 v 28).

When I came home I experienced something akin to a bucketful of cold water being thrown over me when I attended the worship of my own church. Where was the enthusiasm, where was the union, where were the dynamic ideas and energy exhibited at Bristol? I was young. I saw later that this was only the very beginning of ecumenical activity. The one Church and one World idea was only just beginning to stir, at any rate in England.

The leader of the Methodist delegation, Dr Kenneth Meir enjoined us to return home and carry the message. He urged us when we spoke, not to go into matters of theology and detail, but to give a general picture, with some humour and specific experiences. We could not expect to convey in our words all that we had come to learn, understand and hope.

Ecumenicity is to be seen everywhere today. Local Ecumenical projects, joint worship and ventures in faith, and service in the community in many forms are seen in varying degrees up and down our land.

I have been privileged to serve for many years as Secretary to the Morecambe, Heysham and District Council of Churches and still nominally hold that office. Our work has waxed and waned in large measure, with the different attitudes of the changing clergy, and partly due to the increasing burden of maintaining individual causes and some apathy. But in many areas the work is flourishing and expanding.

We were told at Bristol that unity would not come in our lifetime. The Anglicans and Methodists nearly came together, but the General Synod of the Church of England voted against union at the same time as the Methodist Conference voted in favour. There is continuing dialogue between the Protestant, Roman Catholic and Orthodox churches. Much has been achieved, but there are still considerable divisions on matters of theology and order which remain to be agreed. As I write, talks about talks between Anglicans and Methodists have begun.

A really successful venture of the Church in my home town has been Christian Aid. I was asked to take over as Secretary when a Methodist Minister, Rev. R.T.H. Beardsall BA BD, who had started an annual house-to-house collection and other activities, left the town in the 1960s. From small beginnings the present annual campaign raises a substantial sum.

I have recently found in my papers an article from the local newspaper *The Morecambe Guardian* printed in the 1960s, and which I wrote as Christian Aid Secretary. It read:

In many areas of life today there seems to be little confidence. In the international sphere this is plain to see. Increasing leisure, social justice, improving health, education, and countless other benefits do not seem to have enriched the mind and spirit of man. The Church has rarely been subjected to such an attack on the intellectual plane and on basic morality.

Fear, anxiety and apprehension rather than confidence mark the mood of many Christians.

What amazing confidence marks the words of Jesus. This was not because He closed His eyes to the world around Him. He knew what was going on in the world; He knew what was in man in all his evil and wickedness. He faced head on the darkness and shame, the pain, loneliness and agony, the heartbreak of the Cross. And still the confidence. Still the triumphant cry 'It is finished'.

And so the Christian is not overwhelmed. He knows no evil can defeat love, no darkness can conquer Christ. He knows peace is more powerful than war, Grace than sin, the Kingdom of God than the Kingdoms of Satan.

Whence come this confidence? From the knowledge that God reigns. Not man, but God. Not the cleverness of man, but the wisdom of God. Not the skill of man but the purposes of God. Man's world? What pathetic impudence. Here are you and I sitting on a third-rate planet spinning round a second-rate star, revolving with thousands of millions of others in one galaxy amongst millions of galaxies. And all held and fixed on time not by man's skill but by God's power.

And so the Christian is an optimist. He looks all the facts in the face, the pleasant and the unpleasant and discovers God's love at work. And for his justification he points back to that most momentous event of history when the powers of evil tried to drive God out of history. But in an early dawn Jesus rose from the dead. They met Him in the garden, in the Upper Room, on the road, by the sea, on the mountain.

And for 1900 years men have been meeting Him. Everywhere, Christ with men. This is the ground of our confidence. God was in Christ, alive in history and in lives of men.

I do not think there is anything I would wish to alter today, some thirty years later.

Nor do I see any reason for altering another contribution to the newspaper after my appointment as Secretary of the Morecambe, Heysham and District Council of Churches:

The Christian message is a very simple one. There is a tendency to make it difficult and complicated.

The disciples and others who received the message from Jesus himself were not intellectuals nor clever people. Peter was a fisherman. The creeds and a sound theology are important, but Jesus did not ask for intellectual belief.

The Christian message is also often seen as something which

demands effort and struggle, as placing impossible burdens upon us. It should be a burden as wings are to a bird.

Those who lived with Jesus and met him felt better, their hearts uplifted. He made men want to be like Him and gave them a deep and passionate longing that their dreams, longings and desires could come true.

What is the message then? The best description I have ever heard is the acceptance of a gift of the friendship of Christ. It is a gift.

And that friendship survived His death. We find Jesus after the resurrection in the account of meeting Mary in the garden, on the road to Emmaus and elsewhere, transferring the friendship of His earthly days into the Unknown, making people feel he was never far away, that He was present although not physically visible.

And what does the friendship mean? That in every part of life, in joy and pain, in temptation and bereavement, in loneliness and in fear, this loving Friend is with us, sufficient for our every need.

Chapter XXIII

PILGRIMAGE TO THE HOLY LAND – 1958

I had longed for many years to visit the Holy Land. I had sung in Sunday School:

> But if we desire Him,
> He is close at hand;
> For our native country
> Is our Holy Land.

And I still believe that today. I did not realize at the time but I had lived for ten years on the seafront at Morecambe, overlooking a bay with many of the features of the Sea of Galilee. To these I will return.

A lady member of our Church was heard to remark to several people when I returned two years later that I was obviously searching for something I had not found in my life. She was correct in the first part. The search was to try and immerse myself more and more in the places, atmosphere and people of the land where 'He went about doing good', where he was born, lived, worked, completed his ministry, was crucified and from where He returned to His Father.

The call is as strong now as then and my heart is full of joy and anticipation of a third visit in a few weeks' time at Easter. I have been in Jerusalem on Easter Day, but this time it will be spent in Tiberias, not far away, after the first five days in the Holy City. This time, unlike the two previous visits, I shall be able to visit the old part of the city, the Garden tomb, the Garden of Gethsemane, Mount of Olives, walk along the Via Dolorosa, visit Jericho, and much else.

This time I shall not have to be careful about walking down the wrong street in Jerusalem, or opening the wrong door on Mt Zion and risk being shot. I shall be able to visit Bethlehem instead of viewing it from a distance and take the risk of a sniper firing at me as I take a photograph.

I booked through a London travel firm advertising in the *Methodist Recorder* for a holiday and pilgrimage, which was completely new and different from anything my family and friends had experienced. In later years I was to discover as I showed my slides and film and spoke of this and a subsequent visit to Israel, that on nearly every occasion there was someone present who had served in the forces in Palestine during the Second World War, and had in some cases lived for lengthy periods in the lands of the Bible. Some had never appreciated the history and importance of their location, others had taken advantage to the full and were soaked in rich experiences.

A train to London, then to Dover and onward to Calais by ferry brought me to the train for the journey to Marseilles. When I took my seat in the carriage at Calais, I engaged in conversation with a gentleman from London of Jewish origin, and older in years than myself. We talked of normal things from time to time on the journey and I left him at the station at Marseilles. To my surprise he was at the bus stop where I waited for my short journey to the ship. Here he alighted too and walked up the gangway with me. The crowning moment was when the steward informed us that we were sharing the same cabin and carried our luggage there. He had a wonderful sense of humour and taught me the lovely word 'Shalom', the normal method of greeting among his race. The word means 'peace be to you'.

One day, sitting on the deck in glorious sunshine where every prospect was pleasing, I expressed my contentment. He demurred and when I enquired the reason, he said it was Friday. On my remarking that this was no reason to affect the position, he said briefly, 'Friday – the day I have to pay wages!'

The SS *Theodor Herzl*, on which we sailed for four days to Haifa, was part of Germany's war reparations to Israel. Her tonnage was of the order of 10,000. The name came from the founder of the political Zionist movement. Convinced from his own experience in Europe that anti-Semitism would never allow the patriotic Jew to be left in peace, he wrote a pamphlet '*Der Judenstaat*' (1896) advocating that Jews establish their own state. It resulted in the founding of the Zionist movement. He is venerated throughout the Jewish world as the founder of the movement that has led to the establishment of the Jewish national home.

The voyage was extremely pleasant. We sat on the deck in warm sunshine under blue skies. The accommodation was satisfactory and the food very good, apart from one occasion. I had enjoyed a full English breakfast on the first morning and decided to order the same again on the following day. Looks of horror came over the faces of my nearest passengers. An understanding soul gently reminded me that it was the Jewish Sabbath and so I had to content myself with beetroot, cheese, celery, lettuce and similar things which I did not enjoy one bit at that time of day. Kosher food only was available.

There were Jewish students aboard from all over the world, mostly, as with the other passengers, holidaying or visiting family and friends. It is impossible to understand the meaning of their own land to Jews, unless you have talked with them or visited Israel. The Jewish state in Palestine was set up on termination of the British mandate on 15 May 1948. Provisional frontiers were defined in armistice agreements with Egypt, Jordan, Lebanon and Syria. In January 1950, Jerusalem was declared the capital.

We docked at Naples and visited Pompeii, the Roman city engulfed in volcanic lava in AD79. There were two glass cases, one displaying a dog enclosed in lava, and the other a human being caught in the same predicament of trying to escape the molten stream. Both must have been caught in a sudden and violent eruption.

There were channels showing a primitive form of central heating and a crude painting on the back of a door, which only the men were allowed to see. It was surprising to notice that civilization was so far advanced and to see the luxurious lifestyle enjoyed by the Romans, with their attendant slaves. Shades of Frankie Howard in *Up Pompeii!*

We were taken through part of the slums of Naples which had the unenviable reputation of being the worst in Europe. The American 6th Fleet was at anchor in the lovely bay, which has produced the saying 'See Naples and die'.

In darkness we passed Mount Etna on the east coast of Sicily and had a fine view of the isolated active volcano, throwing lava into the night sky. Over 10,000 feet in height, it is the highest and largest in Europe. It was a compelling sight.

And so to Haifa, the port of northern Israel. It was an exciting and emotional moment when the Holy Land slowly came into view, with Mount Carmel rising behind the town. Thoughts of Elijah and his battle with Ahab, Jezebel and the priests of Baal, directed to save Israel from lapsing into heathenism, came to mind. One of the greatest prophets of Israel, he so impressed himself on the Jewish imagination that a belief grew up that he would return to earth as a forerunner of the Messiah. This was the very land where Jesus lived and ministered, and taught, and healed, and suffered, and died, and rose again.

And how much it meant, too, to the returning Jews. An old man with an artificial limb was walking painfully down the gangway. His wife and children had perished in one of the concentration camps of Nazi Germany. His parents and all close relatives had also died in the holocaust. He had come home to die and as he reached the quayside, he crawled along it for some distance, constantly kissing the ground. In such acts is shown the meaning of Israel to the Jew.

Mount Zion Hotel was a large and comfortable place to stay for three days. Lying at the foot of Mount Carmel it enjoyed a clear view over the harbour to the Mediterranean beyond.

On one occasion the hall porter pointed to a passing road sweeper. 'A

London surgeon,' he said, explaining that there was a surfeit of experienced medical men in the country, and the willingness of everyone to work for Israel, and his fellow countrymen, in any capacity. One evening as a few of us sat drinking coffee in the warm evening air on the balcony at the foot of the hotel, I was introduced to a man I had not previously met. We shook hands. He was Richard Tucker, Chief Tenor of the Metropolitan Opera in New York. A guest of the Israeli Government, he was there to carry out a few official functions. He could not be tempted to sing, but gave me his autograph. One evening, I walked up Mount Carmel with another guest at the hotel. We sat among a crowd of a few hundred young Israelis, high up on the mountainside and listened to their folk songs.

The following day the coach left for a tour of northern Israel, largely the Galilee of the Bible. As we left, the guide asked if everyone spoke English. 'No,' I called, 'only one of us speaks English.' As every face turned in my direction, I explained, 'These are all Americans.'

We left a modern city which could have been anywhere in Europe. Passing the ancient city of Tyre, with its ruins, we came into a different world. Oxen were treading the corn in circular motions, children holding the simple implement pressing the grain, in a scene which could have come straight from the Bible. We came to Cana of Galilee. A modern fort-like building stood at the entrance on the main road. It was built of cardboard and had been erected as a film set for *Exodus*, a film telling not of the chosen people leaving Egypt, but the end of the British mandate in Palestine, and the fierce fighting which ensued. Visiting the traditional site of the wedding feast, we saw the large earthenware vessels which were said to be the actual containers of the water turned into wine. My feeling throughout my stay was that although specific identification could not be guaranteed, nevertheless many of the traditional holy and other sites must, of necessity, have been within yards, or at worst a short distance, of the original site.

From Cana, to Nazareth, which retained its traditional atmosphere of antiquity and piety. A population of 22,500 at that time included 12,000 Christians and 10,000 Moslems. The women still drew water from the well, as Mary must have done two thousand years ago. Mary's well was the only well. Today it was surrounded by bougainvillaea, and camels and donkeys stood motionless in the heat. Blind beggars sat cross-legged at the side of the road, leading into the market place, begging for alms.

We visited the traditional home of the holy family, and realized this cave dwelling of limited space had served as the home of our Lord, his brothers and sisters, of Mary and Joseph.

The synagogue was said not to be the original, but with a little crossing of the palms with silver, a few of us gained access to another building. It struck me immediately as being almost identical in shape and size, and other features, with my boyhood Sunday School.

And He came to Nazareth where he had been brought up, and He went to the synagogue on the Sabbath day, as He regularly did.
(Luke 4)

Here was the living proof of the importance of worship. Does God need our worship? Worship feeds our souls, as we worship we become more like the one we come to worship. Worship restores our sense of proportion and of values. Here was material for sermons in the days to come.

And so we came to the road which skirted the northern boundary of Israel and the southern boundary of Lebanon as we headed east. We were told that to step off the road to our left would be to risk our lives by treading on mines. There was a hostile atmosphere. Warning signs told travellers of the dangers, and the bitterness between Jew and Arab became an almost tangible experience. We arrived at Metulla and the artists village of Safed in the extreme north-eastern corner of the country. We wandered round the small community.

Beyond us was the bleak landscape of Syria. It was dry, dusty, arid, rocky and forbidding. Lifting my eyes, I saw the stark vista suddenly arrested by the view in the far distance of Mount Hermon, rising clear and majestic to a height of 9,000 feet. With its peak snow-capped throughout the year, the sun was reflected from it with a burning and dazzling intensity – the site of our Lord's Transfiguration. Not unexpectedly, this is disputed, as with other sites. The Roman Catholics favour Mount Tabor, the scene of an Old Testament battle, on which we gazed earlier, surmounted by a monastery.

It was to a spur of the mountain that Jesus climbed, with Peter, James and John, the three most intimate of his disciples, for that deep spiritual experience, before he set out to Jerusalem, to suffering and to death. There they saw Moses with Elijah, with all their significance as the lawyer and prophet respectively. It was a fruitful source for a sermon in the coming days based on the text 'Master, it is good for us to be here' (Luke 9 verse 33). Peter, James and John were only on the fringe of events, but they were privileged to enter into the glory of the mountain-top experience. Raphael's great picture of *The Transfiguration* shows the other disciples gazing up to the mountain top. Enquiring, upturned faces wondered what was going on. You can imagine the words: 'Come on down, let us get on with things, there's plenty to be doing down here.'

And Jesus, aware that the moment apart was only a time of preparation, to enable Him to enter more fully into the suffering of a needy world, bade Peter and James and John descend with Him from the mountain. His first experience when they descended was to meet a father with his epileptic boy. An immediate and dramatic change. We all need mountain-top experiences to enable us to prepare for life in the valley. But to stay there is not possible. The spiritual air is too rarefied. For Jesus, times apart like this were always times of preparation to enable Him to enter more fully into the needs of the world. They were not times of escape.

And I was brought 'down to earth'. As we stood there, I engaged in conversation with the driver of the coach. He had lived in England. He had lived in Burnley. He had played soccer for the reserve team of my beloved Burnley FC!

As we turned south, we looked out over the vast valley at the foot of the Syrian hills. The area had once been a swamp, where a few Arabs scraped a living from the soil and a little fishing. American technology and know-how had enabled Israeli labour to transform the valley into fishponds and fertile fields, where the harvest was ripe. The course of the River Jordan had been moved. The Golan Heights amply demonstrated its domination of the landscape and the political and physical battles to come, over their ownership and occupation. It was easy to understand the Arabs being jealous, high up on the rocky land beyond, seeing the fertile land and crops below, and their regular habit of opening fire on the workers below, with the consequent loss of life.

Kibbutzim caught the eye. A Kibbutz is a communal collective settlement and a distinctive feature of the country. With a population varying from 60 to 2,000, the 240 settlements had a central dining room and kitchen, communal domestic services and cultural centre. They are predominantly agricultural and by their labour and devotion, the desert is indeed blossoming as a rose. Networks of pipes bring the precious water to the fields, cypress and pine are being planted in their thousands, fruit trees and vegetables flourish. The life of the Kibbutz is shared, it is hard and demanding, and on the borders was dangerous. Rifles were always to hand. But the people are happy, generous and hard-working. I saw a man ploughing with oxen, a rifle over his shoulder. The standard of life is not always high, but the settlers own nothing and are without financial worries. The visitor receives a warm welcome and generous hospitality without charge.

We passed Deganya, the largest of the Kibbutzim.

For the Christian, the Sea of Galilee is a centre of interest and inspiration. Peaceful and unspoiled with the fishermen mending their nets, it presents a scene much as it must have done in the days of our Lord's earthly life, when Peter, James and John left their nets. The only difference perhaps is that as the fishermen toiled during the night sporadic shooting threatened them from time to time. The Syrian hills beyond the quiet blue waters afford ample cover for the marksman. As Dr Snaith said in his Conference presidential address, the Christian's thoughts are not of 2,000 years ago, but of a living presence. Christ is real and immediate, here and now.

And so back to Haifa. I took my leave of my American friends and travelled to the outskirts of Tel-Aviv for a night at a hotel where I sat dressed in my tuxedo, on the marble floor of the patio, dining by candlelight in the warm evening air.

The next day, the ascent along the winding road to Jerusalem. The golden city came into view and here was liquid history. Shepherd's Hotel was my base for twelve whole days, only a few hundred yards from the boundary with Jordan, dividing Israel from Jordan with unmarked boundaries and all their attendant dangers.

The denial of the existence of Israel had the practical result as I have said of preventing me entering the Old City. My visa was not recognized by Jordan. If I had approached Israel from Jordan, I could have travelled through that way, but not in reverse from Israel to Jordan. A divided city. 'O Jerusalem, Jerusalem, that stoned the prophets.'

We visited several synagogues on a Sabbath tour. Without a skull cap, a knotted handkerchief sufficed for me. In shorts and sunglasses, and bearing all the paraphernalia of the tourist, we watched the different forms of worship from the people of the Dispersion. Of particular interest was the swaying of one worshipping group, as they moved backwards and forward, in remembrance of their ancestors who had lived and travelled on horseback on the Russian steppes. Of all standards of learning and background, they had come from far away to settle in the only land they could call home. Often given a few basic materials for houses and agriculture, allocated infertile areas, they were transformed into cultivated settlements within a year.

A few minutes by road out of Jerusalem and we stood on a hillside, looking out over the valley to the distant village of Bethlehem. The red roof tiles of the Church of the Nativity could be clearly seen some two miles away. Built on the traditional side of the 'stable bare', it is now shared by Orthodox, Roman Catholics and Protestants. But a visit was impossible. It was in Jordan. As I raised my camera, the guide gave a quick warning to desist. A United Nations observer had been standing on this very spot only a short time ago and had been killed by an Arab sniper. Here, on the site of the birth of the Prince of Peace, men were still at war, 2,000 years on.

There was sadness that I could see so much within easy reach. I came to know the newer part of the city quite well in twelve days, but the Mount of Olives, the Wailing Wall, Gethsemane, the Church of the Holy Sepulchre, the pool of Siloam, the Way of the Cross, the Garden Tomb, and so much more was beyond my reach in Jordan. There were compensations. The Dead Sea Scrolls, found in the area I was to visit later on my trip to the Dead Sea, were on display behind thick plate and bullet-proof glass, under tight security, in the new Hebrew University. A magnificent view over the city was provided from the top of the YMCA tower where I attended a short Sunday evening service. Although totally immersed in the wonder of it all, I received reassurance and help from the Chaplain's talk on being a stranger, far from home.

In a square, the Orthodox Jews sat around in traditional dress, with their sons, reading the Scriptures in Hebrew. When non-Jews approached they switched to Yiddish. On the Sabbath the road entrances were found to be blocked by stones, and cameras were considered a transgression of the fourth commandment concerning graven images. Across the road from the YMCA was King David's Hotel with a UN vehicle parked outside, a reminder of the political situation. It was at this hotel that Irgun Zvei Leumi, the Israeli terrorist organization, slaughtered many British citizens. I remember today that many of the leading Israeli leaders of recent times, and the present, were guerrillas fighting for their aims, as the PLO and others have done in the past, and still actively pursue today, although the peace process, as I write, is progressing in a way not thought possible only a few years ago.

One evening I walked into the dining room for dinner. A man was sitting alone at a table and signalled me to join him. He was an English solicitor who had left London to settle in Israel and had become in the Israeli Parliament, the Knesset, the equivalent of our Speaker of the House of Commons. A fascinating evening ended in an invitation to visit the Knesset and to attend a lecture he was giving to a party of visiting American professors. Sitting in the Knesset, since transferred to a new site elsewhere in the city, I had to sit with my hands on the ledge of the front row of the balcony, for security reasons. I gazed down on internationally famous figures like David Ben-Gurion and Mrs Golda Meir, both of whom served as formidable Prime Ministers of their people.

An international incident arose during my stay, with an American landing in the Lebanon, Soviet naval manoeuvres in the Black Sea and the American 6th Fleet sailing for the Eastern Mediterranean. The tension was almost tangible and made me very conscious of being in a country the size of Wales, surrounded by Arab countries, which did not recognize Israel, and had sworn to drive every last Jew into the sea. I thought mother and father would be worried, and after an advised visit to the British Consulate, where I was told that in the event of trouble British subjects would be evacuated by sea, I sent a postcard home with this information, hoping to reassure. Father enquired politely of me on my return as to the logistics of executing such a plan in the event of hostilities, and indicated that my effort to reassure them had only increased their anxiety!

And so through the desert to Beersheba, where Abraham dwelt. As we travelled I saw a shepherd leading, not driving his sheep. A reminder not only of the difference from our own country, but of the words recorded in the Bible, of the sheep fold (John 10 verse 1) and the many other references to this gentle creature in the Bible. It was market day in Beersheba – the cattle market. Not sheep and horses and cows, but camels. Squealing, biting, kicking, they were being loaded onto trucks after sale. A couple were heading home across the sand. He was astride the camel, she was walking ahead bearing possessions on her head. Why the lady walking, and the man riding? Why her place some distance ahead of him? Whether in jest or not, the guide's explanation was there were still many mines in the area from previous conflicts and the wife would find them first. A modern hotel rose incongruously from the desert sands, surrounded by Bedouins in their tents, living as they have done for centuries past.

And so down to the lowest point of earth. Through volcanic rocks, treeless, lifeless, without vegetation, the sun burned down on the hottest day of the year in Israel at 43°. Pitiless and a lonely wilderness, the traditional site of our Lord's temptations. One wondered how anyone could possibly survive for forty days and forty nights. We were on the shore of the Dead Sea, 1,290 feet below sea level, and at its northern end 1,308 feet deep. Labourers stripped to the waist were loading sacks at the phosphate factory and I winced just looking at their sweated labour.

The water is 23 per cent salt as against the 4 per cent of the Mediterranean. Cold, clear, refreshing water flows in from the Jordan at the northern end but here nothing can exist because there is no outlet. Another sermon here: a lesson of life, that lack of movement and change spells death, and stagnation. Nothing lives in waters which still had boats at anchor, from the days of British occupation. Beyond, on the far shore, was Jordan. My friend walked into the water, and as so many find, he could sit upright as in an armchair and read his newspaper. Almost impossible to sink, but dangerous to dive, and perhaps be unable to lift your head from the water.

Entry into the nearby caves plunged us into a cold temperature and we were glad to leave. Just a short distance away was the area where the shepherd boy threw the stone into a similar cave, heard a sound of it striking pottery and heralded the finding of the Dead Sea Scrolls. And so we returned at the end of the day to Jerusalem.

The time passed all too quickly and I returned to Haifa for re-embarkation on the SS *Theodor Herzl*. We called at Athens on the way home, where I stayed the night. The 43° Centigrade temperature I had experienced in Israel was a dry heat and did not trouble me, but a night in Athens where the daytime temperature had reached the much lower figure of 90° Fahrenheit, with high humidity, left me lying naked and sleepless throughout the night.

I had met a Cambridge student on the ship and when we anchored off the port of Limassol in Cyprus, we made another friend. Unable to land because of the violent situation with Archbishop Makarios and the Eoka terrorist organization, I could only stand on deck at 5 a.m. and watch a boat approach, containing British soldiers and a man in civilian dress. It transpired that he was a British Army Major, and had been the chief explosives expert in the troubled island. A letter from Eoka had been received informing him that his time had come, and the bomb which would kill him had been blessed by the church in Athens and was on its way. Sir Hugh Foot, the Governor, had given orders for him to be shipped out at once, and he had been smuggled by armed convoy to the ship in the early hours. Everyone who had previously received such a threat had been killed. Ordered not to leave the ship until we reached Marseilles, he insisted on joining us in Athens. We lost him on the Acropolis and just when we were becoming really anxious, he appeared from behind the Parthenon licking an ice cream, and with a pretty girl on either arm. Phew!

Father was a strict disciplinarian, believed strongly in the work ethic and I had not expected him to agree to my 24-day holiday. At that time we enjoyed two weeks in the summer and one in the winter. My holiday, I persuaded myself, was a perk of the boss's son! It was a holiday of a lifetime and one to savour in the days ahead. Often I return in mind to my hotel room in Jerusalem at the end of the first day in the city. I opened my Bible at the first chapter of the Gospel according to St Mark and as I read, it was as if I were reading a tour guide of my own home district. The Bible became so much clearer for me on this holiday, bringing increased knowledge and understanding, but more than that. The person of Jesus became real as I walked in the steps He trod, and having borne in upon me that the Word *did* become flesh, and dwelt among us. I beheld a little of His glory.

The reader may find of interest the following article I wrote, published by the Methodist Youth Department in their monthly magazine of the time, shortly after my return:

Turn you, and take your journey . . . in the Arabah, in the hill country and in the lowland, and in the south, and by the sea shore, the land of the Canaanites and Lebanon . . . Behold I have set the land before you: go in and possess the land which the Lord sware unto your fathers, to Abraham, to Isaac, and to Jacob, to give unto

them and to their seed after them.
Deuteronomy 1 verses 7 & 8.

For many years I had been filled with a deep longing to visit the Holy Land. On several occasions when I had been on the point of making arrangements, the political situation had dashed my hopes. This time I was barely successful, reaching the shores of Israel a mere forty eight hours before the American landing in the Lebanon and the beginning of the Middle East crisis.

Haifa gives the visitor a pleasing first impression of the country, nestling on the slopes of Mount Carmel above the deep blue of the Mediterranean. The golden dome of the Bahai shrine draws the eye incessantly. From the ridge above the city the prophet Elijah, nearly 3,000 years ago, hurled forth his challenge to the priests of Baal.

There is ever a natural readiness to compare the old with the new of any country, but here it is inevitable. 'Nazareth of Galilee, and was baptized of John in Jordon' v 9. 'And immediately the Spirit driveth Him into the wilderness' v 12. 'Jesus came into Galilee, preaching the gospel of the kingdom of God' v 14.

'Now as He walked by the Sea of Galilee,' He saw Simon and Andrew his brother casting a net into the sea: for they were fishers . . . And when He had gone a little farther thence, He saw James the son of Zebedee and John his brother, who also were in the ship mending their nets' verses 16 and 19.

'And they went into Capernaum; and straightway on the Sabbath day He entered into the synagogue' v 21.

'And forthwith, when they were come out of the synagogue, they entered into the house of Simon and Andrew' v 29.

And so to Beersheba on market day. 'And Abraham dwelt at Beersheba.' It is easy indeed to imagine him coming in with his followers from the desert as the Bedouins were doing, on camels and horses, with their sheep and goats, throwing up clouds of dust.

Then down to the Dead Sea and the lowest point on earth. Down through vast valleys and hills, covered with a white volcanic rock, bleak and unutterably lonely under a blazing merciless sun. Here Sodom was engulfed nearly four thousand years ago.

And so finally to Jerusalem, the very history of the Jewish people. 'The city of peace' says the badge handed to me as I descend Mount Zion after seeing King David's tomb and the Room of the Last Supper. And yet but a few yards apart on the Mount the guns of the Israeli and the Arab face each other. From the platform on Mount Zion I can look down into the Garden of Gethsemane lying in the Arab part of the city and which is therefore in forbidden territory.

As I turn I see the site of the High Priest's palace where Jesus appeared before Caiaphas. And then my eyes follow the Way of the Cross back through the city and away to the distant hills hiding Golgotha from view. Below me again is the Church of the Holy Sepulchre. Dominating the view, serene and majestic stands the Mount of Olives.

From a short distance away Bethlehem lies snug and peaceful on the distant hillside.

As I take a photograph the Israeli soldier puts down his telescope in his vantage point and rebukes me, forbidding the others to follow my example. The guide reminds us that on this spot a short time ago United Nations observers were fired on and killed by Arabs shooting from the Monastery across the valley. A United Nations car rushes by on urgent business.

My mind goes back to the Sea of Galilee, to a little hill overlooking the quiet blue waters, and to the words which were spoken from that place. 'Blessed are the peacemakers: for they shall be called the children of God.'

'Neither pray I for these alone . . . that they all may be one; as thou Father art in me and I in Thee, that they also may be one in us: that the world may believe that Thou has sent Me.'

Chapter XXIV

MEDITERRANEAN CRUISE AND THE HOLY LAND
REVISITED

One of my most interesting and life-changing experiences was a Mediterranean cruise in 1960. I travelled via London, from home in Morecambe, by train to Dover, to Calais by ferry, and then on the Orient Express to Venice.

Alighting from the carriage I was met by an officer from SS *Meteor* of the Bergen Line, who assisted me into a launch berthed at the end of the platform. We moved swiftly to the ship, anchored in the Grand Canal. I was one of the last passengers aboard and we sailed shortly after I embarked.

A single port cabin gave me the freedom I enjoyed and a continuing view of land, eastward first, and then westward, round the Mediterranean. The sum of £120 was a large figure in those days, but with shore excursions included, it was twenty-four days of wonderful value.

Our first stop was Dubrovnik in the former Yugoslavia and much in the news at present. Advised that we would see all the signs of a Communist state, we were surprised to find hundreds of children walking in procession to churches, bunches of flowers clasped in their hands, church bells ringing, sunshine and laughter, and a general festive air. It was Holy Week and we were witnessing Christian celebrations under an atheist regime. A walk round the city walls was followed by a coach trip up the mountain road leading out of the city, to a point where we had magnificent views over the Adriatic. At our feet lay the blue dome of Tito's summer residence where he had entertained most of the world leaders of his time.

A member of the crew missed departure and waved frantically from the harbour mooring. He rejoined the ship later.

The Corinth Canal seemed small and of little interest as we approached, but suddenly assumed grand proportions. Cut across the isthmus in 1893 to connect the Gulf of Corinth with the Saromic Gulf, it is just over three miles long, with other dimensions giving a depth of 26¼ ft, a bottom width of 69 ft and a surface-water width of 81 ft. A single-span road and rail bridge, 262 ft long, crossed the canal, one and a half miles from the north-west entrance.

Our ship seemed almost to touch the sides as we glided through and at 3,000 tons, we were told our vessel was about as large as could be serviced.

A short time later we docked in Athens. The Acropolis (including the Parthenon), Olympic Stadium, Temple of Apollo, and other buildings of the Agora and Acropolis were obligatory viewing. The sheer size and beauty of the Parthenon was breathtaking. My high moment in the ancient city was at the Areopagus, and remembering that here Paul preached to the Epicurean and Stoic philosophers, quoting their own poetry to men who knew nothing of the Old Testament.

Ye men of Athens in all things I perceive that ye are somewhat superstitious.

For as I passed along, and observed the objects of your worship, I found also an altar with this inscription 'TO AN UNKNOWN GOD'. What therefore ye worship in ignorance, this I set forth to you . . .

Now when they heard of the resurrection of the dead, some mocked; but others said 'We will hear thee concerning this yet again.'

(Acts 17)

From Athens to Izmir, a coastal town of Turkey, and a journey by coach to Ephesus, through fertile land and houses where storks nestled on the roofs. We saw the remains of the Temple of Diana, one of the seven wonders of the world. According to Pliny, the largest Greek temple ever constructed, it had 127 columns, each 60 feet high. We also visited the ruins of the Stadium, 687 feet long and the amphitheatre mentioned in St Paul's account of preaching in the city.

I was reminded recently, in one of William Barclay's writings, that St Paul's Letter to the Ephesians, rightly called the 'Queen of the Epistles', was the most impersonal he ever wrote, and probably a circular addressed to a group of churches in the province of Asia. In Ephesians the doctrine of the Church is more highly developed than in any other Epistle.

The recent excavations included an Easter Cross, marked on a marble floor. From whichever direction you look, a Cross is to be seen. It was probably made by someone at the risk of losing his life.

And so to the beautiful blue sea of the Greek islands. A donkey ride to the summit of Patmos turned into a hilarious race. The islanders were waiting on the quayside and seemed intent on seeing the largest human on the smallest donkey. A friend and I begged carrots from the galley, and tying them to sticks, held them in front of the donkeys. The donkeys and other passengers were singularly unimpressed by our attempt to gain an advantage.

We viewed the traditional site and actual stone seat of the author of
the Book of Revelation:

I, John . . . was in the isle that is called Patmos . . .

(Rev 1:v 9)

A brief visit to Samos, watching the men mending their nets on the
quayside, preceded our departure for Cyprus, where we indulged in a
local custom of Good Friday, involving hard-boiled eggs.

Anticipation grew as we headed for Israel. Early on Easter Day a
number of us gathered in the observation lounge for a short service,
conducted by a retired Anglican clergyman, the Rev. J.V. Hobbins of
Westgate-on-Sea. I had become friendly with him and his wife. He invited
me to read a lesson on the Sunday following, and I read the account of
Jesus meeting his disciples after the Resurrection, by the Sea of Galilee,
which we had visited on Easter Monday (John 21).

A suitably inscribed New English Bible, which he later sent to me, is
a treasured possession.

As the Holy Land came into view, we commenced the service, singing
the traditional hymn 'Christ the Lord is risen today; Hallelujah!'

Docking at Haifa, we travelled by road to Jerusalem. Jerusalem on
Easter Day! Bells ringing, pilgrims flocking, glorious sunshine, the old
city walls, the Mount of Olives, Mt Zion, the winding road to Jericho,
and so much more. We ate unleavened bread and visited the room which
is the traditional site of the Last Supper. Two small pieces of pillar are
said to be from the original room.

A crack in the door on the other side from where we were standing
attracted my attention, but our guide said that to open it would risk a hail
of bullets from soldiers of the Arab Legion stationed on the other side.
A divided city and we were in the newer part (Israel), unable to pass into
the older part (Jordan). As we walked on Mt Zion I purchased a badge
from a street vendor bearing in Hebrew a verse of Psalm 122: 'Pray for
the peace of Jerusalem' (v 6). We saw on the approaches to the Mount,
evidence of the bitter war between Jew and Arab in 1948, when the
British Mandate ended. And so back down the road from Jerusalem,
passing again abandoned tanks and guns of the earlier conflict.

On Monday I arranged to take the Rev. and Mrs Hobbins to the Sea of
Galilee. He had looked forward to this pilgrimage for many years and
was saddened by the commercial aspects of Jerusalem on Easter Day.
He had expected to find a city of peace and not the noisy, dirty,
cosmopolitan face we saw that day. As a young man these factors little
affected the joy and wonder of being in Jerusalem on Easter Day. I think
too that Jesus must have encountered dust and noise, filth and disease

176

and many of the less pleasant conditions of life during his last earthly days. We took with us the then Treasurer of the Manchester Methodist Mission and his wife. Travel was by sheroot. Almost indistinguishable from an English taxi service, it was however much cheaper, and our driver was a patient, cheerful companion.

The ship had provided an appetizing picnic and as we sat under the willows, at the very edge of the Sea of Galilee, on the traditional site of the feeding of the 5,000, and gazed up to the Mount of Beatitudes, the traditional site of the Sermon on the Mount tranquillity and peace were enjoyed by us all and restored to the heart of my Anglican friend.

I have a letter from the 82-year old Anglican clergyman written to me on 28 April 1965. It is worth setting out in full, expressing as it does the views of a lifetime on a number of important topics, within six small pages of neat handwriting:

Dear John and Rosalie

Dorothy and I were delighted to hear from you again. It added to our Easter joy. Thank you for your very cheery letter. Our love and hearty congratulations on the birth of a little son. What a happy little family! We should love to see them.

As you say time slips away very rapidly. When one reaches my advanced years (I shall be 83 next birthday) the weeks and years simply rush past. One asks oneself at the end of each day 'What have I done today for God for others?' – the answer is too often depressing.

The school holidays end tomorrow and the little boys return for we hope a happy summer term. I always look forward to their return to hear their singing in Chapel and watch them playing cricket. I find a comfortable chair in the cricket field on a summer's afternoon very soothing. I sometimes go to sleep. The small prep school keeps me from 'rusting' and getting too absorbed in my own private affairs. Some day you will be looking for a suitable school for John.

We have not yet been out for a cruise in our little cabin cruiser 'Hobinos'. She is called 'Hobinos' – a nickname given to me by the boys at my last school because I taught classical Greek there. She is a real joy to us. We love taking our friends out for an afternoon on our river 'Stour'. She is fitted with a gas stove and we take our tea and sometimes lunch and spend the afternoons sleeping and reading and watching the water silently gliding past on its way to the sea at Sandwich.

Have you read 'Honest to God' by the Bishop of Woolwich? There is no doubt he is a good sincere Christian and I have found

177

much of it true and helpful. 'Christ was utterly and completely the Man for others because He was love and one with the Father because God is love.' All that kind of thing is good and helpful.

Other parts of the book are puzzling and mysterious. 'Transcendence, immanence, God up there and up there etc denying theologism. The Bishop's 'The New Reformation' is particularly interesting.

I have been reading a lot of mainly 'German Theology' lately. I am not sure I have not been wasting my time. I admire Rudolph Bultman. He is no doubt a very great scholar but his 'Gospel mythology' is at times incomprehensible.

Karl Barth, Bonhoeffer are helpful. I cannot make much of Tillich. I am about to tackle Teilhard de Chardin – the French Scientist.

What does your father in law think of the reunion of the C of E and Methodist churches? I have not followed the discussions very closely but there seem to be almost insuperable difficulties to be solved. If ever it does come about it would gladden the heart of our Lord Jesus Christ whose last prayer was that 'His church might be one'. It would no doubt also rejoice the heart of John Wesley. The main problems seem to be Episcopal Ordination, Apostolic Succession and Sacramental Confession. To many these things are very important. I feel they are non-essentials to the Christian faith.

I often think of you and your good work among the young people of your neighbourhood. It must have its difficulties these days. Do you get many Mods and Rockers in Morecambe? We get quite a few in Margate. These wild teenagers are really very loveable at heart. Their outbursts of violence are due to the fact that they are bored with life. Life seems to have no meaning or purpose for them. Life without God of course is utterly 'meaningless'. The Bishop of Woolwich's chapter (22) in his book 'The New Reformation' 'Starting from the other end' is very good here.

Once again – 'happy memories of our Mediterranean cruise in the Meteor'. I shall remember it until the end of my life. I am still giving lectures with coloured slides on the Holy Land. I have enlarged my library and added many slides bought in London to my collection but only of those places we have visited.

My wife sends her very best wishes to you both. She is a hard worker but enjoys very good health. Old infirm bed ridden ladies enjoy her visits to them. She is a keen member of 'The Mothers Union'. She does nearly all the housework herself and of course takes great care of me. I keep pretty well. My chief worry is and has always been a weak digestion and I have to be very careful what I eat and drink.

Thank you for the cutting by the Bishop of Coventry. He is a good chap and a first rate Christian worker. I enjoyed the 23rd Psalm by the Japanese Woman. I had actually heard it somewhere though rather hurriedly. It is very good and helpful.

Wishing you happy days and a very pleasant holiday at Falmouth in July.

Yours sincerely

J. Vivian Hobbins.

Write again soon. Our very best love to John and Catherine Elizabeth.

We sailed for Crete on the Monday, calling at Knossos. The civilization at the centre of the world in the second millennium BC was almost unknown, when in 1900, Sir Arthur Evans began excavations. Thanks to his research and that of other scholars of many nations, its brilliant culture is now known with amazing fullness and freshness.

Then on to Malta, entering Valetta harbour, which we left for the ancient empty city of Medina, and thence to St Paul's Bay, the traditional site of the Apostle's shipwreck on his way to Rome.

From Crete to Tunis and a visit to Carthage and the ancient amphitheatre. 'The most ruined ruins I have ever seen,' opined an American. Our guide walked with us along the path trodden by the early Christians as they walked into the arena, where the hungry lions were loosed upon them. In Rome the martyrs were allowed shield and spear, but here bare hands had to suffice, before their savaged bodies littered the blood-stained sand. I thought of the strength of their faith.

Lisbon was a joy. Almost entirely destroyed in 1755 by an earthquake, it was rebuilt with gracious, stately buildings, surrounded and separated by vast lawns, trees and flowers. We were shown the spot where the Queen and the Duke of Edinburgh had alighted on a recent visit, and as we sailed up to and from the Portuguese capital we passed the fort from where Vasco de Gama set sail on his momentous voyage to India in the fifteenth century.

After a slightly choppy crossing of the Bay of Biscay, our journey ended in Dover. The sea was as smooth as glass and had been until almost the end of a journey to be savoured and remembered ever since.

Chapter XXV

JOHN AND CATHERINE

I met Rosalie when she came with her mother, father and brother Peter, to Morecambe. Her father had been appointed as a Minister to the Morecambe and Heysham Methodist Circuit, with pastoral care of Clarence Street and Bare churches. They had been at the Methodist Church in Rue Roquepine, in Paris, after living for a time in Lancaster, so that they were not strangers to the area.

We were married on 4 March 1961. Rosalie had worked at the British Embassy in Paris before entering teacher training college and qualifying as an infant teacher. She was a 'daughter of the manse', a child of our minister and because of that and my being inevitably well-known in the town as a solicitor, Methodist local preacher, with a lifetime in one of his churches and also as a golfer, tennis player and as a soccer player in the town's team, it was inevitable that our wedding attracted widespread attention in the town and a large attendance. Rosalie's father conducted the service and her mother's brother, Uncle Walter gave her away.

We spent the weekend in London before flying to our honeymoon destination, Las Palmas in the Canary Islands. Today, of course, exotic foreign honeymoons are commonplace, but over thirty years ago it was something of a novelty. I had never flown before and was not helped in my natural fear when returning. Madrid was a stopping-place on the outward and inward journeys. As we sat in the fragile-looking aircraft of Iberia Airlines, a tyre was found to be punctured and the sight of what seemed little more than a small foot pump being trundled out onto the tarmac to reinflate it, with all the passengers aboard, did nothing to ease my fear.

The temperature was perfect for me, about 70° Fahrenheit, with a soft breeze. The Santa Catalina hotel was all one could wish for.

I am not a practical man and photography is an unknown world, although I later managed a reasonable film and slides of my Holy Land visits. The camera was jammed and the gentleman in the shop seemed to know what he was doing, although I thought it strange that he should be opening it in the shop. In short, we lost our honeymoon photographs.

Our son John was born on 4 February 1962. Many commented happily on the continuation of the family name, but I was quite unconcerned whether we were to have a boy or girl, my only wish being for a healthy child. Catherine was born on 19 November 1964.

In December 1974 our marriage broke up and I left to live with my sister Peggy and brother-in-law Norman for three months, before acquiring my own property. The reason for the breakdown, I accept unreservedly, was mainly my overworking. I was insensitive to the needs of a young bride and the only plea in mitigation I can make is that I was a young professional man, a partner in the family practice, with a connection to build, and countless other interests. My hours of work were ridiculous. A normal day would be to rise at 7 a.m. and work with files and dictating machine, clothed in my dressing gown, until 8.15 a.m. A hurried breakfast enabled me to reach the office at 9 a.m. where I read and distributed all the incoming mail. At 12.30 p.m. I went home for lunch, accompanied by a file of (say) 150 letters, typed in the morning, and all of which I read whilst eating. Returning home for tea at 5.30 p.m., I would invariably be back at the office for 7 p.m. and work for three hours. The position was not helped by the fact that both of my neighbours of roughly the same age worked in 9 a.m. to 5 p.m. jobs.

I had just taken a consultancy, built a new house at Storth, joined the Board of Marsden Building Society as a non-executive director after my father's death, and fully intended, with the urging and full support of my partners, to take life more easily. I have seen heart attacks and breakdowns in health all too often in my profession. I cannot think of one partner in my early days who did not suffer from a smaller or greater ailment, and this applied to other practices in the town.

When I took a consultancy, several close friends told me that I had been heading for an early grave. Anxiety, fear and people-pleasing – these were my companions. I had no financial worries and money was never a dominant factor, or I would have been a wealthy man, with all the business opportunities available to me.

I do not recommend divorce. Whatever anyone may say I learned not primarily as a lawyer but from my personal experience that there is no such thing as 'a friendly divorce'. I speak against my own profession when I say that the clear duty to explore the possibility of a reconciliation before proceedings are started was observed more in the breach than in the honouring.

During my National Service I had been involved in hundreds of divorces, spoken to and taken statements from petitioners and respondents and co-respondents; I saw the misery and unhappiness of so many marriages, and it could have been a factor in my sincerely held belief for many years before I took my vows that although I loved female company, and companionship, I did not want to marry. I also think that my parents' unhappy marriage was unconsciously having an effect and created a

John's Christening 1962
Close families of Mother and Father with Mother's close friend and godmother, Anne

Myself with John and Catherine on holiday in Falmouth.

reluctance to take responsibilities. Thirty-one was pretty late in the early 1960s for settling down.

I identify here with Prince Charles. There was nearly the same age difference in my first marriage; there was no common interest in sport, in music, in recreation. Shopping and spending rather than country walks and views, current affairs and sport. Dancing and gossip rather than conversation.

In my marriage to Rosalie I had felt under some family pressure, at the time, to marry. I was thirty-one, the same age as Prince Charles (to continue the comparison) at the time of his marriage. Rosalie was only two years older than Princess Diana at the time of her marriage. And yet I knew that my father did not want to 'lose' me, and felt a right after all his sacrifices for his children, to continue a relationship which in many aspects was like two brothers rather than father and son.

I am now sure that there was a certain reluctance on my part to marry. I enjoyed female company as much as the next man, and I conclude that it was because of the unhappiness in the relationship of my parents. And too, because I enjoyed the freedom of a single man. I do not ignore an element of selfishness in my attitude and thinking.

Cocktail parties and a social life, large houses and material possessions seemed more attractive than my preferred interests.

With Rosalie, there was a position I have seen in many children of the Manse, where those things which an outsider would consider natural and to be expected did not exist. It must in come cases have partly been through a feeling of suffocation and pressure and unwarranted and unfair expectations.

Rosalie and I had bought an attractive semi-detached house for our first home. It was situated only about 100 yards from the Manse, and that in itself was perhaps a mistake. Owned by an elderly couple, it needed modernizing, and my father really took this work in hand. One evening, some ten days before the wedding, he mentioned that he would need a key whilst we were on our honeymoon, to supervise the work.

A day or two later I told him that Rosalie's mother insisted on retaining the key as she would need it when Rosalie and I were abroad on business and holiday after our marriage. My father could not contain himself and turning to me with his hand reaching for the telephone said, 'Shall I ring and call it [the marriage] off *now*?'

Looking back . . . but then it is easy to be wise after the event. Looking back I also now realize that our mutual interests were virtually non-existent. I had 'married' a safe, attractive-looking daughter of the Manse. The lack of interests outside office and Church, with my wife, were few. I regret my behaviour but I know there was nothing innately evil about it, nor was I materially minded. On the other hand, no one ever spoke to me about the situation, the outcome of which is all too frequently seen – I was the last to find out. There is in my experience, nothing more harmful to a marriage than a lack of communication and interference by in-laws, and this I had in abundance. Even so, my considered opinion, and from the standpoint of today, is that the marriage should not and need not have ended. Those concerned must look to their own consciences.

The final breakdown of my marriage to Rosalie was distressing in the extreme and occurred at Christmas 1974. I had been appointed as a local Preacher to conduct worship at the Carol Service at Central Methodist Church on the Sunday before Christmas. There was a complicated and lengthy Order of Service and I had spent a lot of time in preparation during the week. On the Saturday I could not find the Order of Service and searched the house frantically. Rosalie could not help. I told her I would go into Morecambe and see if I had left it in my office, although certain this was not the case.

On my return the relevant piece of paper lay prominently on a chest of drawers in the bedroom, where I had looked many times. Rosalie had deliberately moved it from my papers and put it there to 'engineer' a reason for taking steps to break up our marriage. When I remarked about the matter Rosalie flustered about a letter which had been written by solicitors to me and that she would get it. This was an undated letter written many months before (and possibly years judging by its condition) and left with her parents. It ordered me to leave the house.

Rosalie told me that on many occasions she had followed me when I left Storth for the office, and spent the day with her parents, returning before I did. She had also consulted solicitors in Manchester and been told that she did not have a case for divorce. Again, one of my partners told me that she contacted him. He was puzzled and said it was as though she used him as 'a whipping post'. Her parents told another partner and his wife when attending a Church concert in which the children appeared that they were unhappy about the marriage.

And nobody, Rosalie, her parents (her father a Methodist Minister with whom I never had a cross word) or friends said a word to me.

I leave it there, except to say that a partner who acted for me reminded me of the alteration in the law since our early days. The old ground of 'cruelty' had become one of 'unreasonable conduct'. He said that only a few days before he had seen a petition by a wife which alleged little more than that the husband had expressed a dislike for two hats she had bought! In other words, the law was a farce and if the party wanted a divorce, it was virtually impossible to stop it on this ground.

I shall never know how I got through the service. Rosalie spent Christmas with her parents, taking the children, and shortly afterwards, on the advice of my solicitor, I left and went to stay, as I have said, with my sister Peggy and brother-in-law, Norman. I lived with them for three months before buying a bungalow in the grounds of the house where I lived with my mother and father until I married. I shall always be grateful for the ready and generous hospitality given to me by Peggy and Norman at this black time in my life.

The chief sufferers, of course, were the children. Access raised constant and continuing difficulties. Blame was often placed unjustifiably on the other party.

On one occasion (a Sunday) I called for John in accordance with arrangements made between the respective lawyers. There was a long wait, and then a tearful, dishevelled Rosalie appeared and said there were no arrangements made. I said there were. She then (I learned next day) tried to phone her solicitor, received no reply, and then phoned my solicitor at home. He told me he had informed her she should not be so silly, arrangements had been made, and she should see John and Catherine were with me immediately.

A real heartache for me was in not seeing my children or hearing from them for many years. In 1988 I received a letter out of the blue from my son which reduced me to tears of joy.

He told me that it was the hardest letter he had ever had to write; that he would understand if I did not reply; that he had always loved me; that he loved me now, and would always love me.

John had sent it from Washington DC (where he was engaged in research) on 21 June 1988. It was addressed as follows:

Mr John Knape
c/o Jobling & Knape (Solicitors)
19 Northumberland Street
Morecambe
Lancashire
United Kingdom.

The letter and the envelope are a treasured possession. John had clearly not known my present address, and in fact the envelope was marked 'Please forward if necessary'.

I have in front of me one of his scholarly papers:

British Foreign Policy in the Caribbean Basin 1938-1945: Oil, Nationalism and Relations with the United States, by John Knape

One of the matters for which I was grateful is that both John and Catherine had excellent educations. Their first school was Lancaster Road County Primary where the Headmaster, the late Mr George

Tomlinson JP, obtained outstanding 11-plus results through the years.

It is also a great happiness to me that I maintain contact with one of John's former teachers, Mrs Beatrice Wilson. I know Beatrice has fond memories of him and he has never forgotten his affection and respect for her, and the influence she had on his life. Beatrice is a dedicated member of our Methodist Church in Morecambe, has held many offices and still holds a house group in her home. I served as Secretary of the Parent Teacher Association and received the following letter in October 1973 from the Headmaster:

31st October 1973
Dear Mr Knape,
   Many thanks for the package containing the Minutes of the Parent Teacher Association received last week.
   I was requested at the Annual General Meeting to convey to you the warm and sincere thanks for the Parent Teacher Association for the part which you played as a member of the Association and in particular the valuable help which you gave us during your two years as Honorary Secretary. I am sure the Association is going to miss this help, but I know that we wish you and your family everything of the best in whatever lies ahead.
   Kindest regards and very best wishes
   Yours sincerely,
   Geo. H. Tomlinson

Only a few days ago (at the time of writing) I received a letter from Beatrice which moved me deeply, but at the same time gave me great strength. I have kept her in touch with the progress of my writing and her interest has been a real factor in my determination to press on with my life story. The contents are a measure of her care, concern, and interest.

9, Slye Rd,
Torrisholme,
Morecambe
LA4 6PA
8.12.97

Dear John,
   Many, many thanks for your Christmas greetings and the 'Bookshelf' leaflet. It's all wonderful news and I'm 'thrilled to bits' for you. You must be feeling very happy. I am really looking forward to reading the book and shall see to it that some of my friends have a copy also.

Wishing you all the best for now and always.
                    Love
                    Beatrice

P.S. I have just had an 'implant' and glaucoma operation on my right eye. The other eye will encounter the same experience in late Jan. or Feb. Keeping my writing to a minimum at the moment, but just had to scribble this note.

The letter was written in lovely handwriting.

Beatrice lost her husband on active flying service during the War and remained a widow and dedicated teacher until her retirement.

I shall probably be in 'hot water' from this modest lady for mentioning her in the way I have, but I can take it!

Catherine attended the C of E school in Storth when we moved there in 1973. She had no difficulty in passing her 11-plus and was in a particularly gifted group that year. John attended Heversham Grammar School. Founded in 1613 it maintained excellent standards and produced a fine type of boy over the years. Being smaller than some schools, they had, as one of the Masters said, 'to try that little bit harder'. John was near the top of his form and excelled at cross-country running.

They later attended the Boys' and Girls' Divisions respectively at the well-known and highly regarded Bolton School.

Poor results in his A levels was the only apparent injury to John. His headmaster told me that he had been repeatedly warned that his potential Oxbridge talent was not being fully cultivated and that the domestic problem had, in his view, substantially affected him. In the event he gained a MA and Ph.D and is currently Communications Manager of the United Kingdom Central Council of Nursing, Midwifery and Health Visiting. We share a common extreme interest in soccer, and John still plays. When at Bolton School he was offered a trial for Bolton Wanderers.

I have not seen John or Catherine now for over four years, after two lovely weekends in London with them. I was so happy, and told John that I intended to write to his mother on my return to say so. It was a friendly, even tender letter, saying how fortunate we should consider ourselves to have two such wonderful children, expressing my joy and happiness for the weekend, and saying that although we would probably rarely meet, I hoped we could be friends.

                                        5th December 1994

Dear Rosalie,

I have just returned home after 2 treasured days with John and Catherine, and cannot go to bed without first writing to you. I shall post it in the morning.

There are so many needful things that I will number them:

1. I enclose a Synopsis of my Autobiography, which I hope you will find of interest.
2. I have sensed for some time in conversations with John, a certain reservation, and which my intuition told me arose from concern about what it may contain. The intuition was confirmed by events.
3. There will be *nothing* within the books cover to cause you or grandma any anxiety. I *must* mention an unhappy divorce and separation from my children for many years, but of any detail, there will be *nothing*.
4. Please read my definition of love near the end of Chapter 34, and before the postscript.
5. In that sense, I love you.
6. You may say that you are not in need. We are *all* in need of love, and caring, and friendship.
7. I offer that to you now, in the future and for evermore, not through any need of my own, but by God's Grace.
8. We have two children beyond my capacity to describe in terms of their ability, character and the joy they bring to us both.
9. They are a credit to you, and I love you for that too.
10. Nothing would please me more at any time than to share with you and/or grandma, now or in the future, and with or without John and/or Catherine, a few seconds, minutes or hours, anywhere you choose, and at any time.
11. Love cannot bear separation.
12. I would give my right arm to hold your hand and grandma's, to give you both a peck on the cheek, and hold out the hand of friendship, and of love.
13. I shall be divorced in a week or two. I cannot live with the ghost of another man.
14. In 23 days I wrote 450 pages of A4. It was done in His strength and by His Grace.
15. I do not intend to have another permanent relationship.
16. I am appointing Ian as an executor and trustee of my will along with John, and David Harrison, the senior partner of Jobling and Knape.
17. There are 2 envelopes with my Will, sealed and marked that they are only to be opened in the event of you and Marjorie respectively, disputing my will.
18. I have told John this weekend, and that I hope he will be able to destroy them, and that they never see the light of day.

19. You may wonder why, in your case. My colleagues confirm me in my view that as you still have a nominal order against me, which I never bothered to have cancelled, you have a theoretical right.

20. Apart from a few recurring legacies, all my estate passes to John and Catherine equally, or the survivor, if there are no children.

21. I am in love with life, joyful, busy, anxious only to serve my God and fellow man.

22. John tells me you are heavily involved in school work and I wish you well. There is no more important work than that of teaching the young.

John and I listened to Donald Soper in Hyde Park on the very point this afternoon.

He and I went to Matins at Westminster Abbey this morning. I enclose a spare copy of the Order of Service, which you may wish to retain. The singing was superb.

I hope I have said most of what I wish.

Please understand I will not press you ever about anything. I repeat – I love you, I love John and Catherine, I love all men.

I ask you to forgive me for anything wherein I have failed you. You are still the girl I married, and that is how I would have it forever.

With my love,
John.

I sent John a copy. This was done on the Monday after my return i.e. on the same day I delivered the letter to Rosalie's home. I had to attend a meeting later that day as a trustee of a charity formed by the Lancashire County Council for young, handicapped children. The venue was only a few hundred yards from Rosalie's home and I delivered the letter by hand, knowing she would be at school. That night at nearly midnight John, clearly under orders, phoned me, and said I had 'violated' his mother's house. He persisted in his complaint, even though I told him I had sent him a copy of the latter and suggested he read it, and he would then see the innocence and sincerity of my action, and we could speak again.

They have not been in touch since. I lost my temper on the Tuesday, and wrote accordingly, regretted it the day afterwards, and send a letter of apology, to no avail. The letter was returned marked 'RETURN TO SENDER'.

Of course I felt released from any undertaking not to include in my autobiography the promise in paragraph numbered 3 in my letter to Rosalie. Neither my prayers nor my conscience, nor the need to give a truthful account would permit it. I have written in a restrained and responsible manner.

Rosalie has remained unmarried. She must deal in her own conscience with her conduct so far as the children and I are concerned.

I sometimes think of my father and this situation. I think he would have said, 'No wonder there are wars.'

And the angels wept.

I give thanks to God for a gifted son and daughter and the joy they bring constantly to my life. Catherine gained an Honours degree in Mandarin Chinese at Oxford (Wadham College) and has recently been awarded her MA. She spent two years in Beijing, speaks several languages, and is currently finishing an advanced course at the London Business School for one of the leading administration qualifications in the country, a Masters degree in administration (MBA). She is involved in strategic management consultancy. Whilst living in Beijing, the Tiananmen Square massacre occurred and there were anxious moments as the British Embassy assisted Catherine's move to Hong Kong.

They are fine children and I am proud of them in terms of human qualities, as well as academic achievement. The reader will gather that for many reasons there is no point in writing at length on my domestic problems in the marriage and for which I believe I have since received God's forgiveness in true repentance.

Access is very often a major problem for separated husband, wife and their children. Many have been the husbands who have called on me professionally on a Monday morning with stories of standing outside the house, waiting for their children, often in pouring rain, for many hours. A cold, a party, a thousand excuses can be made by the parent having custody, usually the wife, for refusing access, and invariably at the expense of the welfare of the children, so often used as weapons by the parents, deliberately to hurt each other. The law cannot legislate for human conduct in such matters.

Apart from the need for reconciliation and forgiveness with everyone, as my Christian duty, I cannot, with my incurable illness, afford to have any resentment or anger. Resentments are a killer for the alcoholic, for it can lead to a drink, and to drink is to die.

Chapter XXVI

THE WIDER FAMILY

In addition to a large immediate family, I have a wide circle of relatives. Cousins Peter-John, Bobby and Sandy come particularly to mind. Their father Dr J.A. Robson set up practice in Wembley, near to the stadium, just before the War. In 1938, aged eight, I spent a holiday with them. They had only just moved and took the opportunity of my visit to see the prominent London landmarks. It was a thrilling experience for me to visit the capital. I saw Buckingham Palace and the Tower for the first time, and visited the Victoria and Albert Museum. Uncle John and Auntie Edith had a combined television radiogramme, and radio (nearly sixty years ago). I saw part of the England v Australia Test Match at the Oval when Len Hutton scored his record 364 runs.

In subsequent years I spent holidays with them in Weymouth. Peter-John and I were keen tennis players and P-J, as he was known, later became Captain of his Oxford College, at this and another two sports, namely squash and hockey.

He was a solicitor and when he died tragically in a hayfield, bereft of the necessary medication for his asthma, Dorset lost a Deputy Lieutenant of the County, a Colonel of his TA Regiment and Commandant of the Dorset Army Cadet Corps from 1973 until 1980. Peter-John was awarded the TD. Educated at Sherborne and Lincoln College, Oxford, he was Secretary of Dorset Hockey Association and played regularly for the county, and Anglo-Scots. He narrowly missed selection for Scotland's national team. I attended his funeral. At the subsequent Memorial Service there were 800 present. The tribute was paid by his brother Bobby, later Air Vice-Marshal R.M. (Bobby) Robson OBE.

Bobby's entry in Who's Who is as follows:

ROBSON, Air Vice Marshal Robert Michael, OBE 1971; sheep farmer; b 22 April 1935; s of Dr John Alexander and Edith Robson; m 1959, Brenda Margaret (née Croysdill); one s two d. Educ: Sherborne; RMA Sandhurst. Commissioned 1955; RAF Regt, 1958; Navigator Training, 1959; Strike Squadrons, 1965; Sqdn Cmdr, RAF Coll; 1968; Defence Adviser to British High Comr, Sri Lanka, 1972, Nat. Defence Coll., 1973; CO 27 Sqdn, 1974-75; MoD staff duties, 1978; CO RAF Gatow, 1978-80; ADC to the Queen, 1979-80; RCDS 1981; Dir of Initial Officer Training, RAF Coll., 1982-84; Director of Public Relations (Royal Air Force), 1984-87; Hd, RAF Study of Officers' Terms of Service, 1987; retired. Chairman: Aerotech Alloys Ltd, 1990-; British Encryption Technology Ltd, 1993- (Dir, 1991-). Chm., Prince's Trust, Lincs. 1993-. FIMgt (FBIM 1980). Recreations: fly fishing, photography. Club: Royal Air Force.

Promoted Air Vice-Marshal in January 1987 he was head of a team reporting on Officers' Terms of Service. It was a highly controversial report which received considerable national publicity. After publication he resigned, to keep faith with the expectations of the officers whom he felt were not being supported by the Air Force Board.

Following retirement he joined the Boards of a number of companies as a non-executive director.

Another relative on my mother's side was Lawrence Turner, one-time leader of the Hallé Orchestra. While I was at Shrewsbury School, the company visited the town for a concert. Shortly before, a few of my friends and I had been discussing the topic of well-known relatives. I said modestly that I only had one, the said Lawrence Turner. A close friend in my House and year, George Wilby, said, 'He's my uncle.' A small world! We visited him after the concert and were rewarded with £5 each, a bonanza for the School tuck-shop.

Uncle Bill was a doctor who served as a missionary in China and married my father's youngest sister Margaret. Dr Eric Isambard Brunel Hawes, to give him his full name and title, was a descendant of Isambard Kindom Brunel (1806-59), engineer and Fellow of the Royal Society.

Resident Engineer of the Thames tunnel at nineteen, he was appointed engineer of the newly formed Great Western Railway and designed and constructed the first line to Bristol, with all the bridges and tunnels. To extend the GWR 'a bit further' he built the first steamship for regular trans-Atlantic travel, the *Great Western*, and the *Great Britain*, the first ocean screw-steamer. These were followed by the *Great Eastern*, until then the largest vessel ever built. The last and greatest of his bridges was the Royal Albert over the Tamar at Saltash, Cornwall.

Isambard Kingdom Brunel was the son of Sir Marc Isambard. Elected as a member of the Royal Society in 1814, he was involved in the building of Chatham dockyard and Woolwich Arsenal. Financial mismanagement and a fire at his Battersea sawmill led to imprisonment in 1821, but he was released by a grant from the Government of £5,000. Undoubtedly his greatest work was the construction of the Thames Tunnel. After many trials and tribulations it was completed after eighteen years in 1843 but the stress and anxiety led to his death in 1849.

When I spent four and a half months at Guildford before my Solicitors Finals, many weekends were spent with Uncle Bill, Auntie Margaret and their three children at Ewhurst Green nr. Cranleigh. Uncle Bill was a dear, kindly, old-fashioned country doctor, and on Sundays we would set off with him on his rounds, returning for lunch at about 3 p.m. He had many distinguished patients including Lord Macmillan, a Scottish Law Lord and godson to one of Uncle Bill's sons. In the evening we watched the Sunday TV play on the BBC, which usually involved Uncle bundling me into the car and overtaking the bus on the narrow country lane as quickly as possible, so that he could deposit me at the next bus stop ahead and return home. I will always look back on those days as important and happy refreshment in my demanding studies.

During my time in Guildford, King George VI died on 6 February 1952. On the day of his funeral, I took an early train to London and stood halfway along the Mall. It was a solemn procession which left a lasting impression on me. The Queen Mother, the Queen and Princess Margaret were in one carriage, wearing long veils but with their faces visible.

The Duke of Edinburgh, the Dukes of Windsor, Gloucester and youthful Kent walked in line abreast. The face of the Duke of Windsor was etched in grief and I wondered about the singular burden he must be carrying. The procession seemed endless as Kings and Queens, Heads of State, and military groups preceeded the gun carriage bearing the coffin pulled by a Royal Navy party, with muffled drums and reversed rifles, on a sombre, dull day which seemed to be in sympathy with the occasion. Emperor Haile Selassie of Abyssinia was an impressive figure.

Another of my well-known relatives by marriage was the late Sir Arthur Pickup who was born in Burnley and married my great-aunt Florence. I remember reading an article about him in my teenage years in the *Picture Post* Magazine. Starting work as an errand boy in the Co-operative Wholesale Society he later became its President. He was also a director of the Manchester Ship Canal Company and the Co-operative Wholesale Society.

Uncle Arthur died in 1960. His home in the Wirral was characteristically called Burn Lea, a practice followed in later years by other members of the family.

I remember visiting our farm with him on one occasion. Father introduced our farm manager David Scott who, quite out of character, was obviously shy and embarrassed as they shook hands. 'I've never met a Sir before,' he said. He need not have been concerned. Uncle Arthur was a quiet, friendly, family man who quickly put him at his ease. He once told me of the time he was travelling by train from London to Manchester. In the same compartment were two gentlemen who talked in loud cultured tones and were clearly trying to impress the other passengers. Eventually they began to speak about their time at Oxford University and turning to Uncle Arthur one said, 'Have you been through Oxford or Cambridge?'

'Yes,' said Uncle Arthur, and saw their faces grow more amenable, until he added, 'through Oxford actually – in a fast car.'

Chapter XXVII

WONDERFUL NORWAY

I am sure a holiday in Norway in good weather is one on which it would be difficult to improve. I enjoyed three such times in this beautiful country. They all involved the car ferry to Bergen, a pleasant enough trip across the North Sea. Bergen has a high annual average rainfall and for me was always just an overnight stay. The fish market on the quay provides live species of every kind, in tanks, waiting for the buyer to choose.

Each holiday was in three of the main fjords. These are the Nordfjord, Sognefjorden and the Hardangerfjord.

In 1984 Marjorie and I enjoyed unbroken sunshine for fourteen days and one of the reasons for not returning was the thought that the weather could not be repeated. In midsummer the sun hardly sets and on that trip was shining on the upper mountain peaks at 11 p.m. Trips by boat along the fjords are a must. The scale of the mountains is considerable – every time on returning to England, we passed the Lakeland mountains which seemed tiny by comparison.

Setting out with no specific plans from Loen on the Nordfjord in 1973, Rosalie, John, Catherine and I drove along a steep mountain road, with snow piled above the height of the car on either side. We did not know then, but the road is opened every year on the first of June, and announced on Norwegian radio. For mile after mile we travelled through the cleared path until we came to a pull-in where I stopped. We had unexpectedly come to the view which is shown more than in any other publicity material of the country, Geiranger, a lovely village nestling at the foot of the mountain. A large vessel looked like a toy at anchor far below.

Ulvik is my favourite place in the country. Descending on a long winding road down the mountainside, to the Hardangerfjord, the visitor finds this delightful village beside the fjord. Cow bells tinkle in the early morning, a seaplane plies for trade, the ferry bustles backwards and forwards to Brimnes on the other side of the fjord. Bicycles can be hired for trips along the road beside the fjord. It is peaceful and the water is usually as smooth as glass.

The owner of the Ulvik Hotel, who was later tragically killed in a cycling accident, would tell visitors during his evening slide shows of the days of the War. German vessels of war sailed up the fjord, with guns blazing, and many of the brave young men of the village died in a desperate bid to defend their homes. Forced labour produced hydro-electric stations and tunnelling. One of these structures outside the village was unfinished and we walked underneath the curved roof. When we had gone a little way, all four of us stopped together, feeling frightened, and hurried out. We all confessed to a sense of evil and terror. Here was something we each experienced which could not be explained and I wondered if it was connected with some wartime atrocity. An uneasy experience.

The Germans provide excellent tourist business, but I have to say my experiences abroad are not inconsistent with stories of towels on deckchairs and aggressive behaviour. The Norwegians do not warm to them naturally, largely because of the War and their temperament, but appreciate their tourist potential. In Switzerland, in 1946, my father, two elder sisters and I were spat on by a group of German hikers as we climbed near Lake Lugano. That was perhaps explained by its proximity to the end of the War the previous year.

At the Ulvik hotel, John and Catherine stood at the entrance to the dining room, anxious to eat. As the door opened, Germans, men and women, pushed them aside, and knocked them to the floor, in the needless rush to get to the tables which were weighed down with food.

In 1984 Marjorie and I were sitting with friends we had met, enjoying a shared table at dinner, when the room was invaded by a noisy group of some forty German tourists who proceeded to conduct their activities with a loud, coarse speech by a man in Tryolean costume. A lady nearby took five large portions of a limited salmon dish and placed all but one on the tablecloth, consuming each portion in turn.

I do not feel at ease with those I have met on holiday. I do not of course wish to appear anti-German for I must remember that my ancestry may well lie there. I speak only of my own experience.

At the Alexandra Hotel in Loen, John and I counted 152 different dishes on the Smorgasbord, or Norwegian cold table. There is no more appetizing sight than a well-prepared Smorgasbord. At Loen too, I enjoyed an early-morning stroll down the lawn to the water and saw the daily seaplane from Bergen fly in to land on the water, and ski to the landing stage. The evening Viking entertainment was fun, with exhilarating music and dancing, a reminder of ancient customs.

Balestrand offers a lovely hotel, reached by ferry. Travel-hungry Americans would arrive by coach, devour dinner and leave before we came down for breakfast the following morning. I heard one elderly gentleman enquire of his wife if they were in Sweden or Norway. The idea of wealthy Americans 'doing Europe' in three or four days is not always correct. My sister who lives in the States speaks of many couples who have worked hard all their lives and saved hard to enable them to make the crossing to Europe for their holiday of a lifetime.

An attractive feature for the tourist are the Pensjonats, government-controlled guest houses, where a good standard and reasonable charges are guaranteed. A journey to the land of the midnight sun was difficult to fit in, but to stand and watch when the sun does not dip below the horizon at midnight must be a sight to remember.

It is an expensive holiday. The Norwegians enjoy one of the highest standards of living and a large number of their three million inhabitants can speak English. A good way to see more of ordinary everyday life is to take one of the milk boats which sail round the villages and hamlets of the fjords. The whole feeling is one of cleanliness, good food, warm hospitality and a clean, invigorating climate.

We visited Voss, rebuilt after German destruction, apart from the historic church which wonderfully survived. A leaflet in the church states: 'We are still filled with wonder that our old church escaped the bombs of the last war, which laid most of the town in ruins, and we are greatly thankful that the house of God has recovered the glory of its past.' A ski lift took us up the mountainside for an unforgettable view. I strongly recommend a Norwegian holiday.

Chapter XXVIII

MORECAMBE: GATEWAY TO THE LAKES

A part from my first four years in Burnley, and two spells of two years each in Storth, I have lived all my life in Morecambe and Heysham. It lies in Morecambe Bay, in north Lancashire, close to the Cumbrian border. With a population in excess of 50,000, it merged with Lancaster on local government reorganisation in 1974, to form the Lancaster City Council. With the port and Heysham harbour it was a municipal borough, with the appropriate motto for a holiday resort and summer playground of industrial North of England: 'Beauty surrounds, health abounds'.

The name is recent, being first used in the eighteenth century, owing to an identification with Ptolemy's Morekambe. In the opinion of many residents, it has never established an identity of its own. At times it appears to try and be a rival to Blackpool, a hopeless task. My own view is that it has not played to its strengths in recent years. Before and after the Second World War, crowds flocked there, many on the annual Wakes week when industrial towns virtually closed down for the week. The hotels and boarding houses were numbered in hundreds.

There was a change from the caricatured severe landlady, with strict meal times, eviction of her guests after breakfast and fairly basic facilities, to the modern en-suite facilities, with every comfort and attraction, such as TV and bars. The numbers have dropped dramatically, leaving problems of DHSS flats in profusion and a general failure to provide the sort of family entertainment demanded today, and found, often at a similar or lower cost, on foreign shores. In my youth we had six cinemas, two piers, and seven live shows, including the Winter Gardens, where a national star appeared weekly. I remember George Formby, Max Miller, Hutch, Wee Georgie Wood, Joseph Locke and many others.

Morecambe's strength lies in its position; only forty minutes in the car takes the holidaymaker to Windermere and the Lake District. The Yorkshire Dales are within easy reach, with Blackpool, its shows and countless attractions only twenty-nine miles away. The promenade offers an ever-changing and unsurpassed view of the hills and mountains.

Those who prefer a quieter place than Blackpool, with unspoilt country in every direction, and the places I have mentioned within close proximity, return time and time again. My former next-door neighbour Bill, who is my age, and has lived in the town all his life, runs a lovely guest house with his wife Marjorie, where the clientele return, year after year. Bill incidentally is a 'sand-grown 'un', denoting that he was born in the town. There are always new plans, which rarely come to fruition, and this is not helped by the conflicting interests of the historic City of Lancaster. A package tour combining both seems excellent in theory, but less than perfect in practice. For me, the glorious sunsets and natural beauty hold me, and, having lived on the seafront in various properties for twenty-eight of my sixty-eight years, I never wish to leave it. Sister Jeanne, who lives in Ohio in the USA, recently told me of visiting a place in Florida famous for its sunsets. She giggled and when asked the reason, informed her friends in a kindly way that they did not compare with those in Morecambe.

The bay can be treacherous and the Queen's Guide, Cedric Robinson, alone is authorized to conduct cross-bay walks. Some years ago the Duke of Edinburgh crossed with horse and carriage from Arnside to Grange-over-Sands during one of his regular stays at Holker Hall for the annual horse trials.

When I was in my teens I kept a fishing line a few hundred yards from the shore, which entailed attendance after each tide to secure the catch and bait the hooks. One day my brother Stuart and Father came with me. On the return journey my legs suddenly 'went' from under me; I found myself knee deep in sand – quicksands. I pulled myself clear, to find Father had grabbed my younger brother and threw him to me. I was screaming in terror when I saw Father up to his waist and still sinking. I lay flat and spread myself, inched slowly towards him and grabbed his hand. By this time the quicksands were up to his chest and after what seemed an eternity, I pulled him, inch by inch, from the sand, both of us ashen-faced and trembling. The quicksands change position constantly and I was not surprised by Father's words to us, 'I don't have to tell you, you never walk out here again.' And we have never done so. Many are the lives which have been lost in various parts of the bay, including horse-drawn carriages, which crossed in earlier times.

The mountains remind me so much of Galilee in Israel and as I gaze at the view I often say to myself a verse (which I repeat elsewhere) of a well-known hymn:

O Sabbath rest by Galilee!
O calm of hills above,
Where Jesus knelt to share with Thee
The silence of eternity,
Interpreted by love!

I have been blessed with four sisters and a brother. We grew up as a close-knit group, who happily spent our childhood days with each other and with many friends who lived in the same street. I have a host of happy memories of those early formative years. Our home for many years was surrounded by sandhills, where excavations had taken place in earlier days and which were capable of giving so much fun and adventure.

Open fields provided football and cricket pitches. There were ponds where tadpoles abounded, a nearby park for paddling, sailing boats and ice skating in winter. We lived near the seafront and the flat, smooth surface of the promenade provided long stretches for roller skating. One of the best swimming stadia in the country was ours to enjoy and all the facilities of a popular holiday resort.

On Saturday afternoons in the summer it was our custom to walk as a family to the West End Pier for the open-air variety concerts held throughout the season. Father was involved in the ownership and when I fished from the end I was authorized to say to the attendant, 'I am Mr Knape's son,' with resulting free admission. Nepotism! If the tide had ebbed, children drew pictures in the sand and visitors to the pier would thrown coins down to them. I often sympathize with the lack of playing facilities for children today such as those I was privileged to enjoy.

During the War, Morecambe was a huge initial training centre for the Royal Air Force. My father was posted there specially, after serving elsewhere at various stations, to oversee the huge task of requisitioning hotels and boarding houses to billet airmen and airwomen. I still have in my possession a handwritten letter from him whilst stationed at RAF Loughborough. This is something of a collector's item as although Father always wrote to us every week when we were away at school, he never sent one in his own hand. This was because of pressure of work and also because we would not have been able to read them. His brain was always ahead of his hand. His letters were eagerly awaited and full of news.

On one occasion his secretary, Miss Dorothy Davies, together with a partner in the firm, Charles Altham, remonstrated mildly with him about his signature on a bank cheque. In deference he signed another, only to find the bank contacting him to see if it was genuine, as they could read his signature. I must not pursue this point too closely. Recently I received a reply to a letter, addressed to Mr J. Thorpe, a name regularly given to my father on letters and receipts.

The letter from Loughborough read:

My dear Children,
      Well here is Daddy writing a letter to you all. I hope you all read
it. First I hope you are all looking after Mummy and being very

good. I know, as you did promise me, you will be doing so.

Well now about the exams. Peggy & John – how has this gone? I should like to know. Mummy has told me some of them.

Daddy has been doing drill again most of this week and next week at this time I should have been posted to the work I am going to have to do. I'm afraid it won't be near home – at first at all events.

It is Church Parade here tomorrow and Daddy is going to read the lessons.

I am Station Orderly Officer this weekend but another Officer is going to relieve me tomorrow morning for an hour so that I can go on the Church Parade.

I hope John has had his hair cut and has taken Stuart to have his done.

The weather here to-day is very cold. It hailed this morning when we were on Parade and it was not very nice.

Daddy was shooting on Wednesday with a Service Rifle. I had to shoot 25 rounds and do you know I didn't hit the target once.

Well dears I think this all – it is a long time since I heard from you. I take it you are doing your elocution, changing your gym slips, slippers on when you come in after tea and keeping the nursery and your boxes tidy.

All a kiss each from Daddy
Your Loving Father
xxxxxx

The well-known Midland Hotel became the RAF hospital with, for the benefit of the superstitious, the Operating Theatre numbered 13. On Christmas Day one year, Father, in Flight Lieutenant's uniform, took us on a tour of two wards, now the dining room, bar and function rooms. One for men and one for women, they were two huge TB wards, with the windows wide open to the strong winds from the sea.

My life was much influenced by the RAF. They had a football team which was in my father's sphere of duties, with an almost international make-up at times. Blackpool was an ever bigger ITC, and the matches between Morecambe and Blackpool contained such stars as Stanley Mortensen of England fame, who scored a hat-trick at Wembley in the 1953 'Matthews' Cup Final. We teased the drill sergeants as they trained their squads on the promenade. 'A waste of shoe leather' we would shout, racing away on our roller skates, often with the NCOs in hot pursuit. The service had a professionally produced magazine.

Father was the Senior Admin Officer, but plainly did much of the work of the Adjutant and the successive golf-playing Commanding

Officers. Father was a wonderful letter-writer, but one day he was puzzled and asked for my schoolboy advice. 'You are a damned good letter-writer,' had said his CO. 'But you *will* split your infinitives.'

'Yes, Sir,' said Father, without a clue about this point of grammar.

I felt quite honoured to be asked to explain the matter to Father.

It may well be the experience of that occasion which makes me immediately aware of a similar mistake, be it on TV, radio or in normal conversation. Actually, I think Father could often obtain extra emphasis in the sentence by splitting the infinitive.

One particular memory I have is of a concert organized in the Winter Gardens for the RAF Benevolent Fund, which raised the sum of £2,000, a splendid figure for those days. The concert was largely his baby, in conjunction with Mr W. Henry Smirk, a part owner with Alderman J.W. Carleton, an outstanding public figure in the town, of the Winter Gardens. The theatre was said to be second only in size to the Glasgow Empire, and the cast list read like a Who's Who of Showbiz. One final touch was needed. Winston Churchill's daughter, Sarah, stationed in the town at the time, was asked to come on stage in the finale and recite an appropriate poem. She refused. Henry Smirk was used to negotiating with all the great artistes of the day and when Father proffered his help, told him he was wasting his time. Father put his hand on her shoulder and said, 'Your father would be proud of you.' She agreed to appear.

Worm's Eye View was a best-selling book of this time, based on the experiences of the author while stationed in Morecambe for his initial training.

The pier was sold to my brother after my mother's death, but was destroyed in the great storm of November 1977. A strong, fine structure, in good repair, and having withstood the elements for many years, it was reduced to a tangled mass of steel and timber – a reminder of the terrifying power of nature. I have a photograph from the *Sunday People* for 13 November 1977, showing my windswept brother standing in front of the correctly described 'Blitzed remains of Morecambe's West End Pier'.

The first grandchild to be born to my parents was Ian, the son of my sister Peggy. Ian is now a partner in the family practice and works at the Carnforth office. When Peggy went into hospital for the birth, her husband, Norman, stayed with us. In the early hours of the morning I awoke with an overwhelming sense of physical relief, the sort a man would imagine a woman experiencing after giving birth. A strong conviction came over me and getting out of bed I went to the door, put my hand on the handle, intending to open it and shout, 'Peggy's had a baby boy.' I suddenly realized what I was doing and refrained from waking everybody. When I came down to breakfast a smiling Norman said, 'Peggy's had a baby boy.' The time of birth and that of my venture to the bedroom door were the same. A case of telepathy?

My story of Morecambe would not be complete without mentioning Mrs Maud Bourne, a lady of small stature but great business acumen, who played a major part in the development of the town in the pre-war years. In the early 1930s she visited Morecambe from her home in Blackpool along with her daughter Nora who now lives in retirement. Mrs Bourne spotted a plot of land ripe for development on the promenade. The result was that she built and ran the Broadway Hotel which was opened in 1936. A leader in its field, it had a range of remedial baths, wonderful swimming pool and luxurious Palm Court. Lupino Lane was prevented from opening it due to the death of his father.

The Headway, Empress, Mayfair and St Winifred's mirrored her huge Blackpool seafront hotel development south of the Pleasure Beach. In 1943 Mrs Bourne, known as the Hotel Queen of the North, sold the Broadway to Thwaites Brewery for £175,000 and returned to Blackpool where she had built about sixty-five hotels. In the mid-1950s the Broadway appeared in the *Guinness Book of Records* as the largest free house in the country. Mrs Bourne died in 1980 aged ninety-nine. She began life with just £18, selling clothes to miners families in Yorkshire.

I met her often over the years and found her a charming and kindly lady. She had that wonderful gift possessed by few – the ability to look at a complicated problem and see through the detail to the heart of the matter. Every project and enterprise she undertook seemed to prosper. She relied much on my father's advice. On one occasion she telephoned him to say she had been invited to appear on the very popular nationwide BBC evening programme *Tonight* to be interviewed by Cliff Michelmore. A car was to be sent to convey her to the studio in Manchester. When she asked my father if she should go, he told her without hesitation to do so. It was a fascinating interview which I still remember in some detail.

In 1993 I wrote to our local newspaper *The Visitor*, which was printed as follows:

Reliving life in Morecambe

I CONGRATULATE you on the note of optimism sounded on the front page of your issue last week.

On the previous Saturday, I walked on the promenade from Seaborn Road to Sandylands Promenade, pushing my grandson in his pram.

It was a fine but rather cold morning, with only a light breeze and ideal for walking. Only about 20 to 30 people passed us, although it was late in the morning.

I have lived in Bare for all but eight of my 64 years, having arrived with my family in 1934, as a boy of four.

As I walked, a host of memories came to mind as I passed each stretch from one road to another. People, events, redevelopment and all manner of things added up to an experience of almost reliving much of my life.

I gazed out too on Lakeland mountains where Wordsworth felt the power of an unseen and eternal presence, and saw the lovely and ever-changing Bay.

I thought of the delightful Happy Mount Park where I now spend as much time as in my childhood, and the golf course where I have spent many happy hours, situated in a green belt area and a fine tourist attraction.

When playing yesterday with friends, one pointed out to me the many small white patches on the course, regurgitated materials from the Oystercatcher, such a happy choice for your masthead.

We all have our trials and worries in life but I feel that those who live in Morecambe should above all have on their lips, as I did during my walk, the word – gratitude.

I wish you well in your mission.

John Knape

During the summer of 1997 I walked from my home in Bare to the Stone Jetty where I fished as a boy. It has of course been completely transformed. It would be difficult to express in words my joy and pleasure on so many gloriously sunny days in walking along the promenade (albeit with the then current works) and sitting with a coffee outside the café at the end of the Jetty. Many day visitors questioned the idea of going abroad for their holidays 'when we've got all this'. There were countless opportunities to talk and enjoy the company. I mention one such encounter.

A smartly dressed gentleman with furled umbrella came to my table which was otherwise unoccupied. He carried a copy of *The Times*. When I spoke with him he said that most of his life had been spent in Africa, this was his first visit to Morecambe, but he climbed regularly in the Lake District. When I enquired about his home location, he said 'Burnley'. I had expected a prosperous place in the South. I explained that I was born in Burnley, and when he asked where I lived there, I demurred saying he would not know, but that it was a road off Manchester Road, called Clevelands Road, and an end-terrace. He asked for the number, and when I said number Sixty-Four, replied that he was to visit a friend in Clevelands Road the following day.

'Number Forty' I think was his reply. It was certainly an even number – about halfway down on the same side as the end-terrace where I was born!

I remember Charles Altham, a partner in the family practice and to whom I refer elsewhere, a former Captain of Morecambe Golf Club and Director for many years, telling me year after year following the visit of the Mayor to the Club's Annual Dinner of yet another disappointment when the matter of security of tenure was raised. There is no doubt in my mind that many interests were vested in those precious green acres of the Club.

As Hon. Solicitor I suggested to the Board in 1979 that I be given an opportunity to negotiate. With little enthusiasm or optimism, it was given. In a sentence, I walked out of the office of the Town Clerk of Lancaster a few days later with the promise of a recommendation of a 99-year lease. The Council confirmed it and it has since been extended. It was perhaps the best service I ever gave to the town and it was done by simply explaining the obvious benefits for the members, visitors and the town in general of having a first-class seaside golf course. No catches, no hidden factors – just plain, straight, sensible talking.

As a pure holiday resort, Morecambe will never see the old times. Everyone is aware of the halcyon years before the Second World War and afterwards when every holiday resort in the country knew good days. I have a teenage memory of a queue three or four deep stretching on the pavement from Happy Mount Park gates to Teal Bay in order to gain entrance during the Illuminations.

Foreign holidays of course brought about the change and decline. It is a fact and there is no point in bewailing that and its permanence.

For natural resources, our bay, the proximity to and views of Lakeland, our ease of access to the Yorkshire Dales, and in every direction from Morecambe are unsurpassed. Morecambe too is ideal for the fifty- and sixty-year-olds who are an ever-increasing and affluent segment of the population, and who for the large part enjoy peace and quiet, a stroll along the promenade, car trips to the Lakes, Yorkshire Dales and shows in Preston and Blackpool. Morecambe also has a good deal to offer a young family in the way of day trips during times of good weather, and the value to the town should not be underestimated.

In the late Alderman R.C. Penhale OBE JP who was a fellow solicitor with my father and qualified in the same year, and was proposed by my father for his well-deserved honour, we had a man of great integrity, a virtue so badly needed, who joined the Council in spite of a tremendous burden of other major responsibilities, simply because he was so greatly concerned about self-interest and lack of disinterested service on the part of many Councillors. He told me so.

Chairman of the Finance Committee (our local Chancellor of the Exchequer), a member of the Connexional Stationing Committee of the

Methodist Conference where only very wise, experienced, and highly thought of appointees were asked to deal with highly sensitive ministerial placings), Chairman of the Musical Festival, a highly successful Mayor, founder of the Abbeyfield Society in Morecambe, and so many other greater and lesser things, he sought only to serve the town and negate so far as it lay in his power to do so, the self-interest and lack of real ability and concern which he had seen in the Council for so long.

Another Councillor I greatly admired was Dr R.B. Wilson. He had his critics, but undertook the chairmanship of the Committee responsible for planning and executing the new sewerage scheme so desperately needed after the War. It could have been carried out at a fraction of the cost in the 1930s. There was little prestige or honour in the task but it was essential to the well-being and health of the population.

It is perhaps invidious to pick out individuals, but there were several men motivated only by a desire to serve the best interests of the town, free from petty thinking and the scoring of party points for whom the old Borough of Morecambe & Heysham should be grateful.

My friends of a younger generation who are involved at a high level in public and private life today speak not just of falling standards, but in many cases of an almost complete absence of integrity, and the pursuance of personal interest.

The attractions of the historic City of Lancaster are many. It was, in my view, a dying city until it received a blood transfusion in the establishment of the University. How hard Blackpool tried to secure it, and how they must envy us!

I am very conscious of the Castle. For many years efforts have been made to secure possession and change from prison use. It would be a tremendous attraction for the whole area, going back to the very roots of our history and monarchy, but clearly political and economic decisions make it unlikely that we shall secure it for tourism and other purposes in the immediate future.

And so I come to the central requirement for the future of the area. The word I use is 'partnership'. I lay at the door of all the political parties the charge of self-interest and party considerations. I refuse to believe that without surrendering important principles, the Councillors of the city and their chief officers cannot get together and work out together a blueprint for a bright, prosperous and happy future, combining *all* our assets. Why do city and seaside have to be blinkered about each other?

I make one suggestion. Is it not possible for a body, a working party to be set up, representative of all the main interests, comprising men and women of ability who know the area and are willing to give of time, money and talent, and produce within a reasonable period, say eighteen months, proposals to lay before the Council and electorate for debate and discussion? Unless everyone tries to suppress their own interests to the common good, it will fail. It is too much to hope that with all we have been given in natural and developed assets we cannot make full and proper use of them?

Certainly one of the outstanding new features in the town are the Coastal Works. They provide a real and effective defence and are well advanced. A letter to me from the Lancaster City Council dated 10 November 1995 reads:

MORECAMBE COASTAL WORKS – IMPROVED PROTECTION

In response to your letter of the 20th October 1993 concerning the above, I write to provide information on coastal protection matters which may be of use to you in lessening the insurance burden to your property by way of the following notes.

i) In recent times Morecambe has suffered severe flooding by a combination of heavy rainfall and stormy sea states. Notably in 1977 and 1983 approximately 2,000 properties were affected in mainly the Bare and West End areas of town.

(ii) After the 1977 event the City Council undertook research work, through Consultants, to investigate a cost effective solution in providing greater protection for the town. The solution adopted was to build a wave return wall along the highway edge of the promenade in the critical areas of town. The effectiveness of this solution was to some extent impaired by planning constraints on height, and of course its design could only address the knowledge and problems known at that time in that it was thought that the return frequency of storms of that severity was of 1 in 100 years and the height limitations made it about 75% effective. A phased programme of implementation commenced in 1980, opposite Happy Mount Park and by 1983 the section through to Thornton Road was completed, but because the work was incomplete and for the reasons mentioned above the Bare area of Morecambe still suffered inundation.

(iii) After the 1983 event it was decided to look again at the solution being implemented. Up to that time the Council had concentrated its efforts on the wave reflection wall

207

programme, with little or no preventative maintenance being done to the primary wall. The conclusions of this review were:

a)   to continue with the wave reflection wall programme;

b)   to commission a structural survey of the existing defences; and

c)   to commission a coastal study with a view to understanding more fully the forces at work in the Bay.

iv)   As a result of these investigations, Morecambe Coastal Works were developed into the package of measures presently being implemented. The extent of these works was modified as a result of the 1990 storm and now encompasses the coastal strip from Teal Bay in the north to Church Point in Heysham Village.

v)   Of the 1990 event it should be noted that on both the 26th and 27th February the storm severity was equal to the two previous events mentioned above and yet the Bare area of town in particular did not suffer anything like the problems previously encountered.

By way of notes, the above I trust provides much of the type of information you seek, but if you or your insurers require additional information please contact my colleague, Mr Eckersley, again.

Yours faithfully,

A. Wrigley
Chief Engineer

The Morecambe Bay Strategy Working Group which hopes to publish a draft strategy by June 1995 would play an important part, with its proposed blueprint taking Bay affairs well into the next century. They will be dealing with pollution, wildlife, the area's heritage and natural beauty and the role of industry, development and transport.

I would be glad to serve. We should enter on such a course with gratitude, zeal and joy in our hearts. This was written in 1995.

A few days ago I was privileged to call at the Tourism Office situated in the old LMS station on the promenade. I use the word 'privileged' advisedly, and confess to amazement at the sight of so much activity in the area, affecting every aspect of life – the environment, fishing, tourism, the RSPB, leisure activities, and many other aspects of life in and around the Bay.

As I write, I have before me and commend to all who care about or are interested in Morecambe Bay, a great deal of literature and reading matter:

Notes on Tourism in Morecambe

1. <u>Statistics from summary report of North West Coastal Resorts Initiative, 1995</u>
   – Total visitor nights in resort   =   2,496,000
   – Total day visits to Morecambe   =   2,311,920
      (+ business and conference trips)
   – Total visitor expenditure in Morecambe   = £104,855,280
   – Direct and indirect jobs resulting from
      tourism in Morecambe   =   5,827

2. <u>Statistics from Planning Service/Engineers</u>
   – total public and private sector investment
      in Morecambe Centre to date (80%
      private sector)   =   £29,500,000
   – Seven phases of coastal defence works   =   £20,000,000
      (=£4.1 million lottery bid?)

3. <u>Morecambe Tourism Service</u>
   Service Head – David Christley
   Staff: Trevor White, Jim Trotman, Jan Lyons, Jane Silvester, Mary Lucas, Barbara Burton (TIC Manager) and Vernon Hallam (Promenade Supervisor).
   The service objectives are to:
   a) Regenerate and sustain the economy of Morecambe by bringing in investment and increasing sustainable employment opportunities.
   b) Promote and market the resort as a principle destination for staying and day trip visitors.
   c) Develop and maintain tourist facilities and improve the resort's physical environment and attractions (Promenade and Foreshore Management plus Happy Mount Park).
   d) Improve the quality of visitor experience through the creation of a resort reflecting quality, diversity and viability (involvement in the resort's regeneration).
   e) Ensure spin-off leisure benefits for local people through the range of leisure and entertainment facilities provided for local persons and tourists alike.

f) Provide an efficient and helpful Tourist Information Service for visitors and for local people.

g) Promote the resort as a conference venue and as a destination for other special interest groups capable of adding a value to the local economy.

'The Lancaster Perspective' is an excellent introduction to the City, Morecambe Bay and surrounding district.

A most attractive Morecambe Bay Diary of Events.

'The Platform' giving a list of events and particulars at the Music and Community Arts Centre. The centre is built round the old hall of the station, leading to the platforms.

A splendid colour brochure 'Morecambe' – showing places to go, things to do, and where to stay.

A letter from Morecambe Tourism which reads:

MORECAMBE –
TOURISM TRENDS AND REDEVELOPMENT

Thank you for your recent enquiry about the resort of Morecambe, which includes the harbour and village of Heysham.

Research work undertaken in 1995 indicates that we now get about 2,400,000 day visits plus about 300,000 staying visitors each year. Also, about 75,000 people stay with friends and relatives. In total, this translates to about 2,300,000 bed nights in the resort each year.

Many of the improvements which have taken place over the past decade resulted from the 1987 tourism survey and the subsequent Regeneration of a Resort document. Also, the floods, most recently in 1990, prompted progress on the coastal defence works. Now about £20 million is being spent on the coastal defence works and Phase IV, the harbour area including the Stone Jetty, opened to the public in June 1995. Phase V, the central promenade will be completed in 1998.

I enclose information on the resort and central area regeneration. By the end of this decade the coastal works will have restored the beaches and North West Water assure us of good quality bathing water. Soon we hope to obtain the Blue Flags.

In preparation for central area redevelopment, 1991 and 1992 saw the demolition of the old Tourist Information Bureau, the old Marineland buildings and the burnt-out pier. Now the new Tourist Information Centre is established in the former station buildings, the Marineland site has been incorporated into the award-winning

Stone Jetty and work is underway on the central promenade area.

As an indicator of change, in 1973, the resort had almost 900 hotels, guest houses etc. but only 80 ensuite bathrooms. Now we have about 120 hotels etc. and about 700 ensuite bathrooms. Many businesses amalgamated and upgraded but some 450 smaller guest houses changed to flats, self-catering units or private residence over the past 20 years. Due to changing markets, about two thirds of our 16,000 bed spaces are now in the non-serviced sector i.e. flats, caravans etc. and 3,500 are in hotels and guest houses. The average length of stay is four to five days and as 80% of our visitors come by car, they normally spend two or three days here and in Lancaster plus taking trips to the Lake District and Yorkshire Dales.

Frontierland Western Theme Park has spent over £4 million on redevelopment over recent years and their new Polo Tower opened in 1995. The old Floral Hall has also been refurbished and turned into a night club and wine bar and the rest of the former Empire Buildings has been redeveloped as a leisure and retail complex. Morecambe Superbowl also opened at Easter 1995 and Apollo 4 Cinema in early 1996. A new yacht club has been built, as a result of the coastal works, and a new bingo club which is operated by Gala Bingo. The Market/Festival Hall opened in the summer of 1996 along with 'The Station', a £1.6 million family pub operated by Tetleys. A new entertainment venue called 'The Platform' opens at the end of 1997.

The pace and scale of redevelopment work has now increased greatly but it will take another two or three years until the regeneration work is complete. We have recognised that markets have changed and we are changing the resort to suit current needs and trends.

Please contact me again if I can be of further help.

Yours sincerely

Jim Trotman
Senior Tourism Officer

Far from my suggestion of forming a Committee we actually have in existence a Coastal Liaison Group, dealing largely with the foreshore; Morecambe Bay Conservation Group, formulating a strategy for the Bay; and a Standing Conference meeting twice a year, which supports the Strategy Group.

I had an opportunity in early February 1998, a few weeks after my visit, to express my thanks and congratulations to the City Council for all their efforts on behalf of the area. The Mayor, Councillor Hilda

Shuttleworth came to our Men's Fellowship at Bare Methodist Church and gave a most interesting, informative and well-received talk about her office. I had been asked to propose a vote of thanks, and this gave me the opportunity of expressing the sentiment which I have mentioned and urging all present to avail themselves of a visit to the Tourism Office and of the splendid literature which was freely available.

Famous Morecambe Personalities

Dame Thora Hird and the late Eric Morecambe are the finest people you could claim as former citizens of your town. Their lives are well documented and need no further words from me.

Dame Thora Hird

I wish the Royal Theatre was still there, Thora! And the Central and West End Piers. We enjoyed thirty-three years of uninterrupted repertory productions at the Royalty, a record for the country at the time. Many readers, I am sure, saw the quite outstanding *South Bank Show* on 13 November 1994, when Melvyn Bragg devoted a whole programme to her, most of it with interviews in the town, and Dame Thora exploring the site of her old home, now entirely redeveloped. The Central and West End piers had gone, her beloved Royalty Theatre removed for a shopping centre, the Winter Gardens closed and so much else.

My outstanding memory is of her sitting on a bench seat with Melvyn adjacent to the ancient St Peter's Church at Heysham, looking out on a typical, beautiful view of Morecambe Bay, the sort which prompted the title of my book. Gently dabbing her eyes, she reminisced and apologized for her tears, excusing herself by saying that it was such a lovely spot. Dear Thora, you shouldn't have apologized. It was entirely spontaneous, natural and delightful. I was reminded again of my words elsewhere in this book on the English stiff upper lip.

It was sad to remember the programme was shown only a few weeks after the death of her beloved husband 'Scottie'. They met when he played in the orchestra at the Winter Gardens. He supported her so lovingly over the years and at the end of the South Bank Show, which I have mentioned, Melvyn Bragg's voice recorded his death and Dame Thora's wishes that it be dedicated to his memory. I remember seeing her in *The Love Match* with Arthur Askey, in London, during my National Service days. Their daughter is Janette Scott, the film star. Scottie was eighty-eight years of age and they had been married for fifty-eight years.

Sunset over Morecambe Bay

Eric Morecambe

Enjoy his repeats. They broke the mould when Eric was born. His superb natural talent, with facial expression and 'gormless' look brought so much laughter for millions. I saw him driving down Lathom Avenue near his old school in Lancaster Road, which was also near the house of his birth. His serious mien reminded me of the other side of comedy. Being funny is a serious business, as Tony Hancock and others remind us.

An appeal organized by our local newspaper *The Visitor* for a permanent memorial has already reached a sum of approximately £8,000 (as at January 1998). The memorial is a sculpture of the famous comedian, to be erected on the seafront depicting him with binoculars and other evidence of his love of birdwatching. Models of birds were recently unveiled throughout the town, with the help of his widow Joan, who has taken a keen interest in the work to record his memory and fame in permanent form.

Eric bought an attractive house for his parents, Mr & Mrs Bartholemew, at Hest Bank, a lovely residential area just outside Morecambe.

Many local residents have written to our newspaper over recent months relating their personal knowledge and experiences of his days in the town. I replay the videos of the *Morecambe & Wise Shows* almost as regularly as the video of *Tom Finney – the Perfect Player*. A commemorative set of stamps was produced for Christmas 1994

Helen Worth (alias Gail Platt).

A reference to well-known Morecambe personalities would not be complete without a reference to Helen, better known as Gail Platt of *Coronation Street* fame. I have known Helen, her father and late mother for many years, and have her permission to say that I dealt with professional matters on their behalf for a long time.

Helen's mother was tragically killed in a road accident many years ago. A lovely lady, I have always felt that Helen obtained her 'bubbly, friendly, sunny disposition' from her mother. Helen's father, now at the grand old age of eighty lives in the resort. Helen has a schoolteacher brother called Neville.

I have in front of me as I write a paperweight, a gift from Helen which I greatly value. In the waiting room of Jobling and Knape there is another gift from Helen, a photograph of 'the Street' characters of years ago, including Ena Sharples and Albert Tatlock, with their autographs.

When I spoke to Helen recently I told her she looked younger than ever, to which she rejoined that she enjoyed 'a bit of flattery'.

A chat with Helen is a tonic, and she is a loyal, cheerful, and altogether delightful lady.

View from a Bay Window

I can sit in my lounge window and be lost in wonder, love and praise, filled with my memories of past and present for as long as I wish. In sixty-eight years I have lived at six different addresses in a short distance of half a mile on the seafront at the east end of Morecambe. Apart from two basements in which I lived during less happy times, I have enjoyed the same view.

Helen Worth – Gail Platt of Coronation Street.

215

Looking to the east, the sunrises over the years have been a glorious beginning to the day during the spring and summer months. Beneath the morning rays lies the golf course, a green belt area where I have spent so many happy hours.

Adjacent to the Golf Club I can see Happy Mount Park, a lovely area where I have, until recently, spent as much time in my later years as in my childhood, when I sailed my boat, ice-skated in winter, played tennis and bowls, listened to live shows and bands, leapt across the stepping stones in the Japanese Gardens, played pitch and putt, visited the autumn illuminations and travelled on the model railway, enjoyed the wonderful flower displays provided by the Parks Department and sat on the grass.

In recent times a distressing period involving a Mr Blobby Theme Park has caused heartache and unhappiness but as I write there are signs of restoration to its former glory and of its proper use by residents and visitors alike. An insensitive and commercially unsound council action has presented a parlous understanding of local needs.

My eye wanders across an ever-changing scene, a still or angry sea or the less attractive sandy bay to Hest Bank where I spend many happy hours with other visiting motorists strolling along the beach, watching the passing mainline trains, admiring the distant views, or enjoying a cup of tea at the attractive cafe. During the past year I have regularly counted 100 cars and more along the short stretch of parking area, but it never becomes congested.

The old Cinderella Home can be seen. This building was a Convalescent Home maintained by Bradford Council for children needing a holiday from that area. It has changed hands many times since then as a restaurant, leisure centre and with other uses, and it is sad that it does not seem to settle into a regular permanent use.

Warton Crag with its limestone quarry reminds me of Friday evening trips with the Church Youth Club by bus to Carnforth, the long walk to the Crag across open fields, and the climb to its summit, and engaging views over the bay and distant countryside, over Lancaster and towards Ingleborough, as well as Lakeland.

In years past Father and I grazed cattle on rented land on the Crag side, and spent many enjoyable evenings 'looking', i.e. inspecting the young two-year-old heifers growing steadily throughout the summer. I remember still with some puzzlement the testing of the soil which found a shortage of lime, notwithstanding an almost continual deposit of limestone dust from the quarry nearby brought by the prevailing north-westerly winds.

The eye wanders round to Arnside Knott, an area of outstanding natural beauty with glorious walks and views over the Sandside Estuary which counts over 130 varieties of birds in a year.

Over the years I have acted for many clients retiring to Morecambe or the surrounding area from far afield. When I asked them the reason which drew them to Morecambe they said without hesitation that it was the birdwatching. The bay itself and Leighton Moss (the latter a bird sanctuary) draw large numbers of 'twitchers'.

Grange-over-Sands immediately opposite my window is a favourite spot for retired people. Its very mild climate is one of the main attractions and with the added advantages of proximity to Lakeland. Sheltered from the prevailing winds, I have seldom encountered a windy day there. Sub-tropical plants grow in some profusion and a long flat promenade is dotted with useful facilities for residents and visitors alike. I have found that its only drawback is the gradient, and many people who retire there are often constrained to move to Morecambe or elsewhere, when inability to drive a car or physical limitations make this necessary.

As the eye wanders along the far shoreline there is always the backdrop of Lakeland mountains, of the Scafell Pikes, Fairfield, the Helvellyn range and much else.

Ulverston, a bay market town and the birthplace of Stan Laurel is visible with its folly on the hill behind the town and smoke rising from the large Glaxo factory.

Along this stretch of shoreline lie Kents Bank and Flookburgh. The latter is a hive of activity for shrimpers and the home of the Queen's Guide for the bay, Cedric Robinson.

And far to the left lies Barrow-in-Furness, with its massive nuclear submarine housing complex clearly visible.

The promenade below my window is a busy thoroughfare with summer days enjoyed by visitors and residents alike. Morecambe was the first resort to provide illuminations and an annual treat was to sit in the window and see the visiting VIP, after the switch-on, sweep by with the accompanying cavalcade on its way to Happy Mount Park. Sadly the illuminations have now ceased.

Memories of roller skating on the lovely flat promenade, or vast numbers of airmen and airwomen completing their drill exercises during initial training in wartime fill the mind.

Britain's bonniest bay hardly describes all it means to me, and with its glorious sunsets, the view from my window of the Bay is one of beauty unsurpassed, of constant interest and wonderful memories.

> O Lord of Heaven and earth and sea
> To Thee all praise and glory be,
> How shall we show our love to Thee,
> Who givest all?

For peaceful homes and healthful days,
For all the blessings earth displays,
We owe Thee thankfulness and praise,
Who givest all.

Chapter XXIX

VERA AND THE SCOURGE OF CANCER

Vera was probably the finest Christian I ever knew, apart from one other person. I loved her until she died from cancer, after 2½ years of marriage.

I went, in September 1975, to Bournemouth on holiday. Bournemouth is my favourite southern resort and Rosalie and I had spent many holidays there with John and Catherine.

The weather was superb; September is in any event my favourite month, with the crisp sunny days always making me feel more 'alive' than at any other time of the year. Lounging on the beach in a deckchair with a novel, I thought of the previous day when I motored through the New Forest playing Beethoven's 'Pastoral Symphony' on my car radio as the sun streamed through the branches. Lyndhurst and a cream tea, strolls alone through glorious woodland, by gentle streams and driving through the ford at Brockenhurst for refreshments at the Splash cafe, immediately adjacent, all came to mind. I thought too about the rest of the week. Rosalie and I had often visited Brockenhurst with the children when on holiday in Bournemouth, and by a democratic vote of 3 to 1 we voted to give the name to our new house at Storth.

Should it be Beaulieu, with all it had to offer and which I had visited many times; Buckler's Hard, where ships for the Armada were built and Sir Francis Chichester left for one of his epic journeys; sitting in the car at the Sandbanks ferry and enjoying the to and fro of the various sailing craft, and particularly as they fought to enter Poole harbour against the ebb tide; pretty Swanage; one or more of the many shows still running; Longleat and the lions; and much more?

It was the toss of a coin to decide whether to settle for any of them or go to Newhaven to see my youngest sister Ann, her husband Don and their sons Alistair and Angus. I went the next day to Newhaven, although somewhat reluctantly. It was here that I met Vera. She had a sad story to tell. She had met Geoff at Cambridge where he was engaged in post-graduate work. Vera was studying Classics at Girton College, which was the last female bastion of the University. Geoff was studying Agriculture and they later lived for some time in Zambia where Alison and Diana were born. Shortly after her return to England, in advance of

219

Geoff, Gregory was born.

There was another lady in Geoff's life and the situation can best be described by saying that Vera stood by her much-loved mother's grave at the funeral, about to give birth (to Gregory), having just been informed by Geoff that he was staying with the other lady in the relationship (whom he subsequently married) and had been informed by the doctor that she was to have a mastectomy. She wished she had been in the coffin, in the stead of her mother. When I think I have problems, I often return in memory to that moment.

We married in the spring of 1976 at Steyne Road Methodist Church in Seaford, Sussex. During the intervening period, after our first meeting, I travelled to Newhaven regularly at weekends and stayed with my sister Ann and Don.

We decided on the purchase of a property at Storth overlooking the Sandside estuary of Morecambe bay near Arnside. It was a split-level house with a half acre of land, on a small elevated site, with five other properties and with glorious views over the bay to the Lakeland mountains. It lay in a virtually unspoilt area of outstanding natural beauty which lies to the west of the A6 between Carnforth and Milnthorpe. The house was only two minutes walk from where I had lived with Rosalie, John and Catherine for nearly two years. Vera's three children by her first marriage attended the local school. Alison, the elder daughter, sat her 11-plus exam in 1978 and failed. In view of the domestic position of Vera's deteriorating condition, we appealed, and on the advice of the Headmistress wrote a brief letter. The reply was lengthy, but a rejection. I seldom saw Vera other than completely equable, but the news upset her and we appealed again. On this occasion I followed my own instinct. I wrote a very lengthy letter indeed in which I set out the position factually in all its sadness and merit.

On a wet Monday morning we travelled to Barrow-in-Furness for a lengthy interview, in a spartan room, with a senior education official. He was understanding and as helpful as he could be, but the tears which I saw trickle down Vera's face were not for effect, yet expressed the frustration and pessimism we both felt. A few weeks later we returned from a holiday to find an enormous pile of mail. Everyone was standing in a group sorting the envelopes when my eyes alighted on one from Cumbria County Council. Concealing it as best I could, I went into an adjoining room and read the contents:

Dear Mr and Mrs Knape
   11+ Appeal – Alison Knape
   Thank you for your letter of 23 June 1978 concerning Alison's transfer to secondary school.

Wedding Day
Gregory, Alison, Vera's sister Phyllis and Alison with Bride and Bridegroom (1976).

You will appreciate that the County Appeals Panel, which allocated Alison to Longlands Girls' School, is normally the final decision-making body on 11+ appeals within the county. However, in view of the very exceptional and distressing circumstances which you have brought to my attention, I have contacted the Appeals Panel again to see if they wish to vary their decision in Alison's case. The Panel was unanimously of the view that, had they been aware of your family's circumstances earlier, they would have realised how severe an effect this must have had for some time on Alison's school work. In the circumstances, therefore, the Panel is prepared to allocate a place at Kendal High School to Alison.

I am sorry that you have had this anxiety, but you can rest assured that the Panel would have, and will now, treat this matter in confidence.

Yours sincerely
Peter Boulter
Director of Education

I shrieked loudly and jumped in the air, with a surprised and puzzled reaction from them all. 'Ali's passed, Ali's passed,' I shouted.

We say the world is small, yet not only were we told it was the first ever successful appeal to this authority, but later Geoff, Vera's ex-husband, recognized the Director of Education's name as an old university friend. There was nothing of concern in this, as Alison had adopted my surname and Geoff was completely unaware of what was going on. There was an extra note of gratitude in our prayers that night and Vera's face was further cause for joy. Vera was to see Alison in her new uniform for Kendal High School for Girls, and some two weeks' attendance, before she died.

During my time in Storth, on this occasion, there were problems at the school relating to the 11-plus exam. The Headmistress, Miss Irene Boyd had a difficult situation on her hands. My own daughter Catherine had attended the school and Rosalie had taught there after we separated. I had never had other than a normal cordial parent/teacher relationship with Miss Boyd, and I was pleased to be able to accept an invitation from the parents of the children attending the school to chair a public meeting in the village, to be attended by a senior official of the Education Authority where the matter could be given a full airing. Briefly, the 11-plus results were disappointing to some. I was in the position of having my own daughter successful in a group of four who passed from six and had sat the exam several years previously, and a stepdaughter who had failed. Perhaps I could speak from a position of balanced neutrality.

There were outspoken comments but I felt that one parent in particular was the source of unfair criticism. Clearly the standard had varied considerably over the years, but with such small numbers it was not easy to assess fairly the uniformity of standards. The child of the parents concerned had failed the examination and with other younger children to follow, they were clearly concerned about the future. The outcome was really a stalemate, but I felt Miss Boyd's reputation had been vindicated and she was grateful for my help.

Vera's first year at Storth found her apparently in satisfactory health, but then began a steady deterioration, involving a ten-day stay in Christie's, a well-known cancer hospital in Manchester. I travelled daily after work, and the children were with Geoff and his second wife Dorothy. A most distressing side-effect of chemotherapy is the loss of hair, particularly so for ladies. Vera had a lovely head of luxuriant auburn hair and found the need to wear a wig at times an unhappy experience, but she never grumbled.

Visits to her doctor became more frequent. Dr Proctor was a kind and able practitioner. Vera asked searching questions and he had difficulty in fielding them, partly from the medical impossibility of definite prognosis and partly because of a pessimistic prognosis which he refrained from disclosing in full. It was arranged for us to see a doctor from Christie's at regular intervals on a Saturday morning at Westmorland County Hospital. The experienced doctor carefully avoided raising or dashing hopes.

On one occasion towards the end, Vera phoned me at the office in deep distress from the pain, which quite uncharacteristically she said she could not stand any longer. I phoned Christie's and they agreed to see her immediately. I dashed home and sped to Manchester where we waited in a large room with some 100 other cancer sufferers. Some relief resulted from the visit.

Vera entered Kendal County Infirmary in the summer of 1978 for ten days. The senior general physician of the Area Health Authority sent for me. I waited for three hours before he could see me, with a perfunctory apology and comment that he had forgotten I was waiting. He peered over his glasses at the medical records and said there did not appear to be much wrong, or to worry about. I had difficulty in restraining myself from an outburst against his utter indifference, and more seriously, ignorance of Vera's condition. As I was leaving a young house doctor rushed after me, stopped me on the stairs and asked if I realized how serious my wife's condition was. I said that I did, but when I told of what his superior had said, he shook his head in disbelief and apologized for the way in which I had been treated.

Vera's sister Phyllis came to stay and on her return to Brighton, she told Vera's father, Ted and Brenda, her stepmother, of her distress and broke down. Ted and Brenda packed at once and came north. Brenda was an experienced nurse and I could not have managed those three weeks before Vera died without their loving, caring and dedicated help, bearing in mind there were three young children.

On the last Saturday morning Dr Proctor called, on his final visit of the day. Normally I left Brenda in the room with him and then spoke to him as he left. On this morning he rushed away and I had to run to catch up. Tears were streaming down his face. He told me that Vera was the last of several terminal cases he had seen that morning and he said that there were times when he felt completely useless. Here was an experienced and caring practitioner showing a usually hidden side of his humanity and caring.

On 17 September I was taking a bath late in the evening. Vera was unconscious and had been receiving morphine on a daily basis. When Dr Proctor had told her that the time had come to administer the pain-killing drug, Vera accepted without protest, knowing what it meant. As I stepped out of the bath I looked through the door and Vera had passed away.

After the funeral, when two wonderful tributes were paid to her, it was necessary to decide on the future. Geoff and Dorothy had gathered something of the seriousness of Vera's condition a few days before she died and Dorothy phoned one evening. Vera did not want them to know and I covered up. After discussion with Ted and Brenda, I said I felt our duty was to tell Geoff and I phoned to say Vera had only a few days to live. Geoff came north on the Saturday, and to the house for a meal before going to nearby accommodation I had booked. He did not see Vera.

She died on the Sunday evening and I phoned Geoff on the Monday morning. The children had stayed the night with my Aunt Ruth who lived three or four miles away. Geoff had the task of picking them up in the car, motoring to Windermere, and breaking the news to them. We waited apprehensively. They returned with pale, tear-stained faces and rushed to their rooms.

Geoff and Dorothy were unable to have a family and had fostered several children, two of whom were with them at the time. The children had gone to stay at Alpheton, nr. Sudbury, on five or six occasions each year, and so the lovely detached farmhouse with ample grounds was a second home. It was agreed that the children should return with Geoff. They would have missed only a few days at their new schools and an immediate break and fresh surroundings were, in all our opinions, probably the least hurtful and harmful way for them.

Geoff and the children left on the Wednesday before the funeral, and

Ted, Brenda and Phyllis early the following week. The house seemed very big and very empty.

I maintained a close contact with Alison, Diana and Gregory for several years, stayed with them regularly and also took them for a week's holiday to Bournemouth. Alison came to Lancaster University to study Marketing and French. We had many happy times together. On many occasions I took her and fellow students to the University campus in the morning, before going to my office. I helped her with driving tuition and our trips to the Lake District enabled her to gain the necessary confidence to pass at the first attempt. Gregory, as I write, has taken up his first post as a doctor at Addenbrooke's Hospital, Cambridge and is shortly expecting to move to King's Lynn. He inherited his mother's intellect, and had ambitions to become a brain surgeon.

Vera's death could well have been avoided. A lump which she found some six months before the correct diagnosis was said by her doctor to be the result of her imagination. Six months later he found his diagnosis to be incorrect. The surgeon's knife did not remove all the malignancy and because of the amount of chemotherapy, no further treatment could be given. We both understood that a five-year period without any adverse developments was required, before medical confidence returned. Vera died from cancer on 17 September 1978 at the age of thirty-seven, after two and a half years of marriage to me.

'John,' said an elderly neighbour, the day after she died. 'You are a religious man. Tell me – I am an old man with heart trouble. I have lived a full and happy life and am ready to go at any time. Here is Vera, a Cambridge classical scholar, organist, pianist, a wonderful mother of three children, who has died at thirty-seven with so much to live for. Why should God take her, and leave me?'

I do not know the answer and I do not know anyone who does. But I do not believe that God deliberately inflicted such a foul disease on such a lovely life. If I did believe that, then nothing has meaning or purpose and there is nothing at the heart of things. There are no glib answers to questions which have baffled better minds than mine, but I offer elsewhere in these pages a few random thoughts on pain and suffering.

I could not express my feelings in a few short words as an epitaph on the headstone to Vera's grave, but eventually wrote:

Her life was a song of praise to the Lord she loved.

Unfortunately, due to an unhappy event, contact with the children was lost, but I maintained contact with Vera's sister Phyllis and, less frequently, with Ted and Brenda who are now advanced in years and suffer indifferent health.

Vera was MA (Cantab), an accomplished organist and pianist, and spoke French fluently.

Here are some of her references:

The bearer, Mrs V.E. Wynn, was on my teaching staff at Kalonga Secondary School. I found her when I came to Kalonga for the first time, and worked with her for a year before she decided to resign.

During my association with Mrs Wynn I found her to be a willing, diligent, and hardworking worker.

TEACHING: French was Mrs Wynn's speciality, she taught it right up to the top form. She is a conscientious teacher who performed her duties efficiently. Besides being a good teacher Mrs Wynn took considerable interest in her pupils and she got to know them individually.

EXTRA DUTIES:Every time I delegated some of my work to Mrs Wynn I was always sure that it would be done willingly, promptly, and very well. However, Mrs Wynn's special field in extra mural activities was music. She is an accomplished pianist and under her direction the school choir gained nationwide recognition. She also helped with playing of games particularly lawn tennis.

Mrs Wynn's departure from Kalonga has left a gap which will be very difficult to fill and I only hope that she will return at some later date.

Yours faithfully,
W.S. Mufana
Headmaster
Kalonga Secondary School
P.O. Box 925
Broken Hill
Republic of Zambia

Mrs Wynn taught English Language and Literature up to 'O' Level from September 1969 to August 1970. She has a pleasant relationship with her pupils and arouses their interest in the work. She was always conscientious and prepared her work well. She is a loyal and co-operative colleague and I was sorry that she had to leave.

I am sure she would be a very valuable teacher in any school to which she is appointed.

R.O. Snook
Principal
Chipembi Girls' School
Box 18
Chisamba
Zambia

Vera's funeral was held at Bare Methodist Church and conducted by the Minister and a dear friend, Rev. Herbert Foster. His address was as follows:

For many years Vera Knape has been a member of the Methodist Church. During the past eighteen months, it has been the privilege of a number of us here to get to know her whilst she has resided in the North West since her marriage on the 2nd April 1976. Vera was an intensely capable person. She was a classical scholar of Cambridge University, well-versed in languages but she was also an ardent evangelical Christian with a deep concern about Christian witness. During the time she has lived in Storth, she has been a member of the Crag Mount Christian Fellowship Group, she has been a member of our Bare Methodist Church Fellowship House Group, she was keenly interested in the charismatic movement revival throughout the church, felt that this had an important role to play in the revival of the world. She was a regular worshipper here with John and the children ever since she came. We shall miss her very much indeed, and the children. During the past few years she experienced many trials and sorrows, not least her own ill-health. A few years ago she had a serious operation and we were all delighted she seemed to make such a good recovery. And then came recurring ill-health, more anxiety and uncertainty about the future. The thing that will always remain in our minds, the minds of those who knew her best, was her deep faith which gave her the assurance that she was able to meet sorrow, and trial and anxiety with a brave heart. Her Christian faith was truly an inspiration. Never once did I hear her complain, never once did I hear her rebel against her circumstances, as well a lesser person might have done although she knew that her earthly life might well be limited to a short span of years. You see she had learned the secret of living a day at a time in dependence upon God, she had learned the secret of making the very most of the present time. She had learned the grace of acceptance. This is one of the most difficult lessons for any of us to learn when you are in danger of being cut off in the prime of one's life, to learn how to accept whatever may come.

227

The person who has learned that lesson is a triumphant person in every sense of the word. Several times she was in and out of hospital but always she maintained a radiant faith from which she derived great comfort and blessing and which brought spiritual strength to others, her loved ones and her friends. In every way she practised what she believed, she was a thoroughly consistent person. I am sure she found great happiness in living at Storth and made their home there a centre of Christian fellowship, which meant a very great deal to those who visited them. Vera was not afraid of death, she knew with a great certainty that nothing could separate her from God's love in Christ Jesus. I am sure that if we had asked her, she would have subscribed to Bishop Ken's hymn which expresses this sentiment. 'Teach me to live that I may dread the grave as little as my bed.' So today, deeply sad as we are at her premature passing, we meet together as Christians and we sorrow not as those without hope, but as those whose strong confidence is in a risen Lord, expressed in that triumphant hymn of faith that we have been singing, being assured of her triumphant eternal life with her Saviour. We feel intensely for the whole family but I know that they want this service to be a song of triumph, the triumph of the Christian faith over circumstances. To John, the children, her parents, sister Phyllis, Auntie Ruth, the whole family, all the relatives connected with them, we extend our very deepest sympathy. I know that in recent days they have been upheld by the prayers and the love of many Christian friends and I know that they will continue to be upheld as we keep on remembering them at the throne of Grace. We know that out of His more than sufficient Grace, God will continue to meet their need. We pray that God will bless all of us as you commit yourselves to Him in faith.

A second address was given by Mr Jim Pratt who with his wife and three daughters were close friends throughout our time at Storth. As a preacher and evangelist for many years he spoke of the sense of victory in Vera's life and faith, breaking through the sadness of her passing and of her wish expressed to him only two weeks before that if she did not recover, and she was ready for either eventuality, she wished her funeral service to be one sounding a note of victory and praise.

Jim spoke of her steadfast testimony and witness over the years since her surgery for cancer, and complete commitment. He referred to her ministry in the open air, and with children; of her testimony at Gospel meetings, Bible clubs and team meetings.

Her favourite verses in the Bible were the last three verses of Habbakuk which spoke of complete trust. In the last few days before her death, although she could hardly speak, she was talking to visitors to our home of Jesus.

He spoke of her faithfulness in the home and service to anyone she met who was in need. Vera, he said, spent a great deal of time in prayer, studying the Word of God, and had a particular interest in the prophecies. The note of victory was sounded throughout the service in accordance with her wishes.

The first hymn was one of our favourites, 'Thine by the glory, risen, conquering Son'. Vera had chosen as her second hymn another Resurrection hymn: 'Awake, glad soul, awake, awake!' but I felt moved to change it to the well-known hymn from the section then named 'Militant and Triumphant' which commences with the words, 'For all the saints who from their labours rest'. Jim had referred to her as a saint and for me the words were appropriate for Vera's service. We closed with the two verses of 'This, this is the God we adore'.

Vera was interred in Torrisholme cemetery. We shall be buried together.

A friend gave us on our wedding day, mounted in a cover, the following sermon. I do not know its source.

A Wedding Sermon from a Prison Cell

Ephesians 1.12 '. . . to the end that we should be unto the praise of His glory'.

It is wholly right and proper for a bride and bridegroom to welcome their wedding day with a sense of triumph. All the difficulties, obstacles, impediments, doubts and suspicions have at least been – I shall not say, thrown to the winds, for that would be to make too light of them – but honestly faced and overcome. Both parties have now won the most important battle of their lives. You have just said to one another 'I will', and with those words you have declared your voluntary assent and turned a critical point in your lives. You know full well all the doubts and suspicions with which a lifelong partnership between two persons is faced. But you have defied these doubts and suspicions with a cheerful confidence, and by your free assent you have conquered a new land to live in. Every wedding is an occasion of joy, joy that human beings can do such great things, that they have been granted the freedom and the power to take the rudder of their lives into their own hands. The children of earth are rightly proud when they are allowed a hand in shaping their own destinies. And it is right that a bride and bridegroom should have this pride on their wedding day. It would be wrong to speak too lightly and irresponsibly about God's will and providence. To begin with there can be no question

229

that it is your own very human wills which are at work here, which are celebrating their triumph. The course you are embarking upon is one you have chosen for yourselves. It is not in the first place something religious, but something quite secular. And so you alone must bear the responsibility for what you are doing, it cannot be taken from you. It is you, the bride and bridegroom, who as a married couple must bear the whole responsibility for the success of your married life, with all the happiness it will bring. Unless you can boldly say to-day: 'This is our resolve, our love, our way,' you are taking refuge in a false piety. 'Iron and steel may pass away, but our love shall abide for ever.' You hope to find in another that earthly bliss in which, to quote a medieval song, the one is the comfort of the other both in body and in soul. Such a hope has its proper place in God's eyes as well as man's.

You have both been abundantly blessed in your lives up till now, and you have every reason to be thankful. The beauties and joys of life have almost overwhelmed you, success has always come your way, and you have been surrounded by the love of your friends. Your path has always been smoothed out before you. Amid all the changes and chances of life you have always been able to count on the support of both your families and friends. Every one has been generous to you, and now you have found each other and have at last been led to the goal of your desires. Such a life, as you know full well, can never be created or entered upon in our own power. It is given to some and denied to others. That is what we mean by divine providence. As you rejoice to-day that you have reached your goal, so you will be grateful that God's will and God's way have brought you hither. As you take full responsibility upon your own shoulders for what you are doing to-day, so with equal confidence you may place it all in the hands of God.

God has sealed your 'I will' with his own. He has crowned your assent with his. He has bestowed upon you this triumph and rejoicing and pride. He is thus making you the instruments of His will and purpose both for yourselves and for others. In His unfathomable condescension God veritably gives His Yea to yours. But in so doing He creates out of your love something that did not exist before – the holy estate of matrimony.

God is guiding your marriage. Marriage is more than your love for each other. It has a higher dignity and power. For it is God's holy ordinance, by means of which He wills to perpetuate the human race until the end of time. In your love you see your two selves as solitary figures in the world; in marriage you see yourselves as links in the chain of the generations, which God causes to come and go to His glory and calls into His kingdom. In your love you see only the heaven of your bliss, through marriage you are placed at a post of responsibility towards the world and to mankind. Your love is your own private possession; marriage is more than a private affair, it is an estate, an office. As the crown makes the king, and not just his determination to rule, so marriage and not just your love for each other makes you husband and wife in the sight of God and man. As you first gave the ring to one another and received it a second time from the hand of the parson, so love comes from you, but marriage from above, from God. As God is infinitely higher than man, so the sanctity, the privilege and the promise of marriage are higher than the sanctity, the privilege and promise of love. It is not your love which sustains the marriage, but from now on the marriage that sustains your love.

God intends you to found your marriage on Christ. 'Wherefore receive ye one another, even as Christ also received you, to the glory of God.' In a word, live together in the forgiveness of your sins, for without it no human fellowship, least of all a marriage, can survive. Don't insist on your rights, don't blame each other, don't judge or condemn each other, don't find fault with each other, but take one another as you are, and forgive each other every day from the bottom of your hearts.

From the first day of your marriage until the last your rule must be: 'Receive ye one another . . . to the praise of God.'

Such is the word of God for your marriage. Thank Him for it, thank Him for bringing you thus far. Ask Him to establish your marriage, to confirm and hallow it and preserve it to the end. With this your marriage will be 'to the praise of His glory'.

Amen.

Chapter XXX

MEMORY AND RAINBOWS

Ever since I qualified as a solicitor I have been convinced that anyone of reasonable intelligence, who is prepared to work hard, can qualify, provided he or she has a good memory. Women are entering the profession in increasing numbers. There was not, in my time, a great deal which was inherently difficult to understand in the law.

When I was working on my course before the Final Examination, the method of teaching was for us to take down in longhand, as quickly as possible, the lecturer's words for one and a half hours, learn the notes that day, and then read the following morning another chunk from the relevant textbook in preparation for the afternoon lecture. We were told, indeed, that if it was possible to commit the notes completely to memory, a pass was virtually guaranteed. Although the lecturers were selective in their material and had analysed the questions from previous years, to note those topics which had just been included and those which had not appeared for a long time (with some success in my case), nevertheless, the learning of the law was largely a memory test.

I am reaping the benefit of my good memory in my later years. I find, with others, that it is extremely difficult to commit new things to memory. It was a common view during my earlier years that a child did not remember very early events. One of my stepdaughters in recent years amazed her mother with a conversation about rabbits which were kept by her father. Her mother insisted that this must have been when she was about twelve months old.

I can remember many details of my first four years in Burnley, in addition to my expeditions to the hen hut! We lived in a stone-built, end-terrace house, in Clevelands Road, off the main Manchester Road, leading into the town centre. Clevelands was to become the name of the house father built in Morecambe in 1938, of another large detached house on the seafront, to where we moved in 1951, and the name of a road which a builder client of my father asked him to name in later years. It is also the name of a hymn tune written by my mother's stepbrother, Uncle Jack.

Next door to us in Clevelands Road lived Mr Hargreaves. I am sure he had a wife but my recollection is of a bespectacled gentleman in a rocking-chair, constantly and gently swaying backwards and forwards, talking to us in a soothing fashion and never without his pipe. It has always been my view that pipe-smokers are calm, reassuring, tolerant and kindly men, who bear the pressures of life lightly on their shoulders. Perhaps Mr Hargreaves was the source of this view.

One unhealthy memory is of walking into the kitchen one day and being ordered out in peremptory fashion. Father was at the sink, with his sleeves rolled up and wearing long rubber gloves. There was a flash of shiny black shapes and I felt a strange unease, a feeling that something almost evil was present. He was a lover of animals all his life and I cannot remember asking him to explain in later years.

A wandering donkey which I tried hard to mount, a local bully who enjoyed running his front bicycle wheel over my feet, a short unmade sloping road beyond the house down which we sped on wooden trolleys, weekend strolls with my parents and two older sisters, pushing my third sister Joie in the pram with Father resplendent in spats, spending a few frustrating days in bed (later remembered as chickenpox) and trips to the small corner shop for mother, are still clear in my memory. Granny and Grandpa lived in Glen View Road which was reached across an open area of ground where goats were kept. Father told us that they would eat anything and proved it by taking sheets of paper from his pockets, and feeding them to the eager recipients. Football and cricket in the street were a constant pleasure.

Here are some of the writings I committed to memory over the years and can recite without difficulty:

1. The hymn of love, in the 13th chapter of Corinthians I (Authorised Version).
2. Psalm 19, which I learned at Primary School, and which we said in morning assembly.
3. The 23rd and 27th Psalms. It was Father's practice to read the latter to us as his last task before we left for the station and our boarding schools at the beginning of term.
4. Anthony's eulogy in Shakespeare's *Julius Caesar.*
5. Gray's 'Elegy written in a Country Churchyard'.
6. Many of Stanley Holloway's monologues delivered in a broad Lancashire accent. At a church concert in my younger days, I was able, suitably dressed, to deliver six of them without identification by many church members.
7. Section 1 of the now repealed Larceny Act 1916 (a lengthy definition of the crime of stealing).
8. Hamlet's soliloquy 'To be or not to be' from *Hamlet.*
9. John's vision of 'A new heaven and a new earth' in the book of

Revelation (chapter 21 verses 1.7).
10. The Gospel according to St John chapter 1, verses 1-14 (the Prologue).

Included in verses of the Bible which I find a constant inspiration are:
1. John 3 verse 16.
2. Romans 8 verses 38 and 39 (my favourite verses in the whole of the Bible).
3. Isaiah 40 verse 31 (a constant source of renewed strength).
4. Ruth 1 verses 16 and 17.
5. Daniel 16 verses 16-18.
6. John 17 verse 20.
7. John 11 verse 35 (the shortest verse in the Bible, and yet one of the most meaningful and moving) – 'Jesus wept'.
8. Job 42 verses 1-6.
9. Micah 6 verse 8.
10. Jeremiah 31 verses 31-33 (possibly the high-water mark of the Old Testament).

I commend them to the reader.

Nostalgic memories of childhood are, however, often found in later years to be different from present reality, and so memory is not always certain and sure. Return visits to the place of my birth and comparison with the visual evidence, seem to reduce both in substantial measure. If I can express this in another way and in specific terms, I would say that the size of the house in which we lived, the length of the slope where we spent hours on our trolleys, the length of the road in which we lived, the size of the gable wall which soared into the sky in childhood, and other physical features, assumed a different and smaller size. The earlier events of those days, the moments which were filled with differing levels of anxious apprehension, and experiences which seemed overwhelming at the time, were now seen in their proper perspective. To coin a phrase, 'Things ain't what they used to be.'

'Be not, therefore, anxious for the morrow, for the morrow will be anxious for itself.' I am reminded again that the only way to live is a day at a time.

A few weeks ago I was joking with a friend about a minor matter of forgetfulness. He said that the first sign of senility was loss of short-term memory. I have suddenly realized that he may be correct. My long-term memory is excellent. I have not yet gone back to living in my past and particularly my childhood. Dates, places and names have never been clearer and in many respects. I consider myself to be at the height of my mental powers. There are historical examples of men who come to their greatness and maturity in later life, and Sir Winston Churchill is a name which comes readily to mind.

Another good example as far as hymn composition is concerned is the Rev. F. Pratt Green, a retired Methodist minister, born in 1903. He is not a musician by training, but served on the committee responsible for the preparation of the new Methodist hymn book. His hymns, all of which were written in retirement, are the best I know for expressing the eternal truths in modern language. He leaps into *Hymns and Psalms* sub-titled 'A Methodist and Ecumenical Hymn Book', first published in 1983 and now used in most Methodist Churches, with twenty-seven hymns to his name, all sung to familiar and well-loved tunes.

It is, however, quite easy for me to forget something of a minor nature during the day, such as purchasing a loaf of bread, or of forgetting to check if the kettle is full before switching on. I recently experienced 'a nuclear meltdown' in the kitchen as a result of this lapse.

I shall probably increasingly have to turn to mnemonics as a means of assistance. Throughout my life they had afforded invaluable help in examinations and in many other ways, including my preaching. Last week we had a very mixed wet and sunny spell of weather, and for several days witnessed a large number of rainbows of differing lengths, including one great overreaching arc, stretching across the bay. In order to remember the colour of a rainbow, I have committed to memory 'Richard of York gives battle in vain'. The first letter of each word reminds me of the seven colours of red, orange, yellow, green, blue, indigo and violet.

On one occasion, when a child, the crock of gold at the end of the rainbow nearly became a reality for me. Returning from Barrow-in-Furness in the car with my father, I saw in a field we were passing what seemed clearly to be an arched rainbow touching the grass just over the wall. I pleaded with Father to stop and leaping over the wall I ran towards the spot. There was no thought of material gain in my young mind but the certainty of a wonderful discovery. As the rainbow retreated from me, and after trying several times to touch it, I turned disconsolately to the car and had to come to terms with myself and Father's gentle but knowing smile. He did not need to explain.

I know that my store of memories made a large contribution in my School Certificate (now GCSE) examinations, in Greek grammar (my master explained that they were paradigms or tabulated infusions of a word, but worked to the same end), in Divinity (or RE), to remember the fruits of the Spirit (Galatians 5 verses 22 and 23) and in other subjects.

I have unconsciously committed to memory over the years a large number of the hymns in *Methodist Hymn Book with Tunes* which was in use until *Hymns and Psalms* was published in 1983. I very much welcome the new book prepared by the Faith and Order Committee. I quote from the Preface:

The publication of *Hymns and Psalms* owes its origin to a decision of the British Methodist Conference of 1979, which resolved that a new hymn book should be prepared, to embody the best traditions of Methodist hymnody and to be a contribution to the life and worship of the universal church. The same Conference empowered its Faith and Order Committee to encourage as wide a participation of other churches in the project as should prove practicable. The present committee has been greatly heartened by the degree of participation by many denominations in its work; and it has become increasingly aware of the potential of this book to build from accepted denominational traditions towards a richer sharing of our diverse interests and our common heritage. The Methodist Conference has been able to scrutinise the various drafts of this book to ensure that the Methodist emphases are present within it, and has authorised it as a successor to the *Methodist Hymn Book* of 1933; agreeing also to its full title, *Hymns and Psalms, A Methodist and Ecumenical Hymn Book.*

The numbers of the hymns in the old book are so familiar that I could name very many of them. The new hymns, songs and tunes are to be encouraged, particularly for our young people, but they can never replace for me and at my age, either in word or tune, the great hymns of Charles Wesley and others. These are a constant source of spiritual resources to me. Only a short time ago I found a 'gem' in the form of a tape, at an annual pre-Christmas book display arranged by Kendal and District Christian Literature Society at our Church. I play hymns constantly in my car and at home, but recent expeditions have left me looking largely at a mix of old and new words and lines. The 'gem' was a tape made by the Choir of the Methodist Central Hall, Westminster singing twenty of the hymns of Charles Wesley. It is playing as I write and I draw freely on the riches which are offered.

My memory has also enabled me to retain and repeat the words of very many hymns in the old Methodist hymn book, recently replaced, as I have mentioned earlier.

Chapter XXXI

THE NEW MONASTERY OF OUR LADY OF HYNING

Hyning Hall has played an important part in my life, and I commend a visit. Situated just off the A6 near the M6 junction at Carnforth in Lancashire, it was from about 1935 until 1973 the home of Earl Peel. The last Earl was a charming man and great public benefactor. After the War, when building materials were in short supply and regulations very strict, he was prosecuted at Liverpool Assizes for their breach. Standing in the dock he was told by Mr Justice Lynskey, in imposing a very heavy fine, that if it had not been for his fine record of public service a custodial sentence would have been imposed.

It is now the Monastery of our Lady of Hyning, occupied by Bernardine Cistercians. The published leaflet of events states: 'As a community of Cistercian nuns we seek God through our daily life of prayer, work and fraternal charity. Each day we come together to celebrate the Eucharist and the Divine Office, and at these times we are closely united with our brothers and sisters throughout the world as we bring their needs before the Lord. Our work of hospitality allows us to welcome those who wish to share in some way the peace and prayerfulness of our monastic guesthouse.'

Although I have stayed there, I do not now do so because living only fifteen minutes journey away by car, I feel I should not deprive others who come from every part of the land of the opportunity.

A time in the simple but peaceful chapel, a browse among the excellent stock of books, a visit to the small room where tea, coffee and biscuits are freely available on a self-service basis, a chat there if others are present and many of the world's problems are settled, a walk round the delightful grounds, all make for a staple diet of reflection, prayer and spiritual renewal.

The vegetable garden is a source of much of the kitchen produce. A continuing mystery is when the spotless premises are cleaned, and how the immense work in the grounds is carried out, much of it by elderly nuns.

I often call two or three times a week.

On a lovely sunny day in 1994 I sat on a garden seat behind the Hall with Sister Mary John. I remembered, with Marjorie beside me, that it was here we had our first 'date' in 1979. Marjorie already knew Hyning. Sister Mary John imparts a serenity which restores one's faith in humanity and the love of God. She knows all my unhappy story and when I related in late summer my miracle of recovery in July of that year, she listened in silence and quietly said, 'And now, John, the most important thing is humility.' She meant, by these words, that I must understand all that had happened as the work of God, and not the greatness of John.

I would feel remiss if I did not also mention the love and wise counsel shown to Marjorie in particular by Sister Mary Lawrence who died in 1990. Marjorie and I have been instrumental in making known the benefits of Hyning to many members of our own church at Bare in Morecambe. Our last minister, Rev. Andrew J. Hill and Carol his wife, arranged quiet days there and first visited as a result of a word in season from us.

Rev. Graham Vickers who came to Bare in September 1994, is aware of the attraction and work of the community, and has arranged 'Quiet Days' when up to thirty people can be accommodated.

Hyning will play an important part in my life in the coming days as I journey on my pilgrim way. It has become almost a second and spiritual home.

The Hyning or Monastery of Our Lady of Hyning.

Chapter XXXII

BOREDOM

Jesus told a story of a man who spring-cleaned his life. The man drove out of himself all that was evil and unclean and left a life that was clean and sparkling and fresh and new. And that was how he left it. He put nothing in the place of what had been there before, and we learn that the last state of the man was worse than the first.

I find in my personal experience today that most people can be divided into two categories – the overworked on the one hand and the bored and frustrated on the other. There are not many people I meet who seem to live a full, balanced, useful and contented life.

Our society is becoming more vicious and violent by the day. Any television news programme or newspaper will testify to the truth of that statement. I have been deeply disturbed in the last few weeks by the degree of force and demonstration emanating from normally law-abiding citizens of villages and ports connected with the export of live animals from our shores.

I believe a vicious and violent society is the result in large part of boredom and frustration in employment or unemployment, and large numbers are finding physical outlets that could destroy it. There are, of course, many who practise violence for its own sake, but an increasing number are turning to hooliganism, burglary, political and racial demonstration and persecution, drugs and alcohol, because they are seeking outlets for their boredom.

I know several people who have large houses and all the material possessions anyone could desire, but have no zest for life. They have come to the feast of life without appetite and found only emptiness.

Repetition, too, adds to the number of the bored and frustrated. Performing one simple function in a factory for eight hours, five days a week, being a minder of machines, even being a mother, can through constant repetition beget indifference and detachment. And boredom comes to the activists as well. People throw themselves into causes which are lacking in real worth just to keep busy and not have time to think. Anything to pass the time.

Again many are bored out of their minds by amusements and entertainments to fill up the hours. This evening's television programme on Channel 4 had seven programmes advertised between 11.05 p.m. and 2.50 a.m. dedicated to sex and erotica, nudity, a lesbian strip club, and what is described as a 'ritzy brothel'. What gullible fools we are!

I was told as a young man that technology and science would give us more leisure time, and so should that be one of the aims of so-called progress. But too often it results in more emptiness to fill.

Even wars can be the result of boredom and depression. The Crusaders and Hitler respectively are examples. The former were stimulated by love of God, but also by love of money and treasures, and the tedium of their lives. Mediocrity and poverty helped to promote a huge following for megalomaniacs like Hitler.

Humanism, Communism, dictators have all failed. And so have education and a tolerant permissive society.

What must the Christian do?

He must proclaim unceasingly that the Way of Christ is the only way in which the kingdoms of this world will be transformed and become what Jesus came to proclaim – the Kingdom of God here and now, on earth.

Life is never a bore nor dull nor empty when filled by the Grace of Christ. When life is filled with Him and the virtues of truth and honesty, justice and peace, things which are lovely and of good report, there is no room for anything beyond the love of God and love for all mankind, and service to both.

Chapter XXXIII

A SENSE OF HUMOUR

During my life, I have occasionally met a man or woman, often formed a friendship, but felt somehow that there was a missing ingredient. Sometimes it has been pointed out to me and at other times it has suddenly become clear to me. It is a sad deficiency.

I refer to the lack of a sense of humour.

I can think immediately of a dozen people during my life who had this defect of character. A leading politician of today comes to mind. In several of the cases in my own personal experience the person concerned has been an only child, with over-protective parents, not allowed to mix and play with other children in a normal way.

I feel a deep sorrow for them.

Taken from a magazine produced for RAF personnel in Morecambe during the War, and edited by a professional journalist.

Why I Cling to Life

(The following is a copy of a letter sent by a subscriber to a well known Hospital in answer to their appeal for funds)

For the following reasons I am unable to send you a larger cheque. I have been held up, held down, sandbagged, walked upon, sat upon, flattened out and squeezed by the Income Tax, the Super Tax, the Tobacco Tax, the Beer Tax, the Spirits Tax, the Motor Tax and by every Society, Organisation and Club that the inventive mind of man can think of, to extract what I may or may not have in my possession – for the Red Cross, the Black Cross, the Ivory Cross and the Double Cross, and for every Hospital in town and country.

The Government has governed my business till I don't know who I am, where I am, or why I am here at all.

All that I know is that I am supposed to be an inexhaustible supply of money for every need, desire or hope of the human race, and because I will not go out and beg, borrow or steal money to give away, I am cussed, discussed, boycotted, talked to, talked about, lied to, lied about, held up, hung up, rung up, robbed and damn near ruined.

The only reason why I am clinging to life at all is to see what the hell is going to happen next.

The following were the regulations for a Burnley cotton mill office in 1852:

Office Staff Practices

1. Godliness, Cleanliness and Punctuality are the necessities of a good business.
2. The firm has reduced the hours of work, and the Clerical Staff will now only have to be present between the hours of 7 a.m. and 6 p.m. on weekdays.
3. Daily prayers will be held each morning in the Main Office. The Clerical Staff will be present.
4. Clothing must be of a sober nature. The Clerical Staff will not disport themselves in raiment of bright colours, nor will they wear hose, unless in good repair.
5. Overshoes and top-coats may not be worn in the office, but neck scarves and headware may be worn in inclement weather.
6. A stove is provided for the benefit of the Clerical Staff. Coal and Wood must be kept in the locker. It is recommended that each member of the clerical Staff bring 4 pounds of coal each day during cold weather.
7. No member of the Clerical Staff may leave the room without permission from Mr Rogers. The calls of nature are permitted and Clerical Staff may use the garden below the second gate. This area must be kept in good order.
8. No talking is allowed during business hours.
9. The craving of tobacco, wines or spirits is a human weakness and, as such, is forbidden to all members of the Clerical staff.
10. Now that the hours of business have been drastically reduced, the partaking of food is allowed between 11.30 a.m. and noon, but work will not, on any account, cease.
11. Members of the Clerical Staff will provide their own pens. A new sharpener is available, on application to Mr Rogers.
12. Mr Rogers will nominate a Senior Clerk to be responsible for the cleanliness of the Main Office and the Private Office, and all Boys and Juniors will report to him 40 minutes before prayers, and will remain after closing hours for similar work. Brushes, Brooms, Scrubbers and Soap are provided by the owners.

13. The New Increased Weekly Wages are as hereunder detailed:

Junior boys (to 11 years)	1/4d
Boys (to 14 years)	2/1d
Juniors	4/8d
Junior Clerks	8/7d
Clerks	10/9d
Senior Clerks (after 15 years with owners)	21/-d

The owners recognize the generosity of the new Labour Laws but will expect a great rise in output of work to compensate for the near Utopian conditions.

A Methodist local preacher moved to a new area of the country. He was appointed to conduct worship at a small country chapel some ten miles from where he lived. His reputation for preaching a sermon never less than forty minutes in length had gone before him.

There was no public transport and he did not drive. Nothing daunted, he set out in good time to walk. The weather was atrocious.

On his arrival he found only one person present, an elderly lady who greeted him warmly. No one else arrived.

He announced the hymn before the sermon which was No. 339 in the Methodist Hymn Book with words by Charles Wesley (to the tune of Wrestling Jacob).

> Come O Thou Traveller unknown
> Whom still I hold, but cannot see.
> My company before is gone
> And I am left alone with Thee;
> With Thee all night I mean to stay
> And wrestle till the break of day.

'Not likely,' said the old lady, as she gathered her coat and handbag and made for the aisle. 'I'm off.'

Chapter XXXIV

TIPS FOR LIVING

I hope I have learned many important lessons through my experiences and can pass on a few in the anticipation that they will be of help to others.

I have tried to draw from my sixty-eight years of life a few pieces of wisdom, help and enjoyment which I have received, learned or found to be true in my own experience on a variety of subjects.

I have also expressed opinions I have formed. I stress that they are my personal views.

An Inspiration for Daily Life

I have in this year of grace 1998, found a source of great personal and spiritual strength. It is in the picture of Jesus as portrayed by Frank Topping. Frank lost his faith in early years, but studied theology for eight years and was ordained a Methodist minister in 1930. He is widely known to millions for his radio and TV programmes, his stage partnership with Donald Swann, and devotional books.

He came with his simple one-man show to Trinity Methodist Church Morecambe in 1994. Portraying the characters involved in the Crucifixion of Jesus, he left an indelible picture on me which I find myself bringing into focus whenever I feel hurt or see injustice, and suffering, and pain.

Jesus, standing still, in the presence of the jeering crowd, reviled, and spat on. Jesus condemned by Pilate, flogged and in terrible physical condition. Jesus, forsaken by his disciples, and denied by Peter. Jesus who had taught and healed, and loved, hated and abandoned. Jesus, without sin, an object of ridicule. I see His eyes above all, Jesus standing motionless, with those gentle, loving caring eyes, soaking in all the violence, sin and evil like a sponge, absorbing all that the world could throw at Him. And He loved them, and died for them. He died for each and every one.

When I survey the wondrous cross,
On which the Prince of Glory died;
My richest gain I count but loss,
And pour contempt on all my pride.

Were the whole realm of nature mine,
That were an offering far too small;
Love so amazing, so divine,
Demands my soul, my life, my all.

Isaac Watts (1674-1748)

Letters to the Editor

In recent years I have felt an increasing interest in writing instant letters to the Editor in the pattern of 'Disgusted of Tonbridge Wells'. It is probably due in part to semi-retirement. I try not to reply the same day.

In August of 1994, I read with interest of Enoch Powell's forthcoming book which was to question the orthodox view that the Gospel according to St Mark was the first of the Gospels to be written, in about 70 AD, and which is largely contained in both St Matthew and St Luke.

He also questioned the death of Jesus by crucifixion and raised the case for his having been stoned by the Jews. Always to me a fascinating man, I could not help but feel that his great intellect in Greek (he was a Professor of Greek at Sydney University at the age of twenty-four) did not entitle him to automatic authority in another field.

I wrote to *The Independent*, and my letter was published as follows:

The gospel according to Enoch Powell
From Mr John Knape
Sir: It will be interesting to see if Enoch Powell (report, 17 August) deals in his forthcoming book with some words of the Roman historian Tacitus. My education in the classics at Shrewsbury School obliged me to commit to memory:

. . . one Christus, who in the reign of Tiberius had been condemned to death by the procurator Pontius Pilate.

I do not think that leaves' much room for a lapidation.
Yours faithfully,
JOHN KNAPE
Morecambe, Lancashire

As I hand in my manuscript I hear with sadness of the death of this great man.

In September 1997 an immigrant peer wrote a main article in the *Daily Mail* asserting that there was no class distinction in this country. In the feature 'Saturday Essay' we read:

> Peter Bauer, the immigrant son of a Hungarian bookmaker, is an economist of international repute and member of the House of Lords. No one is better placed to answer the question: Is our nation still stifled by a class system?

My reply printed five days later was as follows:

Accent on Pride

Most British people are classed as soon as they open their mouths. I was born and have lived in Lancashire nearly all my life. I was educated privately for two years before going to a council school and the local grammar.

I started at Shrewsbury at 13 with a strong Lancashire accent. Though I was a good scholar and sportsman, the word 'oik' followed me for four years. When I came home after my first term, three friends called to see me, but I had already lost my accent. They stayed for two minutes and I never saw them again.

I am all for letters from readers provided they do not seek to rush into print and their contributions flow from a considered view and firm conviction. Editors clearly use this popular part of their publication to sell more copies, carry out a particular policy, and often studiously avoid expressing the paper's view, or favour one side of an argument. Good fun.

A friend writes immediate and forceful letters to release frustration or anger but does not post them.

Education

I am convinced that the best help any parent can give to a child in secular education is to encourage extensive reading. When I was between eight and sixteen years of age I read anything and everything I could lay my hands on. Father had to take his newspaper from me when he came down for breakfast. I remember vividly the stories of the Battle of Britain in the headlines of the *Daily Mail* in August and September of 1940. Biggles and Leslie Charteris ('The Saint'), *Pilgrim's Progress* and Bulldog Drummond all came the same to me.

One day my father banished from the house my pile of copies of the *Beano, Dandy, Hotspur, Rover, Adventure*, and others. I hid them and went stealthily to a building site across the road, when it was deserted, sitting in a corner in the sun. Within reason anything goes, and produces vocabulary, a great unconscious acquisition of knowledge of all types, a self-confidence arising from an acquired ability for self-expression, and an unending source of pleasure for the remainder of life.

Computer games and all the other popular pastimes of today, combined with the generally held view among the young that learning and study are not 'cool', hold the seeds of problems for the future.

Retirement

Another of my father's 'pearls of wisdom' was that on retirement a man either died within six months or lived to be 100.

I have seen the truth of his remark. I was speaking recently to a man about to retire who spoke excitedly of all the hobbies and interests which lay before him, and which presently he would take up. I heard a few weeks ago of another man who had not moved from his armchair except for meals and bed for two weeks since retirement. His wife had already been driven to distraction by his repeated whining, 'Whatever am I going to do now?'

Monday morning with no work to go to is, for some, a horrible spectre of the future, and for others the virtual end of life. What a terrible state of affairs. Some are borne down with too much work, others yearn for employment and self-respect, and that is understandable; but to moan and fear retirement with all its opportunities and advantages is nothing less than a sin.

The Stiff Upper Lip

Recently I turned on Radio 5 (which I heartily recommend for those interested in news, sport and discussion). John Cleese and the writer of the script of the outstanding film *A Fish Called Wanda* were talking about England and the Englishman. They said they were proud of their origins and would not wish a change, but there was one characteristic of our island race which was unhealthy, and caused deep problems for many – the English 'stiff upper lip' attitude.

I knew boys at school who had entered prep school at six or seven, hardly saw their parents where the father worked abroad, often spent holidays with relatives or friends and seemed to be very lonely. One boy asked me, 'Do you love your mother and father?' It typified many at public school.

You must 'take it on the chin', 'be a man' and similar; all deny the importance of being able to talk about emotions and feelings, and share these things with those near and dear to us, and bring them to the surface. The rooms of psychiatrists and psychologists are full of those who have suffered breakdowns by reason of their inability to express their feelings, bottling up of emotions, absence of purpose for or reasons for living, and without the sense of a Higher Power in their lives and the world.

National Trust

The year 1995 marked the centenary of the founding of the National Trust as any TV viewer or newspaper or magazine reader will know. There was some controversy as might be expected in respect of Britain's top fund-raising charity, bringing in during 1993 £78.7 million but needing £165 million for essential repairs in 1995. The Trust urgently needs new members and funds and as a member for many years I commend it to all.

Although it has only two properties in my own County of Lancashire, it is a different story in Cumbria where the total protected estate is 131,000 acres – one quarter of the National Park. There are other buildings and farms over which the Trust holds restrictive covenants, enabling it to control any potential development or alterations.

Three-quarters of a million members help the Trust in its important and overriding aim to preserve property entrusted to it. Although fiercely independent, the Trust works closely with the statutory Government organizations which are active in Cumbria.

I particularly recommend Fell Foot Park at Newby Ridge described in the Handbook as follows:

> An 18-acre park and garden in the process of being restored, with lakeshore access and magnificent views of the Lakeland fells. Good shows of daffodils and rhododendrons. Boat launching, rowing boats for hire, picnics; ideal for a day's outing.

TV Soap Operas

I remember with great affection, Gail Platt of *Coronation St* fame, and her real life family. I love the programme and so does the majority of the nation. Great entertainment, much wisdom from and for life are all captured for the viewer. After a hard day's work it is a time of real refreshment.

I have been privileged to know Helen (Gail) and her family for many years. Helen is a Morecambe girl. I count her father as a good friend of many years standing. Helen's mother was a vibrant, bubbly personality, and has passed her gifts to her daughter. She was tragically killed in a road accident many years ago. My law firm proudly portrays a large signed photograph of the cast in our waiting room and I treasure a paperweight, a personal gift from a lovely lady (and see Chapter XXVIII).

Hidden Talents

I have never met anybody in my life completely devoid of talent. However basic their education, training, physical or mental abilities, there is a uniqueness about every soul on earth. I know one lady who would always be bottom of the class, except for one gift. She has a love for and winning way with children. Her life has given much joy to others and personal satisfaction to her from the use of this one gift. Jesus spoke of the use of whatever talents we might possess.

Work and Worth

I worry about the young people I see around me who have never had a job, do not seek one and never wish to work for the rest of their lives. There are large numbers of older, healthy people who take State benefits when fit for work, and in some cases could readily obtain employment.

The Queen Mother speaks of service being the rent for our place on earth.

The safety net for those who need it is vital, but we shall increasingly have to address our economic minds to a shrinking workforce and an increasingly elderly population. Here there is a great example to set for the more fortunate in our society. 'What's in it for me?' is the question on the day the Chancellor of the Exchequer rises to his feet with his budget proposals.

I feel that the very wealthy and the moderately wealthy could make a gesture which would benefit society far beyond the amount they would contribute in taxes.

It amazes me that some of the highest paid people in our society today award themselves huge pay rises without considering their effect on the ordinary man or the unjustified nature of the award in some cases. Clearly out of touch with reality, they are ignorant, selfish and disturbing of a just and peaceful society.

249

Understanding the Bible

In mid-December 1994 I heard Derek Jameson in a phone-in radio show say that he could not understand how anyone could be blamed for failing to believe a book which contradicts itself at every turn (the Bible). What a foolish man, and what a failure to understand the very basic elementary facts about the greatest book in the world.

In 1953 Her Majesty the Queen was presented with a Bible only a few yards from the spot where my son and I were sitting a few weeks ago at matins in Westminster, with these words: 'Here is wisdom, this is the Royal law, these are the lively (living) oracles of God.'

There is a difference between knowing about the Bible and knowing the Bible. But what of the Bible itself?

There are many intelligent guidebooks to the proper understanding of the great book. My favourite is *A Guidebook to the Bible* in the 'Teach Yourself' series of the 1950s which is now out of print. The fly-leaf reads as follows:

'This really is the book I have been looking for.'
The Rev. Dr Leslie D. Weatherhead
(Minister of the City Temple, London)

'I strongly recommend it to all who want to read their Bible with understanding: it is first rate, and it contains a very large amount of information in a very small space.'
The Late Archbishop of York

'Quite the most comprehensive and readable popular introduction to the Bible that I have seen and it is scholarly and up to date.'
Professor C.J. Mullo Weir, D.D.
(Glasgow University)

'Very well done. It represents fairly, and with sufficient accuracy, the kind of critical position which is now widely held and should be generally known. I shall recommend it.'
Professor C.H. Dodd, D.D.
(Cambridge University)

'A most serviceable handbook.'
Professor Edgar P. Dickie, D.D.
(St. Andrews University)

It would be difficult to pay greater tribute.

In his sermon on the Second Sunday in Advent (Bible Sunday) the Canon in Residence of Westminster Abbey, the Reverend Dr Donald Gray, made the following five points. He advised me with a smile as we shook hands on leaving the Abbey, that I could gladly set down his five principles without fear of breach of copyright. I commend them to you. He prefaced the five points by saying that it is essential to know something of the history, characters, principles and other aspects of the Bible for a proper understanding.

1. Do not try to read it at one go. Don't have a guilt complex convincing yourself that you have to spend hours reading Holy Writ, out of a sense of duty. There is no merit to be achieved or Everest to be conquered by reading the greatest book in the world at one sitting. It is in fact many books on widely differing subjects.

   Many large family bibles are still found, without being usefully used.

   Don't start at the beginning (Genesis) and read through to the end (Revelation).

2. A good knowledge is necessary. There is the account in Acts 8 of the Ethiopian eunuch who was reading in his chariot from Isaiah. Philip asked him if he understood what he was reading. 'How can I, except some one shall guide me?'

3. To obtain maximum benefit we need guidance. There are very many good commentaries; there is the Bible Reading Fellowship, and other guides. In the Alternative Service Book of the Anglican Church there are two sets of three lessons appointed for each Sunday, offering a logical and connected sequence.

4. Obtain a modern version. I recently counted twenty-eight versions in my small local Bible shop in Lancaster. My own preference is for the Authorised Version but I recognize its 300-year-old language is a hindrance to many young people today. For my service of recognition as a fully qualified Local Preacher in 1961 I chose the Revised Standard Version which retains much of the fine language of the Authorised Version but again would not be suitable for many young people today. The Revised English Bible found in most Churches today is a fine translation.

5. Think and read carefully what is God's word *but* mediated through the pen of men and women. It is not infallible. It is not a totem. You will not find a text for your day or need of the moment by simply opening the Bible and expecting an instant remedy or immediate advice. It is not white magic. All of us need help and guidance. Read, mark, learn and inwardly digest. You cannot master the Bible in five minutes.

I would also add to the address of the learned Canon (partially influenced by his reference to guidebooks and commentaries) the use of daily notes such as those provided by the International Bible Reading Association.

Speakers' Corner

I refer to this fascinating place, busy every Sunday afternoon, in Hyde Park. The following are jottings I made on my visit with my son John during December 1994, and the first occasion since my National Service in 1952-54. I hope they will give the reader who has never visited, a glimpse of the proceedings.

Jottings from Speakers' Corner – 4/12/94

1. Orthodox Jew waving flag of David, separated by only a few yards from Yasser Arafat advocate with PLO flag – berating the USA.
2. Christian Atheist banner and podium prominent. No time to listen.
3. Syndicalist – advocating that if you want a pair of shoes, you should be able to enter a shop and take one! All in favour – I need a new pair.
4. The 'Fellowship of controversy' is alive and well. Lord Soper's legs have gone (had to be lifted onto his step ladder) – but the voice is strong, the mind as keen as ever, and the twinkle present in the eye.
5. Heckler: 'Now, about the House of Lords.'
   Lord Soper: 'Yes, I put your name down twice, but they wouldn't have you.' And so much more.
6. Continues to stress that Jesus spoke far more about the establishment of the Kingdom of God than personal salvation.
7. Berated Tony Blair about his children's education.
   Said his son would pass five RC schools on the way to the chosen one.
8. Insisted education be dealt with at local level and not by central Government.
9. Evolution and not Revolution in everything. Pacifism still the call.
10. Thinks Arthur Scargill a nice man, retain Clause 4, and the only answer is Socialism.
11. Castigated the Government.
12. Drew *young* heckler's attention to the fact that he *was* interested in reincarnation – and pointed out it was likely to be of more immediate importance to him than the questioner.

Vintage Soper. Had to see him after forty years absence.

Feeding the Seagulls

I have just returned from a walk along the seafront. The morning has been sunny. A fresh wind, blue sky, high tide and an above-average temperature for mid-February have enhanced the usual view across the Bay. It was not quite as clear as on some occasions but all my favourite places were plainly visible. As it is Saturday, the golf course was busy and eight wind-surfers were busy getting their craft ready.

I took a larger amount of bread than usual, as a loaf I had bought several days ago was suspect. My final destination was the slipway, some 200 yards from my home and which I can see as I write at my desk. The seagulls seem to know that food awaits them and with my first steps at the top of the descent, a few rose from the water and circled me. I have enjoyed doing this from my earliest days.

But not for me the simple task of throwing the bread on the ground and departing. It is an art, to be developed and honed, a time to savour and not to rush. With the fresh wind, navigational skills are required by bird and feeder alike. I throw the bread upwards, sometimes several pieces at a time, into the wind. The seagulls swoop down or fly forward according to their position and on most days catch in their beaks the larger proportion thrown to them. Passers by stop and watch. The residents of Lakeland House, a high-rise block of flats across the road, view from their balcony seats. The shrieks of the gulls masks the noise of the traffic. If the tide is on the ebb and some distance from the shore, there are often items of greater interest on the edge of the tide and in the rocks for them. A simple but delightful pleasure and one appreciated by many local residents.

When I have been away from Morecambe over the years, several people have remarked that they can tell I live at the seaside. Apparently I talk of seagles instead of seagulls, because of their familiarity. The types vary throughout the year and some are more contentious and noisy than others. But all are friends.

Modern Aids

Although I recognise their use and my age, I feel I will never come to terms with and dislike many aspects and features of:
1. Portable telephones.
2. Ansaphones.
3. Cash dispensers.
4. Word processors.   ) The preparation of my book
5. Photocopying machines.) would have been a difficult task
) indeed without them.

The reason is quite simple, if unacceptable today. They all lack the personal touch.

The Chain Reaction

Anyone can test the theory of the chain reaction in daily life. If I drive down a road in busy traffic and allow someone from a side road to enter in front of me, it is my experience that he or she will do the same.

If I am in my local shopping centre and hold open a door for a shopper it is my experience that most people say 'Thank you' and immediately change from looking after No. 1 and become aware of and helpful towards others.

I firmly believe that when the chips are down in serious circumstances, most people are good at heart. It is usually pressures of work, money, family problems and a hundred other things which made them appear so often as irritable, scowling and looking after their own selfish interests.

Recently I have travelled a good deal by train in inclement weather and with poor travelling service. On each occasion I have found myself sitting with an older lady travelling to or from family. Kindly eyes and disposition and a warm intelligent interest in, and concern for people and events, have manifested themselves.

They have strengthened and restored my faith in human nature.

Anxiety

There must be very few people alive to whom anxiety is a stranger. My reader will not have had to be very discerning to note that my favourite author on religion is the late Dr Leslie Weatherhead. He is the writer of *A Prescription for Anxiety*. Over the years I have read and skimmed through dozens of books on the subject, but never one to equal his.

Many of my friends to whom I have loaned one of the many copies I keep for the purpose have thanked me for it, and have spoken of the great help they received from its pages.

There can be few greater commendations than those on the flyleaf of one print:

'I have always wanted a book of this kind that I could safely commend to depressed and worried folk, and now I have it.'

Professor L.W. Grensted

'I am delighted with this book; it is vintage Weatherhead! Here is the thoughtful Christian answer for all those oppressed with anxiety.'

J.B. Phillips

'Anxiety is such a ubiquitous and chronic ailment that multitudes will thank God for sending to them through His servant this prescription for their malady.'

Professor James. S. Stewart

'The best that Dr Weatherhead has done. I am not looking at it from the learned side, but as a book likely to be helpful to ordinary people. It lives up to its title.'

Dr S. King Hutton

'It is specially valuable because it is written by a man who has plumbed the depths of anxiety and depression in his own experience. Having passed through the shadows himself, he is able to write with a large understanding and full sympathy.'

Dr Ernest White

'No book I know brings out so thoroughly not by argument, but by personal illustration the tremendous value of the Gospel and our religious faith for anxiety conditions.'

Professor J.G. McKenzie in the *British Weekly*

'He has not done better than this. *Prescription for Anxiety* is a contribution to thought and practice.'

The Methodist Recorder

The cover depicts a sea with distant mountains and varying shades. At the foot of the flyleaf are these words:

The picture on the dust cover was painted by the author to symbolise man's emergence from the darkness of anxiety to the bright uplands where God's purposes are finally fulfilled.

Looking Round Churches

In spite of declining congregations, many people still enjoy looking round our great Cathedrals and Churches. I have found a booklet *What to look for in an Old Church* by J. Hope Unwin a great help. First published by SPCK in 1934, my copy is a 1964 reprint.

Another excellent booklet to be found in very many churches I have visited is *Acceptance* by Vincent P. Collins. In many places I am told it is the best-selling product on the bookstall. It is published by Anthony Clarke of Wheathampstead, Hertfordshire. The copy in front of me is priced at 65p and is a fourth (1990) printing.

The National Lottery

As I write I detect a feeling that people are already seeing the dangers of an almost insane pursuit of a weekly multi-million pound prize. Nor do I believe that the money it produces for good causes will result necessarily in the best outcome. Jockeying for the funds will spread corruption and other evils, and many smaller charities will suffer.

I believe money in itself to be neutral and if anyone offered a pools or other win to a good cause with which I have connections, I would not refuse it.

People really *do* believe they are going to win £15 million and probably live on the thought from week to week. What a way to live.

Lakeland Treasures

There are an almost limitless number of places of interest and pleasure in the Lakeland area and it is perhaps invidious to mention only a few.

I have however found the following a particular source of enjoyment:
1. Abbot Hall, Kendal. The Gallery & Museum.
2. Brantwood, on Coniston Water. The home of John Ruskin.
3. Cartmel Priory Church.
4. Holker Hall.
5. Leighton Hall.
6. Levens Hall.
7. Muncaster Castle.
8. Sizergh Castle.
9. Brockholes between Ambleside and Windermere and owned by the Countryside Commission.
10. Fell Foot, Newby Bridge.

I recommend the various *Walks for Motorists* books of circular routes.

An excellent book for those who wish to visit Retreat Houses is *Away from It All* by Geoffrey Gerard BA FRS(Edin) MIEE (Lutterworth Press).

Knowing How

Among my father's papers I found this story from an address at the Sunday School prize-giving:

> How many of us look back with thankfulness on those influences for good in our lives that emanated from the words and example of our Sunday School teachers? And so you teachers be encouraged in your work by the thought that you are influencing these young lives for good, and in the years that lie ahead these young people will look back with grateful hearts on their days in Bare Methodist Sunday School.
>
> And to our young people – just a few words. Learn your lessons well. They are going to stand you in great stead in the future. You have come here to-night to receive your prizes which denote regular attendance and good conduct at Sunday School. One of the best messages that I can give to you is to learn your lessons well.
>
> Our old Methodist preachers used often to quote in East Lancashire a story said to be true of the town of Burnley. A certain factory had been stopped for a fortnight by reason of some defect in the engine which the engineers could not detect. Great hardship was being suffered by the employees and despite all the efforts of the engineers the mill could not be started. Eventually an expert from London was called in. Going into the engine room he asked the engineers briefly the cause or what they considered was the cause of the trouble, and taking hold of a small hammer he tapped a steam valve and then told them to start up the engine. The engine started. Some weeks afterwards the firm received a bill. The bill amounted to £54, and the firm gratefully paid the account, but as a matter of interest asked the engineer if he would itemize his account. The account was returned itemized as follows:
>
> | | |
> |---|---|
> | Expenses from London to Burnley | £4 |
> | To knowing how | £50 |

Eat Morecambe Bay Shrimps

Eat generously of this delicious delicacy of my home town! Shrimp picking was originally a cottage industry, with groups of ladies working dextrously round tables in cottages around the centre of the town.

Two or three months ago I bumped into Bob Baxter outside my newsagent. He is a member of one of the original Morecambe fishermen families, and holds the Royal Warrant for the product. He had been talking on the telephone that very week with my cousin Air Vice-Marshal 'Bobby' Robson, and Lord Justice Rose (both mentioned elsewhere in my story) about his shrimps.

When I stayed with my cousin Bobby in January 1995 while completing the research into our family history mentioned in an earlier chapter, his wife Brenda knew how to please me by serving us each with a carton of 'the lovely grub'. They were *delicious*.

Potted shrimps are sent to all the London Royal Palaces each week. In earlier days, Mr Morley of Lord Street had the Royal Warrant sign, almost covering the front of his modest terraced house. Potted shrimps were sent to Winston Churchill during the War.

Enter the Common Market regulations. The possibility of Morecambe shrimps being prevented from travelling through the post brought Sir Mark Lennox-Boyd, our constituency MP, to Mr Baxter, along with Christopher Soames, of ample girth, and (then) Minister of Food. Reassurances were given by both, but the coup d'état was delivered by Mr Soames who, when asked if his gastronomic reputation had included the consumption of Morecambe Bay shrimps, said, 'Eaten them my boy? I was brought up on them.'

I reproduce the following article with permission from the *Financial Times* for 25 April 1992:

Peeled in the pink with pride
Nicholas Lander meets the Lancashire producer of a British seafood delicacy.

When your product has been made by the family business since 1799, bears the name of your home town on its label, and has earned two Royal Warrants as purveyors to Their Majesties The Queen and The Queen Mother, pride in the product is justified.

Bob Baxter, proprietor of James Baxter and Son, Morecambe Bay, Lancashire, hopes he has pride in his product sufficient to see off the two new threats to his speciality food business (and to many similar businesses throughout Europe): EC interference from Brussels, and the wave of new food legislation which seems to make no distinction between small, independent food producers and industrial giants.

His family – thanks to the combination of a fishing grandfather and a grandmother on the commercial side – monopolised the Morecambe Bay fish trade. Until the early 1950s Morecambe was an important seaside location: weekend trains in the summer season disgorged 800 visitors every 15 minutes at Morecambe station. The Baxters ran wet fish shops, five large restaurants, fishing boats and a famous potted shrimp business.

As a lad, Bob Baxter used to look on to a bay filled with more than 100 small fishing boats; on my visit there were just six. He has spent 45 years in the family business, selling the retail outlets ahead of Morecambe's decline as a seaside resort; he now runs a business with a £500,000 turnover which includes more modern frozen foods, but it still produces the traditional potted shrimps.

The shrimps live in the sandy estuaries of the rivers between north Wales and the Solway Firth. Baxter only buys those trawled by professional fishermen in the traditional 25 ft boats.

Twenty stone of shrimp is a good catch for the eight-hour voyage. Once on board, the shrimps are cleaned and cooked in boiling sea water. Later they are hand peeled by the fishermen and their wives in approved premises, then delivered to Baxter.

Kathleen and Doreen, with more than 35 years' experience between them, take over. In a small room, no bigger than a domestic kitchen, the shrimps are re-cooked in small batches in spiced butter – the recipe is a trade secret – and allowed to cool. Then 2oz cartons are filled with 1¾oz shrimps each, and ¼oz butter lovingly spooned across the top to seal and protect the contents.

The process is swift: out of the sea and into the pot in a maximum of 36 hours. It is simple, too: there is only one quality standard. Asked by a potentially important customer to produce potted shrimps to a slightly lower specification, Bob Baxter refused.

On a busy day Kathleen and Doreen fill 750 pots; in a good year, 150,000. In the past, the weather was the biggest obstacle – not merely storms, but changes on the sea bed occurring every eight years. In 1991 the shrimp catch was reduced by 40 per cent.

Baxter now feels that the obstacles are multiplying, and that they are increasingly man-made. Like most professional food handlers he cares about hygiene and safety: the shrimps are regularly analysed by an independent laboratory, and his formica-topped tables were replaced by stainless steel long before any directives appeared. But he has no truck with the sentiment expressed by a government health official, that the main drive for quality should be fear of prosecution. For Baxter, the priorities are a good product and a satisfied customer.

Last year, as recession was also affecting sales, two new obstacles materialised. First, the EC decided to classify the one-man 25ft trawling boats as 'factory ships'. Although not yet passed into law, this directive could lead to the end of the immediate boiling of the shrimps in sea water, an important part of the traditional process. Instead, the small fishing vessels would be required to carry huge quantities of fresh water and ice on board.

Then the new Food Safety Act, by initially proscribing mail order business and stipulating that all deliveries to wholesalers be made by refrigerated transport, threatened to break the contact between Baxter and his customers. The second stipulation means that he can no longer supply his retail or restaurant customers with fresh potted shrimps; they now have to make do with frozen shrimps. (There is, though, no significant difference in taste: at certain times of the year the shrimps are frozen to ensure a constant supply.)

Fortunately for all small-scale UK food producers, the ban on mail order business was lifted, allowing it to continue to the 'end-user': the private customer. For Baxter this was critical: local trade now accounts for only 5 per cent of his entire production. In late 1991 he placed an advertisement in a national newspaper offering ten 2oz pots at £19.90 inclusive of packing and postage. £4,000 worth of new business was the result.

There has been speedy repeat business from grateful customers. If he can maintain momentum, Baxter plans a small modern unit to handle mail orders.

I recently came across the following in the *Morecambe Guardian* newspaper for 10 June 1960:

Shrimps for Royal Duke

Mr R. Baxter of the Morecambe fish merchants' firm of James Baxter and Son made a special journey to Wales on Monday with a small consignment of shrimps. They were for a very special customer, the Duke of Gloucester, who was the guest of Brigadier Mainwaring at St Asaph. The Brigadier had ordered Morecambe shrimps at the request of the Duke.

When I showed it to Mr Bob Baxter he commented that he thinks he made the delivery in an E-type Jaguar.

Law and Order

There is grave public concern today about law and order. In the last few days I have read of exemplary sentences of considerable severity. I think the powers that be would find it difficult to understand the depth of public relief.

'Love the sinner, but hate the sin' is a good maxim. Whilst compassion, love and understanding must always be shown, and the reasons for terrible misdeeds sought out, the most important ingredient of discipline is essential. My Latin learning and the English dictionary tell me discipline is training of the mind that produces self-control, orderliness, obedience and capacity for co-operation. Its usual connotation infers in many minds the wrong impression of harsh regulations and authority.

Some people advocate the return to National Service as one remedy for the ills of today. There may be some merit in the proposal, although I hope not for the two-year period for which I served. Twelve months is the ideal period and some University students would be better served by this form of education, learning and service than in the way some spend their 'year out'.

I was extremely fortunate, as the reader will have read, but for others it was too long a period for many reasons. I am aware that for some National Service was a time of boredom, but for most the benefits were plain to see in later years. I was not alone in seeing the benefits, and the 'National Service man' could be readily identified in those and the immediately succeeding years by, in general, his mannerly bearing, tidy appearance and reasonable conduct.

Work

The late Rev. Jimmy Dinsdale, a retired Methodist minister was one of the old school. Following him along the promenade to church one lovely Sunday morning, I saw him stop and turn to the shelter which was full of residents and holidaymakers reading their Sunday papers. Tapping his walking-stick on the ground, he thundered in his Scottish accent, 'Have you read what's in your Bible today?'

He was a mentor of one of our ministers during a difficult period. The minister concerned repaired often to his home for sound counsel.

In a children's address, which forms part of our normal morning worship, he spoke of a boy vigorously polishing a pair of shoes until they shone: 'There is salvation in work,' he said.

Beware the Misquote

As a young advocate I appeared in Court as one among others, opposing the grant of planning permission to a man who intended to open a garage on the main road into Morecambe from Lancaster.

I represented the vested interests of others along the same route. My case rested on the fact that the applicant had indicated he would run the business on his own. With illness in mind, and the 1,001 things that man is heir to, I went on to quote the Bard in referring to 'the slings and arrows of outrageous fortune'. A nice turn of phrase I thought (and not unaware of its impressive look in the local press) only to be reported as saying: 'The slums and avenues of outward future'. I can't read shorthand but although I now smile, I thought more at the time about a pair of boxing gloves and the three School House Championships I had won at my weight.

In Hyde Park in the 1950s, as I have mentioned elsewhere, I heard Lord Soper reply to a questioner who asked what he thought of the Royal Family. He said, 'I think on the whole, they do a good job,' a reasonable reply. 'But they are not perfect and I wish for instance the Duke of Edinburgh didn't play so much polo on a Sunday.' The next day a national newspaper carried the banner heading: 'Methodist Leader makes violent attack on Royal Family.' I heard and saw this for myself, and *know* what the media can do when so minded.

Funerals and Hymn Tunes

I have left clear instructions for my funeral and advise others to do the same. At a time of sorrow, it is a help to executors and family.

My instructions are for: two favourite Bible readings, the first to be from the Old Testament and beloved of my father. The second is a resounding proclamation from St Paul of the love of Christ.

My choice of hymns sing of God's free Grace for all sinners and the request for an inextinguishable flame of love to be kindled in our hearts until death.

Some weeks ago, our new Minister announced one of them and referred to a well-known tune 'Hereford' to accompany it. 'But,' he said smilingly, 'We are not going to sing that one. We are going to sing "Wilton".' And so say I. That is the tune I have chosen. I have made it known that if it is not so played, I will turn in my coffin. As we left the church two friends complained that we had not sung 'Hereford'.

My dear father used to say that certain hymns were 'wedded' to certain tunes, and if the organist did not agree and played another, my father would on occasion put his hymn book down on the pew ledge as a temporary mark of protest.

The Methodist Recorder – *A Good Read*

I have always been an avid reader of this weekly treasure house of

Methodism. It is coveted by other denominations and I commend its weekly wisdom and spiritual riches. I must disclose a personal interest. In 1984 the following appeared:

> Mr John Knape, a local preacher and member of Bare church in the Morecambe and Heysham circuit, has been appointed chairman of the Marsden Building Society. The society is described as the largest 'Lancashire-based building society' with assets in excess of £80 million. Founded in 1860, its policy is to remain independent as a strong regional society with the emphasis on personal service. Mr Knape, admitted as a solicitor in the Supreme Court in 1952, is secretary of Morecambe, Heysham and District Council of Churches. He has held most church offices, including local preachers' secretary and has served on several District committees.

In December 1994 in the Christmas issue the following appeared:

> A former Morecambe lawyer, Mr John Knape, has written his autobiography *Satanic Mills to Galilee*. Written in Bunyanese-style it took him 23 days with 450 sheets of A4 paper, cataloguing his own battle against illness, the tragedy of his young wife's death from cancer, and the trauma of divorce. Mr Knape qualified as a solicitor in 1952 and went on to become senior partner in a firm of solicitors, founded by his father. A local preacher for more than 30 years he has been a regular worshipper at Bare Street church for over 60 years. The book, which shines with a faith for the future was a 'cathartic experience', said Mr Knape. 'To have completed it has given me a terrific feeling of fulfilment and I feel renewed and invigorated.' He hopes the book will be published next year.

Initiation

Many different bodies, societies, clubs, associations and other organizations have forms of initiation for new members. The Freemasons are perhaps the most notable example of the practice. It is wise to take them in good part.

The ceremony for a new boy at Shrewsbury School was 'the sacrifice'. This involved having one's head pushed down the lavatory basin, and held there, whilst the chain was pulled. The degree of unpleasantness varies, but I look back on my own experiences without displeasure, and I think they did me no harm.

Handel's Messiah

A great experience was to hear the Huddersfield Choral Society in Handel's *Messiah*. A local lady, Mrs Ellen Brook, had been the Lady Mayoress of Huddersfield many years ago. She had a record of never having missed a performance for thirty years, and her usual arrangements fell through at the last minute. I was glad to take her to my favourite musical experience. In a cafe that day, my good friend Leslie Morgan was lunching with a group of local Building Society managers, who had previously kindly invited me to join them (as a Building Society director) at their regular meetings.

Leslie was going to Bradford that evening. But were we not bound for Huddersfield? No! For the first time in memory the performance had been transferred to Bradford because of urgent repairs being carried out at the Huddersfield Town Hall. He gave us a history lesson on the way, guided us to our destination, and was a good companion on the return journey.

The lovely dresses of the ladies of the choir, the tremendous volume of their singing, the pre-Christmas atmosphere and air of anticipation, all made for a memorable evening. I recently attended a small performance in a local church, on a day when approximately 150 choirs around the country joined together in separate performances, for the benefit of their local hospices. The radio was on in the church, linking all the events, and each began after a countdown from 10.

I never cease to be amazed that it was written in twenty-four days. When he wrote the Hallelujah chorus, Handel speaks of having seen the whole of heaven open before him.

I was recently brought to earth when telling a friend with some pride that I had written my life story in longhand in twenty-three days. He said that was no big deal and referred to Handel's twenty-four days. Some difference! I have LP and 78 recordings, and never cease to feel my spirits soar to the realms above on its every hearing. I always look to see how many young people are in the choirs, looking to the future. I am encouraged.

Since I wrote these words our minister at Bare Methodist Church, Reverend Graham Vickers, has written his letter in the February 1995 issue of our church magazine, *The Messenger.* The choir's singing clearly had the same impact on him and Mrs Vickers:

THEIR SOUND IS GONE OUT INTO ALL LANDS

One of the high points of my Christmas activity – still fresh in my memory some six weeks later – was undoubtedly the evening which

Pam and I spent in Huddersfield Town Hall listening to Huddersfield Choral Society sing *Messiah*. Tickets were like gold and there was not an empty seat. It was a great privilege indeed to be present.

It was interesting to sit for some time beforehand and watch the audience come in, then the choir, row by row, together with the orchestra, the Northern Sinfonia on this occasion. A burst of applause greeted the leader, the principals and the guest conductor, Stephen Barlow. Then total silence – a moment of anticipation to savour what was in store.

I was totally unprepared for what followed: two verses of 'Christians, awake, salute the happy morn'. The sheer volume of sound that reverberated around the hall, the massed choir singing as one voice, the orchestra, the great organ – I've never heard it sung like that before! Inspiring and emotional – although it's interesting to note that during Sir Malcolm Sargeant's era with the Huddersfield Choral Society (1932-1967) the traditional Christmas hymn was always conducted by the chorus master, Sir Malcolm refusing to conduct 'that jingle'.

Handel's oratorio was in effect a dramatic Bible study in three parts on the theme of the Messiah:

Part One: The prophecy and realisation of God's plan to redeem mankind by the coming of the Messiah.

Part Two: The accomplishment of redemption by the sacrifice of Jesus, mankind's rejection of the offer, and mankind's utter defeat.

Part Three: A hymn of thanksgiving for the final overthrow of death.

There was a time when virtually every chapel choir in the North of England had its annual performance of *Messiah* – and Morecambe was no exception. Those days are gone, perhaps thankfully. The village choir's 'rendering' of the oratorio could often be interpreted in various ways! But Huddersfield was perfection – a tingling experience.

I hope that over Christmas – and as the new year dawned – you too in whatever way felt the inspiration of God's spirit moving within your heart and mind, exciting you with a deeper awareness of the beauty and harmony of his love for you – a renewal of the faith that in 1995 'the Lord God omnipotent reigneth . . . King of Kings and Lord of Lords: Hallelujah!'

With every blessing.

Yours sincerely,

Graham A. Vickers

A Smile

On one occasion I was at Deepdale, the ground of Preston North End Football Club, with Father and companions to see a normal league fixture. Turning round for no apparent reason, I saw two familiar figures in the seats immediately behind me. George Formby and his formidable wife, Beryl were sitting there. The troubles of later years were still not apparent but in repose George had a sad, sad face. The Lord loves a cheerful countenance as well as a cheerful giver, and so do I.

Dogmatism

It is an unwise habit to assert something as indisputable. In his book *Who Moved the Stone?* Frank Morrison set out to prove that the Resurrection of Jesus could not have happened and was a myth. After the utmost research and study, he was led inescapably to the conclusion that Jesus *was* raised from the dead.

Always be open to reasoning and enquiry and questioning. Is there a God for instance? If, as I have said elsewhere, we knew with absolute certainty that there was, we would be robots, with no room for our own personalities and the choice of making or refusing a free loving response to the love of God.

It is not easy to believe in God. There is a hiddenness and so much in life to make faith, and the kind of God I, as a Christian believe in, a difficulty; but at its lowest, my experience of life fills me with a strong feeling that there must be something more to life and the amazing universe in which we live. I cannot accept that it all just happened and life has neither meaning nor purpose.

The Flaw in Modern Soccer

Every soccer supporter is entitled to express his views, and they do. Whether it be to cast doubt on the parentage of the referee or the giving of unequivocal advice, he is never short of offers of help. I hold strong views however on a matter which I believe goes to the very heart of our English game and is responsible for its decline in recent years to a far greater degree than anything else. A large claim.

My views are twofold:

1. The recent tightening of the rules, as applied in the World Cup of 1994 has been seen as a way to bring back the Matthews, Finneys

and Bests of football. I disagree. I have already mentioned one. In the video of *Tom Finney, The Perfect Player*, Jimmy Hill refers to a statistic about the great outside right. It has been calculated, he said, that 'Sir' Tom was fouled on an average of just over every four minutes. It did not stop his genius.

2. The modern defensive systems and methods of stopping attackers can never defeat the winger with ball skills. Finney and Matthews again. If they beat, as they did so often, two or three opposing defenders, there were no possible defences or tackles to counteract them.

Away with wingless wonders and the all-purpose player. Bring back the winger and the excitement of the game, and the goals.

The 'If Onlys' of Life

As I draw near to the end of my earthly life, I am allowing my mind to wander over life's broad canvas. At every turn I see the need to express my gratitude for all those whom I have met in the journey, influencing my life.

I no longer have regrets. There is such a futility about the 'if onlys' of life. There is a divine, over-reaching and over-arching plan, and though the path before me may be clouded and dark at times, though I may not understand, God is not confused, and He knows the outcome of His good providence.

> Who fathoms the eternal thought?
> Who talks of scheme and plan?
> The Lord is God! He needeth not
> The poor device of man.
>
> Here in the maddening maze of things,
> When tossed by storm and flood,
> To one fixed ground my spirit clings;
> I know that God is good!
>
> I long for household voices gone,
> For vanished smiles I long;
> But God hath led my dear ones on,
> And He can do no wrong.

I know not what the future hath
Of marvel or surprise,
Assured alone that life and death
His mercy underlies.

And if my heart and flesh are weak
To bear an untried pain,
The bruised reed He will not break,
But strengthen and sustain.

No offering of my own I have,
Nor works my faith to prove;
I can but give the gifts He gave,
And plead His love and care.

And so beside the silent sea
I wait the muffled oar;
No harm from Him can come to me
On ocean or on shore.

I know not where His islands lift
Their fronded palms in air;
I only know I cannot drift
Beyond His love and care.

John Greenleaf Whittier, 1807-92

Physical Features

A favourite saying of my father when someone's unusual physical features were to be seen were the words: 'He (or she) is some mother's son (or daughter).' A reminder of this is found in the story of Samuel's choice of the young boy David as King:

> But the Lord said unto Samuel, Look not on his countenance, or on the height of his stature . . . for the Lord seeth not as man seeth, for man looketh on the outward appearance, but the Lord looketh in the heart. (1 Samuel 16)

Detaching with Love

Sometimes in life we come across people who are vexatious. We are taught in our Christian faith to love others, but this does not mean necessarily 'to like'. You can still love even if you do not like, because love involves the giving of oneself whether the element of liking is there or not. It is perhaps best exemplified in the Bible story of the parable of the Good Samaritan.

There are those who rub us up the wrong way, get up our nose, get on our nerves for reasons we cannot always explain. I believe there is nothing wrong in detaching ourselves with love.

Prayer

A hymn contains these verses:

>   Prayer is the soul's sincere desire,
>   Uttered or unexpressed,
>   The motion of a hidden fire
>   That trembles in the breast.
>
>   Prayer is the simplest form of speech
>   That infant lips can try;
>   Prayer the sublimest strains that reach
>   The majesty on high.
>
>   Prayer is the Christian's vital breath,
>   The Christian's native air,
>   His watchword at the gates of death;
>   He enters heaven with prayer.
>
>   O Thou by whom we come to God,
>   The Life, the Truth, the Way!
>   The path of prayer Thyself hast trod;
>   Lord! Teach us how to pray.
>   Amen.
>   James Montgomery, 1771-1854

The importance, power and influence of prayer cannot be over-estimated.

There are countless books on the subject dealing with the various aspects of Adoration, Praise, Confession, Petition, Intercession and so on.

The most important part and the highest form of prayer, which needs to be practised, is that of listening to and not speaking to God.

Indeed, a mind cleared of all else, concentration on opening the heart to the incoming power and presence of the living God, ever ready to enter, if we open the door and invite Him in, are essential for preparation and growth in the spiritual life.

The Daffodil

In the last few months when I have lived on my own I have had a vase of daffodils in my lounge. They have always spoken to me of spring, of new life, of Resurrection.

Their colour is always fresh and they strike me as simple and uncomplicated. They cost little, and, if tended well, last a long time. Buy a bunch today!

The Press

I shall deal briefly but with firm conviction about the Press. May we be preserved from any attempt ever to muzzle the Press. Better the not inconsiderable consequences of breach of privacy, exaggeration, witch-hunting and much more, than the attempt to suppress so much that the Press uncovers in the increasing corruption, lack of integrity and general laissez-faire of so much of our national, public and local life.

Go on Holiday to Bournemouth

I was brought up to believe that Bournemouth was inhabited by wealthy people of Semite origin, and I did not visit it until after marriage, with my wife and children.

It has so much to offer. A lovely long sandy beach with safe bathing (I know not its EEC standing so far as pollution is concerned); live shows, fine shops; the incomparable New Forest; Salisbury Cathedral, Christchurch Priory and its environs; Longleat; Beaulieu, Buckler's Hard and Brockenhurst come immediately to mind, and are in themselves the source of a wonderful annual break.

Freemasonry – A Gentle Caution

I may lose some well-loved friends by this title and content! My personal view of Freemasonry coincides with that of the Methodist Conference which has considered reports prepared on the subject on several occasions. The objection is on the grounds of its exclusivity. Let me say at once that I know many fine public-spirited men who give freely of time, talent and money to the laudable charitable and other objects its members generously support.

A friend from childhood and former co-partner in Jobling and Knape, who succeeded me as Senior Partner in 1973, is a senior figure in Freemasonry. He travels weekly to London on important business on their behalf in spite of having suffered severe heart attacks in recent years. Colin has cut down his commitments and workload appreciably. He was Treasurer of Sefton Road URC for many years; Chairman of the Governors of his old school, the George Fox School in Lancaster, for several years (the Quaker movement founded by George Fox is strong in this part of the country); he was a friend of Sir Charles Carter, the first and outstanding Vice-Chancellor of the University of Lancaster, who in turn was a friend of Harold Wilson. Colin advises and supports many good causes. He has made a remarkable recovery.

Colin and I lived in the same road (Stuart Avenue, named after my brother at the behest of my father's builder client) and have grown up in the same area and, in many respects, the same way. His father, the local Registrar of Births, Marriages and Deaths, was a senior local figure in the scouting movement. I registered the birth of my son Andrew John with him in Cheapside, now redeveloped as part of the Arndale Centre and close to the home of dear Dame Thora Hird who recently featured in a moving *South Bank Show* which I describe elsewhere in my story. Colin has been the butt of a few good-natured jokes in the office about his Freemasonry. Trouser legs have been rolled up, but he has always taken it in good part.

Why then my objection? Exclusivity, as I have said. And Charles Altham.

Charles was one of nature's gentlemen. He qualified as a solicitor at exactly the same time as me. We went on the same course, Charles to London, and I to Guildford. Charles had wanted us to go together but I feared it may have been at the expense of our studies. I passed through sheer hard graft, Charles through knowledge acquired, first at the old Burnley firm where my father was first articled and then in Morecambe. A fine spin bowler for Lancaster CC, a Captain of Morecambe Golf Club, choir member at the church I have attended for over sixty years, Charles and his first wife Phyllis, who died of TB of the stomach during the War, acted as babysitters for my parents. He taught me to play chess and bowled to me in the nets at Morecambe Grammar School. We always went together to the first day of the Old Trafford Test Match.

When my father died, his support was beyond the telling. On the way back from the farm where we had been planning the auction sale, I expressed doubt about my ability to run the practice. 'Of course you can,' he said. There are not many Charles Altham's around. He never showed the slightest sign of resentment about any nepotism in the practice. Charles was untidy and not the greatest speed merchant, but as a 'back-room' boy was priceless, and it is one of my great regrets that I never really told him of my affection.

But back to Freemasonry, which practises the custom of 'blackballing'. If one person votes in a totally confidential ballot against an applicant, that person is refused membership. Charles was blackballed. He was certain he knew the reason, which made it worse.

They look after each other in a wonderful way, they give freely to charity, some of my best friends are numbered in their ranks, but I would never ever accept membership. I understand it is by application and not invitation, and many have wondered why I have not joined.

In Chapter XLIII I give my definition of Christian love. It is:

A deep and genuine concern for the well-being of all with whom we come into contact, who are in need, irrespective of colour, class or creed, and whether the element of liking is there or not.

Freemasonry does not, in my view, qualify on those grounds.

Music

My taste and interest in music is narrow. Introduced to Handel's *Largo* at an early age, it has remained my favourite piece.

The peak of all music for me is Handel's *Messiah*. I still find it hard to believe that it was written in twenty-four days. It has lifted my soul many a time. The Huddersfield Choral Society conducted by Sir Malcolm Sergeant and with Isobel Baillie as soprano, is one of the several recordings I possess, including LP and 78.

In village choir and hall, or mighty cathedral, at Christmas or Easter, it never fails to make me realize that here in itself is cogent evidence for a benevolent Creator. Handel's *Messiah* or Beethoven's *9th*, could not have just 'happened'. The agnostic I can understand, the atheist I cannot. Arrogance is spelled out to me when a man says with unqualified assertion: 'There is no God.'

Mozart I find a delight, enhanced by the knowledge that he was writing well-turned keyboard minuets at the age of five, violin sonatas at seven, and symphonies at eight. Beethoven towers for me, with Handel and Mozart. The genius of a man who could, stone deaf, write his *9th Symphony* is beyond my understanding.

Endlessly I play tapes of hymns I love, and particularly those of Charles Wesley. 'Methodism was born in song,' and worship is greatly enhanced by God's gifts of music and song, the means by which we are often best able to express that which is inexpressible.

There is nothing like music for lifting the soul to the very gates of Heaven.

I have changed my attitude about music over the years, as in so many other things. I regret discouraging John and Catherine from *Top of the Pops* on BBC1. I still dislike the extremes of my experience, grand opera at one end of the scale and heavy metal at the other. In between there is a large area I enjoy provided there exists an element I describe as harmony or tune. 'Puppet on a string' with Sandie Shaw, which won the Eurovision Song Contest, is a favourite and sits well with Kenneth McKellar singing Scottish songs, and particularly my favourite, 'My love is like a red red rose.'

There are classical composers of renown such as Benjamin Britten and Shostakovitch where I just cannot recognize anything to enjoy. I feel there are few people who love and are moved more by music and few who understand less about it. Tolerance is necessary. Everyone to their own.

One matter does concern me. A few weeks ago I attended a meeting in a public hall. A disco for teenagers (well supervised) was taking place in the hall but it was difficult for those in the adjoining room to hear themselves speak. Not only was the volume tremendous, but unlike ballroom dancing there was no break. I cannot believe, looking at the youngsters late on in the evening, many of whom appeared slightly disorientated and shell-shocked, and thinking of the modern 'Walkman' that physical and emotional damage will not be caused in some measure in the future.

I remember a true case of two young children living near Heathrow airport. The sound level on one occasion was above 120 decibels, and the children were found running round in circles, having lost control temporarily of their faculties. Noise is certainly a problem of modern society, and not just in the musical sphere.

The Monarchy

Everyone seems to be expressing a view on the future of the Monarchy, so I might as well add my 'two pennorth', as we say in Lancashire.

My mind goes back (and I do not think an apology for repetition is required) to that so public and yet so private moment on 2 June 1953 when our young Sovereign pledged herself to the service of her peoples in the solemn oaths of the Coronation Service in Westminster Abbey. The moment I remember (and have already mentioned) most vividly of all was when she was handed a Bible with the words:

Take this book, the most valuable thing this world affords. Here is wisdom; this is the Royal law; these are the lively (living) oracles of God.

I focus my mind on that and all its implications. Personal morality, petty squabbles, press interference and public speculation on this and that were transcended by that declaration, by superb music and song, by colour and pageantry and ceremonial, the whole pervaded by the mystique that surrounds not only the Throne but more importantly, the God we worship.

I had the opportunity to take a seat along the route of the Coronation procession, working as I did in the Directorate of Legal Services in Northumberland Avenue, between Trafalgar Square and the Embankment (I digress for a moment to note that the offices of my family practice are in Northumberland *St*) during my National Service.

I chose instead to accept an invitation from Cousin Tom and their daughter Ann to their home in Esher, and thence to a neighbour's house where there was a gathering of neighbours round their colour TV set. I had wanted to see the Coronation service, and never regretted my decision. The beginning of a new Elizabethan era was proclaimed by the media. A young Sovereign, a future following the throwing off of the last dull shackles of post-war Britain which promised so much, was to be our heritage.

When I watched with millions the wedding of Prince Charles and Princess Diana I did not share the overwhelming adulation and joy which was exhibited. It did not 'feel right' for many reasons, and what Prince Charles said on the occasion of their engagement did not 'sound right'.

I wish Prince Charles had not been involved with another woman. I wish Prince Charles was not so involved in his interests including recent peripheral spiritual matters and gurus. I wish Princess Diana had been able to see that her real needs, particularly because of her unhappy childhood, could never have been met by the flimsy medical and other remedies with which she flirted. How I yearn that they might have seen an uncomplicated, true picture of Jesus and had accepted what is afforded to us all, a gift of the friendship of one who loves them and will never fail them, however fickle the support and loyalty of those on whom they depend.

Spare us from a presidential type of government, and let us retain, build upon and strengthen all that is good and noble, and let us pray for and support our Sovereign and the whole Royal Family, that they may seek the highest possible level of sacrifice and service to the Commonwealth, a tremendous force for good in the world, making up a quarter of its population, of so many tongues, and colour, and ways of life.

God save the Queen.

Horoscopes, Superstition and Other Rubbish

There is no need to waste much time on horoscopes, although a very large number of people reply on them implicitly. Others I suspect read them daily with reservations. They incline to believe them if favourable, and not otherwise. Harmless fun? Perhaps. As for superstitions, I walk under ladders, but I know someone who will not get out of bed on Friday the 13th. I cannot reconcile either with a loving, purposeful Father.

A few days ago in the large bookshop in Lancaster there was a section headed 'New Age'. Underneath were headings which included:

Tarot	Nostradamus
Astral	Witchcraft
Iching	Dreams
UFO	Magic
Ghosts	Mystery
Life After Death (Not the Christian view)	

I would not personally spend five minutes of my time in reading the books found there, apart from an interest in the study of dreams.

Blackberrying

The word may not be in the *Oxford Dictionary* but everyone knows what is meant by 'blackberrying', and most people seem to have tried it at one time or another. I think back to the pleasures in my childhood of collecting chestnuts and picking mushrooms, but blackberrying is something which has never ceased to give me pleasure down the years. September is my favourite month, with a slight 'nip' in the air on a sunny day making me feel more 'alive' than at any other time. And in my part of the world that is the best month for blackberries.

I have never yet met anyone who can pick them more quickly than I can, and have issued many challenges. One of the secrets is to stand still when a large number are seen on a bush and not be tempted to walk along, looking for even better bunches.

Another secret is the location. I lightly proclaim to friends that I will leave in my will, details of a spot on a country road near my home where blackberries grow in profusion, and have done so throughout my life. The bushes are spaced well apart and so do not attract the attention of passing motorists. I collected several pounds there last autumn and gave pleasure to friends who either made jam or mixed them with apples for delicious pies – with cream.

The blackberry bush is an invader and predator and spreads rapidly, thereby denying it a friendship with farmers. With modern tractors and machinery many hedges are now cut neatly and quickly about the time of harvesting, and it was only after a year or two of avoiding such places that I discovered that pruning did not remove the fruit entirely, but rather revealed them to the picker more clearly in many cases.

Wellingtons and old clothes, sandwiches and flasks, plenty of good strong collecting receptacles, a fine day, and September days can be a great experience and pleasure.

In a recent nature film on television I was amazed to see how many birds, insects and other creatures depend upon the blackberry bush in deepest winter. So leave some for others.

Regional Accents

I have recorded the problems I encountered at Shrewsbury School with my Lancashire accent. I love regional accents and the only one with which I have difficulty is the Geordie, largely, if not entirely, because of not hearing it overmuch in my part of the country.

In the old *Northern Daily Telegraph* newspaper of my teenage years, published in Blackburn and bought on a Saturday for its extended reports on the Burnley and Blackburn Rovers soccer games, there was a weekly article in Lancashire dialect. Translation was a slow but fascinating process.

Albert Leeming had the broadest Lancashire accent I can remember. A local poultry farmer, he often called to see Father at lunchtime in the old days. He once suspected Father of 'taking the mickey'. Discussing the finer points of the receding breeding potential of the cock, which he kept with his hens, Father asked him for the remedy he applied. 'Tha dubbs it'. On further inquiry as to the full procedure, he explained: 'Tha gets 'em bit legs, off wi its wattles, dubs it in cold watter, and its reet.' A more genteel description reveals the rather cruel practice of removing the major part of the poor creature's comb with a penknife (a very painful procedure I would think), holding it upside down by the legs, immersing the head in a bucket of cold water, shaking vigorously and releasing.

A very rude, but regularly used question of Albert's to anyone looking crestfallen, and which I leave to the reader's imagination was: 'Ast tha seen thi 'arse?'

It would be a dull world if we all spoke the Queen's English, although I still feel an Englishman is categorized as soon as he opens his mouth. Let us keep our accents.

Short-Term Memory

Some months ago I was told by a friend that one of the first signs of senility was the loss of short-term memory.

Very recently, my good friend Group Captain R.G. (Bob) Nuttall OBE RAF (Retd.) copied 333 pages of handwritten copy for my story. Frankly, I was afraid of the originals being stolen or destroyed in some way. It was a great relief when he completed the work in one uninterrupted spell of several hours in spite of indifferent health, and I was able to leave the copies in his home.

Afterwards he gave me a ticket for a Remembrance Day Service of Commemoration which he had helped to organize, where he was officiating as MC and receiving the Mayor and other local dignitaries before an all-ticket audience of 600, which could have been sold out several times over.

Clad in best suit, poppy in buttonhole, aftershave liberally spread and shoes highly polished, I parked on the seafront near the town centre and strolled along the promenade towards the brightly lit and welcoming venue. Taxis were discharging their fares, people were arriving on foot. I was early, with time to read my programme, look around and meditate.

The young lady who politely took my ticket looked puzzled. After some hesitation she said, 'I'm sorry, sir, this event was last night.' And it was. I had lost myself in the intensity of my writing efforts. The event taking place was a controversial Council-approved event – a tinker's wedding. 'Have you heard the one about the retired Solicitor who . . .'

A day or two ago I left my car a few streets away from home. I had met two friends who had been walking towards my house, and accompanied them. For a few panicky minutes I ran round the block where my house stands and suddenly remembered where I had left it. I had been about to phone the police.

I think my friend is correct. Certainly as we grow older we talk more about earlier years, and here I can certainly say from the experience of writing my story that my memory of earlier days is as clear, if not clearer, as at any time in my life.

Only this week I replaced my kettle. It had been used on my gas stove. I had put it on the flame unfilled, with a consequent 'nuclear meltdown'. I bought a new electric kettle and, preoccupied, I placed it on the gas flame. You have been warned!

Talking to Children in Church

Every preacher has his own method of conveying a spiritual or moral message to the children. We have black bags and brown paper parcels, containing unexpected surprises, and visual aids are increasingly used.

The Rev. P.W. James had a ready wit. A small boy on a station platform. The passenger in the train hands him, through the window, a shilling for two cakes from the adjoining stall. As the train starts to move, the boy runs alongside the man, one cake in hand, tosses a sixpence into the carriage and says, 'Sorry sir – they only had one.'

Mother gives Johnny a lovely large red apple and a smaller green apple. 'One for you, and one for Mary.' Mary receives the green apple. 'Now, Johnny, if that had been Mary she would have kept the green one.'

'Well she's got it, hasn't she?' said Johnny.

The Politics of Envy

The writing of my autobiography has been a time of unmitigated joy, fulfilment and renewal for me. But not for some. We talk about finding our true friends in time of trouble, but I would be less than honest if I did not say the same is true in times of what may to others appear to be worldly success.

Of course I have enjoyed being the subject of conversation in many areas where I move and am known, but I know my real and lasting aim has been to try and help others through the Slough of Despond which nearly, if not all of us, pass through at one time or another in life's journey. Some people appear to avoid disaster and misfortune, but not many, and even in those cases appearances can be misleading.

It has saddened me to find that people I have known all my life and regarded as real friends are full of envy, have deliberately told lies and spread rumour about its contents, have ignored me, have in one case said publicly I sought only personal glory and reputation. I have been called a hypocrite to my face in the most unfair circumstances. These things no longer have the power to hurt in any real way, but make me sad for those concerned. I really can pray for those who use me spitefully and often stand appalled at the thought of the state of their inner lives.

And I do not apologize for saying that in more than one instance those involved are ordained clergymen. In one case it was a man who had wrongly misjudged me and had come to an instant decision when we first met, and had drawn a wrong conclusion. There was no element of apology although the opportunity offered itself. I would not have my reader think other than that in the vast majority of cases people have genuinely looked forward to the contents being of help to them, and been glad for me, but the need of the human soul for forgiveness and cleansing has never been clearer to me. Envy is a particularly nasty human trait.

In one case a person has lived in fear of me mentioning or attributing something to him or her, ever since news of my writing being in hand became known.

It has prevented the healing of a breach which I was particularly anxious to bring about, and will almost certainly affect the long-term mental health of both persons involved.

It is not inappropriate for me to say as a Methodist I have come to see the value of confession and absolution, particularly in the Roman Catholic Church. It is an essential element of the programme of recovery in Alcoholics Anonymous, to which I will come.

The Incomparable Christ

More than nineteen hundred years ago there was a Man born contrary to the laws of life. This Man lived in poverty and was reared in obscurity. He did not travel extensively. Only once did He cross the boundary of the country in which He lived; that was during His exile in childhood.

He possessed neither wealth nor influence. His relatives were inconspicuous and had neither training nor formal education.

In infancy He startled a king; in childhood He puzzled doctors; in manhood He ruled the course of nature, walked upon the billows as if pavements, and hushed the sea to sleep.

He healed the multitudes without medicine and made no charge for His service.

He never wrote a book, and yet all the libraries of the country could not hold the books that have been written about Him.

279

He never wrote a song, and yet He has furnished the theme for more songs than all the songwriters combined.

He never founded a college, but all the schools put together cannot boast of having as many students.

He never marshalled an army, nor drafted a soldier, nor fired a gun; and yet no leader ever had more volunteers who have, under His orders, made more rebels stack arms and surrender without a shot fired.

He never practised psychiatry, and yet He has healed more broken hearts than all the doctors far and near.

Once each week the wheels of commerce cease their turning and multitudes wend their way to worshipping assemblies to pay homage and respect to Him.

The names of the past proud statesmen of Greece and Rome have come and gone. The names of the past scientists, philosophers, and theologians have come and gone; but the name of this Man abounds more and more. Though time has spread nineteen hundred years between the people of this generation and the scene of His crucifixion, yet He still lives. Herod could not destroy Him, and the grave could not hold Him.

He stands forth upon the highest pinnacle of heavenly glory, proclaimed of God, acknowledged by angels, adored by saints, and feared by devils, as the living, personal Christ, our Lord and Saviour.

We are either going to be forever with Him or forever without Him. It was the incomparable Christ who said:

'Behold, I stand at the door, and knock: if any man hear my voice, and open the door, I will come into him, and will sup with him, and he with me.'

(Revelation 3:20)

'I am the way, the truth and the life: no man cometh unto the Father, but by me.'

(John 14:6)

FOR

'There is one God, and one mediator between God and men, the man Christ Jesus.'

(1 Timothy 2:5)

THEREFORE

'Believe on the Lord Jesus Christ, and thou shalt be saved.'

(Acts 16:31)

Coincidences

I give two instances:

I finished writing the manuscript of my book in a car park next to the well-known restaurant of Miller House in Bowness-on-Windermere. It was about 7.30 to 8.30 a.m. when I began. It was raining heavily and in darkness apart from the interior car light. The reader may think they were hardly ideal circumstances for inspired or intelligent or thoughtful writing. I can only say I agree, but I was still enveloped in that atmosphere of the twenty-three days of which I have written.

When I had finished I determined to go to the Parish Church at Hawkshead to give thanks, to spend a short time in meditation, and generally dwell upon the happenings and events of the last four weeks. It was far from high summer and all was peaceful and quiet.

I was alone in the church for some time. I was conscious that Wordsworth came to Hawkshead at the age of eight when his mother died in 1778. After his father's death he lived in the village with his 'dame' Anne Tyson, until he went up to St John's College, Cambridge in 1787. He went to the grammar school close by. A chapel existed in the twelfth century. The massive pillars and rounded arcades of the present church are to be found nowhere else in England.

After a short time, a lady entered and busied herself with a new altar cloth. About to leave, I walked towards the altar to admire the stained-glass windows. I wished the lady good day, and fell into conversation, in my eagerness to tell about my proposed book. In my hand was the synopsis which I prepared months before for any publisher who might be interested. I handed it to her, so that she could read the short first page about the purpose of the book, and which mentioned Wordsworth and the Lakeland mountains and hills. She turned to the second page, and saw the mention of Shrewsbury School. She asked me 'Did you know Mr Charlesworth?' I think I have it right when I say that her daughter was married to a relative of Mr Charlesworth. I must confess to some uncertainty, because I was so taken aback by her question.

Some months ago, as an old boy of Shrewsbury School, I ordered an eagerly awaited book *Behind the Headlines*. Michael Charlesworth can perhaps claim to know, and be known by more Salopians than anyone living today. His sixty-year association with my old school has seen him in the varied capacities of schoolboy, master, housemaster, headmaster, bursar, editor of the Newsletter, and assistant secretary of the Old Salopian Club. I wrote to ask if he could assist me with an extract from school records to enable me to finish part of my own writing about the school (my soccer prowess!). I have had a continuing correspondence with him, and I received a postcard in which he said that I appear to have received a deal of inspiration for my book.

I duly acquired a copy of the autobiography and feel badly that I could not reciprocate as I had promised. In November 1997 I wrote to explain the position and that publication was now proceeding. Typically I received an early reply on a postcard, showing a painting of 'Speech Day at Shrewsbury' by John Alford, in which he said that he looked forward to the publication, and generally thanking me.

The lady, I met, is a widow, who came to live with her husband on his retirement as a Bank Manager. He died over two years ago from cancer. I spoke to her of Vera, and her death from the same disease. We shared painful experiences. Some call such happenings, a coincidence.

In January 1998 I was handed a letter by the old family friend who, in my view, saved my life in May 1997 and is mentioned elsewhere. On the reverse side was the name and address of the sender and the address side was marked 'Please forward if necessary'. The name was Bob Makin. My friend has lived at the address for twenty-nine years and I knew the previous owners for very many years. They were members of my Church, and their daughters were in the Youth Club, Sunday School and other activities where I was a leader and worker.

And then my memory once again came to my aid. The letter was addressed to Mrs— née— and I spoke to Irene Lynch, my first Sunday School teacher, of whom I write fully elsewhere in these pages. The name was faintly familiar to her though she could not have been around for very long.

My mind suddenly went back to my Sunday School days in the 1930s, in the original church building, which was rebuilt in 1959 and converted into a Church Hall and other rooms. We were only eight or nine years old but I recalled Bob for one reason only. We were asked one afternoon to 'sign the pledge'. I do not know whether this was connected with the Rechabites. As the reader would expect, coming from a traditional and strongly Methodist home and background, alcohol was evil and the thought of it made me shiver and slightly frightened. In the light of Chapter XXXV the reader will be forgiven for being shocked, but I would remind him that it is an illness as much as cancer or TB or asthma.

Bob, however, open and frank, said he would not sign. A surprised teacher, very much taken aback, asked for the reason. As if it were yesterday I can see Bob's open countenance say, 'Because I like the taste of beer.' I do not remember him apart from this one occasion. I offered to return the letter and when doing so mentioned this occasion.

A week or two ago in early January 1998, only seven to ten days after my letter was despatched, I was leaving my flat for church when the telephone rang. It was, of course, Bob!

'Are you back in England then?' I asked. The call sounded so clear it could have been a local one. 'No,' came the reply. 'I'm speaking from South Africa.'

Bob said his recent phone bills had been horrendous and that he intended to make a tape covering all that had happened to him since the event I have mentioned. I promised to reply in like form. I have just received the tape. He has relatives in the part of the town where I live. All will have been revealed by the time of publication of my life story.

I could regale my readers with literally dozens of similar and even more unusual events during the course of my writing. They strengthen a view I have long held that there are more things in Heaven and earth . . .

I draw strength from the element of mystery in so many parts of life and this helps me to realize that man is far from being God.

Chapter XXXV

ALCOHOLISM – RECOVERY WITHOUT CURE

I anticipate that many of my readers will have turned to this chapter first. I hope they will stay to read the rest from the first page.

My decision to write this book will have been well-served, if it assists even one person, who suffers from the incurable and life-threatening illness of alcoholism, which I must carry to the grave.

It was a matter of profound relief to me, when I was told, and came to understand, that the alcoholism which came close to ending my life, was something for which I was not to blame any more than if I were a cancer victim, a diabetes sufferer, or one who had contracted by whatever means, any one of the incurable diseases, which afflict mankind. Those men and women who have known me throughout my life, and those closest to me would accept unreservedly that I was the last person they could imagine, as one who would ever have a drink problem, much less be classified as an alcoholic.

A man in a dirty raincoat, tied with string, under a canal bridge, sleeping rough, with seven days growth of beard, is the sort of person they would have in mind. Not a respectable professional man, with a lifetime of service to his clients, a man who professed to be a Christian, a preacher of the Gospel for over 30 years, one who had attended and served his Church, in nearly every capacity, for a lifetime. A man with a drink problem, who had incomprehensibly allowed himself to stray away from his principles, a member of a denomination whose public symbol was of a wine glass with a cross drawn across it? Yes, perhaps this might be the horrible truth, but the shame, the wrongdoing, the bad example, the hypocrisy, the disillusionment resulting from the revelation of such a respected member of the community.

But John was and is an alcoholic, with a determination, and the help, to enable him to maintain the present arrestment of his affliction, and not to take another drink as long as he lives. If he has not had a drink for nearly 2 years now, how can I as a neutral observer, be expected to understand that the exercise of will-power is not sufficient, and that if he should take a sherry at a social gathering, within weeks his condition will almost certainly be worse than the one which brought him to his knees, and a rock-bottom experience?

Once more: 'The alcoholic at certain times has no effective mental defence against the first drink. Except in a few rare cases, neither he nor any other human being can provide such a defence. His defence must come from a Higher Power.'

Along with war, and other addictive drugs (for it is one), alcohol has killed millions of men and women, caused havoc in countless lives and families, and caused untold misery to dependants of the men and women who live with, or whose lives are touched by, its inevitable results. But I am not anti-drink, although I was brought up as a strict Methodist, and saw it as the devil's kingdom.

On a day trip to the Isle of Man, sailing from Heysham in 1938, aged 8, I needed to go to the toilet, and father directed me through a large room, where a number of tall men were holding glasses in their hands, speaking in raised voices, and with laughter on their lips. Something about the scene frightened me, I disliked the horrible smell, and rushed to the toilet and back, relieved to get back to Daddy. Until I was 31, I would no more have thought of consuming even a tiny drop of alcohol, than jumping off the Tower at Blackpool. I could sit with my friends, the other team members of the soccer side for which I played, in a public-house on returning from an away game, and match the pint of bitter they drank, with a pint of orange juice. I could do the same in the company of my tennis club friends, but to partake of the foul concoction of alcohol, was beyond the pale.

Apart from disliking the smell and the thought of tasting alcohol, whatever would my family, friends and acquaintances say if John had a drink of alcohol; this almost perfect example of respectability, who had signed the pledge in Sunday School at the age of 7 or 8, confirming that he would never partake? What of my Sunday School Superintendent, who had spoken to us of the widespread display of posters on billboards throughout the land asserting 'Beer is Best', and the wise and brave individuals who had taken a stand by adding to the end of the slogan, 'left alone'.

When I first became engaged to be married to Rosalie, I announced to my fiancée with some bravado, that when on honeymoon, I intended to smoke a cigar, and drink a glass of red wine. Six months later I did so, and then remained a total abstainer for many years.

Let me quote again from 'Alcoholics Anonymous', the 'bible' of the fellowship of Alcoholics Anonymous:

'Here are some of the methods we have tried: drinking beer only, limiting the number of drinks, never drinking alone, never drinking in the morning, drinking only at home, never having it in the house, never drinking during business hours, drinking only at parties, switching from scotch to brandy, drinking only natural wines, agreeing to resign if ever drunk on the job, taking a trip, not taking a trip, swearing off forever (with and without solemn oath), taking more physical exercise, reading inspirational books, going to health farms and sanatoriums, accepting voluntary commitment to asylums – we could increase the list ad infinitum'.

It is a progressive illness, which affects almost every organ of the body. It has baffled doctors and psychiatrists, scientists and ministers of religion. It is no respecter of persons and affects people of every kind, in all walks of life. Doctors, priests, members of the aristocracy, accountants, manual workers, scientists, lawyers and every kind of person in society can be an alcoholic.
Is there an answer?
I know there is. A.A. says:

'Rarely have we seen a person fail who has thoroughly followed our path.'

The path is the Twelve Step programme of A.A. which I have set out later. It is a promise which I have seen being fulfilled in my life and the life of others. I am not going to burden the reader with a drunkalogue. I could take up the rest of my work in detailing the long catalogue of troubles I encountered because of John Barleycorn, and even when I found A.A., because of my failure to give myself to their simple programme. Several periods of sobriety were interspersed with periods of drinking, but let one experience point to the baffling, cunning, powerful and patient nature of the illness.

I was returning from an important business meeting. I had been attending A.A. meetings on a regular basis and had not had a drink for over 2 years. I felt mentally and physically fit. The day had been successful. The result of my labours had been a personal and financial success for many good people. It was a lovely spring evening, and summer beckoned. A lovely meal would be waiting for me, prepared by my loyal and caring wife. God was in His heaven, and all was right with the world. A drink was the farthest thing from my mind. When I was only 4 miles from home, I glanced towards a line of shops at the side of the road – I saw the off-licence shop. The mental defence of my Higher Power failed me, because I did not call on or use it. I turned the corner and parked. With 3 cans of lager I returned home. Within 3 weeks, I was in a worse stated than over 2 years before when I had my last drink, proving the truth of the A.A. teaching of the progressive nature of the illness.

I learned in the end that the only way to get hold of the 12 Steps was to get on my knees and surrender. If there are two truths more important than others they are that half measures avail *nothing* and that I have yet to see a happy recovering alcoholic living a useful life who has not been 'in the gutter'. I know. I was there.

I am not a bigot. Alcohol, in moderation, and for most people can be one of the pleasures and lubricants of social life, enhancing its quality, providing relaxation and generally contributing to human happiness. Even for someone who permits the occasional excess, the worst outcome is often a sore head the next morning, and sometimes a promise that it will never happen again. But, and I stress, for the alcoholic, the man or woman who has passed that invisible line which separates the social drinker from the alcoholic, who is powerless over the alcohol, to drink is to die.

I am here today, because after several failures, I have learned finally to surrender, and give myself with real and genuine honesty to the simple programme of A.A. I *know* that half-measures availed me nothing. unless medical science comes up with some new discovery, I can never be cured, but my illness is arrested a day at a time, if I stay away from that first drink. And is not a day at a time, the way for everyone to live? I think so. Yesterday has gone. Tomorrow is an unknown quantity. We have today, waiting to be filled with love, and joy, and usefulness, and service to our fellow man.

In July of 1993, I had been living in the basement of my house. My living conditions were indescribable. My study was two foot deep in empty cans and bottles. The carpet was soaked in urine. The walls were wet, because I had not opened windows, nor switched on the central heating. I had not washed for months, nor changed my clothes, in which I slept on a torn and sodden mattress. I thought nobody saw me when I sneaked out for more food and more drink. I had 'the shakes', an aching body and was unable to sleep, except in a drunken stupor. I was at the bottom, and ready to die.

On 10th July 1993, Marjorie went to morning worship at our Church, when she heard some words which greatly moved her. At the close, she crossed the road to the newsagents shop of her friend Margaret, who said 'Are you alright?'. 'Yes, why?' to which Margaret replied 'You look different'. Marjorie said that the only way she can describe her feelings at that time was that she felt 'two stones lighter'. Returning home she spent the afternoon completing her favourite crossword, the general knowledge one in the Sunday Express, and in reading. Just before 6.20 p.m. she turned on the television for the much-loved 'Songs of Praise' programme on BBC1. A previous programme was just ending on one of the channels, and showed a Third World starving child. The face of Christ was then superimposed upon it. There followed a picture of a wounded soldier (probably from Bosnia) with half his face blown away, and the face of Christ became superimposed upon him. Finally there came everyone's idea of an alcoholic, sitting on a park bench, with seven days growth of beard, a dirty raincoat, and a can of lager held to his lips. And the face of Christ covered him.

The next few minutes are something of a haze to her, but she went to the table, scribbled a short note to the effect that she loved me, and asked me to telephone her. I had been thinking for an hour or more about my love for her, and through the semi-stupor was yearning for an end to this state of affairs, and for our coming together. Marjorie pushed the note under the door which separated us.

Although in 2 years I had hardly ventured up the steps between us apart from looking for mail, because it was pointless as there was no access, and although it was late on Sunday afternoon, and there could not have been any post, which occasionally I sought to retrieve, something impelled me to walk up the steps, to the note. Within minutes I telephoned her, the lock was removed, the bolts drawn, the heavy metal door opened, and I sat in our lovely lounge overlooking the Bay, in disbelief and with muddled mind.

The following morning, Marjorie contacted my G.P. Dr Graham Orr, the senior member of a local practice, who had been my doctor for 20 years or so, and knew me inside out. He came late that evening at great personal inconvenience, and asked me if I realised how ill I was, and whether I would place myself in his hands. I readily agreed and asked in the conversation if I could go to Harvey House, an Alcohol Dependency Unit of the nearby Lancaster Moor Hospital, where I had attended A.A. meetings over the years. He said I was too ill to go there, words which brought home to me the seriousness of my condition. He wanted me in Royal Lancaster Infirmary for a week of intensive treatment (presumably and mainly for detoxification) and then we could consider my suggestion. Marjorie packed a case that evening. She later told me he had asked her at the door as he left, if she realised the seriousness of my condition and implied that I was in a terminal condition unless something was done. I could have only 2 or 3 weeks to live.

On the Wednesday evening he came again, a busy G.P. showing care and concern. He had secured a side ward in the Infirmary, the last available bed, where I would enjoy a measure of privacy. Not only that, but Dr MacIlmurray and Dr Gaskell had agreed to treat me. The former is head of our local Hospice, and a busy general practitioner; the latter a fairly recently appointed Consultant Psychiatrist specialising in alcohol-related problems, and whom I had seen twice, in company with Marjorie, in the immediate past. I enquired of him the date of admission. 'Tomorrow' was the devastating reply. I prevaricated, pleading several important matters to be dealt with, and intimating that I had expected a wait of 3 or

4 days. He stood up and in most uncharacteristic fashion, used some very plain words, indicating that he now had to telephone his two professional colleagues, with the consequent embarrassment to him, and the knowledge that he had wasted their time.

When he left, Marjorie and I talked, and realising my foolishness, I telephoned the surgery the following morning, apologised, and asked if the bed was still available. A sharp negative reply indicated that as soon as he had left me, he had contacted the hospital, and asked for the bed to go to a more deserving case.

Whenever I had stopped drinking previously the craving left me at once, and there was no difficulty in staying stopped. On this occasion something told me that after such a lengthy period, to stop at once would be harmful to a body which had become so anaesthetised by, and tolerant to, alcohol. For two weeks Marjorie bought me an ever decreasing number of cans a day, until I had reduced my consumption from 4 tins to a tiny can of 1% lager (little more than water to an alcoholic) which I consumed on the 24th July 1993. I realised that I was an idiot to be drinking at a level which had no effect, and which I did not want, and as I went to bed that night I resolved, that there would be no more. I have not had a drop of alcohol since that day nor wanted one.

Dr Orr told me that if I had stopped immediately, there was every possibility that I would have suffered a heart attack. I can do no other than see yet again, the hand of the God of my understanding. Marjorie and I visited his surgery at intervals for several months. Dr Orr would smile, and shake his head on seeing me. There was no physical examination, no talk of medication, but a clear indication that he could not understand or explain my condition and experience, on any known medical grounds. Marjorie enquired on more than on occasion if he believed in miracles, and asked if he believed my recovery was a result of divine intervention.

Some 3 or 4 weeks after I took my last drink, I drove to my golf club, a few hundred yards from where I live, and walked to the practice ground, some 100 yards from the car park, holding 3 or 4 balls and 1 club. After half a dozen shots I dragged myself back to the car, in a state of exhaustion. Today I play 2 or 3 rounds a week, engage in normal Church activities, undertake an appreciable amount of work for my father's legal practice where my nearly 50 years of knowledge and experience is appreciated, am involved in charity work, attend 2 A.A. meetings on a weekly basis, read widely, take every opportunity of travelling to my beloved Lake District (a 40 minute car journey), walk moderately, and visit and meet with a host of friends.

I waken every day with a full agenda in front of me, but without the pressure to do it all that day, with a quiet joyful zest for life, and gratitude to God for his mercy and forgiveness; and the willingness to love and serve my fellow man. The workaholic and alcoholism have passed away, and all things are made new. Thanks be to God.

Alcoholics Anonymous was founded in Akron, Ohio, as a result of a meeting between Dr Bob and Bill W. In 1938 The Twelve Steps of recovery were written. Because I believe this suggested programme of recovery is the only answer for the true alcoholic, I set it out as follows:

1. We admitted we were powerless over alcohol – that our lives had become unmanageable.
2. Came to believe that a Power greater than ourselves could restore us to sanity.
3. Made a decision to turn our will and our lives over to the care of God as we understood him.
4. Made a searching and fearless moral inventory of ourselves.
5. Admitted to God, to ourselves, and to another human being the exact nature of our wrongs.
6. Were entirely ready to have God remove all these defects of character.
7. Humbly asked Him to remove our shortcomings.
8. Made a list of all persons we had harmed, and become willing to make amends to them all.
9. Make direct amends to such people wherever possible, except when to do so would injure them or others.
10. Continued to take personal inventory and when we were wrong promptly admitted it.
11. Sought through prayer and meditation to improve our conscious contact with God as we understood Him, praying only for knowledge of His will for us and the power to carry that out.
12. Having had a spiritual awakening as the results of these Steps, we tried to carry this message to alcoholics, and to practise these principles in all our affairs.

(The Twelve Steps are reprinted and adapted with permission of Alcoholics Anonymous World Service, Inc. Permission to reprint and adapt the Twelve Steps does not mean that A.A. has reviewed or approved the content of this publication, nor that A.A. agrees with the views expressed herein. A.A. is a programme of recovery from alcoholism – uses of the Twelve Steps in connection with programmes and activities which are patterned after A.A., but which address other problems, does not imply otherwise.)

If the word 'alcohol' in step 1 is substituted by the word 'life' and the words 'other alcoholics' in step 12 by the words 'anyone we meet who is in need' we have in my view a programme for a happy contented life for everyone.

There are over 300 groups in Great Britain alone, a vast network of people who could not recover without the help of fellow sufferers. A vastly experienced doctor in the field of alcoholism told my wife that he had been studying and working with alcoholics for some 15 years, and was no nearer understanding them at the end, than at the beginning. It takes one to know one, and most sufferers will tell you they only feel free, comfortable and understood, in the presence of others like themselves. Their drinking stories may be different, but the Peer of the Realm, the tramp living rough, the priest, doctor or lawyer, and all shades in between, find identification, in sharing their experience, strength and hope.

Alcoholics Anonymous saved my life, and I know personally of at least 50 others, who can say the same. The number is multiplied world-wide. In 1976 the total membership was conservatively estimated at more than 1,000,000 with almost 28,000 groups meeting in over 90 countries. In 1993 the number of A.A. groups had risen to a conservative 90,785 in 145 countries. I believe this is only the tip of the ice-berg so far as the true number of alcoholics is concerned.

Psychiatrists testify to the importance of the need for a psychiatric change to arrest the allergy, which expresses itself in an inability to stop the craving for alcohol, and is set up whenever the first drink is taken. Recovering alcoholics are sick people getting well, not bad people becoming good. There are many helpful agencies assisting people with drink problems, and I would not wish to detract from the excellence of their work, but A.A. is clear that the alcoholic can never safely drink again. Some can hardly face this truth at first, but come to live happy useful, and fulfilled lives.

Trembling, despairing, nervous and tragic wrecks, are often transformed into people who are self-reliant and contented, living full and contented lives. I shall die with the illness, but if I stay away from the first drink on a daily basis, the illness will be completely arrested. This differentiates it from other incurable diseases. It cannot be cured, but can be arrested. I know people who have not had a drink for 30 or 40 years, but still 'pay the premiums' on their insurance policy, by attending A.A. meetings.

Let me tell you of 2 other events in my life since July 1993, and which I will call spiritual experiences.

In the spring of 1994 after enjoying a very happy nine months of life and marriage, recovering my health and strength, participating again in sporting and social activities, 'mending fences', carrying out professional work for my legal firm, reading extensively, and generally rejoining the human race, I began to feel the need to complete step 5 of the spiritual programme of A.A. The fourth step involved making a searching fearless moral inventory of myself. It is recommended that it be done in writing. From my earliest day in the Fellowship I had neglected to follow the suggested steps of recovery. It seems incredible to me now, but I was one of the not inconsiderable number who thought it was sufficient to 'put down the drink' and that this was the reason for attending A.A. meetings. Such people will almost certainly drink again, or end up with a wet brain, or if they are fortunate, die. I had prepared a mental inventory many times over the years, and shared it with the God of my understanding, as we refer to Him in the Fellowship. I felt I had received the forgiveness, promised in the two following steps.

I knew there was something wrong because I had drunk again and nearly died. A friend in A.A. to whom I shall be ever grateful referred me to page 292 of the 'Big Book' book entitled 'Alcoholics Anonymous' and which, as I have already said is the 'bible' of the Fellowship. The appropriate part reads as follows:

The day before I was due to go back to Chicago, a Wednesday and Dr Bob's afternoon off, he had me down to the office and we spent three or four hours formally going through the Six-Step programme as it was at that time. The six steps were:

1. Complete deflation.
2. Dependence and guidance from a Higher Power.
3. Moral Inventory.
4. Confession.
5. Restitution.
6. Continued work with other alcoholics.

Dr Bob led me through all of these steps. At the moral inventory, he brought up some of my bad personality traits or character defects, such as selfishness, conceit, jealousy, carelessness, intolerance, ill-temper, sarcasm and resentments. We went over these at great length and then he finally asked me if I wanted these defects of character removed. When I said yes, we both knelt at his desk and prayed, each of us asking to have these defects taken away.

The picture is still vivid. If I live to be a hundred, it will always stand out in my mind. It was very impressive and I wish that every A.A. could have the benefit of this type of sponsorship today. Dr Bob always emphasised the religious angle very strongly, and I think it helped. I know it helped me. Dr Bob then led me through the restitution step, in which I made a list of all the persons I had harmed, and worked out ways and means of slowly making restitution.

The friend came to my house one evening, and we knelt in the corner of the room I have previously described, now restored to a quiet restful study, lined with books, personal photographs and memorabilia, and furnished simply, but attractively, and including the desk where I am now writing. We knelt together and said the prayer of step 3, handing my will and life over to the care of God as we understand Him.

For the following 2 to 2½ hours, I poured out my life story. It was almost as though someone was doing it for me. Just a day or so before I had remembered again, the experience with which I started this book, and realised this was almost certainly the source of my anxiety and fear through the years. Things I had done, matters of resentment, guilt, selfishness, immorality, conceit, jealousy, bad temper and all the other character defects from which I suffered, poured out in a seemingly unending stream. The pride and self-dishonesty which had prevented me doing this before, were removed, and although we are told there are naturally things we will have forgotten, and which may not be intended to be uncovered at the time, I did not remember more than one or two comparatively small matters, at a later date.

I finished speaking, exhausted verbally and mentally. We sat in silence for a few minutes. My companion gently said 'Are you ready to have God remove all these defects of character?' I was more than ready to have them removed from me, all the wreckage of the past.

'Then', he said 'we can take step 7'. And kneeling together, I said: 'My Creator, I am now willing that you should have all of me, good and bad. I pray that you now remove from me every single defect of character which stands in the way of my usefulness to you and my fellows. Grant me strength, as I go out from here, to do your bidding.'

I had completed step 7.

There fell on me a great physical sense of peace, my whole body seemingly soothed, and at ease. Then after some minutes the mental release flooded in and continued for several days. I could echo the words of the man on page 292: 'If I live to be a hundred, it will always stand out in my mind'. I could now begin a new life.

And now must come my third experience – 'must' because it is still of recent and painful memory. For 2 or 3 months Marjorie and I had grown increasingly apart. I do not think she was as conscious of it as I. After feeling in July 1993, that a wonderful, happy and fulfilling future lay before us, when I could repair the damage, and make up for so much of the past, I became more and more conscious of what I can only describe as the suffocating aura of my wife's first marriage. There was for me, a constant and critical comparison in all I did, or tried to do. We had always been able to speak openly of each other's previous spouses, but this was different. Marjorie had enjoyed 25 years of a happy first marriage. A day came when I realised there was no longer the relationship which had previously existed. I did not share it with Marjorie or anyone, but for a week I wept inwardly, not shedding tears. I was very sad, but not depressed. It lasted a week and prevented me attending the farewell service at Church for our departing minister on the Sunday evening.

On the Monday as I woke, I felt my spirits rise. Driving to the beach at Hest Bank, a favourite place for visitors and residents, I walked out on a tideless beach in glorious sunshine, for a great distance. With every moment, I felt surer and surer that I was on the brink of some vital experience. A conviction came that I should go to the lovely Anglican church at Kirkby Lonsdale, where I have often meditated. After an hour there, I was moved to go to another favourite spot, by the viaduct at Arnside. As I travelled the road from Kirkby Lonsdale I suddenly felt as though hands were upon me tearing away a mass of grey strands of rubber, which had been enveloping me. It was rolled into a ball, and in the manner of an inflated balloon being released without a tie, it sped away, a clear physical sight to my eye, until it seemed to disappear to the farthest corner of the Universe. Deceived? Imagination? Wishful thinking? No, no, no.

I believe with all the conviction of my heart that God had a purpose in that experience, for my life. Never for one moment since August 8th 1994 have I ceased to feel so sure of God's purpose for me, such peace of mind, and mental vigour, such awareness of my life being in His hands. Nor have I lived one day other than as fully as possible, and with the certainty of God's hand leading me on the road. I called out, and startled myself, with praise to God. 'Thanks be to God' I shouted, quite involuntarily. Brother Lawrence speaks of the sanctification of the secular as I have already said, of feeling as much as home washing the dirty dishes in the Refectory, as when kneeling at the Communion rail. That God-consciousness, experienced for varying spells throughout my life, became in my 64th year a living, daily, constant Presence. The blind man could not explain his returned sight. 'Whereas I was blind, now I see' . . . I can only plead his explanation.

I wrote this chapter thus far in 1994/5 and the remainder in recent weeks.

It is absolutely vital for anyone who wishes to understand the problem of alcoholism, to realize that medical science to date cannot offer a cure. For countless diseases and illnesses, medical science has found a cure. This will continue. Perhaps the biggest hope today is that the time may not be far away when *all* the various types of cancer can be cured, and not only some, as is the case at present. But as yet, medical science has *not* found a cure for alcoholism.

But for the alcoholic there is a difference. Although a cure has not yet been found (and pray God it *will* be found one day), it can be arrested and there can be recovery, *provided* the alcoholic does not take another drink. Alcoholics Anonymous says in its 'bible' that an alcoholic cannot *with safety* take another drink. There may be a few rare exceptions, but *I* would prefer to say 'An alcoholic can *never* take another drink.'

There, then, is the big difference. I may contract cancer and be cured. I am an alcoholic and can *never* be cured (unless medical science discovers one in the future), but I can have my incurable illness arrested, and need never be troubled by it again *PROVIDED* I never take another drink. And that is the big problem. The addictive nature of the illness is such that most alcoholics will go to any lengths to get a drink when the craving comes upon them. They will beg, borrow or steal. They will hide bottles in almost inconceivable places. Most people would stand amazed at the cunning, scheming and dishonesty to which an alcoholic, who wants a drink, will go.

I know of a case where an elderly alcoholic lady was often found the worse for drink most nights in bed in the house where she lived with her son and daughter-in-law, who were normal social drinkers. She never left the house and they were bewildered. It subsequently came to light that she poured gin from the drinks cabinet into her hot water bottle before retiring at night.

I know another case where an elderly man lived with his daughter and son-in-law in similar circumstances. They had a large orchard, and the man had resorted to taking a bottle from the drinks cabinet, where there was a regular store, and tied it to a tree in the orchard. He could then walk into the garden, pull down the bottle with his walking-stick, take a drink unobserved, and return to the house.

It is the *first* drink, not the second or subsequent one which activates the allergy and causes the trouble.

And more. I will not say, because it would be untrue, that all the agencies which help the problem drinker are a waste of time. But the only one of any use to me is Alcoholics Anonymous, because it is the only one which says you cannot with safety take another drink if you are an alcoholic.

Often, the patient in an alcoholic unit, or receiving treatment elsewhere is given a choice of agencies for aftercare. AA will always come last, because the alcoholic in 99 cases out of a 100 will see that with the others, he may be able to control or limit his drinking, and cannot imagine life without it. The prospect for someone who has drunk in the pub (or to a lesser degree at home) from an early age, not being able to have a drink again, is unendurable. Whatever shall I do? He cannot envisage a life without drink.

Step 2 of the AA programme is so important. There are twelve Steps and they hang together, but I know many friends who found the realization that a 'Higher Power' could restore them to sanity gave hope at last.

And even more. Narcotics Anonymous and Gamblers Anonymous have adopted the twelve-Step programme of AA, substituting the words 'drugs' and 'gambling' for 'alcohol'.

And still yet more. It has been calculated that those who finally arrive at AA are only 2 per cent of the total with the incurable illness, and of that 2 per cent only another 2 per cent *do* recover.

I know some fifty people who have found recovery out of the hundreds I have met in AA. One man has not taken a drink for over forty years, and several men and women for fifteen, twenty and more years. They are those who attend AA meetings *regularly*. That is to me absolutely vital. It is plain to see that the increase in the number of women who are alcoholics has increased dramatically.

It is not for nothing that the AA 'bible' describes alcoholics as cunning, baffling and powerful. I would add 'and patient', because the craving will lie dormant, very often for months or years, and then comes a sudden temptation or impulse when the alcoholic is 'off his guard'. AA tells us that at certain times the alcoholic has no mental defence against the first drink. His defence must come from a Higher Power.

And there is yet still more. When an alcoholic who has arrested his incurable illness for any length of time, takes a drink, he *starts* in the same condition where he finished before. It is not a slow slide again into misery, but an accelerated deterioration, and eventually either certain death or a 'wet brain'. In the latter case the person concerned must be 'locked up' for life, and is as helpless as a baby. Many will tell you death is preferable, so far as they are concerned.

I know of a recovering alcoholic who had not taken a drink for many years but visited from time to time, in the hospital where she lived permanently, a lady who had been on the same course of treatment for three months in an alcoholic unit. He handed her a box of chocolates. She began to eat the cardboard and left the chocolates.

Several older GPs have told me that in their training at Medical School little of help was said about the confirmed alcoholic. He was regarded as a hopeless case, and the doctor would be better employed in spending his time and skill on more deserving cases. It is good to know the situation is changing. Many GPs today still have little time for the alcoholic, probably in large measure due to pressure on their own time.

I am grateful to have had the time and skill of a GP who was sympathetic and as near to understanding an alcoholic as possible without actually being one. It is a truism about alcoholism that 'it takes one to know one'. Only the person himself can really say if he is an alcoholic.

I know of a retired doctor of great skill and caring who opened an alcoholic unit within the large hospital for which he was responsible, and said that although he had been studying the illness and patients for some sixteen years, he was no nearer solving the problem or fully understanding the alcoholic than when he began.

Alcoholism is an illness of body, mind and spirit. I have said elsewhere that if any of the three are unwell, the whole man will be affected. I have never lost my faith even in the darkest hours of my life, since a spiritual experience during morning worship at the church I have attended for sixty-four years. I was seven or eight years old, but the experience is as clear to me today as then.

My father told me, on one occasion, that my mother never had a day's illness in her life, apart from the period when my youngest sister was born, and she nearly died after six months of great suffering. This, of course, was not sickness in the normally accepted way. I believe I inherited my mother's constitution, and that this, along with my love of playing all kinds of sport and keeping physically fit, probably enabled me to survive the physical devastation of this incurable illness.

Dr Orr told me that alcohol attacks every organ in the human body, but they can recover, apart from the liver. I understand only a small part of the liver is required to enable a person to survive. A friend tells me his doctor has told him he has only a tiny part of his liver operating. It is sufficient to enable him to live a normal life, but further slight damage will kill him.

The reader will gather that the incurable illness alcoholism is not something to be taken lightly.

But even after these experiences I had not reached my 'rock bottom', the phrase used by the alcoholic where he or she is very often at death's door, broken in body, mind and spirit and intent only on self-destruction.

But I was to enter that living hell again within 12 months.

In A.A. there is a mnemonic often used, and important to remember and practice:

H
A
L
T

Never be hungry.
Never be angry.
Never be lonely.
Never be tired.

297

I do not find the following brief reference to my second broken marriage easy to write, nor do I think it is necessary to dwell on the details other than in giving a truthful and honest account of my life story. It is now needful that I speak of such details.

Marjorie lost her first husband Derek on 8th October 1978. He was drowned in the Bay during a fishing expedition. Vera had died from her cancer only 3 weeks before on 17th September 1978. After the funeral, and dealing with necessary matters, I went to stay for a few days on the South coast with Vera's father and stepmother (I never knew Vera's mother, who had died several years before). As a result I did not know of Derek's death which was a great tragedy for the local community, as well as the family. His death however resulted in a lot of gossip and I had to bear the hurtful experience of snide remarks, as did members of my family. In October 1994 I moved to my present home. As I have said Marjorie and I had grown increasingly apart. I had felt more and more very much in second place in her life. Suddenly, within a few days I felt impelled to leave with a haste which would have appeared unseemly and hasty to an uninformed observer. In almost indecently short a period I felt gloriously happy in a comfortable flat with a view over my beloved Bay to the Lakeland Mountains from lounge, kitchen and one bedroom. I know there are husbands and wives who live, on the surface with little in common, but are very happy. But for most, I believe there must be a measure of common ground and interests.

In the case of Marjorie my divorce petition referred almost entirely to comparisons with Derek. I will confine myself to one. In August 1994 on a glorious summer day Marjorie reluctantly agreed to a run in the car to a place of her choice. During the outing she mentioned Derek's name and mostly in comparison with me on 34 occasions. I counted them because she had mentioned him so often in the weeks prior to that August date. It had taken me 14 years to appreciate that I came second to him, to her children, and then to her grandchildren. I love company and being with people, but I also enjoy time alone, to be still and to follow where my natural inclinations lead me.

It was now that I was able to write 450 pages of A4 in longhand in 23 days, hardly sleeping or eating. It was now I visited Lakeland whenever possible, played golf, and tried to cultivate and assimilate the things of the spirit. A pilgrimage to the Holy Land with 21 other fellow Christians lifted me to new heights, my book was with the publishers, and when I returned there was their verdict that it was good, and tears flowed readily. But then the anger at feeling used. It had been agreed that the matrimonial home would be sold. It was vested in joint names in equal shares but Marjorie, through her Solicitors, claimed a 7/10ths share. Although I was entitled to claim a share in another property formerly owned by Marjorie, her late husband, and parents, which was free of mortgage I decided, and I feel generously, not to make a claim. Unfortunately for my anger and sobriety, Marjorie's daughter and her two young children moved to the former matrimonal home almost immediately after I left. When my solicitors protested strongly, and as the reader will appreciate, for very good reason, as a threat this represented to an early and successful sale, Marjorie's solicitors replied, and I quote:

'As regards our client's daughter Jane living at 449 Marine Road. This is correct. However, she is only living there to look after our client and keep her company in view of her poor health.'

Marjorie's daughter and her two young children stayed in fact, for nearly 1½ years, moving from one of Marjorie's flats. I never knew or enquired about Marjorie's finances but I am conscious of having discharged thousands of pounds of bank loans she incurred while I was living apart from her on an earlier occasion.

I was known by my close friends as 'The chauffeur and cheque book'. I learned fully and not in part that money does not bring happiness. I had been in the fortunate position all my life of not having to budget and economise, watch the pennies, and I give thanks for the freedom I enjoy today from the shackles which bind an increasingly materialistic world. I am pleased that Marjorie is now taking an active part in Church life. During our 15 years of marriage we had to pass through five broken marriages of her two children, and the heartache and sheer misery of it all will I hope be healed for her by a comforting God. I accept my faults. I do not wish to apportion blame. There are few relationships where the blame all rests entirely on one party. I pray for Rosalie and Marjorie, have asked for God's forgiveness for my shortcomings, and would like to be friends with them both for the remainder of my days. I have shared so much, including the good times, with them both.

And so the inevitable happened. My incurable illness returned and I nearly died. But for the care and attention of a family friend whom I can never repay my physical condition had brought me to the point of death.

There were few other friends who cared. While walking one day along Newmarket Street, a long and narrow thoroughfare from my flat to the shopping area of Princes Crescent, I noticed as I neared my flat a distant figure of a well-built lady. She was the only other person in the street, usually very busy at that particular time. As we drew nearer, and I was almost at my flat, I recognised her as a stalwart and faithful and indefatigable worker for A.A. I knew I had to get to a meeting of A.A., it was of vital importance for my survival. I believe the hand of God was upon that encounter. The meetings of her group were still on the same day and I would of course be welcome. Here was a lady who had not taken an alcoholic drink for 17 years and had helped so many with a similar problem.

I was back where I needed to be, and I gave thanks from a grateful heart.

> When shall I see the welcome hour
> That plants my God in me
> Spirit of health and life and power
> And perfect liberty.

That hour was with me.

On 13th December 1997 I went with my eldest sister Peggy to the Lancaster and Morecambe Crematorium to look at the Remembrance Book and think and pray about my youngest brother on the second anniversary of his death. Only a week or two before I had established with the Staffs C.C. that the computer had not correctly recorded the verdict of the Inquest. Stuart died of gunshot wounds, but because of all the circumstances the Coroner found an Open verdict, and the foul rumours were largely stilled.

Why Stuart? Always bright and breezy, nothing seemed to bother him. And can we not all speak of like things

I offer to my reader the contents of Chapters 36 and 37.

Chapter XXXVI

PAIN AND SUFFERING

A s I have said elsewhere, I thought I had all the troubles of the world heaped on my young shoulders, until at forty-one I found I had in fact lived a privileged life, shielded and protected from any real pain, problem or suffering.

But the death of my father at the early age of sixty-four, a bitter divorce, the loss of my son and daughter for ten years, the death of Vera at the age of thirty-seven through cancer, my twilight life through ten years of being an 'on and off' suffering alcoholic to the point of death, a second divorce when I thought the final years of my life were to be tranquil and lived in matrimonial harmony, the death in 1985 of my younger brother, found with a shotgun by his side, and serious present health problems with my family, enable me to say that I am no stranger to the experience of pain and suffering, and can at least identify in some measure with those who have suffered much more.

It is a vast problem which so often is neglected, avoided or skimmed over. I cannot offer a final solution nor can I find anyone who can. I have mentioned earlier that on the morning after Vera's death from cancer at the tender age of thirty-seven with so many gifts and qualities and so much to live for, I was unable to give a clear answer to my elderly neighbour who, ailing and with a full and fulfilled life behind him, was ready to face his Maker, and unable to understand what had happened.

But I believe there is a road to peace and faith even in such a difficult area. It may surprise the reader that I turn to Job. 'He's a Job's comforter' has come to mean a person who tries with little or no success to offer comfort and advice to someone in real trouble. Job never did find the answer of why the innocent suffer. To him as to me it remained and remains a mystery but I can affirm today that my experience of God in my latter years convinces me that God's character and justice and nature, are deeper than the understanding of man, that I am content to leave in the hands of Him whom I have come to know what is to many the final unanswered question, and that the divine justice and love does not willingly inflict suffering and pain upon the objects of His love.

Friends of mine recently lost their 34-year-old son. A fine young man, about to take over his father's legal practice and allow Mark to take a

301

well-earned retirement, this estimable man, Simon, was struck down by lung cancer in 1994 and died within three months. Why? Why? Why?

I told his mother and father that it was not a sin to be angry with God. The vicar who conducted the funeral service spoke honestly of the fact that although we were giving thanks for Simon's life and paying tribute to his qualities, we were met to mourn the loss of a promising, happy, young life, which offered so much for the future, through the foul scourge of cancer. He told Margaret, Simon's mother, on the day of Simon's death that he was going home to have a bath and while soaking was going to tell God a thing or two about what he thought. I would find it very difficult to deal with pain and suffering if I did not believe that this is God's world, and I am a child of God. Would a father willingly inflict pain and suffering on His child?

At the end of the day I can go no further than affirm with all my heart that I have in these latter days been granted such a deep personal experience of God that I can echo Job's words and find them a sufficient answer this side of the grave:

> I have heard of thee by the hearing of the ear.
> But now mine eye seeth Thee.
> Wherefore I abhor myself,
> And repent in dust and ashes
>   (Chapter 42 verses 5 & 6)

It is no real surprise to me now that in many ways I find this book of Job unique in its beauty and brilliance. It is not just a story with an unknown author or place in the timetable of history, a book alone in any attempt at classification. It has been described as a book of philosophy, poetry, drama, morality and nature rolled into one. We do not even know if the book was written by a Jew, but it meets with Jonah and with Ruth in voicing a protest, and strays from the original thinking of orthodox Judaism.

I cannot and will not believe that God punishes sinful man with blindness, hunger, and wretchedness, while the prosperous healthy man is being rewarded for his uprightness and goodness. Thousands of examples in my life scream aloud against such a view.

Job's friends try to comfort him. They speak of seeking forgiveness and make clear that they consider his suffering is because of his sin. But Job has seen the innocent suffer and the wicked prosper, and he rejects the argument and view of his friends. Job does not hesitate to cry aloud about the cruelty and injustice inflicted on him but he will not 'curse God and die'. In all his agony and pain and suffering he can still cry out with those words we all remember in Handel's *Messiah*, 'I know that my Redeemer liveth.'

In chapters 38-40 Job is shown the limits of human knowledge. Question after question shows the infinite power and wisdom of God and Job sees his own smallness. Who is he to question God? Who is he to assert that the good should be rewarded and only the evil punished?

I can only say, and really I should not use the word 'only', that if I could understand the ways, the mind, the intentions and the acts of God, He would not be the God of the universe who I know is beyond my understanding, and thought, and imagination. 'I know in Whom I have believed, and I am persuaded that He is able to keep that which I have committed unto Him against that day.'

Here is mystery.

God, with man, is working out His plan. I know Him well enough to say *that* is sufficient for my path ahead.

I *know* in whom *I* have believed, and all will be well.

Chapter XXXVII

WHEN YOU'RE DEAD YOU'RE DONE

Mrs Harborthe-Forshaw, for so I shall call her, wears the most enormous, beautiful, flower-bedecked hats, beloved of Ascot but a constant puzzle to her husband, who is happy to indulge her female interest. At Easter her bonnets rise to the demands of the day, and outshine the earnest efforts of her friends at church.

The church will be full, everyone goes at Easter, the Vicar will notice, she had always gone to church on lovely Easter Day. The church bells seem more cheerful, summer approaches and somehow she feels it is right to be present; there is something which strikes a chord in her heart and meets a largely unrecognized craving of the heart. Yes, it is good to go to church on Easter Day, even though apart from Harvest Festival and Christmas, she will not be seen again until next Easter.

Some of course have no wish for life after death. When they die they will have had quite enough of this business of living, thank you. H.G. Wells said he could not understand why people found the prospect of a final personal death unendurable.

A mother lost her son, killed in action as one of that brave breed of pilots in the Battle of Britain. To those who would comfort her she replied that her son had lived for over twenty clean, happy and glorious years, and then died for his country. What more could she ask? I do not find myself at home with that view.

My reader, I cannot prove there is life after death by the methods of science. But neither can you disprove it. I do not believe in life after death because I can prove it, but I am always trying to prove it, because I believe in it. I look at the richness of the lives of Mother Teresa, St Francis of Assisi, St Paul and a thousand others. I refuse to believe that when laid in their graves, that is it. The brightness of their spirits was not extinguished like a gutted candle.

'What shall it profit a man if he gain the whole world, and loses his own soul,' asked Jesus.

Above my personal inner conviction, above the hunger of my heart and the testimony of my reasoning, there lies the resurrection of Jesus himself. Let no one doubt that the Christian faith stands or falls on the *fact* of the resurrection of Jesus Christ. Frank Morrison began to write a book, to prove that the Resurrection of Jesus Christ was a myth. It is well known that as he wrote the book, he became convinced of its truth.

In John Masefield's play *The Trial of Jesus*, Pilate's wife asks the centurion if he thinks Jesus is dead. 'No lady, I don't.'

'Then where is he?'

'Let loose in the world, lady, where neither Roman nor Jew can stop his truth.'

That is my conviction, and I rejoice in the conviction that life does not end in futility and in dust, but that death opens the door on life and love and God.

One of the most compelling proofs of the resurrection of Jesus is the transformation of the disciples. How else can you explain the change in a group of frightened, disillusioned men who only days earlier had forsaken, fled or denied any connection with Him? Within such a short time these men, the very people who were in the best position to know if it had been otherwise, were changed into a band of brave, courageous individuals, prepared to go to the end of the world, to the suffering and death which faced many of them, for His sake.

No! Jesus *did* rise from the dead and by so doing broke the power of the grave, opened the door on love and life, and proved that life does not end in futility and failure and final death.

Chapter XXXVIII

SCIENCE, TECHNOLOGY, EVOLUTION, BIG BANG, AND ALL THAT JAZZ

The Jew of the first chapter of the book of Genesis, the first book of the Bible, was not a scientist. Nor did he pretend to be.

The subject I disliked most at Morecambe Grammar School was Physics. Mrs Siddle was an excellent teacher of the subject and proved it by her results; but to me, it was all Chinese. I could recite Archimedes' Principle. At least I got as far as when an object is totally or partially submerged in a fluid, it displaces a volume of fluid which weighs the same as the apparent loss in weight of the object.

I had not then begun to learn Greek which was the language I came to love when I began seriously to study Classics at Shrewsbury. I was then much more at ease with the great scientist's shout of delight from his bath. 'Eureka', I then knew this meant he had found whatever it was he was seeking, but he could have fooled me. At Shrewsbury, I only had a few Physics lessons, these being in my first year before I moved into the classical stream for ever.

The only event I remember from Mrs Siddle's class was the day Hobson, the class joker, crept under the laboratory benches from the back of the room, out of view from Mrs Siddle's higher-placed bench, and placed a tiny live mouse behind her apparatus. The entire class could see the scene slowly unfolding, but not Mrs Siddle, the intended recipient. She returned to her seat without detecting it. As we watched with bated breath, the mouse slowly emerged in front of the Bunsen burner. Mrs Siddle froze, but with commendable courage, did not scream. Nor did she stand on her chair and pull up her skirt, which was in any event not long enough for that purpose.

The only event I remember in the Physics class at Shrewsbury was when our teacher said, when speaking about the origin of the universe, 'Gentlemen, it is just possible that we are not here.' I hoped that was not the case and his comment disturbed me greatly. I was due to play soccer later that day.

Sir Charles Darwin is an Old Boy of Shrewsbury, his theory of evolution was a regular topic of conversation and I gathered that, in the opinion of most of the boys, it destroyed religion. His recognition of the change of the mutability of species through descent was met with serious

306

acceptance. He not only assembled the vast material and convinced the world, he inaugurated a new science through the study of variation and heredity. By his integrity of judgement and analytical logic, he built his theory on a factual basis. Later discoveries have meant some modification, but the wealth of relevant fact remains.

The first man to persuade me that there was no conflict between Science and Religion was Professor C.A.Coulson FRS MA Ph.D. (Cantab) D.Sc. who wrote a book of that title. An outstanding Vice-President of the Methodist Conference in 1959, the highest office open to a layman in the Methodist Church, he was a humble man of a clear and professed Christian faith. He was Professor of Theoretical Chemistry at Oxford from 1972 and prior to that, Rouse-Ball Professor of Mathematics at Oxford from 1952-72. He was also Chairman of Oxfam from 1965-71 and a member of the Committee of the World Council of Churches Central Committee from 1962-68. He was known as an expert on the Quantum theory and Theoretical Chemistry, and wrote three general books and many articles on Science and Religion. Professor Coulson was a man of towering intellect and stature; the latter I observed at the Methodist Conference in 1961, which I attended as a representative from north Lancashire. He sat a few seats away from me in the Conference Hall.

I have kept a report in the *Methodist Recorder* of 19 September 1968 of a speech made by Professor Coulson when he gave the inaugural lecture on Faith and Technology at the inauguration of the Luton Industrial College.

They are well worth repeating and remembering. Under the heading 'Men of machines and sons of God' it said:

'Change is something wonderful, something far more wonderful than the human race yet realises,' were memorable words in Professor Charles Coulson's inaugural lecture on Faith and Technology at the inauguration of the Luton Industrial College last Saturday. 'I see industry making use of the best possible faculties that people can bring to it, releasing man from the burden of physical toil so that deeper parts of his spirit may have time to blossom and to grow, making possible richer and deeper worship, I see his spirit released as his body has been released so that he may sing God's praises in a new tone. We have a basis of certainty and hope in the midst of change.'

Professor Charles Coulson with impressive simplicity and equally impressive scholarship instructed and delighted his 'students' with facets of a world in change. Perhaps the most significant factor in the changes that were now sweeping the world was that man himself was controlling them. His knowledge of the processes of growth and of life is such that not only does he begin to paint a picture of his own past, but of his own future. He has learned how to create new mutations. Medically we are beginning to control things in our conquest of diseases.

'The first industrial revolution took away the great need of man to work by the sweat of his brow. In the second industrial revolution, which is happening round us, we are learning how to make machines which do the thinking for us. Many of the major decisions which are being made to day – and will be made in the future – will be made by computers. Man has in this sense almost worked himself out of the need to use his physical body. In large measure he is in the process of working himself out of using his mental faculty'.

These changes, said Professor Coulson, raised fundamental questions: 'What is a man? What is man for? To these there is the Christian answer, Man is a child of God, but it has to be remembered that a child grows up. God wants us to use new knowledge for change. We can have the kind of confidence that will make us flexible and open minded, to be able to accept the new knowledge, new responsibility and changes, because we know that this is God's will. 'If behind all these tumultuous events I could not have the confident knowledge that this is God's world, I should find it vastly more difficult than I do to come to terms with things.'

Science, technology and industry were tools to serve a higher end than making the machine our saviour. Properly directed they can be part of the saving grace of God himself. For such a purpose the college here has been founded: to seek to know the hidden spring which, when released, will sweeten relationships, and will ensure that changes for man's betterment are made for man's betterment. Let us not be afraid of change.

Many people will have been fascinated recently by Professor Stephen Hawking, a brilliant man in the field of Theoretical Physics. In appearance, he seems to be severely handicapped, both physically and mentally. He is in fact a disabled genius who refuses any comparison with Einstein. The technology with which he is able to communicate the spoken and written word has to be seen to be believed and, I understand, is to be further enhanced. The affliction from which he suffers is Motor Neurone Disease, and he is a tireless worker for the Motor Neurone Disease Association.

Professor Hawking claims the possibility of the universe being finite. His recent book, *A Short History Of Time* has already, as I write, exceeded seven million in sales, although very complex in context, as one would expect with such a subject. He further considers this subject is not incompatible with the existence of God, but makes clear he is a scientist and not a theologian. Pointing to the comparative amount of GNP (Gross National Product) spent on resource and development, he draws attention to Great Britain, at one time, being second only to the USA. Japan has now replaced us and he points to their outstanding progress and success. Professor Hawking thinks that the disease from which he suffers will soon be understood and possibly brought under control, but it is unlikely to be able to reverse his own condition.

In personal terms, this brilliant scientist courageously speaks of his greater happiness, now that technology has eased the constraints of his disease, given him a sense of purpose and increased the quality of his private life from one of despair. The professor has triumphed over despair, confessing that before he was able to leave hospital he wanted to die. He confesses in fact to being a born optimist. He enjoys music and takes great pleasure in knowing that he is now recognized as existing.

Turning to the serious and worrying subject of genetic engineering, he does not expect much advancement in the next 100 years, but feels it possible that in 200 years the position may be different, and that in the future we may be able to produce human beings by methods of control and design. He finds this a worrying aspect. I suspect the reasoning behind his concern is the nature of man.

In a fascinating programme broadcast in the *Horizon* series on BBC2 (14 November 1994) we saw a team of scientists in Cambridge, California, Italy and Tenerife starting the first practical experiments aiming at proving the 'Big Bang Theory'. It was clear that the scientists were making such progress that written material was almost out of date before publication. Interestingly, all were asked at the end of the programme which question they each would put to God if they could ask Him. Each question differed from the matter of structure to quantum, although one said he would rather discover for himself. The point is that, in spite of the progress, the programme made clear man is still far from understanding the origin of our galaxies. 'In the beginning, God.'

The Big Bang theory is now generally understood, and the fact that scientists claim to be within a short distance of bridging the narrow gulf between their present knowledge and that which will take them to full discovery of the centre of the ever-expanding explosion, they see as the source of the universe.

When the first Russian astronauts returned from space they said they had not seen any evidence of God.

The Reverend Ken Clapham, an Anglican Vicar of St Cuthbert's, Over Kellet, nr. Carnforth, addressed our Men's Fellowship during a recent session. His subject was the American Space Programme and he spoke from an intimate friendship with, and knowledge of, some of the American cosmonauts who have walked on the moon. He had visited them in Houston, and two recently visited the church school under his pastoral care. Some of the children were a little disappointed that one of them landed in a helicopter on the school playing field, wearing a lounge suit, when they had anticipated a space suit.

He told us that eight out of the twelve men who had walked on the moon were committed Christians. This information was given to me by the Reverend Ken Clapham. He received it in person from the late Colonel James Irwin of the Apollo 15 mission in July 1971. Colonel Irwin was the eighth man to walk on the moon.

In a report describing how he and Neil Armstrong gave thanks to God after their lunar bug, with only seconds of fuel remaining, settled safely on the moon, Buzz Aldrin humbly wrote: 'I opened the little plastic packages which contained bread and wine. I poured the wine into the chalice our church had given me. In the one-sixth gravity of the moon the wine curled slowly and gracefully up the side of the cup. It was interesting to think that the very first liquid ever poured on the moon and the first food eaten there were Communion elements.'

I am clear that the first chapter of Genesis was never intended to be a scientific description of the founding of the universe, and certainly not in seven days. The central truth which the writer sought to assert is in the first four words: 'In the beginning, God.'

Religion and Science are not mutually incompatible. They are seen increasingly as partners. In my simple way I see the scientist seeking to answer the question 'How?' and the theologian the question 'Why?' We should urge on the scientist to explore in every realm. Of what value is a faith, which cannot bear searching scrutiny?

Chapter XXXIX

BODY, MIND AND SPIRIT

I believe with all my heart and with absolute conviction that the problems of Society today throughout the world are largely because body, mind and spirit are out of harmony. If any one of the three is not in tune, there are problems.

First, the body. I live on the seafront and regularly see groups of children from the local high school taking 'exercise' along the promenade. I assume they are supposed to be jogging. Many of the girls and boys are obese. Most run on their heels at little more than walking pace, panting and puffing, red-faced and miserable. In most groups only a few are slim and athletic. I see crisps and chocolate in their lives and all manner of excesses, and I fear for their future health.

Many of the low points of my life have coincided with lack of physical exercise. I try now to play two rounds of golf every week. I once read that golfers are the fittest athletes of all because walking strengthens the heart muscle. I must say that at sixty-eight, when reaching the brow of the 13th, the awareness of my panting sometimes takes away momentarily a little of the magnificent view of Bay and tide and Lakeland mountains. I walk a lot.

Sleep does not seem as great a need. After thirty years of taking a small number of sleeping pills I am sure now I can dispense with them, but am taking my doctor's previous advice when so minded, and reducing them slowly. I regret I ever allowed myself to become dependent on them before I was first married as a result of 'wedding nerves' and the relationship between my father and Rosalie's mother.

My ability to fall asleep in my armchair now is perhaps more to do with age than anything else, but I am sure my physical and mentally relaxed state at all times is a large factor in the equation.

There is nothing in the line of food which I dislike. Nothing. And so I try and eat the healthier items. I eat chicken instead of fatty red meat, drink semi-skimmed milk, control my intake of chocolate and cream, do not need and so avoid sugar in tea and coffee, eat plenty of fruit and vegetables on a daily basis, and only brown bread. I do not wear spectacles.

My mind feels sharper than ever. My long-term memory is excellent but I confess to a recent deterioration in the short term. I remember, as I have described earlier, events when I was four years old, but can forget to buy a loaf of bread. A 'friend' told me recently that the loss of short-term memory is the beginning of senility! I take a lively interest in TV, current affairs and read newspapers and books avidly.

I attend a meeting of Alcoholics Anonymous weekly, take a full part in church activities, go to the Lakes whenever I can, write five or six letters almost every day, make constant use of the telephone and do not begrudge the bill, and mix easily (unlike some times past) with people of all ages and from all walks of life. I feel I have become a little nearer to my father who was the greatest 'mixer' I ever knew.

One of my fathers-in-law, who lived into his nineties, always spoke of having something to which he looked forward, be it holiday or a lesser event. He rightly, in my view, gave this as a partial explanation for his longevity.

And what of the Spirit?

The answer lies in worship, prayer, meditation, the constant practice and awareness of the presence of God, and in love and service to our fellow man.

The technology and other inventions of our day have affected body and mind. The materialism of our day has affected the spirit of man. If only man would really understand and accept that you cannot take it with you, that there is more joy in giving than receiving, that getting and getting we lay waste our powers, that love is better than hate, kindness than greed, that time is short and precious, that there is nothing wrong with the world, that life is a precious precious gift, that violence, hatred, prejudice and so much else only detracts from the wondrous gift we have all been given, then we would begin to see that we really *can* have the Kingdom of God on earth.

Whatsoever things are true, whatsoever things are honest, whatsoever things are just and pure and lovely and of good report; if there be any virtue and if there be any praise, think on these things.

Chapter XL

BEYOND MY WILDEST DREAMS
(Written on Christmas Eve 1994)

The pocket Oxford Dictionary defines the word 'reconcile' as 'make friendly after estrangement'. In 2 Corinthians 5:19 we read: 'God was in Christ reconciling the world unto Himself.'

In December 1994 I attended a normal meeting of Alcoholics Anonymous where I had been asked to share my experience, strength and hope in the usual manner. The venue was the group room where I had attended my first meeting of AA in August 1983. Due to unavoidable causes, I had postponed my 'share' in the two previous weeks. It was not without significance.

I have now reached that stage of maturity and experience in life where I can get to my feet, and provided it is a subject on which I have knowledge, can speak without previous preparation or notes. This is something I would never do deliberately if preparing for an occasion when I had received a specific invitation where preparation was required.

Before leaving for the meeting I selected some twelve Christmas cards from those I had received in the preceding few days. I opened by saying that there was only one topic for me that evening, to speak of one of the promises of our Fellowship, that it would bring about things 'beyond our wildest dreams'.

On the previous Sunday I had been troubled by the realization once again that there was a continuing breach with my stepchildren, Alison, Diana and Gregory, the children of my beloved Vera, children who meant so much to her and also to me, and who themselves responded by calling me Daddy and asking to adopt my surname at school so that they would be 'like the other children'. The reason for the break is not really relevant, but concerned money, and my impulsive reaction to a situation where I felt I had been treated less than fairly. There was a complete absence of contact for three years and the only information I received about them was through Vera's sister Phyllis, who in turn heard from her father Ted.

On the Sunday I suddenly felt the pain of the separation. At once I sat at my desk, and wrote to Geoff and Dorothy, speaking of Christmas, the need to heal the breach, and saying I would give the proverbial right arm to see them all again. I placed in the envelope the current publicity about my book, with synopsis and other items of interest. I went to the local

Post Office and posted the letter in time for the early morning collection the following day. The following morning the postman delivered a card from 'Geoff, Dorothy, Ali, Di and Greg'. I wept. It had clearly been posted before my letter. The next day I phoned. Dorothy answered. A genuinely warm conversation followed with her and with Geoff. The children were not at home.

I could feel such peace and joy rising in me as we spoke. All was well and plans were made for the future. I replaced the receiver back on the rest, switched on my record player and heard the words ring out: 'O come let us adore Him.' To which there was only one reply: 'O come let me adore Him.'

I also received a card from Jeanette Brandwood and husband Brian. Jeanette was my secretary at the Marsden Building Society when I had my Chairman's office over the Lancaster branch. Her contribution to what I achieved was substantial. It was so good to receive her card too after a long break. Her husband Brian had been transferred from Heysham Nuclear Power Station to Sizewell in Essex, shortly after I left the Society.

I feel my main input was in the area of instilling confidence and raising morale which was at a low ebb. A loyal and able staff were lacking in direction and leadership. It was a period of my life I look back upon with great pleasure.

Regular visits to all the branches, personal chats with staff at every level, a time which worked to my advantage in that boom period of the 1980s, all contrived to create a buzzing, successful, happy staff and Board. I felt completely fulfilled. Branches were opened, profit increased and the crowning moment of my period of office was the opening of our new computer centre a mile from our Chief Office.

A few days ago I received a letter from the then Chief Executive of the Society, Eddie Shapland. I served on the sub-committee of the Society which interviewed Eddie for the position of Assistant General Manager in 1979. I have his letter and CV in front of me as I write. The latter reads as follows:

Dear Sir,
<u>Assistant General Manager</u>
I wish to apply for the above position which is advertised in the April edition of the Building Societies' Gazette. I enclose full personal and career details and would confirm that I will be available for interview at any time.

My daytime telephone number is Burnley 25025 extension 287.
Yours faithfully
E Shapland
E. SHAPLAND A.B.S; A.M.B.I.M; D.M.S.

Full Name: Edward Shapland
Date of Birth: 3rd April 1946
Married: Two children aged 9 years and 6 years
School: Burnley Grammar School
Career: Joined the Burnley Building Society from school in 1962. I have worked in most head office departments and have experience in all aspects of building society work. In 1973 I was appointed assistant accounting manager. In this position I have responsibility for all the Burnley's 600,000 mortgage and investment accounts.
I also teach Building Society Management part-time at Preston Polytechnic College.

Professional Qualifications:
Passed final associate examination of the Building Societies Institute May 1973
Passed diploma in Management Studies 1974-77
Associate Member British Institute of Management 1977.

Present Salary: £7,148 per annum with effect from April 1979.

The letter received in December 1994 reads:

14th December 1994

Dear John

Many thanks for your letter of 3rd December 1994. I was very pleased to learn that you are feeling much better and are on top form.

The pace of change in the building society movement continues to accelerate and it would be impossible to update you fully on matters which have occurred since we last spoke. 1994, particularly, has had its highlights, but also has had a number of very sad occurrences which you may have heard about through your visits to Morecambe Office. Rather than trying to record everything in a letter I perhaps will take the opportunity of telephoning you before Christmas and then I can update you on some of the things which have happened to the Marsden.

Overall, things are progressing forward in a very positive way and the Society is going from strength to strength.

I would be very interested to read further chapters of your autobiography and, as I say, hope to speak to you before Christmas.

Kind regards
Eddie
E.Shapland
Chief Executive

We had many applications but did not make an appointment for several months for reasons I need not relate. Eddie was clearly my first choice with not only the obvious potential for great things, but also the invaluable asset of being a Burnley man employed at the Burnley Building Society, one of the most respected building societies in the country. Several of his directors were great friends of my father. Henry Cooper, a former Chairman, was the best man at his wedding, and Jack Butterworth, an 'institution' in the building society movement, was a close friend.

Miss Muriel Jobling, daughter of Mr George W. Jobling (to whom my father was articled) was a partner in the firm of Southern, Jobling and Ashworth and dealt with the contentious merger with the National and Provincial Building Society on behalf of the Burnley Building Society. This merger took place in 1982 some two years after Eddie joined 'The Marsden'. It occurred long after my father's death but I often think of what he would have thought. He held the Burnley in such high esteem but he was also very friendly with Mr Dennis Howroyd who was joint Chairman of the National and Provincial at the time of the merger. It would have needed the judgement of Solomon, but then many people would have said that was exactly my father's role. Eddie's letter was a very big Christmas present.

I spoke to Cynthia on Christmas Eve. The 'right hand' of the Chief Executive at the Building Society, she is the sort of person without whom you feel an organization could not function. She had a wealth of experience accompanied by a deep knowledge of individuals, their quirks and their strengths. She broke down as I said I had not known of the death of her husband Clive from a heart attack. Once again I could identify through my own experience, and made a promise to call and see her in the New Year. I had previously written to her at home after receiving Eddie's letter, to say that she would never type a letter that had brought such joy (and tears).

Again on Christmas Eve I thought a lot about my father's death, the manner of which I describe in Chapter XVII. I felt moved to phone Ted Mitchinson, our former farm manager, and Edith, in whose arms my father died. Edith answered my call and she spoke intimately of the things you would expect. Edith said again she would never forget the day as long as she lived. I enquired of their children and arranged to visit them early in the New Year.

I mentioned I was to visit the luxury Gilpin Country House Hotel in response to an invitation from friends. This hotel is only about a mile from Ted and Edith. The invitation was from Dennis Howroyd (to whom I refer earlier in this chapter) and his wife Dorothy, and contained within a Christmas card I received a few days ago. Almost beyond belief.

Marie Gorst had been much on my mind in recent weeks. Marie is an elderly widow who lives in Staveley near Kendal. Her sons, Gordon and Malcolm, both worked for us in our farming days and then had their own farms. Gordon is the elder son. I phoned a garage in Staveley under the pretence that I was checking Marie's address, not having seen her for some time. Having been assured she was still alive, I phoned but there was no reply. I phoned her son Gordon and he answered, delighted to hear from me. He said how delighted Mother also would be. Gordon then shocked me by telling of the death of his wife from cancer a year or two before. Again I could identify. Here was a chance with Marie to restore a friendship which so far as I knew may have been extinguished by her death. Gordon was staying with his mother in her bungalow at night now because of her state of health. His farm was just a few hundred yards away along the Windermere road. I visited Marie in the January and we had a wonderful joyous reunion for which I will always be grateful.

Lois and David Roberts sent a welcome card saying they are looking forward to my autobiography. David, Dwin Wilson and I ran a 70-strong Youth Club for many years. David was our best badminton player. We were great friends over many years and I know David must rightly have been disappointed in me in recent years. He made the shortest speech for a bride's father I have ever heard at her wedding reception which I attended many years ago. We shared so much. I miss him greatly. Another miracle.

Cousin Bobby (a retired Air Vice-Marshal) reminded me that I am to stay with him and Brenda at North Rauceby after the New Year to pursue family lineage (see Chapter II). See this same chapter also to explain a card from Roger Knape 'and all the Knapes'. What a story – nine years without a word and then a phone call while I was actually referring to the matter in my book.

Several cards from members of Alcoholics Anonymous arrived or were given to me at meetings. I remembered some would probably be calling on Christmas Day when I was to hold open house, particularly for those spending Christmas on their own.

Cards from golfing colleagues whetted the appetite for bitter battles ahead and much psychological warfare!

A card from Lakeland Laundry reminded me of my reward, to collect after Christmas – kisses from three ladies in return for three small boxes of chocolates I left.

Good old reliable Richard and Beryl never forget their Christmas card. Beryl is the daughter of the late Rev. Arthur Marshall, minister of our church from 1953 to 1959. In his last year he saw the fulfilment of a dream with the opening of our new Sunday school and church hall. I used to find Beryl very attractive and was sure I was her ideal man (why did I so often get this wrong along with other male members of the youth club) and had just begun to chase her round the kitchen at the youth club. I should have known better. She never *did* let me catch her. Richard's best man was taken ill on the Friday night and I was asked to substitute on the following day. This gave me a good line for my speech when surrounded by other ministerial colleagues of the bride's father – the Law was heavily outnumbered by the Prophets.

Jennifer and George's card came too. Jennifer reminds me of my Aunt Ruth, insofar as she can get more news on a postcard than most people in a letter. Jennifer's card was crammed with news. George (the Rev. G.W.Barton) has been stationed at Victoria Hall Sheffield, to take effect in 1995. This is a priority appointment and so does not go through the normal stationing procedure. He will not be far from Cliff College where he spent two years. He will be going back to inner city life like his previous work in Liverpool which has been broken by a spell in Southport where he succeeded the Rev. John Harris BA as Superintendent. John was our minister at Bare from 1981 to 1989. George and Jennifer's card incidentally reminds me that I am getting old. Their daughter Catherine is in her final year at Oxford, and Deborah in her first year at Bristol. My daughter Catherine went to Oxford and so I fulfilled, through her, my own unfulfilled ambition. Jennifer reminds me my sister Joie has been with them at Markside Road from time to time whilst visiting family.

There was a card from John Harris as well! He thanks me for wishing him well on his retirement. I would like to place a bet that he will not be short of preaching invitations!

A card came from another sister, Jeanne, resident in Cincinnati, Ohio, USA since her early twenties. Carmosino, her Brazilian-born husband, is a doctor who retired, returned to work because of an allergy diagnosed when taking up gardening as a hobby, only to fall victim of further ill health and had to retire again. Jeanne promised to phone over Christmas. I remember that calls from her sound like local calls, although we are approximately 4,500 miles apart.

Sister Ann also sent a card mentioning ill-health. She has worked so hard as headmistress of an infants' school for many years. She has just received her P45 on retirement through ill health. Don, her husband, has diabetes. They are leaving for a seven-day holiday in Austria over Christmas.

There is a card and note of thanks from Beatrice Wilson who recently celebrated her eightieth birthday. I brought her round to my flat recently and forgot she is not well. I talked for too long and too much. She was, as I have recorded, my son John's teacher. I remembered telling John I would be bored stiff again listening to her singing his praises! She insists he was conscientious, well-behaved and well-mannered, and with obvious ability. He must have got it from his mother! Anyway Beatrice must have been correct about his ability. I now proudly address letters to Dr A. J. Knape MA.

I have written this chapter on Christmas Eve, for the large part of the morning, but in some part before, during and after viewing *A Christmas Carol* by Charles Dickens on ITV. I pray that the words of my work may in some small way reflect the spirit of Christmas so gloriously portrayed in the Dickens classic. I pray that they may echo the words of Bob Cratchett: 'We thank you for this day of love and joy.' I pray they may help us to say more often the words of Ebenezer Scrooge himself: 'God forgive me for the time I've wasted.' I pray we may all say each and every day the words of the crippled Tiny Tim: 'And God bless us all, everyone.'

The theologian talks of the sanctification of the secular. Brother Lawrence writes (I repeat yet again) of feeling as at home when washing the dirty pots in the refectory, as when kneeling at the Communion rail for the Blessed Sacrament. I thank my God that I can speak of a new and present experience of the consciousness of His presence in all the tasks and duties, the pleasure and the joys, the sorrow and the pain, of daily life. I give thanks to Him that in these latter days I have come to know the Spirit of Christmas so wonderfully encapsulated by Charles Dickens, in every moment of my waking life. May love and gratitude and service mark all my remaining days, whether long or short for what I have received. And to him be all the praise and all the glory.

Christmas has indeed been beyond my wildest dreams.

Apart from my Christian duty and desire, it is part of my continuing programme of recovery from my incurable illness that I make a list of people to whom I need to make amends, and having done so, make such amends, except where to do so would injure me or others. To the best of my knowledge I had made amends some time ago. Mostly it was simply a case of being seen to be well and going about my life and business in a normal, conscientious, useful and happy manner. Except, that is, for Aunt Ruth. She had been offended some years ago and we had not met or spoken during that time.

Apart from Marjorie she above all others was the one to whom I wanted and needed to make amends and be reconciled. I was her godson. I spent countless holidays at the Kilmarnock home of Uncle Andrew and Aunt Ruth, as well as visiting and staying there with Father and our farm managers on our Scottish expeditions, to which I refer in my farming story. When Father died in 1971 I felt a special duty of protection and care towards her. It was to be near Father that she had moved to Silverdale from Scotland. On the death of my wife Vera in 1978, Aunt Ruth asked me to go and live with her; at the time I was living only some two or three miles away.

On the day before Vera's funeral I motored over to see her. It was early evening and I will never forget the sight which met Ted, Phyllis and I in her garage. She had been toiling since early morning without rest or refreshment to complete four wreaths she was preparing for Ted and Brenda, Phyllis, Vera's three children, and myself. My sister Peggy had gone with her to buy the flowers and other items which went into their preparation.

Aunt Ruth had no gardening or horticultural skills when she married Uncle Andrew fairly late in life. His main business was that of a knitwear manufacturer in Kilmarnock, but as a hobby he ran an 8-acre nursery with a large area of greenhouses producing tomatoes, and all manner of vegetables and flowers for sale on the site and at Glasgow market. On many occasions I rose at 5 a.m. to gather the produce, travel to Glasgow for delivery, and return mid-morning for breakfast. Aunt Ruth had acquired tremendous skills in every area of the business in a very short time.

She was a lady of many parts. An accomplished pianist, she also played the saw most effectively, recited monologues in dialect, was a charming and brilliant hostess, cooked 'out of this world' and was the centre and hub of the family life which she valued so highly. A great letter-writer, she had a host of friends all over the world, and until recent years regularly spent much of the winter in Glendale, California with her many American friends. In 1952 Uncle and Aunt called on my father at our offices in Morecambe en route for Germany to see Manfred, a former German prisoner of war who had worked in the nursery during the War and had become almost a son to them. Tragically Uncle Andrew died there. When they called at our offices in 1952 I had received the previous day, as I recall earlier, notification of having passed my Solicitors' Final Examination and was able to share the good news with them.

After over twenty years of widowhood she married an American, Stuart Condie, from California.

This then was the lady I just had to see but felt I never would. She lived in a lovely residence for the elderly in Ewhurst, in deepest Surrey, which is partly owned by my cousin Joanne and her husband Paddy. It was to Joanne's home that I used to repair at weekends during my months in Guildford before my Final Examination, and which I describe in more detail elsewhere.

For reasons which are too hurtful to mention I had laboured for several years under the impression that I was persona non grata with Aunt Ruth, and at Ewhurst, not, I hasten to add, in any way because of Joanne or Paddy. Aunt Ruth's mental condition had been deteriorating for some time and she could not be said to have any really lucid intervals, though physically well. She received quite heavy sedation. This then was the gracious and loving person I had not seen for so long and whom I had greatly hurt. Here too was a situation which had been allowed to fester and continue, when honesty and truthfulness would have resolved the problem long ago.

My father advised me in my early days at the office that there are situations which should not be left, and this was certainly one of those. Everyone can remember proposed visits which were left too late, letters which were never written, telephone calls never made, and which in many instances were too late. I can remember more than one occasion where I visited clients immediately they contacted me about a will and was able to have them completed just in time to avert serious family and other problems. Inevitably there were times too when a perfectly ordinary situation turned into a difficult one because of an entirely unexpected injury or death.

Joanne told me that Aunt Ruth was 'not going to die tomorrow' and Bobby had told me a few weeks before that she could live to be a hundred. Her physical health was good and it was the mental condition which caused the concern. I arranged with Joanne to visit Aunt Ruth in January. Joanne met me at Guildford station and our journey to the Old Rectory at Ewhurst evoked so many happy memories of my six months in Guildford and the so happy Sundays with Uncle Bill, Auntie Margaret, Joanne, Marc and Hugh. The conditions under which Aunt Ruth lived could not have been bettered and I was deeply impressed by the obvious care and love of the staff, the happiness of the elderly residents, the comfort of the home, and the general atmosphere which for me reflected Joanne's character and goodness. I am sure the same goes for her partner. Joanne's son Charles was there and it was good to meet and talk to him.

And so I walked into the room to see Aunt Ruth dressed in a lovely pink, sitting in an armchair in a delightful room. I can only leave to the reader's imagination my feelings as I held her hands and kissed her. For some two hours I sat, sometimes with Joanne, sometimes with just the two of us. I showed her photographs and newspaper cuttings and talked of Uncle Andrew and a hundred other things. I cannot be sure of the extent of her appreciation and understanding. Certainly talk about Uncle Andrew with whom she enjoyed the happiest of marriages evoked no response. I even mentioned meeting them in the Isle of Man before the Second World War when they had just met. My father had taken me on one of the popular day excursions from Heysham.

There were three memorable moments. For part of the time I sat in silence as Aunt Ruth was clearly dozing, but consciousness kept returning for short periods. Firstly she mentioned Aunt Marth' Ann. I do not think any other living member of the family will remember her but she was

Martha Ann Knape, a daughter of Councillor John Knape, my great-grandfather who came from Wisbech as a child, as I record earlier. I remembered the countless occasions Aunt Ruth used to mention her. She was clearly a special person and this is borne out by the following report of her death in the *Burnley Express*.

Loss To Bethel Church
Death of Mrs Walter Smith

Bethel Primitive Methodist Church has lost one of its most valued workers by the death which occurred last Thursday, of Mrs Walter Smith, of 10, Colne Road Burnley. Aged 54 years, Mrs Smith had been in failing health for the past three months. A daughter of the late Councillor John Knape, who was superintendent of the Sunday School and a circuit steward at Bethel, she maintained the family association with the church, and played a leading part in many of its spheres of young ladies' classes, of which she was the teacher. She was indefatigable in her efforts in connection with it, and was held in great esteem by its members. Before her marriage she was a chorister, and her services as an accompanist at children's concerts were frequently requisitioned. She was prominently identified with the ladies' Wednesday afternoon meetings at which she also acted as accompanist. At the sales of work promoted by the church she was always an industrious helper, assisting in the organisation of the refreshment stall. Among other departments of the church, the Ladies' Missionary Auxiliary found in her a warm supporter, and she fulfilled the duties of secretary to that body with distinct ability. Much sympathy will be extended to the widower, Mr Walter Smith, who is society steward at the church, and to his son. The funeral will take place this morning at Burnley Cemetery.

Secondly, I showed Aunt Ruth a photograph from the *Burnley Express* of a vehicle built by John Knape of Bank Top Garage and Motor Works in Burnley. Registered in June 1906 it was called 'The Habergham' and the name was displayed on the side. I do not think Aunt Ruth would have been able to read the name but she said aloud and very distinctly 'Habergham, Habergham'.

Thirdly and far more importantly for me, when we were alone at one moment and she appeared to be showing some mental reaction, I held her hands, looked into her eyes and said, 'I love you, Aunt Ruth.'

She screwed up her eyes, gazed straight into mine and said unhesitatingly, 'And I love you.'

It was a moment to dream about, to return to for the rest of my life in memory, in gratitude, in love, in thankfulness to anyone and everyone.

'God was in Christ reconciling the world unto Himself,' I had said as I commenced to write on Christmas Eve. And here for me was complete and absolute proof. Thanks be to Him.

Chapter XLI

JOY IN DAILY LIVING

I have a friend, somewhat older in years, who has an outlook on life which prompts him occasionally to say about some venture or other mentioned in conversation, 'Well it helps to pass the time, doesn't it?' He is basically a happy man who has lived a full life, but the words sadden me.

I have played golf with those who are glad to spend four hours playing the regulation 18 holes, and then repair to the 19th hole for refreshment (not always alcoholic by any means) and to spend two hours settling the affairs of the world. There are those in comparison who would rather complete a round in two and a half to three hours, spend a short time in the clubhouse and repair home for other tasks and interests.

There is a wide gulf in attitude to life. In only one period of my life can I remember wishing time would pass. When I qualified as a solicitor and took the few steps open to me to speed up my call-up to the RAF for National Service, it was with a feeling that here was a period of my life to get out of the way as soon as possible, a necessary evil which prevented me applying and using my training of the previous five years in gainful employment. My life's main purpose and work in the form of my chosen profession was being being diverted from the chosen path. I quickly changed my mind and look back upon my two years of National Service as a time of great fulfilment, experience and happiness, not least because of being able to practise my chosen profession, but also for many other reasons, including eighteen months spent in London, working hard and playing hard. I had the real reward of friendships (some of which last to today) with Scottish and English solicitors, about fifteen in number at any one time.

A full day's useful work was joined to acquiring a knowledge of the places of interest in the capital and beyond its boundaries, enjoying its varied entertainment and shows, watching cricket and soccer at the highest level, making many friends, and enjoying a change from five years of strenuous work and study.

I was determined not to shirk my duty. It is ironic that the son of the founder of the firm was the only articled clerk who completed his National Service. Flat feet and all sorts of petty ailments gained exemption for many people, usually as a result of a persuasive letter and doubtful medical reports by doctors who must have stretched their consciences to and beyond their limits. No 'Your country needs you' feeling of duty as portrayed in Kitchener's famous advert for the First World War was about at this time. I felt sorry for young men who, in my view, shirked their responsibilities, and lacked the courage to do their plain duty.

During 'square bashing' I wished the two years away, although as I have related it did not present any problems to me. Little did I realize how precious time is. Reader, I urge you to live a day at a time, filling every hour with useful and fulfilling work, hobbies and service.

We can all think of areas of living where we have wasted time. Let me emphasize there is a time for leaning over a country gate 'to stand and stare'. I am not advocating planning every moment of every day and behaving as though every single second were held in trust for the glory of God, or the service of our fellow man. I think young people will have to face the question in the future in the area of computer games, CDs, videos and a host of other time-consuming, and in several areas, addictive pastimes.

But in one area we are all affected. I speak of TV and would like to give a specific example. The BBC and ITV programmes for Boxing Day 1994 did not contain a programme of real interest to me. They were nearly all films, and at the moment when I had so many matters requiring attention, an enjoyable evening with a film, to relax, not take too seriously and usefully spend in getting away from the demanding rigours of an ordinary working life, were not on my agenda. The only exception was the *Dave Allen Show* which I did switch on, but, most out of character, was unable to sit through because I was falling asleep and so went to bed.

Instead of viewing on Boxing Day I wrote 17 letters, edited some 20 pages of my story, played Handel's *Messiah* from beginning to end and read 30 or 40 pages of a book by Elizabeth Goudge, one of my favourite writers. I felt so much better than I would have done viewing half-heartedly.

At the age of sixty-eight I regard each day as a precious gift from God, twenty-four hours waiting to be filled with all manner of activities and interests, including peaceful sleep, and an honoured place for recreation. Looking back over just two months since I moved into my present home, I am not a little surprised both at the speed with which time has passed and, somewhat incongruously, the amount of living I have done and things I have accomplished.

I can say with honesty today that the only thing which gives me cause for a measure of anxiety is the speed with which time passes, and I am told it gets worse as the years pass.

I have made a list of some of the things which fill my mind with joy at the beginning of each day, and any activity throughout its working hours that may spread the gift of God to a grateful soul, and which I am sure most people could extend in their own particular way:

1. Waking in a warm and comfortable bed with the day stretching before me, full of opportunities for service, love and friendship.
2. My health and the knowledge that I can see, walk and run, and even as a senior citizen play with ease a round of golf or take a 5-mile walk.
3. A cup of tea. I remember clearly the Reverend R.T.H. Beardsall BABD, a minister of my circuit, giving a fascinating talk in which he showed that in drinking a cup on waking, we were in debt to half the world almost before the day had begun.
4. The simple pleasures of washing, shaving and dressing with warm water readily at hand.
5. A start to the day with a few moments of quiet prayer assisted since 1956 by *A Diary of Private Prayer* by John Baillie DD D.Litt. STD, sometime Professor of Divinity in the University of Edinburgh.

There is a page for morning and one for evening of each day of the month. Here is the one for the sixth day (morning) which is for the day I am writing these words:

Oh God, who hast proven Thy love for mankind by sending us Jesus Christ our Lord, and hast illuminated our human life by the radiance of His presence, I give Thee thanks for this Thy greatest gift.
For my Lord's days upon earth:
For the record of His deeds of Love:
For the words He spoke for my guidance and help:
For His obedience unto death:
For His triumph over death:
For the presence of His Spirit with me now:
                                        I thank thee, O God.
Grant that the remembrance of the blessed Life that once was lived out on this common earth under these ordinary skies may remain with me in all the tasks and duties of this day. Let me remember –
His eagerness, not to be ministered unto, but to minister:
His sympathy with suffering of every kind:
His bravery in face of His own suffering:
His meekness of bearing, so that, when reviled, He reviled not

again:

His steadiness of purpose in keeping to his appointed task:

His simplicity:

His self discipline:

His serenity of spirit:

His complete reliance upon Thee, His Father in Heaven.

And in each of these ways give me grace to follow in His footsteps. Almighty God, Father of our Lord Jesus Christ, I commit all my ways unto Thee. I make over my soul to Thy keeping. I pledge my life to Thy service. May this day be for me a day of obedience and of charity, a day of happiness and of peace. May all my work and conversation be such as becometh the gospel of Christ.

Amen.

6. The daily reading from my 'Words for Today', the notes on bible readings prepared by the International Bible Reading Association.

7. The reading for the day from the 24-hour book, a valued companion for many of my alcoholic friends. It contains a necessary reminder of our incurable illness, a short meditation, and a brief prayer.

   I have learned the importance for me of starting the day with a quiet time for five and six minutes, and which sets the tone for the day. I know the difference when I have inadvertently forgotten either.

8. Three meals a day.

9. Playing at regular intervals throughout the day a tape called '20 Favourite Hymns' (Wesley) by the Westminster Central and Epworth Choirs. Only recently acquired, my soul soars at every playing.

10. The news bulletin and weather on TV.

11. Ever-changing views across the bay, with tide and cloud, and bird, and the backdrop of the Lakeland mountains.

12. My car and the ability to visit so many places in a day when needful.

13. Family and friends.

14. The arrival of the post.

15. The flowers on the window sill.

16. Work to do and the power to do it.

17. Newspapers and books which I can read without spectacles.

18. Letters to write. I find more and more of my friends find this less and less attractive, but I give thanks for the fellowship of the pen, and the joy of giving and receiving.

19. The photographs and pictures in my home with reminders of people I love and reminders of other happy days.

20. The simple comforts of home.

21. The telephone and its opening to friends and for necessary duties and tasks.

22. A good 'lie-in' from time to time and particularly on Saturday mornings, a residue of my working life at the end of a busy week.

    I listened to a young lady on a train journey recently who spoke of her routine of getting up on a Saturday at her usual weekday time of 5 a.m., completing all her usual chores and then returning to bed and luxuriating in the time available to her.

23. The thrill of waking in the knowledge that it is Sunday and the joy of worship, or an evening meeting of Alcoholics Anonymous, or an evening enjoying the hospitality of friends.

24. An awareness of the sun, moon, planets, stars, galaxies and the whole universe which shows our earth as a grain of sand on the seashore. 100,000 million stars in our galaxy alone and 400,000 million galaxies in the universe. What a Creator!

Dear reader, I have already written enough to show the real truth – the list is endless.

Yes God is good!

When all thy mercies, O my God,
My rising soul surveys,
Transported with the view, I'm lost
In wonder, love, and praise.

Unnumbered comforts on my soul
Thy tender care bestowed,
Before my infant heart conceived
From whom those comforts flowed.

Ten thousand thousand precious gifts
My daily thanks employ,
Nor is the least a cheerful heart
That tastes those gifts with joy.
                    Joseph Addison (1672-1719)

Chapter XLII

EASTER PILGRIM TO THE HOLY LAND

I travelled on a third pilgrimage to the Holy Land in 1995. An account was given in four editions of my Church magazine *The Messenger* and I set them out as follows:

Part One

As I write, the peace process involving Jew and Arab seems to be making little progress, as the mission of the U.S. Secretary of State, Madeleine Albright to the Middle East seeks to breathe life into the Middle East initiative, after the suicide attacks that have killed twenty Israelis since late July.

In 1958 I was handed a badge in Jerusalem on Easter Day as I climbed Mount Zion. It was inscribed in Hebrew, 'Pray for the peace of Jerusalem' (Psalm 122).

I have had the privilege of three visits to the Holy Land, in 1958, 1960 and most recently in 1995. On the first two I travelled alone, and was frustrated by an inability to enter the old city of Jerusalem, and many other places of Christian interest. Jerusalem was divided between Israel and Jordan.

In 1995 I joined a small party (22 in all), most of whom were members of Lanchester Methodist Church in County Durham, where the minister at the time was Rev Keith Harbour. Many of our readers will remember him as a former minister of our Church at Torrisholme. He was in his tenth and final year at Lanchester. Pilgrimages of the type I undertook were advertised in the Methodist Recorder and the travel agents put me in touch with my friends at Lanchester. It was a happy arrangement.

Travelling by coach from Lanchester we flew from Gatwick and landed in Tel Aviv at Ben Gurion airport on the 9th April 1995 where our splendid guide Jacob welcomed us for the short journey to our hotel in Jerusalem.

The first day was spent sightseeing in Jerusalem, visiting the Mount of Olives with its splendid view of the city. We remembered that Jesus did not spend a night in Jerusalem until his final visit. In the afternoon we travelled the short distance to Bethlehem, noticing the very poor living standards of the Arabs compared with those in Jerusalem. We passed the traditional site where the shepherds grazed their sheep, and spent some time in the Church of the Nativity, gazing quietly at the traditional place in the stable of old. This visit had not been possible for me on my previous visits, when I could only stand on the hillside in Jerusalem and gaze across the valley at the red roof of the Church of the Nativity. I remembered that I had put my camera to my eye, to be stopped by the guide who said a U.N. official had been standing on the same spot a few weeks before, and killed by a sniper firing from the valley below.

The following day we travelled down the steep road from Jerusalem to Jericho, to the Dead Sea area. Jericho is the oldest city on earth. We remembered the parable of the Good Samaritan as we passed the inn of that name.

The Dead Sea is the lowest point on earth. There are medicinal elements in the black mud which has resulted in the growth of a busy commercial centre. Most of the party entered the water and experienced the unusual sensation of floating, unable to sink and able to read a newspaper if desired. (Care must be taken; it would be extremely difficult to surface if anyone were to dive in.)

A short journey brought us to Masada, passing the cave where the Dead Sea Scrolls were found. Masada is a desert fortress where Herod was buried. It was here that the last remnants of a Jewish resistance force held out against the Romans after their occupation of Jerusalem in 66 B.C., until 73 A.D. It is a terrible story of the children being put to death by their own fathers when it was realised that the fortress was about to fall, then the women; and then the men, in small groups, in their determination not to surrender.

It is difficult to understand how they were able to survive for so long with such a limited area for growing crops and general survival.

As we returned to Jerusalem I pondered on the courage which had moved this small band of Jews to resist the mighty Romans, whether wisely or not, and that they must have been sustained by their faith in God.

Part Two

Our party spent most of Holy Week in Jerusalem. The city began to fill with pilgrims from around the world. It was also the time of the Passover, of such importance to the Jew. The narrow streets of

Pilgrims on the Mount of Olives – Easter Week 1995. Immediately below – the Garden of Gethsemane. In the distance – the Dome of the Rock.

the old city were crowded from dawn to dusk.

On all three of my visits to the Holy Land I have been able to climb Mount Zion and see King David's Tomb and the traditional room where the Last Supper was held. There are pillars said to come from the original room. My mind went back to 1958 when in that same room I was about to open a door when stopped by a guide. He said that I would have been met by a hail of bullets fired by the troops of the Arab Legion, stationed a few yards away in the then divided city – Jerusalem the city of peace. King David's Tomb lies on the summit of Mount Zion. **Jesus is still to be found and a Christian with open heart and mind may still encounter Him, the living Lord.**

We travelled to the Mount of Olives on Good Friday and walked down the slope where Jesus shed tears over the city before His entry into Jerusalem, and entered the Garden of Gethsemane. The Church of All Nations and a huge rock traditionally (and here we can be fairly certain of accuracy) mark the spot where Jesus knelt alone, sweating blood, the fate of mankind resting on His shoulders. His words 'My Father, not as I will but as Thou wilt' showing his trust and dedication. **Engulfed in tears, hardships, fears and temptations, we too can find power to overcome the temptations and suffering.** The Cave of Betrayal or Grotto of Gethsemane marks the spot where traditionally the Apostles slept when Jesus was betrayed by Judas, and arrested to be crucified.

Modern Jerusalem is built over several previous civilisations. I did not find Jesus along the crowded Via Dolorosa on Good Friday, which was certainly not the short path to the Cross where He was crucified, and which today is filled with cries of the shopkeeper. Nor did I find Him when walking through the Valley of Kidron where David shed tears when he was cast out of Jerusalem by his own son, and through which Jesus was led in chains; until I realised that here, the Ruler of heaven and earth, robed in power and majesty, submitted like a lamb to the bonds of wicked men.

The possible sites of the dungeon where Jesus was imprisoned between the times He was shuffled between Pilate, Caiaphas and Ananias, deserted by His friends, exhausted, weary and derided, brought home a little of His loving heart, enabling all men to free themselves of self-will, lust for power, bound to Him and redeemed from all that makes us unhappy.

The Church of St Peter in Gallicantu marks the traditional site where Jesus turned to Peter, who had denied Him thrice, and by His loving gaze enabled Peter to repent and become a new man, ready to suffer.

332

EASTER PILGRIMS IN JERUSALEM 1995

Ray and Val Hill, members of the Lanchester Methodist Church, working at Dipton currently on Sunday mornings, both local preachers, Ray also runs Lanchester Chapel football team. Val is the group leader.
Martin and Rhoda Joyce, both members at Lanchester, Martin is a church steward and Rhoda organises the book stall.
Marjorie and David Hughes, both members at Lanchester, David is choirmaster and often becomes involved in circuit musical events.
Audrey Potts, Rhoda's sister.
Wendy Hughes, Marjorie and David's daughter.
Joan Atkinson, member at Grange Villa and has various jobs there.
Edna Shields, East Stanley, A local preacher.
Mary Ord, member at Lanchester, has been involved with Night and Day group.
Patsy O'Brien, member of Lanchester All Saints RC Church.
Peter Rogers, member at Lanchester Methodist Church and church steward.
Bob Armstrong, member of Dipton.
Maurice Clavert, Bob's son-in-law.
Katherine and Anne Crinson, sisters both from Lanchester, Anne is a member at the Methodist Church, Katherine now lives, works and worships in York.
Rita Wood, member and steward at Tanfield Lea Methodist Church.
Mildred Horner, Rita's friend.
Mary Murray, member at Lanchester, involved in Christian Endeavour and famous explorer of 'down under'.
Rita Hewitson, Mary's friend.
The Author and our guide **Jacob**.

Lithostrotos marks the traditional site of the crowning with thorns and the mocking of Christ. Jesus stands degraded, derided, blasphemed and appeared ridiculous, the butt of human evil, reduced to the level of a fool, and yet continuing in love.

The Chapel of Flagellation marks the traditional site where Jesus was scourged, half beaten to death, covered in wounds, undeserving His suffering, driven by love for all mankind and for me. **Ruined personalities, disease and misery and all the torments of hell in eternity – from these He can redeem us as we claim Him in faith. All things are made new.**

The Chapel of Condemnation marks the traditional site where the Cross was laid on Jesus. The church of the Holy Sepulchre marks the traditional site of the Crucifixion. The actual distance which took Jesus from his condemnation by Pilate to His death would be much shorter than the Via Dolorosa. He would be in a long line of others, crucified and intended as a warning from the Romans to all would be offenders.

The Garden Tomb fits the biblical description and we entered the small entrance to the spot where the body of Jesus is said to have been laid. From the gloomy grave He emerged as the Prince of Victory.

And so on Easter Saturday we left Jerusalem for a week in Tiberias and in Galilee.

Part Three

Our happy band of pilgrims left Jerusalem on Easter Saturday morning en route to Tiberias on the Sea of Galilee which was to be our home for four days. The way lay again down the steep road from Jerusalem to Jericho along which we had travelled on the first day of our stay in Jerusalem on the way to the Dead Sea.

We passed once more the Inn of the Good Samaritan before turning north towards Jericho. In the distance as we left the Dead Sea area I could see both there and around us the bleak rocky landscape. In 1958 I had visited Beersheeba at the southern end of the Dead Sea, a place where Abraham lived for a time, and I remembered the camel market where the 'Ships of the Desert' squealed, and kicked and bit.

The visitors to the market left for their desert tents with the husband invariably riding on the camel, and the wife walked well in front and bearing on her head the purchases from the market. When I asked about this apparent lack of chivalry, I was told that there were still land mines about from the war. The ladies would find them first!

This area around the Dead Sea is composed of bleak rock, with neither vegetation nor animal life. In 1958 it was the hottest day of the year in Israel (43° Centigrade), but a dry and not uncomfortable heat. It is the traditional site of the temptation of Jesus in the wilderness.

Jericho dates from the early Bronze Age (c. 2900 B.C. to c.2300 B.C.) and is probably the oldest city on earth. We sat in the main square taking refreshments and basking in a lovely temperature of just over 70°. The Bougainvillaea and other plants and flowers lay in profusion round us. It was difficult to believe that this peaceful quiet place housed many of the dreaded Hamas, the suicide Arabs dedicated to driving every last Jew into the sea.

On our right, along the whole route, was a fence showing the boundary established by the Jews during the last conflict, the notoriously unstable West Bank, guarded by Israeli troops.

Our hotel in Tiberias, a large town on the Sea of Galilee gave views, from its proximity to the Sea of Galilee, to the distant hills of Syria and Jordan. We rested on the Saturday evening.

Easter Day. We travelled the short distance to the Mt. of Beatitudes, the traditional site of the Sermon on the Mount. In the spring the hills for miles around the lake are covered in grass and a carpet of wild flowers. And so it was for us. In the open air outside the beautiful Church where the Roman Catholics were worshipping, we stood together in glorious sunshine looking out over the blue water, and sang the Easter hymns with all our hearts.

Jacob, our guide, a Christian, asked me to read the Easter story from the Gospel according to John. Jesus was no historical figure at that moment, but an immediate and living presence. This was a time to return to often in the memory.

As we left I looked down to the shore and saw the trees at the lake side where, in 1960, I had shared a picnic with the Rev. J.V. Hobbins, and his wife. He was a retired Anglican clergyman who had looked forward all his life to his visit to the Holy Land. We were on that occasion only in Israel for Easter Day and the Monday. He had been so disillusioned by Jerusalem with the crowds, the noise, the heat and the ever present beggars and souvenir sellers. I arranged a picnic from the ship, docked in Haifa, and we travelled in a sheroot (an Israeli taxi but much cheaper than ours). With us were the then Treasurer of our Manchester & Salford Mission and his wife.

The peace and beauty, very much as it must have been in the days of Jesus, restored him completely, and all was well. I later stayed with him and Mrs Hobbins in Canterbury where he was an authority on the Cathedral and taught me much.

Later in the day the coach parked at the foot of Mt. Tabor and luxury taxis took us at frightening speed round the hair-pin bends to the summit. This is the traditional site of the Transfiguration of Jesus according to the Roman Catholics and seemed, situated as it was in that part of Galilee where Jesus spent much of His ministry, more convincing that Mt. Hermon which I had been told in 1958, was the site. Mt. Hermon is in Syria and we gazed on that earlier visit at its 9000 ft., snow-capped all the year round. It was to a spur of that mountain that Jesus is said to have gone with Peter, James and John, the three most intimate of his disciples, before setting out for Jerusalem, to suffering and death.

Part Four

Our second day in Tiberias, as with all the previous days was one of blue skies, a temperature of about 70°, and with the spring flowers and the trees in the shade of green which only comes at that season, we spent the larger part of the day sailing on the tranquil waters of the Sea of Galilee. The wives of the crew had made lovely brooches and other decorations from sea shells, available at very reasonable prices; the men were friendly and cheerful, 'God was in His heaven and all was well with the world'.

The 'Galilean lake' or 'Syrian Sea' can change very rapidly and become rough and dangerous within a short time, as the wind blows through a funnel between the hills. We remembered Jesus stilling the storm, but this was not such a day. My mind went back to my previous visits, when the Galilean fishermen, still using boats similar to those of New Testament times, went out at night with their lamps aloft, often to be shot at by the Syrian soldiers on the other side. In 1958 and 1960 fishing was more dangerous than in the days of Jesus.

> O Sabbath rest by Galilee!
> O calm of hills above
> Where Jesus knelt to share with thee
> The silence of eternity
> Interpreted by love!

I have quoted this verse previously. It was the inspiration for the title of my book.

Many of us lunched on the St Peter fish served at the lakeside cafés.

On the third day we drove north to the Golan Heights, presently occupied by Israel but the scene of bitter conflict in recent times. The Syrians were able, from the summit, to dominate the whole of Northern Israel, and often shelled the River Jordan valley. We could see the Israeli soldiers in their observation post on the summit, from where they could see all the way to Damascus. Here too is the boundary with the Lebanon. On either side of the road, warning signs told of the minefields which surrounded us. The River Jordan starts at this point, a confluence of three other rivers. All around was evidence of fortification and recent conflict.

We set off from Tiberias on the only poor day for weather. It was windy and cloudy, and disappointing for those hoping to stroll round Nazareth. I had seen Mary's well (we know it to be the one she used as it is the only one in the town), the home of the holy family, and the synagogue where Jesus spoke ('Is not this Joseph's son?'). The town has grown rapidly, is occupied in part by a large Arab population, and predominantly Christian.

From Nazareth we travelled to Cana, visiting the Synagogue, and the site of the wedding feast which Jesus attended. Even the earthen jars were said to be the originals where Jesus turned the water into wine.

On the coastal road, journeying to Tel Aviv, we stopped at Caesarea Philippi. This was the residence of the procurators of Judaea, and so the official residence of the Roman Province. Herod built temples, baths, a theatre, a hippodrome and aqueducts, still extremely well preserved. We walked along the aqueduct parallel with the Mediterranean. This was the busy and only safe port on the Palestine coast.

It was from here that Paul sailed to Rome.

And so to Tel Aviv, a city to rival any in the world with fashionable shops, night life and all the trappings of modern luxury city life. Most of us spent the two days sunbathing and swimming on the glorious sandy beaches. On the second day our coach took us to Ben-Gurion Airport from where we flew back to Gatwick after a memorable time.

Chapter XLIII

WHAT'S IT ALL ABOUT ANYWAY?

And so I come towards the end of my journey. I wrote in the foreword that the aim of my writing was to answer the question so many ask: 'What's it all about?' I also mentioned the Lakeland hills, where Wordsworth felt the power of an unseen and eternal presence.

It is 7 a.m. on Saturday 19 November 1994 as I write these words. My daughter Catherine's thirtieth birthday. I hope she has received my card and Marks and Spencer vouchers. I look forward to speaking to her on the telephone this evening, rejoicing in the knowledge that I will be with her a week next Saturday in London, staying overnight with my son John, before returning the following day.

I am sitting in my car as dawn breaks over Lake Windermere. My vantage point is a popular public car park presently deserted but which, in a few hours, will be full of visitors. The parking area is close to the main road from Windermere to Ambleside and provides extensive views in daylight, along England's longest lake, with Ambleside to the east, and Bowness-on-Windermere to the west. The journey has been through the darkness, accompanied by fairly heavy rain, so that I have not been able to enjoy the usual lovely views on the journey from Morecambe. Instead I have been listening to my tape of twenty favourite hymns of Charles Wesley from the Methodist Central Hall, Westminster. I know the words and have enjoyed joining in with the choir.

I realize now that I must answer the question which I posed, and, by implication, inferred I could answer.

Yesterday, I completed the writing in longhand of approximately 450 pages on A4 paper, and which I started exactly four weeks previously. I have written of my experience in the first chapter. It was on 21 October, after returning from a round of golf, when I felt the urge to begin. I know that when I look back in the coming days on those four weeks, I will continue to be amazed that I could write so much in such a short time, with little sleep, few signs of tiredness and buoyed up by a burning desire to write. At times I came to my senses, unaware momentarily of the day or time. There were tears of joy and tears of sadness, with a total immersion in the experiences and story I was trying to tell. From an original intention to rent a Lakeland cottage for three months and write

338

in complete isolation, I had completed the task I set myself, sitting at my study desk at home. I have read of the compulsion which can come upon a writer when the spirit moves him. And now I have experienced it for myself.

I remembered again from early days the incredulity with which I received the knowledge that George Frederic Handel wrote *Messiah* in twenty-four days. 'I did think I saw the whole heaven open before me,' when he wrote the 'Hallelujah' chorus.

As I drove along the Kendal by-pass to an elevated position above the market town, the first faint signs of the dawn appeared on the tops of the distant Lakeland mountains. I felt the need, after my exertions of the previous days and the prospect of a removal on the following Monday, for an escape to my beloved Lake District which I expressed in a brief note to my sister, and pushed through the letterbox of her home a short distance away, on my route northwards. And I thought of Wordsworth again, and of the power he felt in the Lakeland hills, of an unseen and eternal presence; and I thought too of my pending divorce.

A few days ago, I visited an elderly retired Methodist minister, the Reverend David Pike MA BD, at his bungalow in Bare, where I also live. David is the 'other person' to whom I refer in the first sentence of Chapter XXIX, where I write of my late wife, Vera. I speak of him in a way which he would disclaim, only to make me the more certain of its truth.

David does not preach now, because of advancing years. He will never really know, and I am aware of others of a like mind, the profound effect he had on my life in the years of his retirement. He is a member of the choir, takes a very full and active part in the life of our Bare Methodist Church and until a year or two ago played golf. I can see him now in his unchanging way in the pulpit at the beginning of his sermon. Having read his text, he removed his spectacles, placed them in (I think) his left-hand pocket, and from a great intellect and profound faith, proclaimed the good news of the Gospel, always with an eye to the practical implications and lessons for daily life. They were moments to savour and to return to often in the memory. Behind them was a time of careful preparation and prayer, and an affirmation and deep conviction of the eternal truths of the word of God.

I have, on occasion, regretted that his sermons were not recorded on tape for the greater benefit of many. It is to my knowledge, from another source, that he has prayed for me every day for several years. I find that comforting, but also very humbling.

When I visited him on the occasion I have mentioned, he spoke of recent events in my life but the words which stuck in my mind was when he spoke of me 'winning through'. And there you have it.

That *is* what it's all about.

It's all about Pilgrim in the second-best book in all the world – John Bunyan's *The Pilgrim's Progress* from 'This world to that which is to come'. It is the word of a genius which succeeding generations of Christians will treasure, while time lasts.

And in what way, dear reader, have I won through?

As I have already said, until the age of forty-one I did not have a real problem in life, although I often thought to the contrary. Since then, some would say I have had my fair share. I repeat that the death of my father at the early age of sixty-four was a shattering experience. There followed a painful divorce and the loss of my children for ten years. My second marriage ended after two and a half years with Vera's death from cancer. Next came, from 1981 onwards, varying periods including one of twelve months and another of two years of sobriety, when the incurable illness of alcoholism, cunning, powerful, baffling and very patient, had me in its grip. A miracle on 10 July 1993 started me on the path of recovery. A spiritual experience in the spring of 1994 delivered me from all the wreckage of my past life, and August 1994 saw a very real experience of the power and consciousness of God in every situation of my daily life. In 1995 my younger brother died from gunshot wounds.

I have won through, not through any merit of my own, but by the triumph of His Grace. You will see it in *The Pilgrim's Progress* and you will see it in the words of Charles Wesley:

> Thy sovereign grace to all extends,
> Immense and unconfined;
> From age to age it never ends;
> It reaches all mankind.

> Throughout the world its breadth is known
> Wide as infinity;
> So wide it never pass by one,
> Or it had passed by me.

You will see it in the words of the former slave trader John Newton:

> Amazing grace (how sweet the sound)
> That saved a wretch like me!
> I once was lost, but now am found,
> Was blind, but now I see.

And what of the future?

The triumph of *His* Grace.

Henry Drummond in his book *The Greatest Thing in the World* says:

> Everyone has asked himself the great question of antiquity as of
> the modern world:
>
> What is the *summum bonum*, the supreme good?
>
> You have life before you, only you can live it. What is the noblest
> object of desire, the supreme gift to covet? He says that when Paul
> spoke of faith, hope and love, and concluded 'the greatest of these
> is Love' it was not an oversight. Drummond states unequivocally
> that the supreme work to which we need to address ourselves in
> this world, is to learn love.

My own definition of love, and I do not know if the words are solely
mine, or picked up on life's journey is: 'A deep and genuine concern for
the well-being of all with whom we come into contact, who are in need,
irrespective of their colour, class or creed, and whether the element of
liking is there or not.'

I end with these words. I cannot remember where I read them but I
think they are in a book attributing them to Dr Edward Carpenter, former
Dean of Westminster Abbey:

> Seek not the end of love in this act or that act, less it become an end
> in itself; but seek this act and that act, and thousands of acts whose
> end is love. And so shalt thou at last attain that which thou desirest;
> but when these are all past and gone, there shall yet remain unto
> thee, a great and immortal possession, which no man can take away.

Author's brothers and sisters

Chapter XLIV

THE TRIUMPH OF HIS GRACE

A nd so I draw near the end of my life's story up to the present time. I give thanks to God, revealed uniquely in Jesus Christ, by the power of the Holy Spirit.

I give thanks to all my family and friends, those still living, and those who have entered upon the higher life.

I give thanks to all those friends and colleagues whom I have met on life's way, and for all the help, advice, care and friendship which has been freely given.

I give thanks for all those with whom I have come into contact in my earthly pilgrimage, and ask for understanding and forgiveness from any I have offended.

They have all brought me to the point where I can affirm with confidence the words of St Paul when he wrote:

> I am convinced that neither death, nor life, nor angels, nor principalities, nor powers, nor things present, nor things to come, nor height, nor depth, nor anything else in all creation, shall be able to separate us from the love of God which is in Christ Jesus, our Lord.

I said in the Foreword to my story that its aim was to answer the question: 'What's it all about?'

It is, as I said in the last chapter, a matter of 'Winning Through'.

It is also about the acceptance of the Love of God, freely offered to us all and the enjoyment of that love by loving God in return, and in love and service to our fellow man.

Therein lies true happiness and contentment, and victory over this life.

> O for a thousand tongues to sing
> My great Redeemer's praise,
> The glories of my God and King,
> The triumphs of His grace.

A FINAL AFFIRMATION

I will not cease from mental fight,
Nor shall my sword sleep in my hand,
Till we have built Jerusalem
In England's green and pleasant land.

William Blake, 1757-1827